I0759392

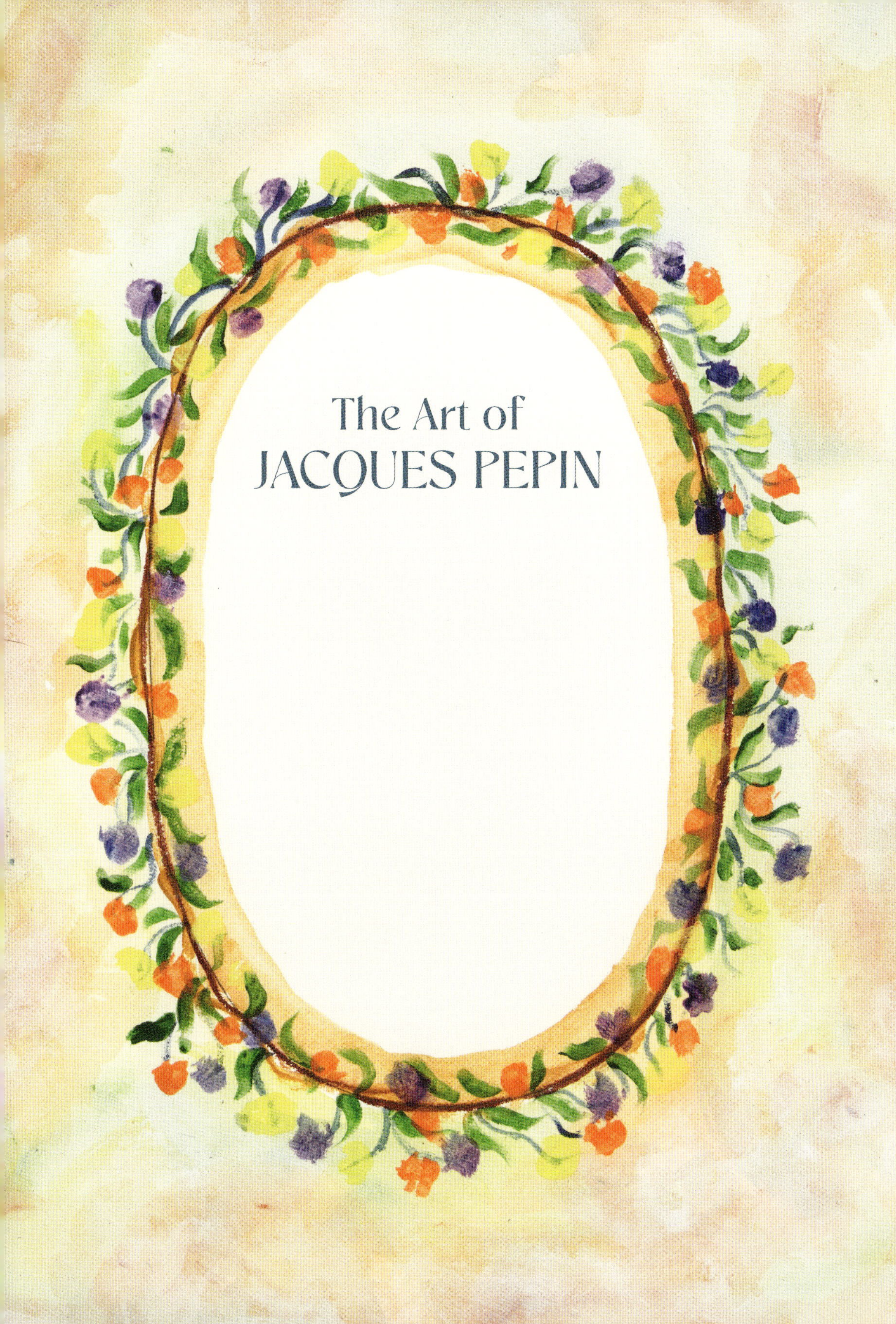

The Art of JACQUES PEPIN

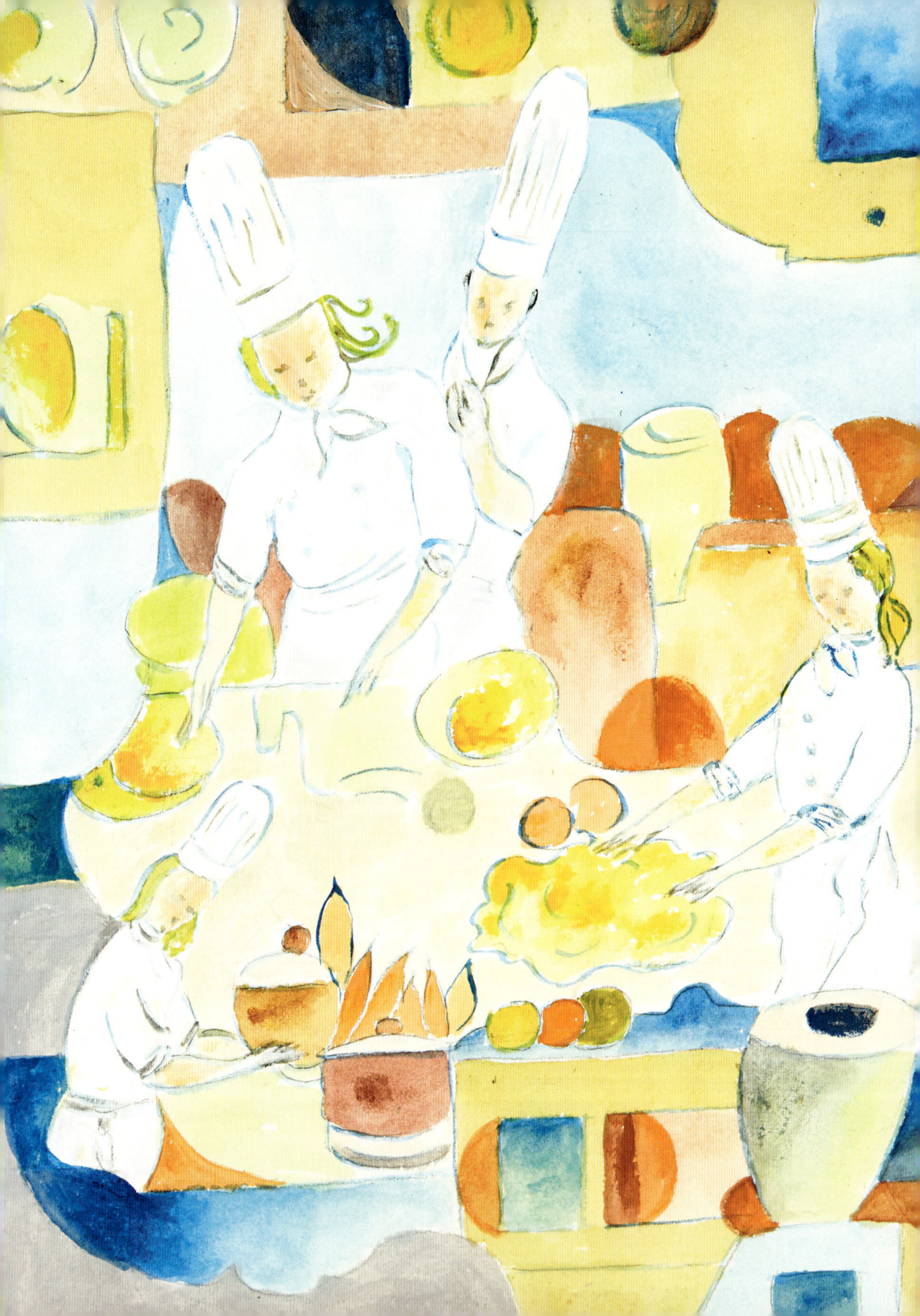

The Art of JACQUES PEPIN

THE COOKBOOK

Favorite Recipes and Paintings from My Life in the Kitchen

Text and artwork by Jacques Pépin
Artwork curated and photographed by Tom Hopkins

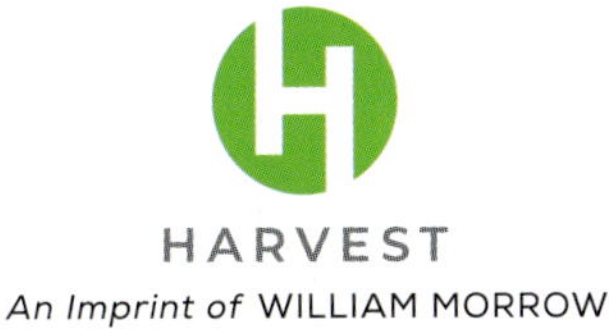

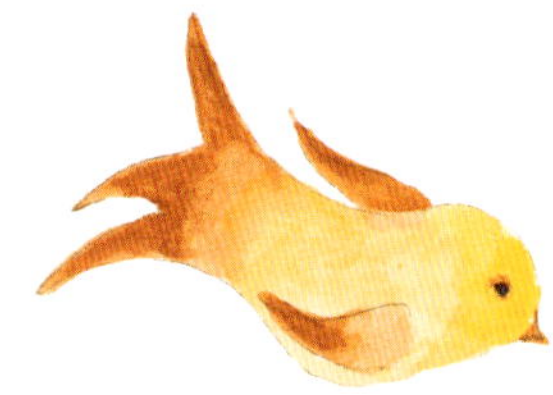

HarperCollins books may be purchased for educational, business, or sales promotional use. For information, please email the Special Markets Department at SPsales@harpercollins.com.

FIRST EDITION

Designed by Melissa Lotfy
Photography by Tom Hopkins

Some illustrations were previously published in another format.

Library of Congress Cataloging-in-Publication Data has been applied for.

ISBN 978-0-06-342024-3

25 26 27 28 29 PCA 10 9 8 7 6 5 4 3 2 1

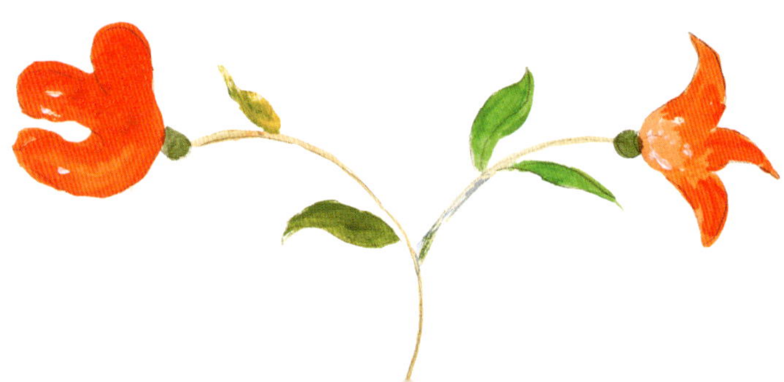

"to my dear friends of the Pétanque family.
Thank you for the support, fun, and love
you bring to me."

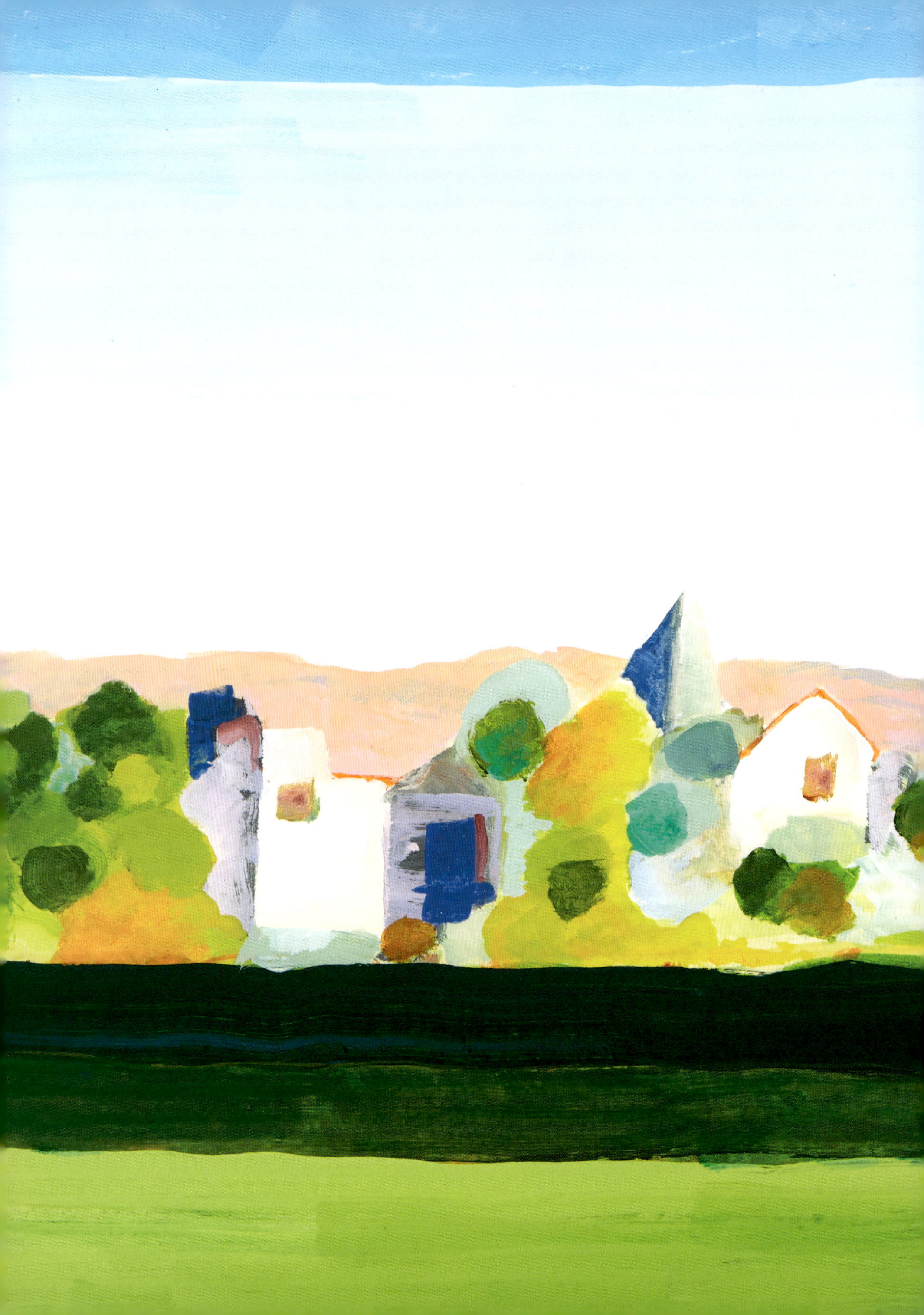

Contents

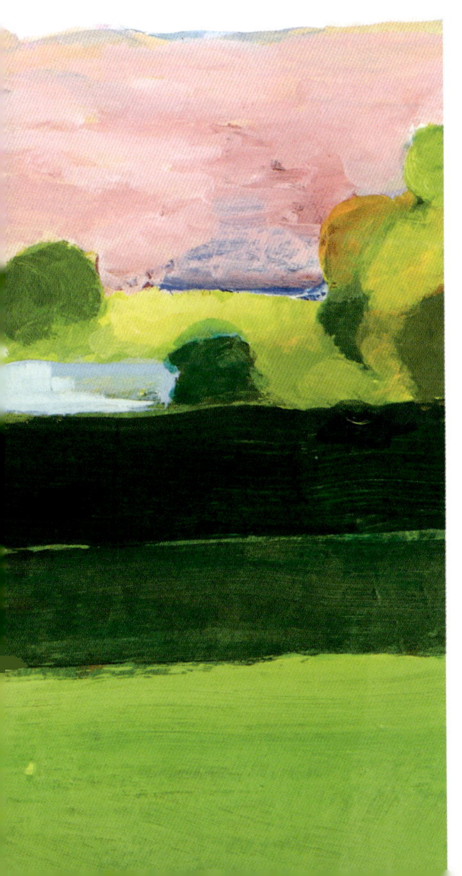

Serenity Landscape, 2016

Artwork

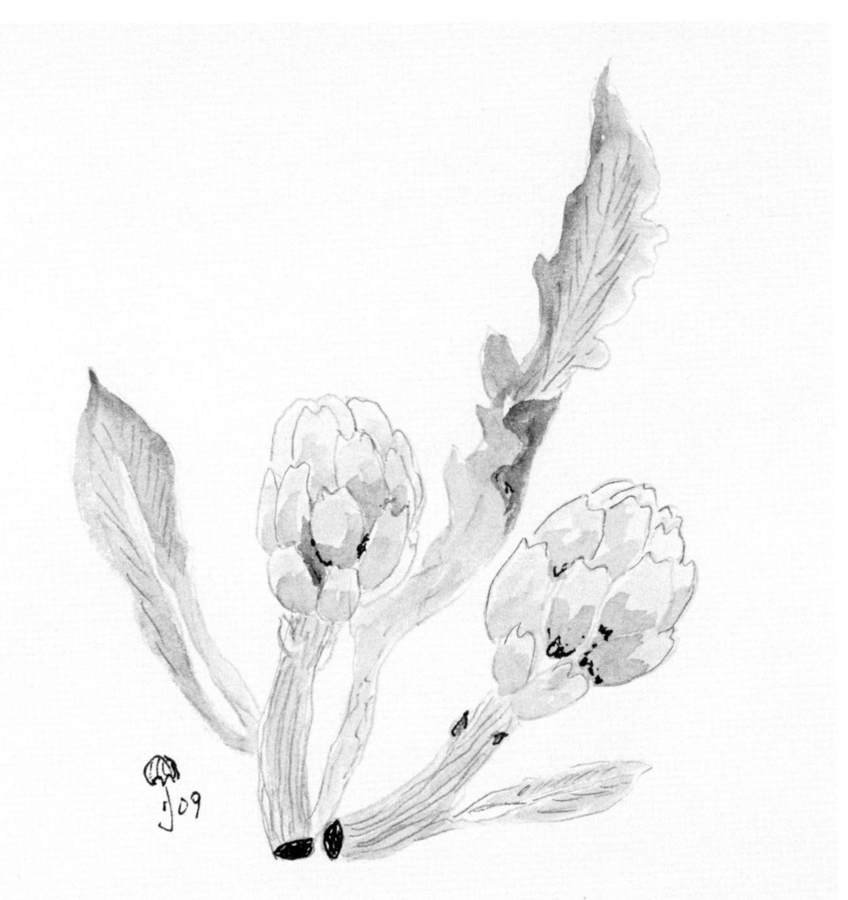

Artichoke 2, 2009

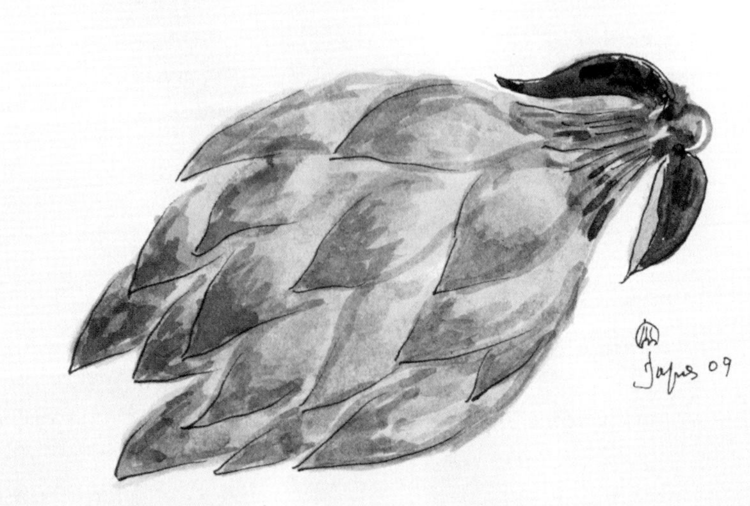

Artichoke, 2009

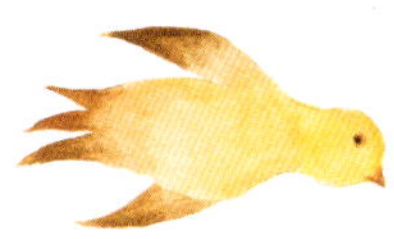

Introduction

THIS BOOK COMBINES my two main passions in life—cooking and painting. Of course, I have other interests and devotions, like playing boules with my friends, foraging for mushrooms, listening to music, and reading, but my two primary passions remain cooking and painting. I think of each of them as a form of art. While painting is a solitary art form, I share its results when I display my drawings and paintings. And of course, cooking can be both solitary and communal—and like painting, the results are shared with many others. When I cook, I always think about the people who will eat what I cook. And I am especially happy when I teach—the ultimate form of sharing food, and an art form in itself. In *Remembrance of Things Past*, Proust recounts that touch, sight, smell, taste, and hearing are important to the artist, and they are essential to the chef as well. There are memories of the senses as opposed to the memories of the brain. These memories are immediate, often unexpected, and very powerful. I am walking through the woods with my dog, and suddenly I smell wild mushrooms. Instantly I am eight years old again, walking in the woods with my brothers and father, looking for mushrooms.

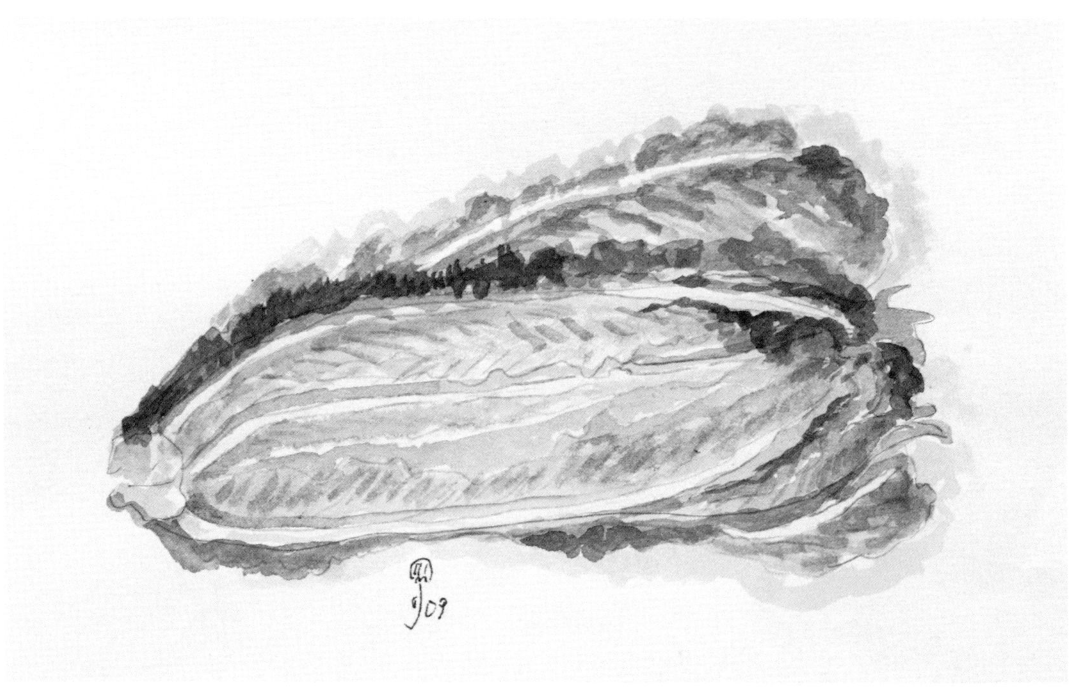

Romaine Lettuce, 2009

I am a cook by trade, and it is what I am best at. Cooking is my métier, and I have cooked professionally all my life, from age thirteen. I have made a living from cooking, teaching cooking, writing books on cookery, and demonstrating cooking on television. And I've always been in a kitchen, as far back as my memory goes, from helping my mother along with my brothers at about the age of six.

I have also always liked art and have always enjoyed looking at paintings. During my working years in Paris in the 1950s, I spent many afternoons at the Louvre Museum, probably because it was free and a place to go during the afternoon break from my kitchen work. It grew on me, and eventually, I started reading about painting and art and returned to the Louvre again and again, as well as to the old Rodin Museum on Rue de Varenne and L'Orangerie Museum in the Tuileries Gardens, where I could stand for hours in front of Monet's enormous *Nymphéas* (*Water Lilies*). I was hooked but did not actually start drawing and painting myself until after I came to the United States at the end of 1959.

I enrolled at Columbia University to learn English as a second language and would end up studying a variety of subjects there for the next thirteen years. In addition to the requirements I had to follow for my degree, I had a couple of elective courses to choose from; I took drawing for one semester and sculpture for another. I enjoyed the experience greatly, and several of the drawings and sculptures in this book go back to that period.

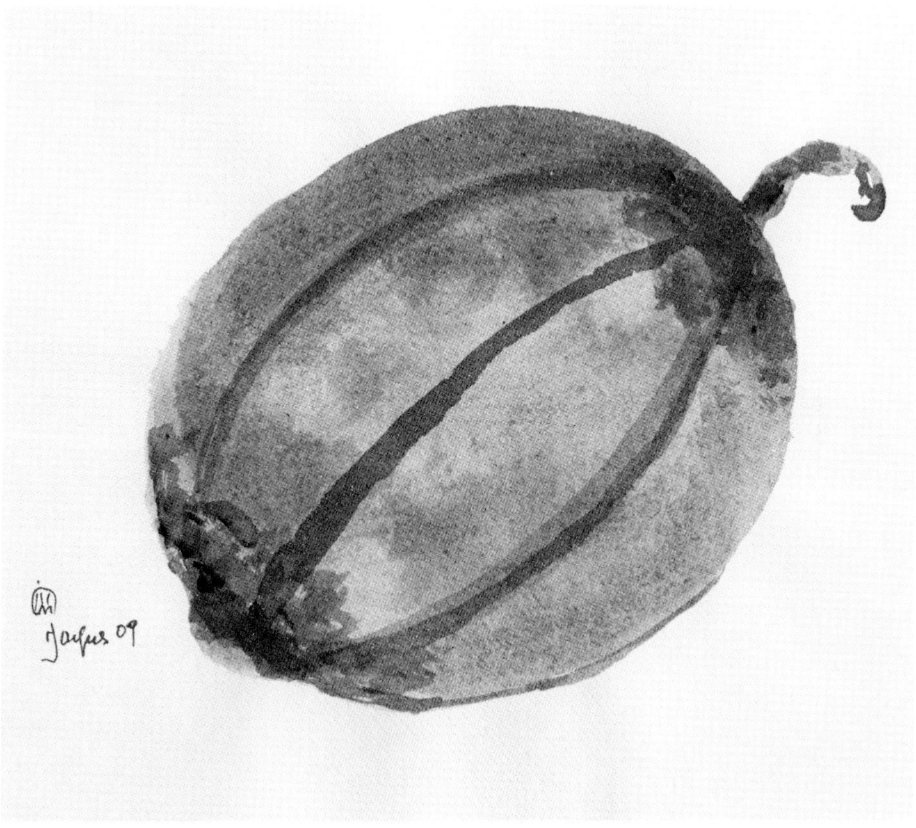

Melon, 2009

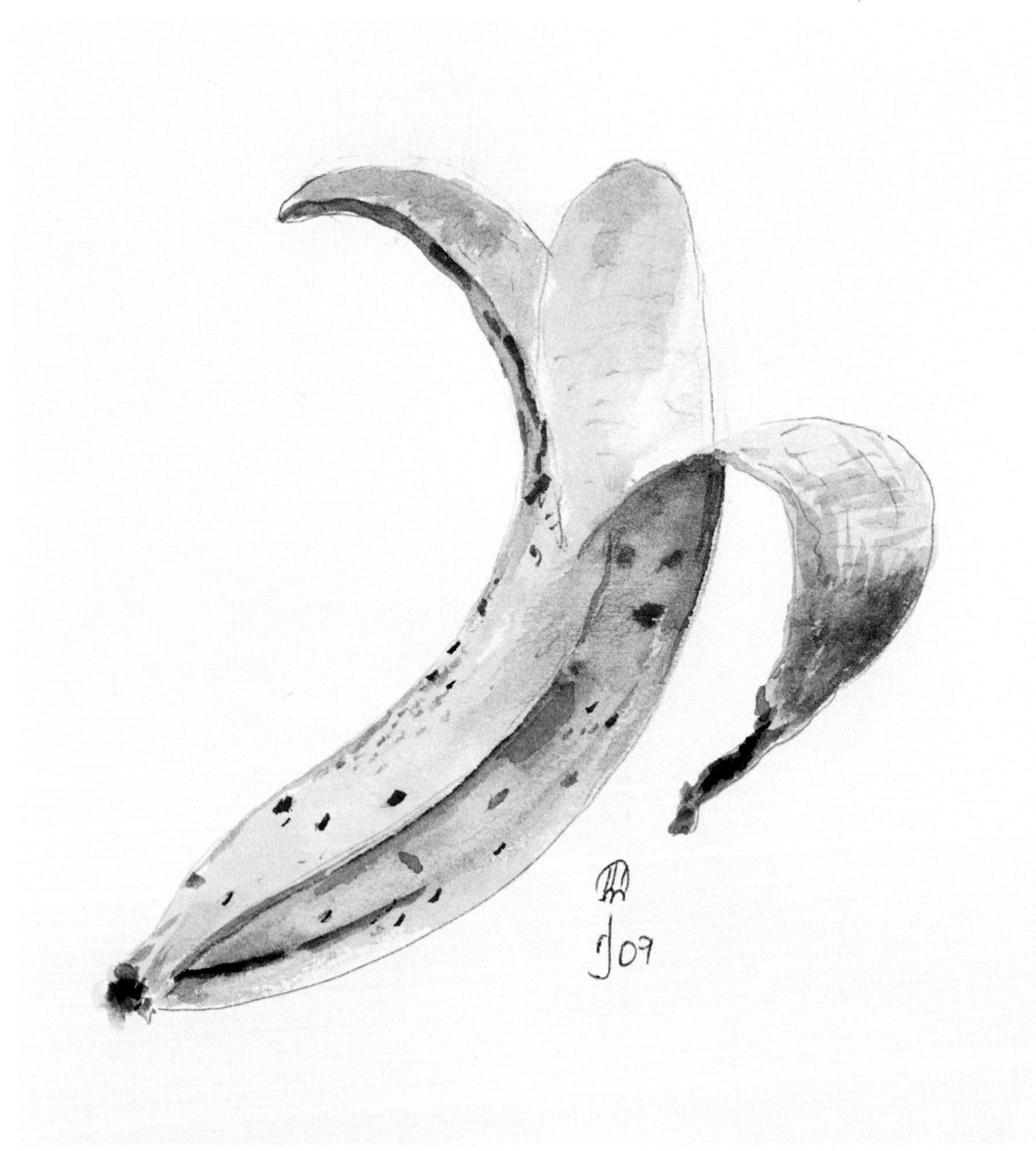

Banana, 2007

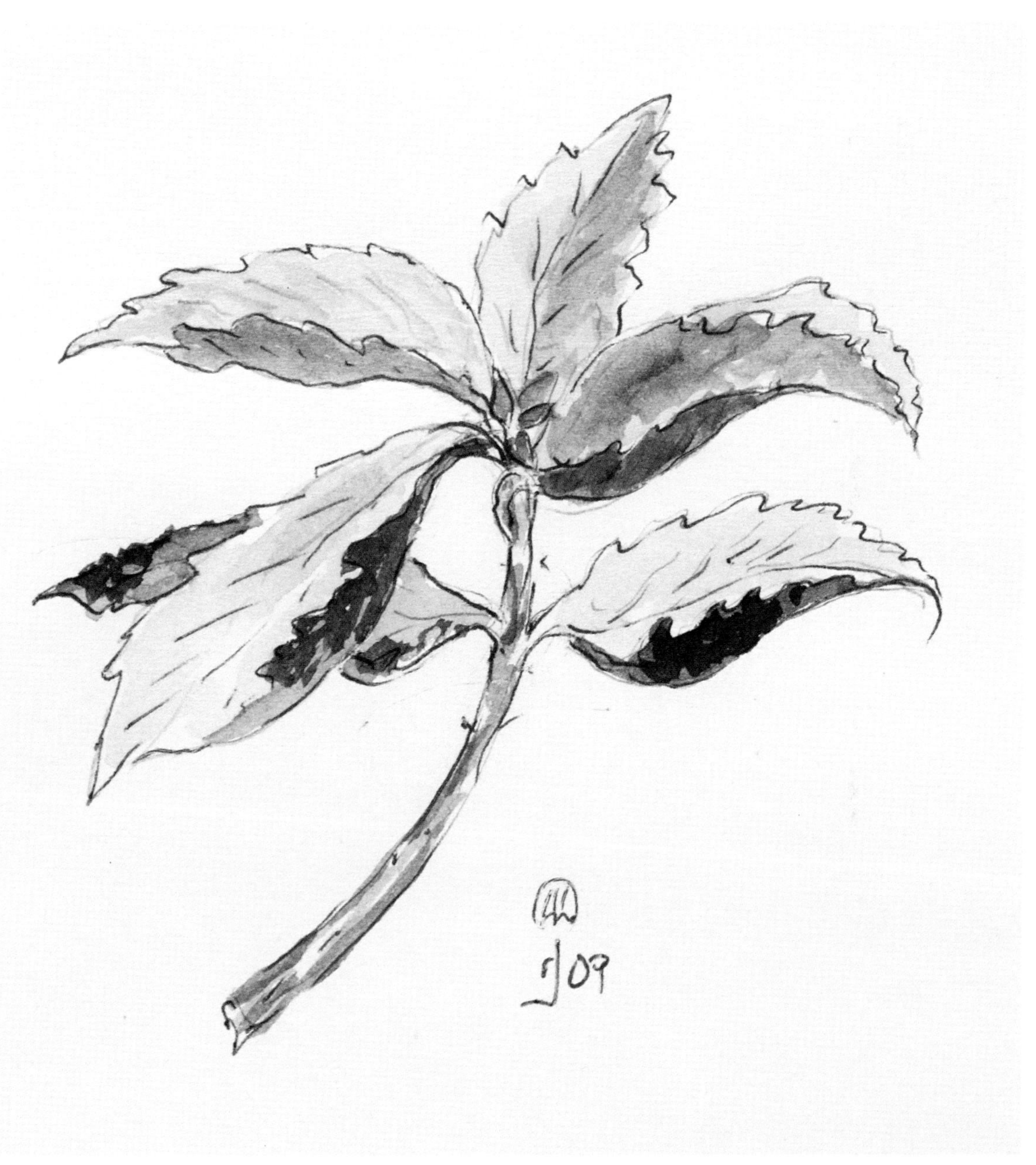

Basil, 2009

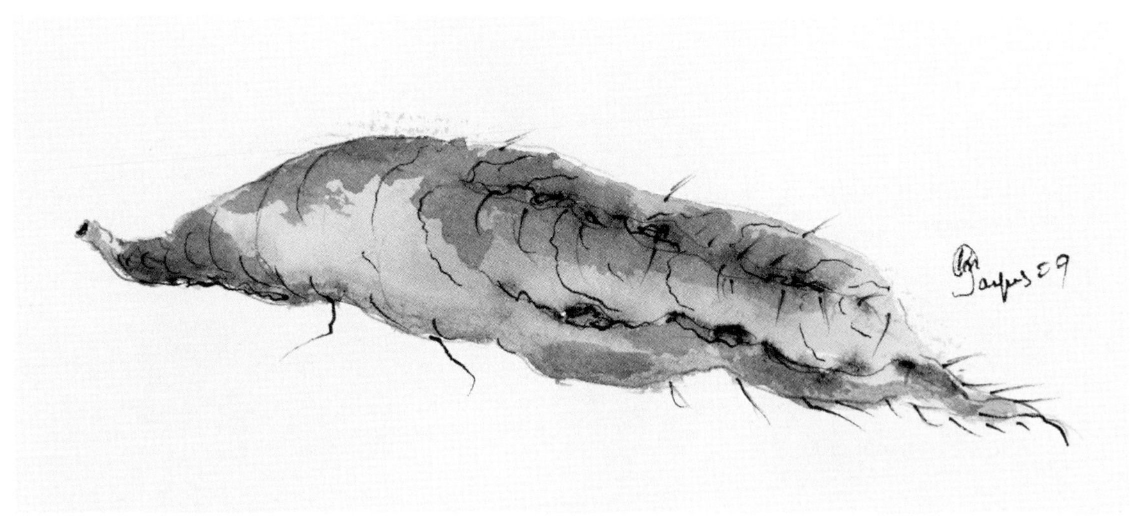

Sweet Potato, 2009

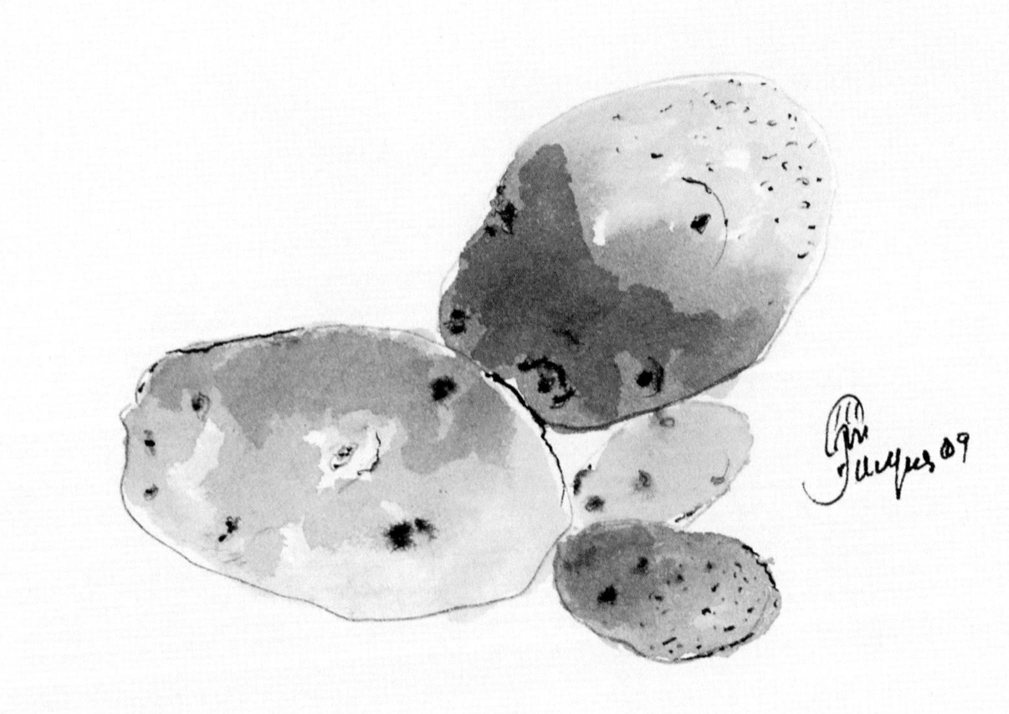

Potatoes, 2009

By the summer of 1962, a group of friends, including my dearest friend, Jean-Claude, rented a house in Woodstock, New York, for our summer weekends. It was an artists' summer gathering place and soon we—Jean-Claude, our friend Charlie, and me—started repairing old furniture, drawing, and painting, as well as cooking together. It was fun; we had no rules, and our paintings were mostly inspired by the impressionists and the countryside around us. It would take me many years to dabble and try my hand at abstract or other types of nonrepresentational painting. It is great fun to fill the plates with paint rather than food, and it is certainly more permanent.

For me, painting is for pleasure and fun, and I paint only when the mood strikes me. I often get frustrated when I start a new painting, but occasionally the painting takes hold of me, I react, and I end up with a satisfying result. The same thing happens from time to time in my cooking. I know I am more skilled as a cook than a painter because my knowledge of the techniques, ingredients, and the process of cooking is much vaster than my knowledge of the mechanics of painting. I have spent years in the kitchen learning, but I have never taken the time or found the patience to spend years in art school learning the processes or science of painting. I am usually in control of my cooking, but I do not always control my painting or drawing as easily. Unlike in cooking, where I can usually fix a mistake, I have no recovery strategy in my art when something goes astray, except to paint over it. I have found that when I paint, especially nonrepresentational painting, I have no measurement, no way to estimate or assess whether the painting is good. I have learned to stop when it satisfies me.

I don't know whether my painting has helped my cooking or whether my cooking has benefited my painting. All I know is that they live in harmony. Both are a different expression of who I am, and both enhance my life considerably. Paul Valéry said something about poems that I apply to painting, "A poem is never finished, it is just abandoned," and the same can be said for a painting. Through the years I have painted over many of my works, but when the painting survives a couple of years of hanging, I usually do not touch it again. In fact, I often look at some of my old paintings and wonder, How did I do that? Not that they are necessarily better, but they surprise me because I do not feel now the way I felt then, and I would not be interested or even know how to do the same type of work now. I would love to be able to taste food that I made forty or fifty years ago, but food is evanescent. You cook, you eat it, and it's gone—except for the memory. However, the old paintings remain. The eyes of the artist visualize and see shapes that the average person does not see, just like the palate of the chef can perceive and "taste" combinations of ingredients before he goes to the stove.

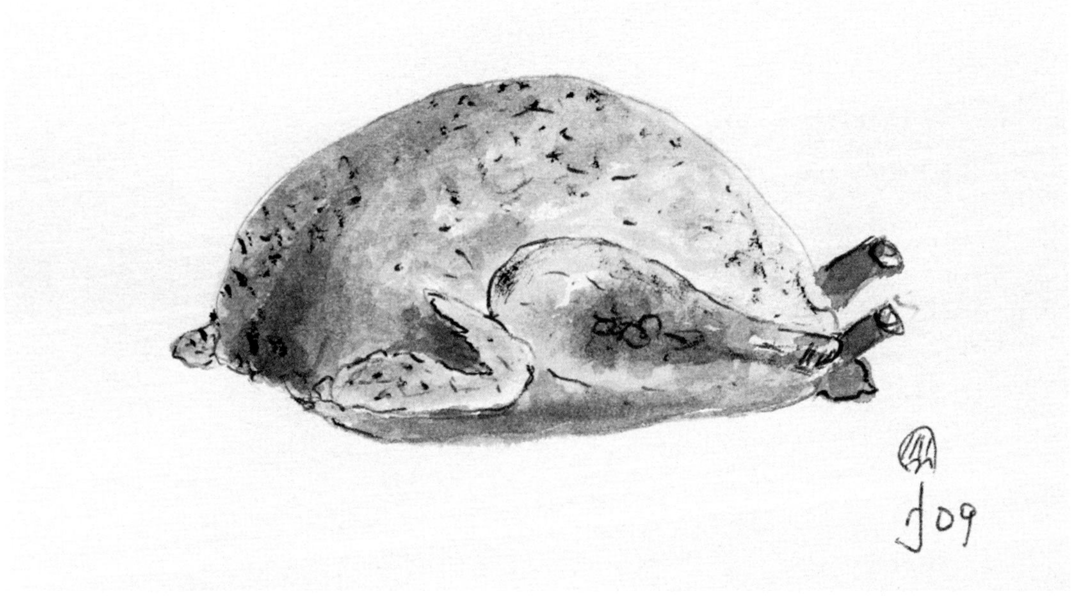

Chicken Ready to Roast, 2009

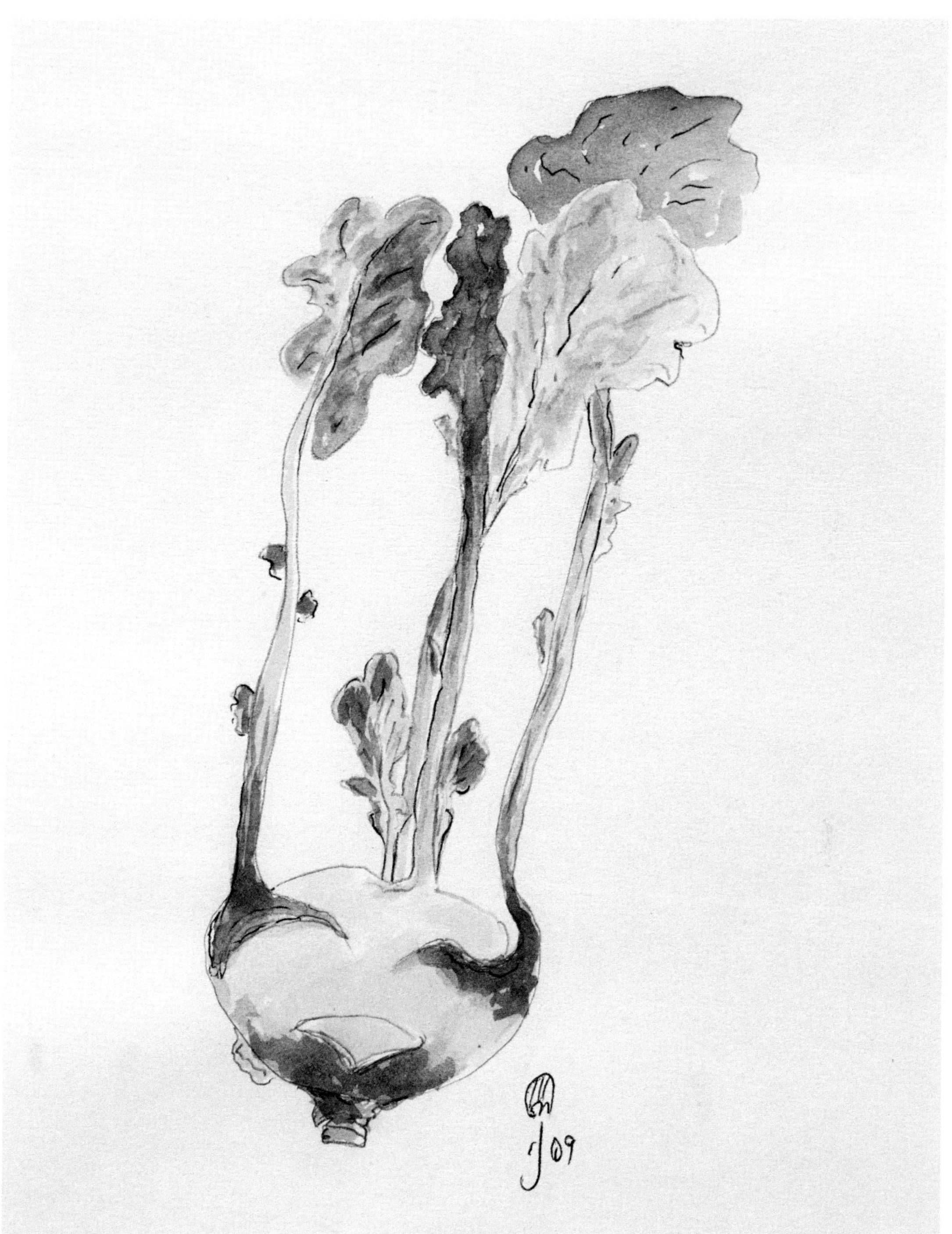

Kohlrabi, 2009

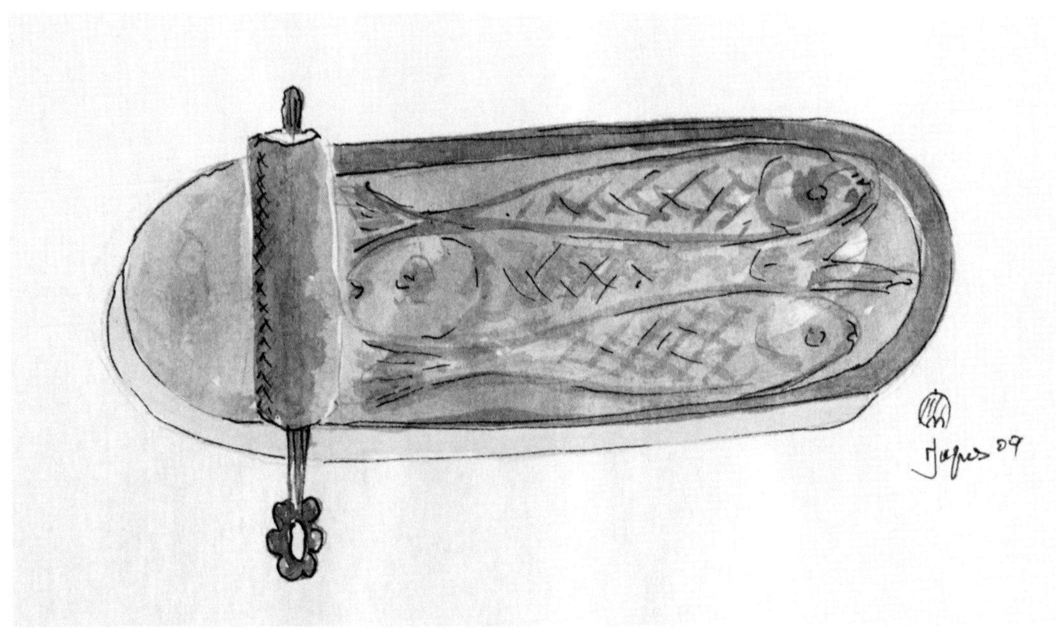

Sardines, 2009

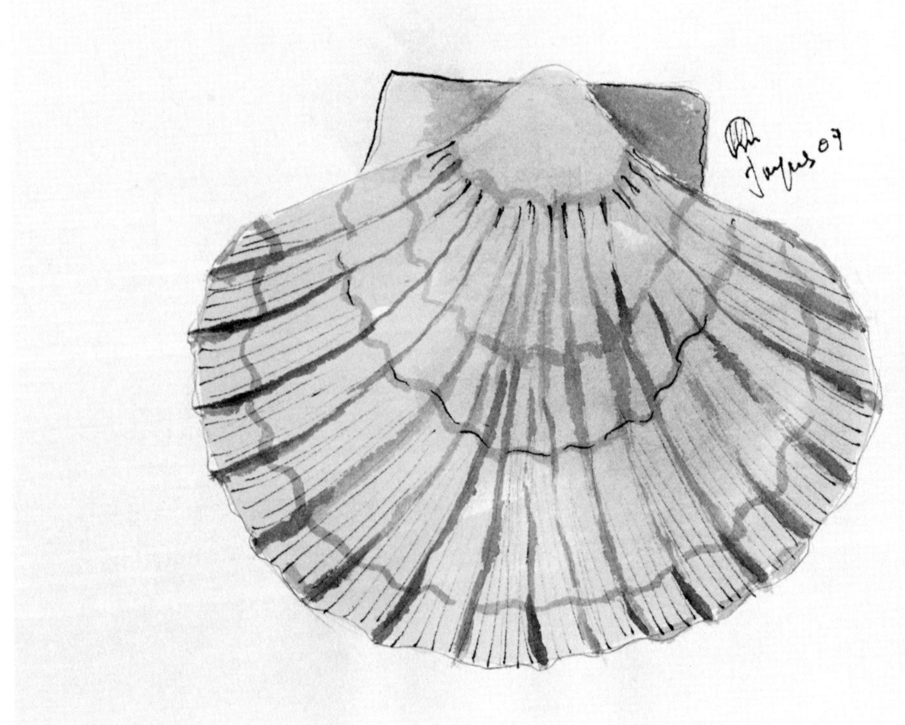

Scallop, 2009

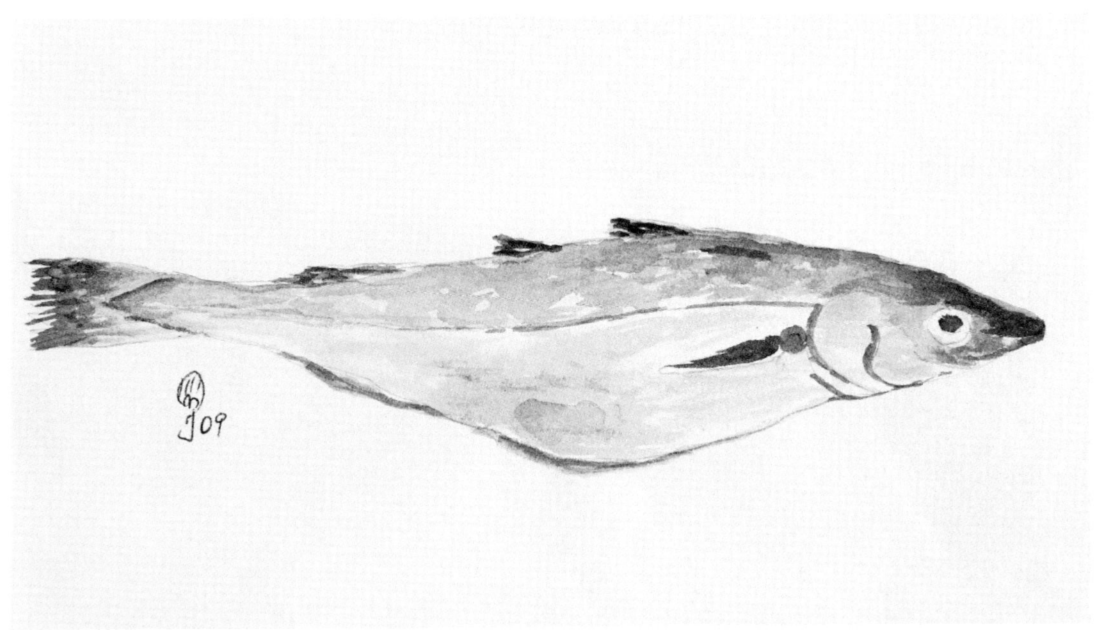

Whiting, 2009

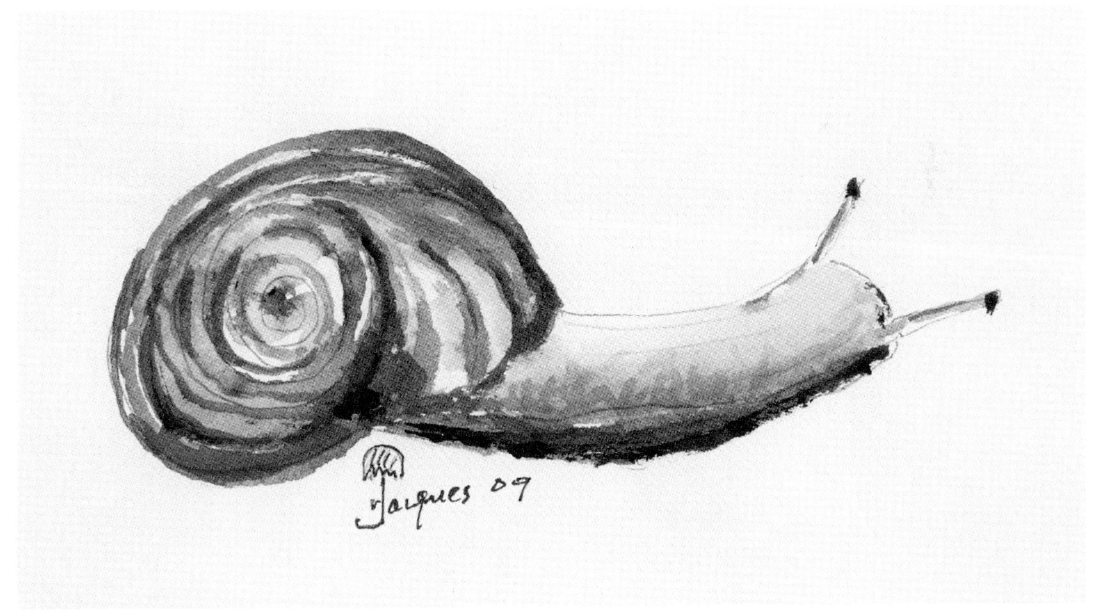

Snail, 2009

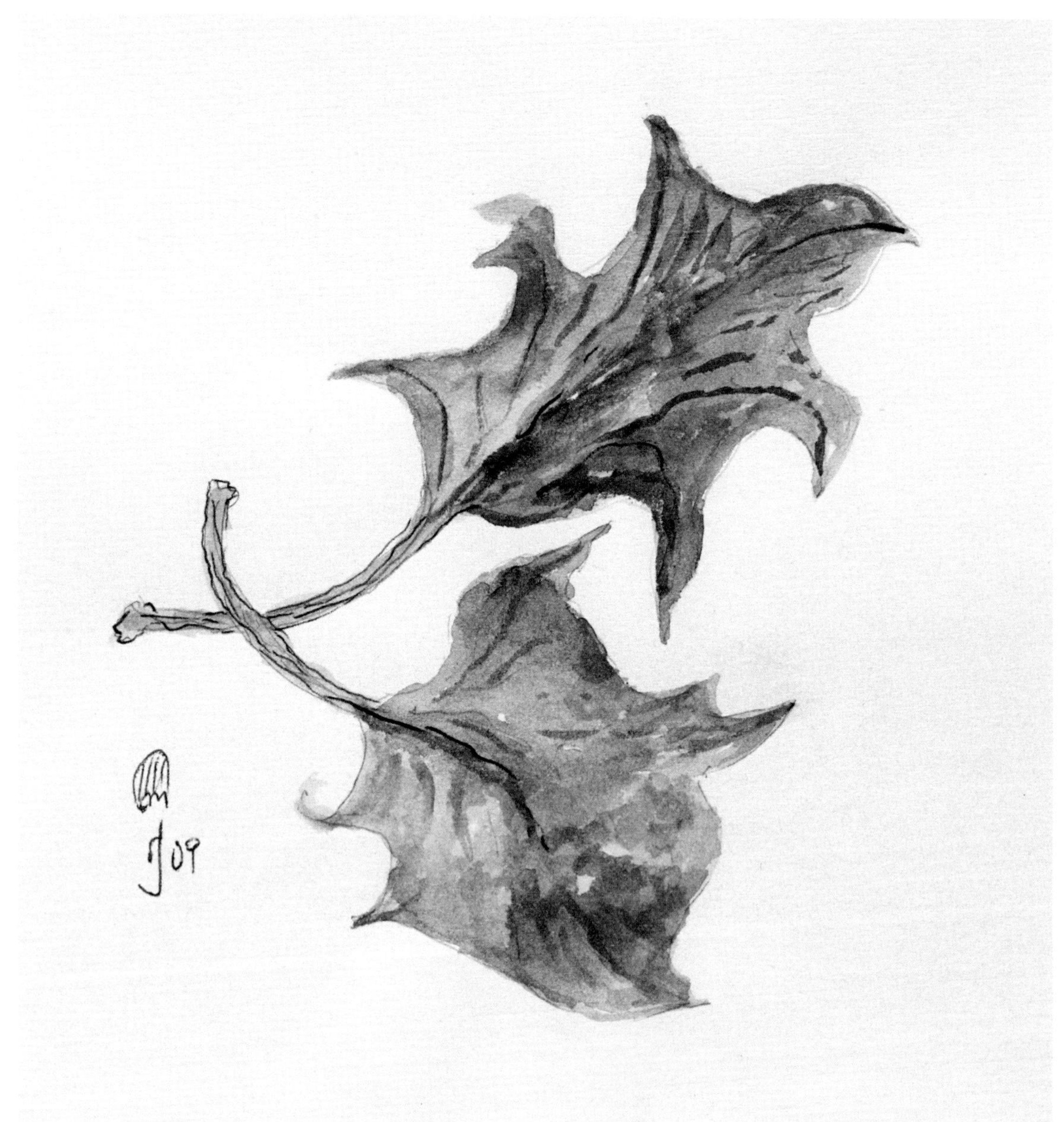

Spinach, 2009

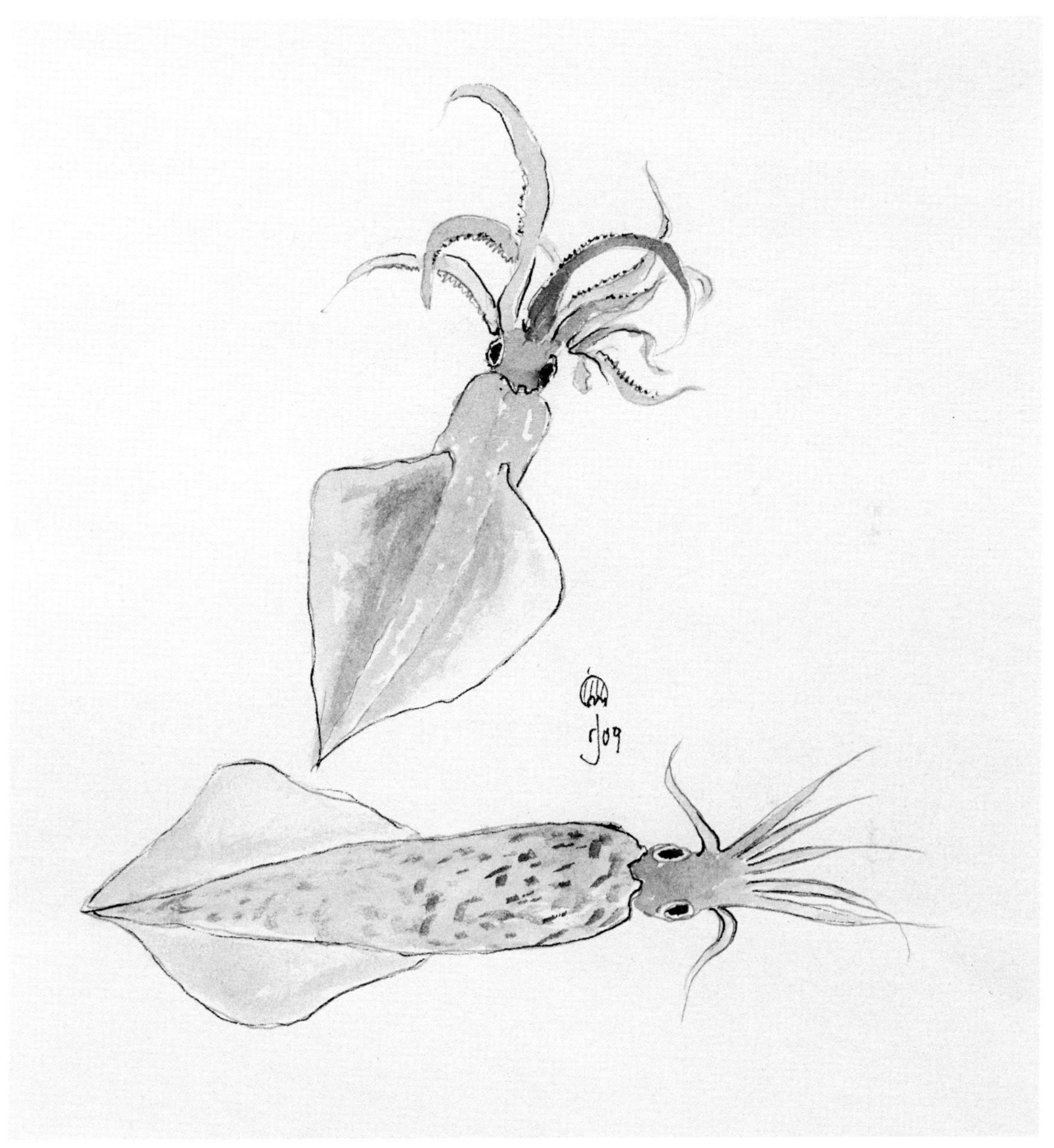

Squid, 2009

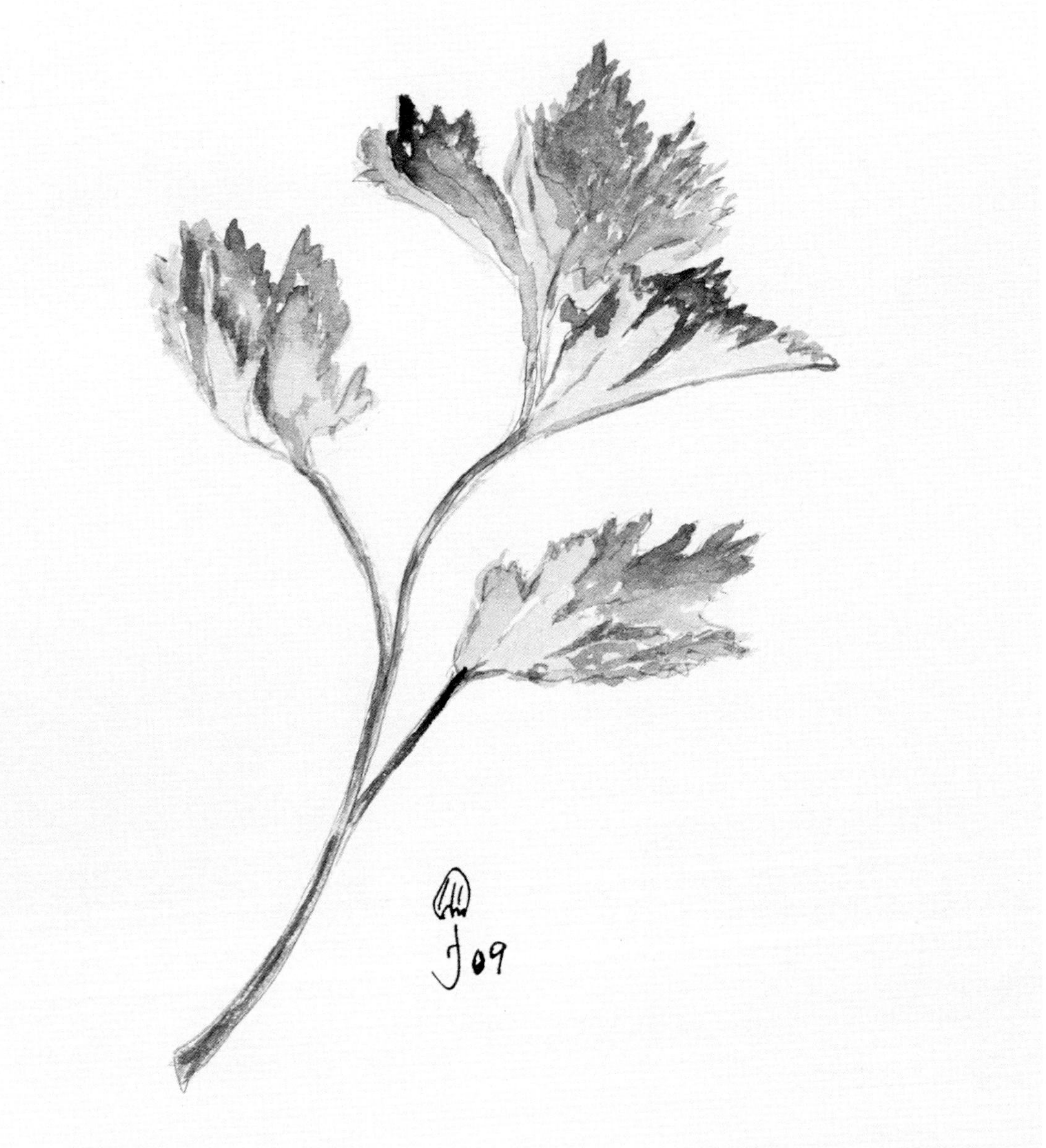

Parsley, 2009

Starting many years and many books ago, I began using my illustrations, drawings, and paintings to complete my cookbooks. For *Essential Pépin*, I drew about 250 black-and-white illustrations to insert throughout the book. All the books I have authored in the last ten years have many of my paintings and drawings, from *Heart & Soul in the Kitchen* to *Quick & Simple*, *Art of the Chicken*, *Poulets & Légumes*, and *Cooking My Way*.

Throughout the years I have given many of my paintings, drawings, and menus to friends and to organizations raising money for one charity or another. Many of my paintings have disappeared; some have been discarded and some painted over. In this book, I want to pair some of my artistic works with my recipes. And I want to share the food through the art of teaching how best to make those recipes. The recipes chosen are from various moments in my long history of cooking at home and writing cookbooks. They were selected because even though they may be from a very different time in my life, they reflect the way I cook now—simply, with economy and an aim to use whatever I happen to have on hand. I never want someone to feel put off by a complicated list of ingredients or a rigidity about swapping an ingredient for what you already have in your refrigerator or pantry. You can note that salt is always finer sea salt as opposed to coarse kosher salt, unless otherwise specified, and butter is always unsalted. I typically use a mild-tasting olive oil, but may occasionally call for extra virgin—most often in salads. Of course, you can use what you like best.

I have tried my hand at painting on tiles, making mosaics, and sculpture. In the '60s and '70s, I painted strictly in oil, but for many years now I have painted with acrylics, whether on canvas or paper. I often dilute the acrylic paint to use it as a "wash" and have used crayons and markers as well to create my menus. My art has even appeared on some plates, which really connects both mediums I work in.

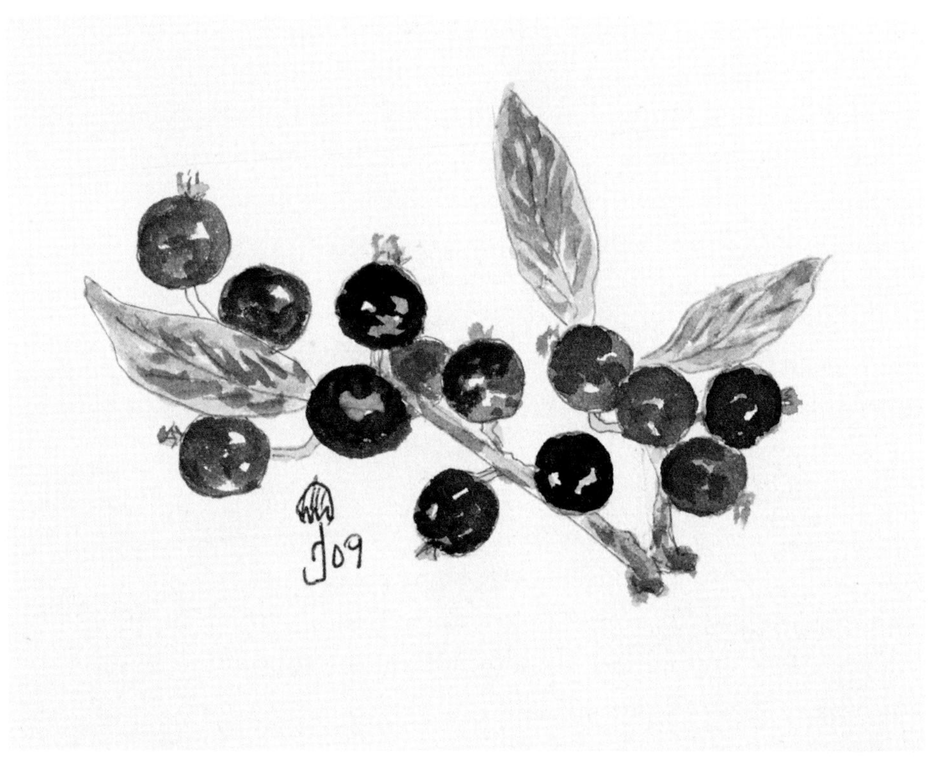

Blueberries, 2009

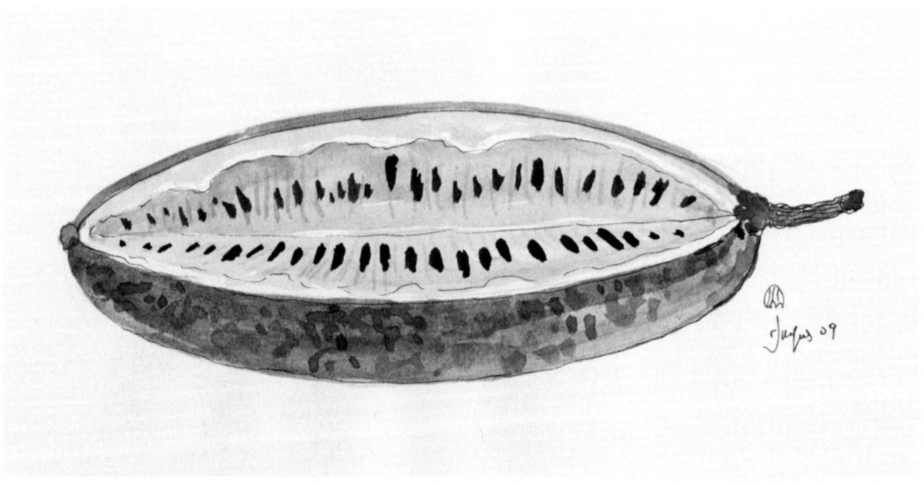

Watermelon, 2009

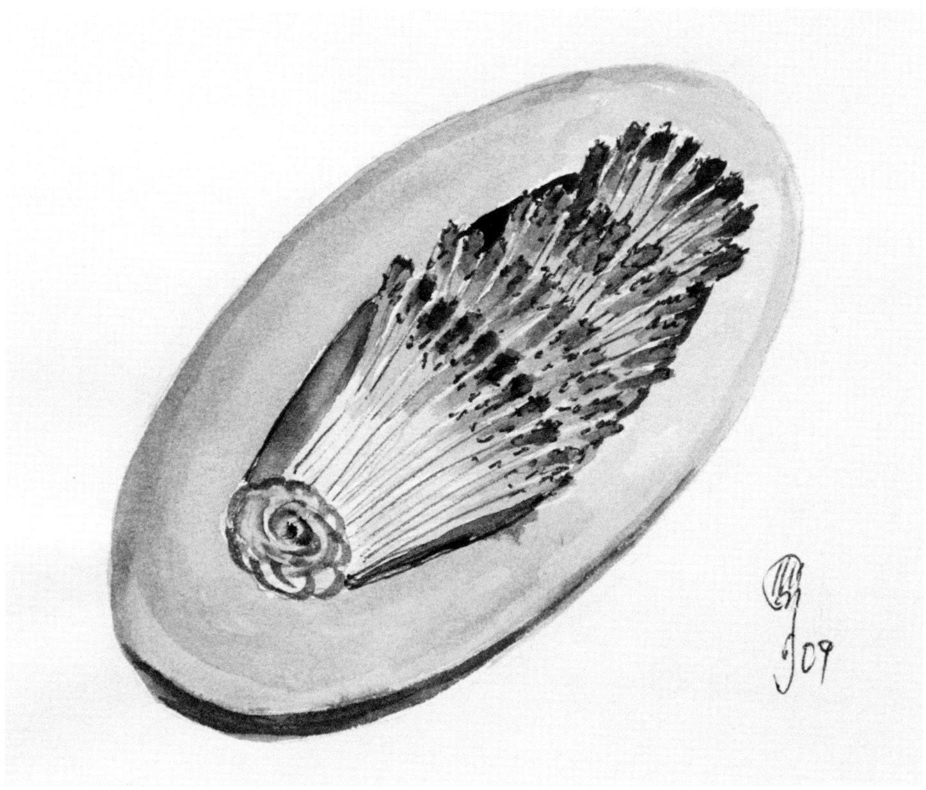

Asparagus on Platter, 2009

I believe that most of my paintings, especially the nonrepresentational ones, are kind of abstract representational and, most of the time, go back to scenes of a kitchen, buffet, living room, dining room, or food and kitchen tools or equipment in one form or another. The pattern and impression that seems to be emerging from the canvas represents food, most of the time, in shape, confirmation, or contour. I cannot escape myself. My "arts" are intertwined.

When the time came for us to pair the artwork with the recipes in this book, the choices turned out to be very arbitrary. We rarely agreed on a combination where the style, color, spiciness, texture, or feel of a recipe would fit a specific painting. Furthermore,

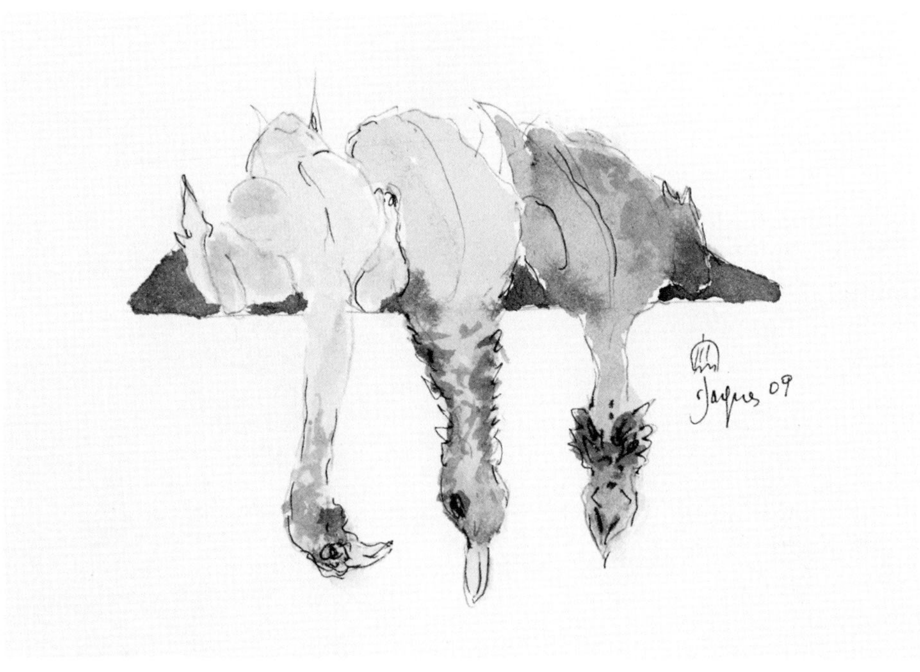

Dead Fowl, 2009

a cookbook, to be useful, must be divided by courses or subjects, such as soup, salad, meat, and fish, and to match each recipe with a specific work of art was futile and unworkable. Yet, somehow, most of us agreed that the dessert chapter should be paired with flowers. The light, colorful, delicate recipes often containing fruit seemed to fit the graceful elegance and lightness of flowers. So, the book is divided into five chapters—soups and salads; eggs, pasta, and vegetables; fish and shellfish; poultry and meat; and desserts. Each chapter features its own work of art. Black-and-white drawings, mosaics, and sculpture for the first chapter; next, drawings of animals, vegetables, and fruits; next, landscapes and seascapes; next, abstracts; and finally, flowers. It is my hope that people will choose their own pairing by creating menus combining my recipes and paintings to reflect their own taste and sense of style. Happiness is in my kitchen and painting studio.

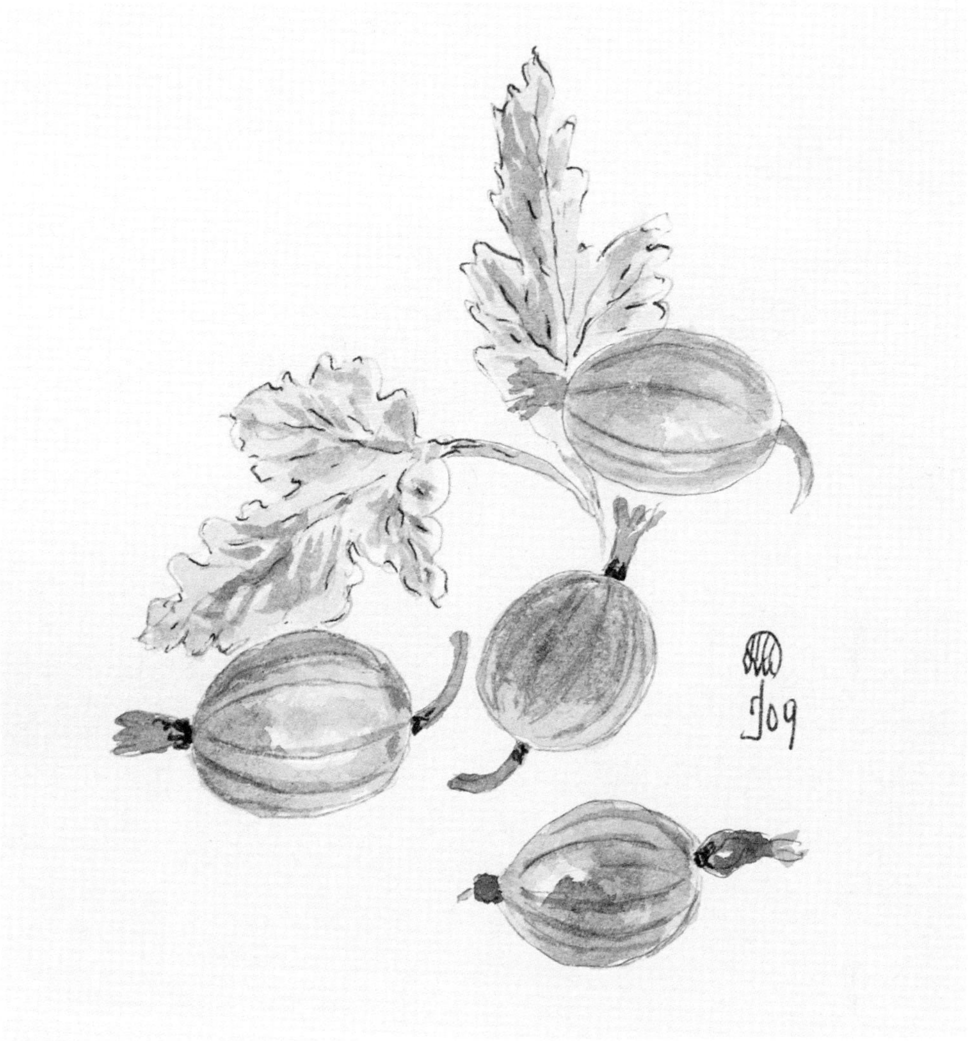

Gooseberrries, 2009

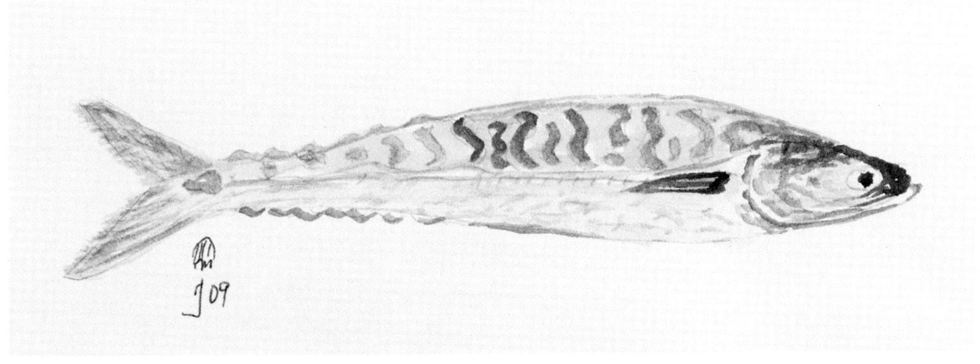

Mackerel, 2009

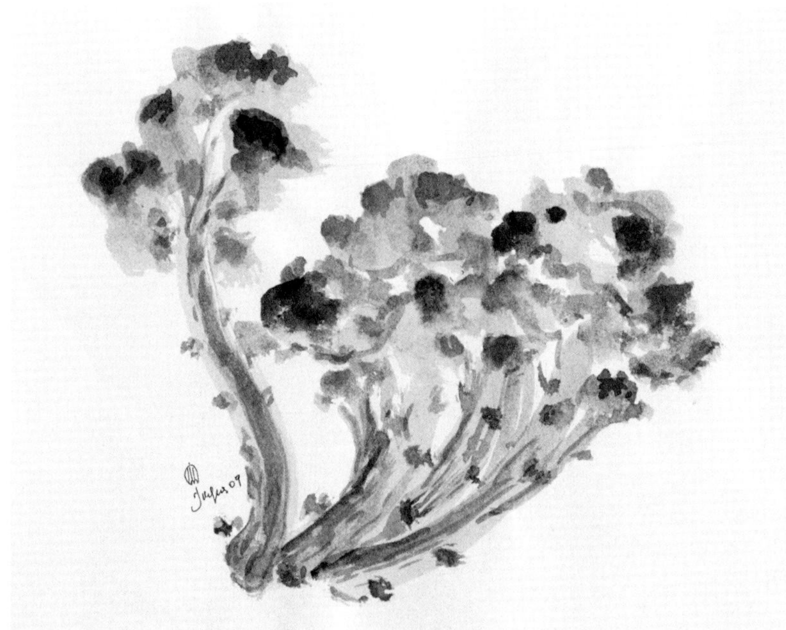

Broccoli, 2009

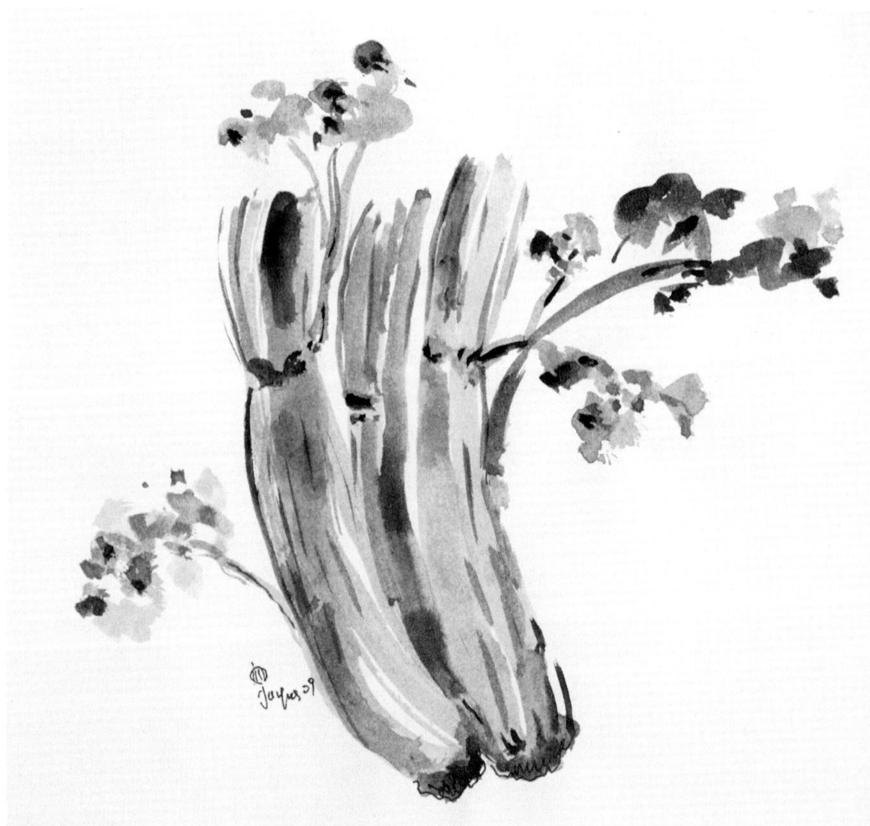

Celery, 2009

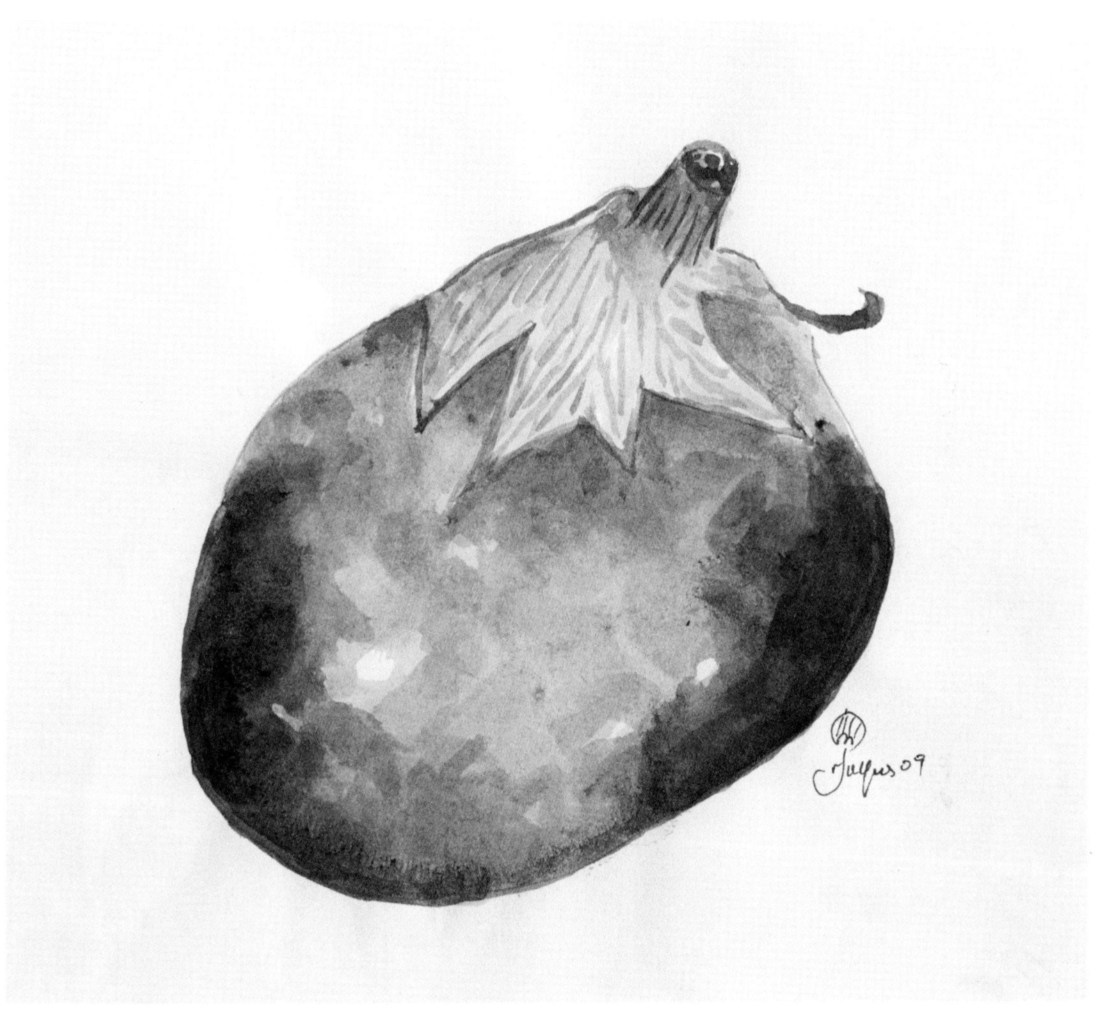

Eggplant, 2009

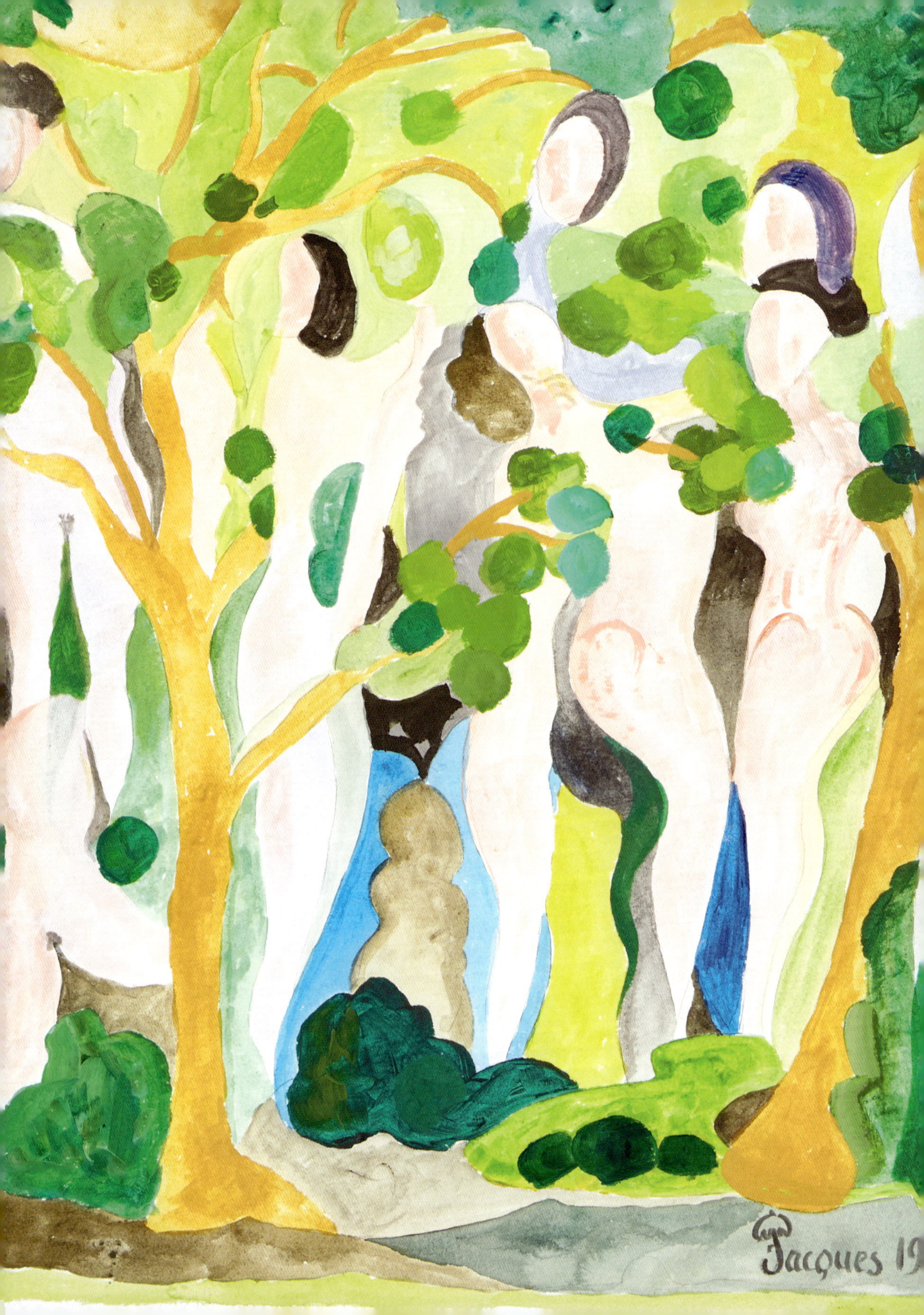
Jacques 19

Soups & Salads

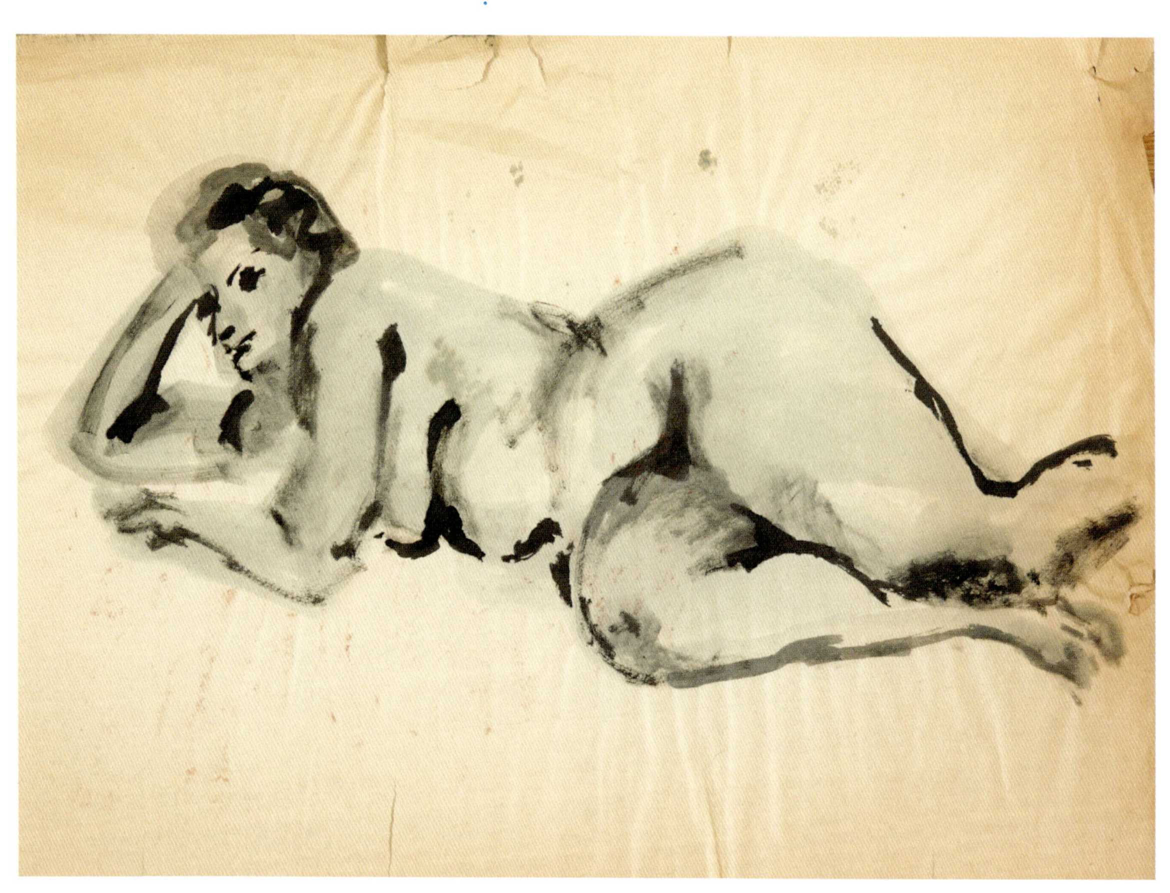

Lying Model, 1964

GLOSSY YELLOW PEPPER SOUP with ASPARAGUS GARNISH

This elegant soup, essentially a puree of yellow peppers garnished with spears of asparagus, is the perfect opener for a formal dinner, but it could also make an excellent lunch served with some nice bread. The soup's gloss and creamy texture are achieved by emulsifying the mixture with a handheld immersion blender (or in a regular blender) before it is served.

Serves 4

8 ounces asparagus, preferably large stalks with tight heads

3 yellow peppers (1⅓ pounds), halved, seeded, and cut into 1-inch pieces

1 large potato (9 ounces), peeled and cut into 1-inch pieces

1 large onion (8 ounces), peeled and cut into 1-inch pieces

3 garlic cloves, peeled

1 teaspoon salt

1½ teaspoons sugar

¼ teaspoon freshly ground black pepper

2 tablespoons butter

2 tablespoons extra virgin olive oil

▸ Peel the lower third of the asparagus stalks and discard the trimmings. Cut the asparagus on the bias into slices ¼- to ½-inch thick. (You should have about 1½ cups.) Bring ½ cup water to a boil in a saucepan over high heat and add the asparagus pieces. Bring the water back to a boil and boil the asparagus for 30 seconds. Drain, reserving the cooking juices, and set the cooked asparagus pieces aside in a bowl.

▸ Place the yellow peppers, potato, onion, garlic, salt, sugar, and pepper in a large saucepan and add 2 cups of water. Bring to a boil over high heat, add the reserved asparagus cooking juices, cover, and reduce the heat to medium. Cook for 30 minutes, or until the potato is easily pierced with a knife.

▸ Add the butter and olive oil and emulsify the mixture with a handheld immersion blender until it is smooth and creamy. Add the reserved asparagus, heat through, and serve.

LENTIL & BARLEY SOUP

This comforting winter soup is one of my favorites and could be a hearty meal in itself when served with a beautiful, crusty bread, a glass of wine, and a piece of cheese. This recipe serves more than four, but it is more economical to make it in larger batches and freeze what is not needed. When you are ready to eat the soup again, thaw it, heat it through, and enjoy a second time.

Serves 8

1 pound dried lentils, washed and drained

4 quarts chicken or beef stock

1 leek (8 ounces), cut into ½-inch pieces and washed (about 3 cups)

1 large onion (8 ounces), peeled and cut into ½-inch pieces

2 hot Italian sausages (about 5 ounces total), cut into ½-inch pieces

2 carrots (6 ounces), peeled and cut into ½-inch pieces

½ cup (4 ounces) pearl barley

5 large garlic cloves, peeled, crushed, and coarsely chopped

1 tablespoon herbes de Provence

1 tablespoon salt

½ teaspoon Tabasco sauce (optional)

½ cup grated Swiss cheese (optional)

▸ Place the lentils, stock, leeks, onion, sausages, carrots, barley, garlic, herbes de Provence, and salt in a large pot and bring the mixture to a boil over high heat. Reduce the heat to very low, cover, and cook gently for 1½ hours, or until the barley is cooked.

▸ Emulsify the soup with a handheld immersion blender for 8 to 10 seconds to make the mixture somewhat creamy, but still chunky. (Alternatively, place 2 cups of the soup in a blender or food processor and process for 20 seconds. Combine the puree with the remaining soup.)

▸ Add the Tabasco, if using, to the soup. Serve in bowls, garnished with the cheese, if desired.

This soup tends to thicken as it cools. When reheating leftovers, thin, if necessary, by adding some water.

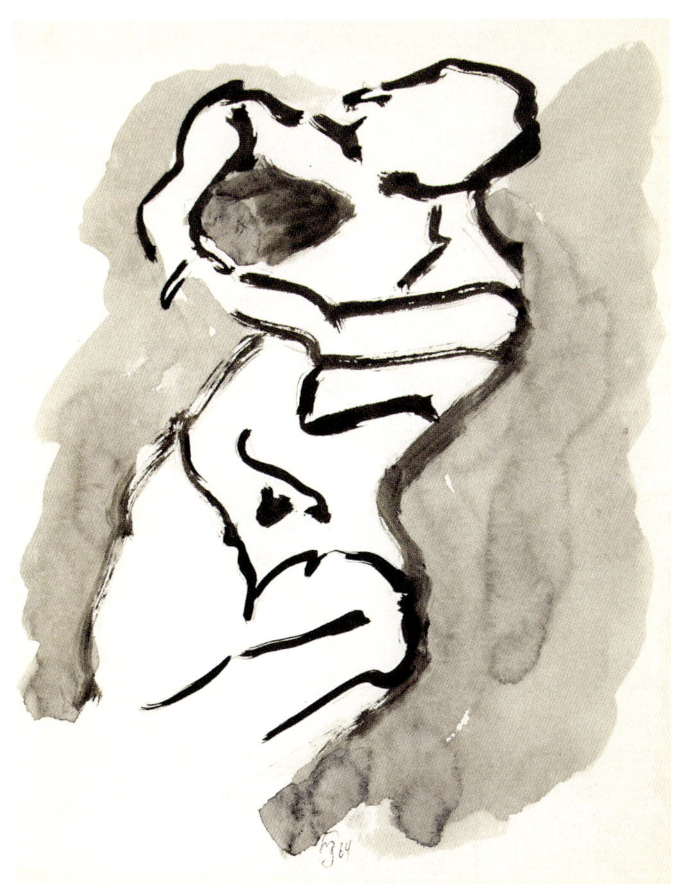

Turning Model, 1964

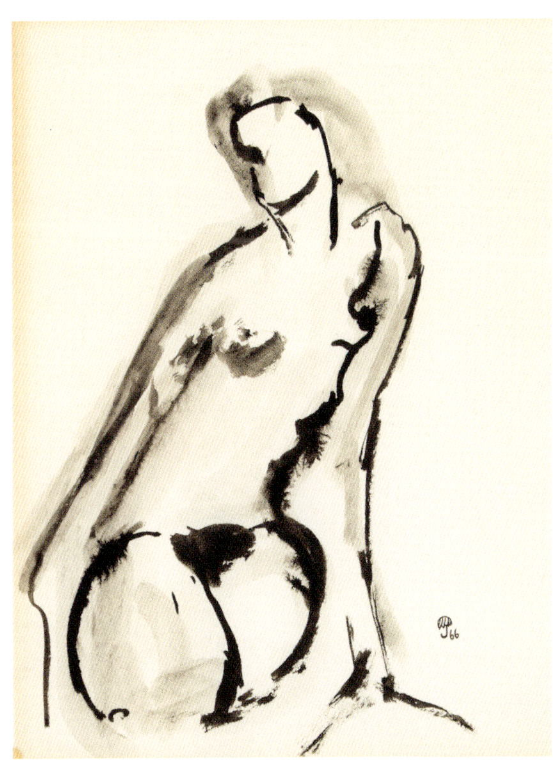

Model, 1966

BROCCOLI CREAM with TAPIOCA

This cream of broccoli soup is made with the heads, or crowns, of broccoli; the stems are cut into a julienne and served as a garnish. The soup is thickened with pearl tapioca—tiny, glistening jewellike balls—which are cooked on their own first in a lot of water. The tapioca makes a great addition to the soup. On its own it is quite mild in flavor, but it enhances the taste of the broccoli, adds to the sheen of the soup, and gives it a satisfying texture. The cooked tapioca tends to thicken and stick together after sitting awhile, but its pellets can be loosened again by adding a little water.

Serves 4

¼ cup pearl tapioca

2 heads broccoli (about 1¼ pounds)

3½ cups chicken stock

1 medium onion (6 ounces), peeled and cut into 1-inch pieces

1 teaspoon salt

¼ teaspoon freshly ground black pepper

⅓ cup heavy cream

▸ Bring 4 cups of water to a boil in a medium saucepan. Add the tapioca, bring the mixture back to a boil over high heat, cover, reduce the heat to low, and simmer gently for 20 minutes. Drain the tapioca in a colander, then rinse it under cold water for 15 to 20 seconds to stop the cooking. Set the tapioca aside. You should have about ¾ cup.

▸ Cut the broccoli heads from the stalks and set them aside. Peel the broccoli stems to remove the fibrous outer skin and cut the stalks into 2- to 3-inch chunks. Cut these chunks into ⅜-inch-thick slices, then stack the slices and cut them into ⅜-inch sticks. (You should have about 1¼ cups of broccoli sticks.) Bring the stock to a boil in a large saucepan over high heat and add the broccoli sticks. Bring the stock back to a boil and boil the sticks for about 1½ minutes. Remove the sticks with a skimmer and set them aside. Add the broccoli head pieces and onion to the stock, return the mixture to a boil, and cook, covered, over low heat for 12 minutes.

▸ Transfer the contents of the saucepan to a blender or food processor along with the salt and pepper and blend the mixture for 45 seconds to 1 minute, until smooth (you could also use a handheld immersion blender).

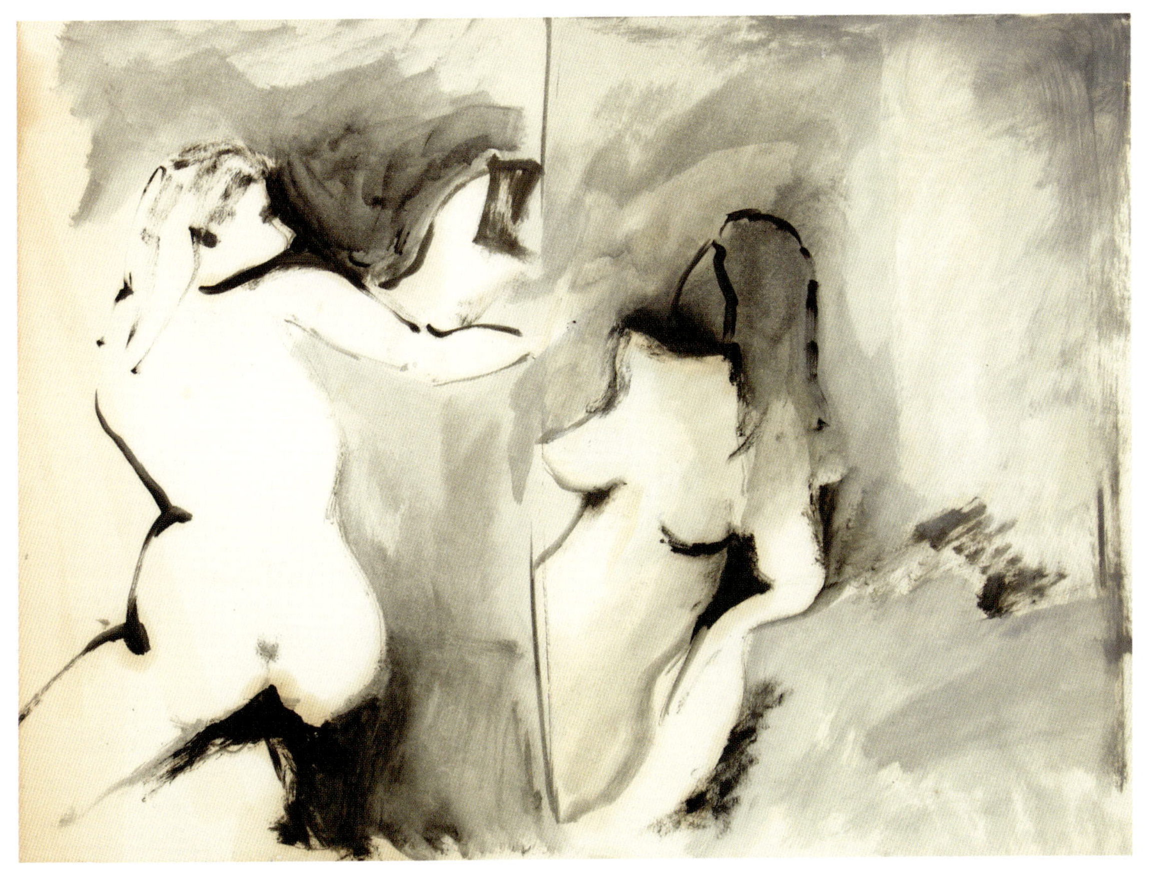

Two Nudes, 1966

▸ At serving time, place the broccoli soup in a saucepan. If the reserved cooked tapioca pellets are sticking together (as they tend to do after sitting awhile), add 2 to 3 tablespoons of cold water to them, and mix it in until they separate. Add the tapioca to the soup along with the broccoli sticks. Stir in the cream and bring the mixture to a simmer. Serve immediately.

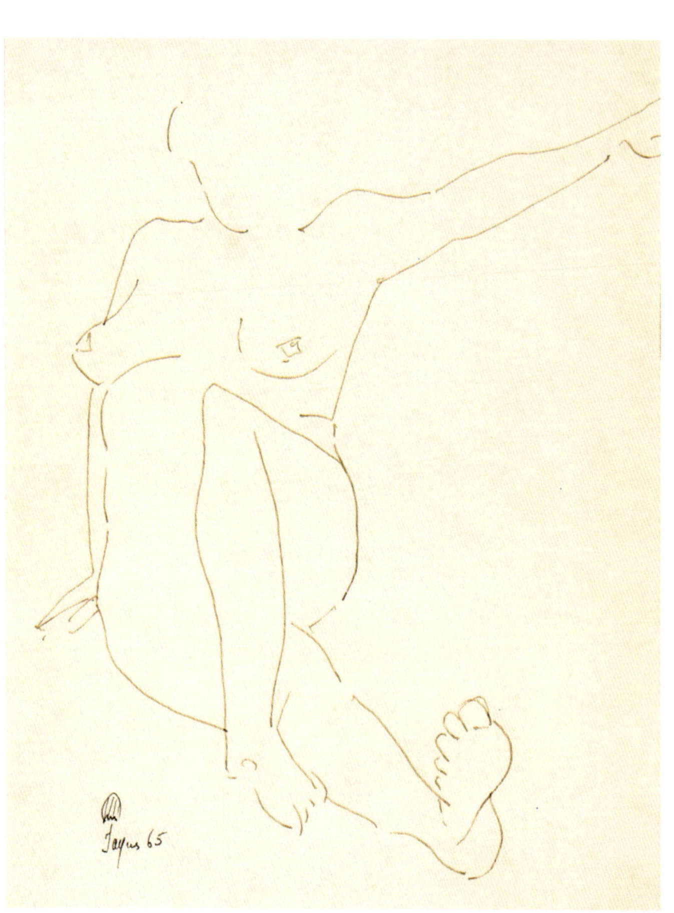

One Line Nude, 1965

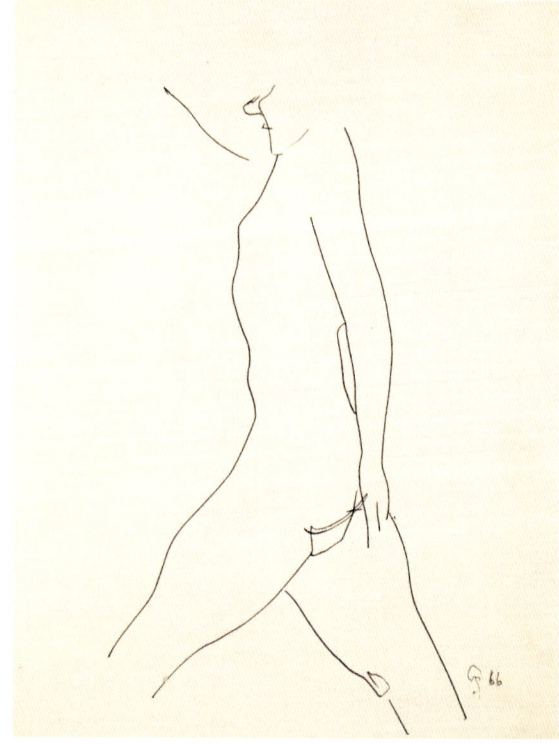

Walking, 1966

COLD CORN SOUP

This corn soup can be served hot as well as cold. It consists simply of onion, corn kernels, and potatoes—which act as a thickening agent—cooked together in water, then pureed in a food processor, and finally, finished with half-and-half and chopped chives to create a type of corn vichyssoise. One advantage of this soup is that it can be made ahead; it will keep, refrigerated, for 4 or 5 days (in that case, however, I would not add the half-and-half until just before it is served).

Serves 4

1 tablespoon butter

1 tablespoon corn oil or other neutral oil

1 medium onion (6 ounces), peeled and sliced (about 1¾ cups)

8 ounces potatoes, peeled and cut into 2-inch chunks

4 large ears sweet corn, husked and kernels removed (3½ cups)

1 teaspoon salt

1½ cups half-and-half, cold

2 tablespoons chopped fresh chives or tarragon

▸ Heat the butter and oil in a large saucepan. Add the onion and sauté for 2 minutes. Mix in the potatoes, corn kernels, salt, and 2½ cups of water. Bring the mixture to a boil, cover, reduce the heat to low, and boil gently for 30 minutes.

▸ Using a handheld immersion blender, puree the soup in the saucepan; alternatively, transfer the soup to a food processor and process until pureed. Stir in the half-and-half and chives. Refrigerate until serving time.

▸ To serve the soup hot: After pureeing the soup in step 2, add the half-and-half to the soup in the saucepan and bring the mixture to a boil. Mix in the chives or tarragon and serve.

SPICY GAZPACHO

This spicy gazpacho is a favorite in summer when my garden produces more cucumbers than I can use. Using a spicy tomato juice or Bloody Mary mix makes the recipe very quick and easy to execute. This can be made ahead and is best served cool but not too cold.

Serves 4

2 cucumbers (about 1½ pounds total)

1 cup diced sweet onion

2 large garlic cloves, peeled and crushed

1 teaspoon salt

4 tablespoons extra virgin olive oil

2 cups spicy tomato juice or Bloody Mary mix, such as V8

2 tablespoons chopped fresh chives, for garnish

▸ Peel the cucumbers, halve them lengthwise, and remove and discard the seeds. Cut them into coarse pieces. Place in a food processor along with the onion, garlic, and salt. Add 2 tablespoons of the olive oil. Process to liquefy the mixture. Add the tomato juice and process a few more seconds. Divide into bowls, drizzle with the remaining 2 tablespoons of olive oil, and top with the chives. Serve.

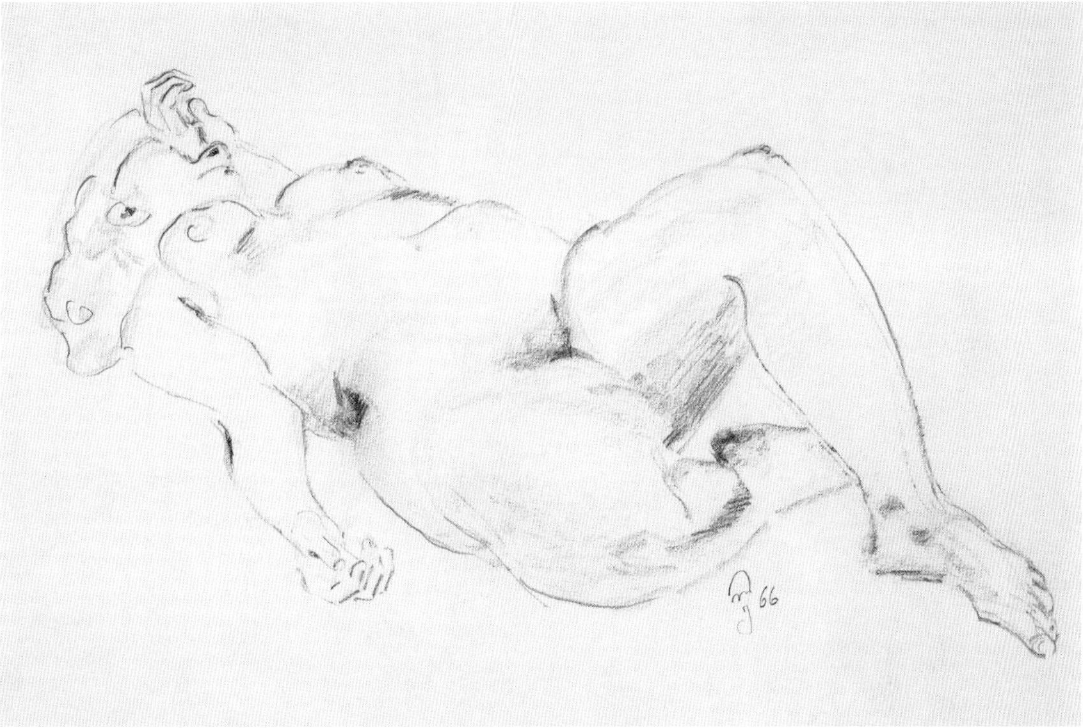

Leaning on Back, 1966

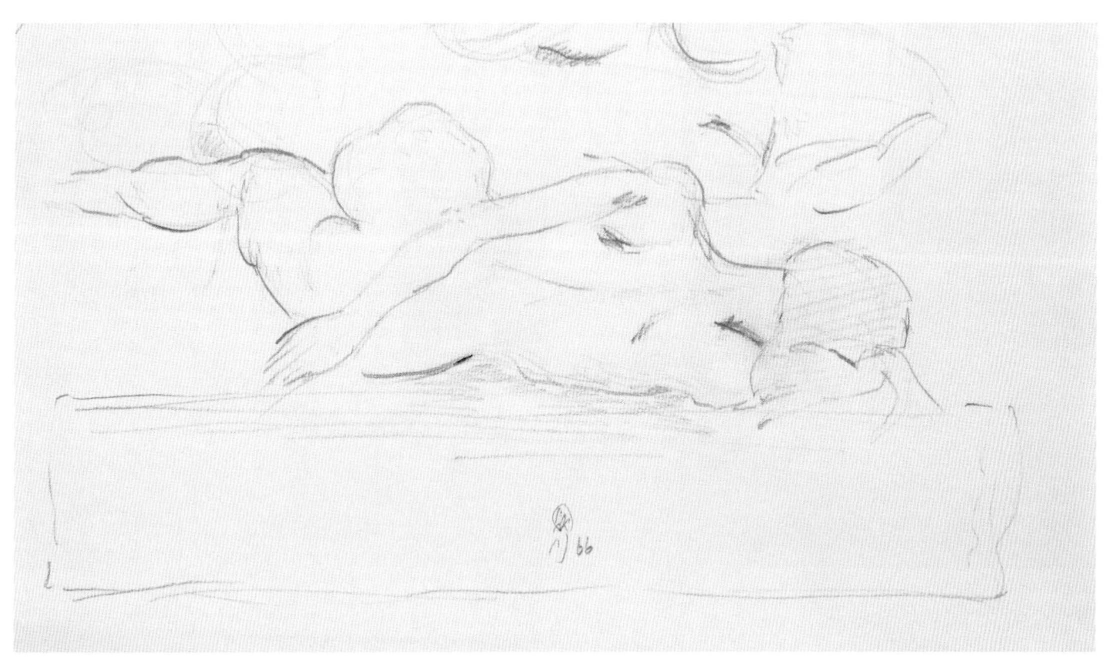

Model Back, 1966

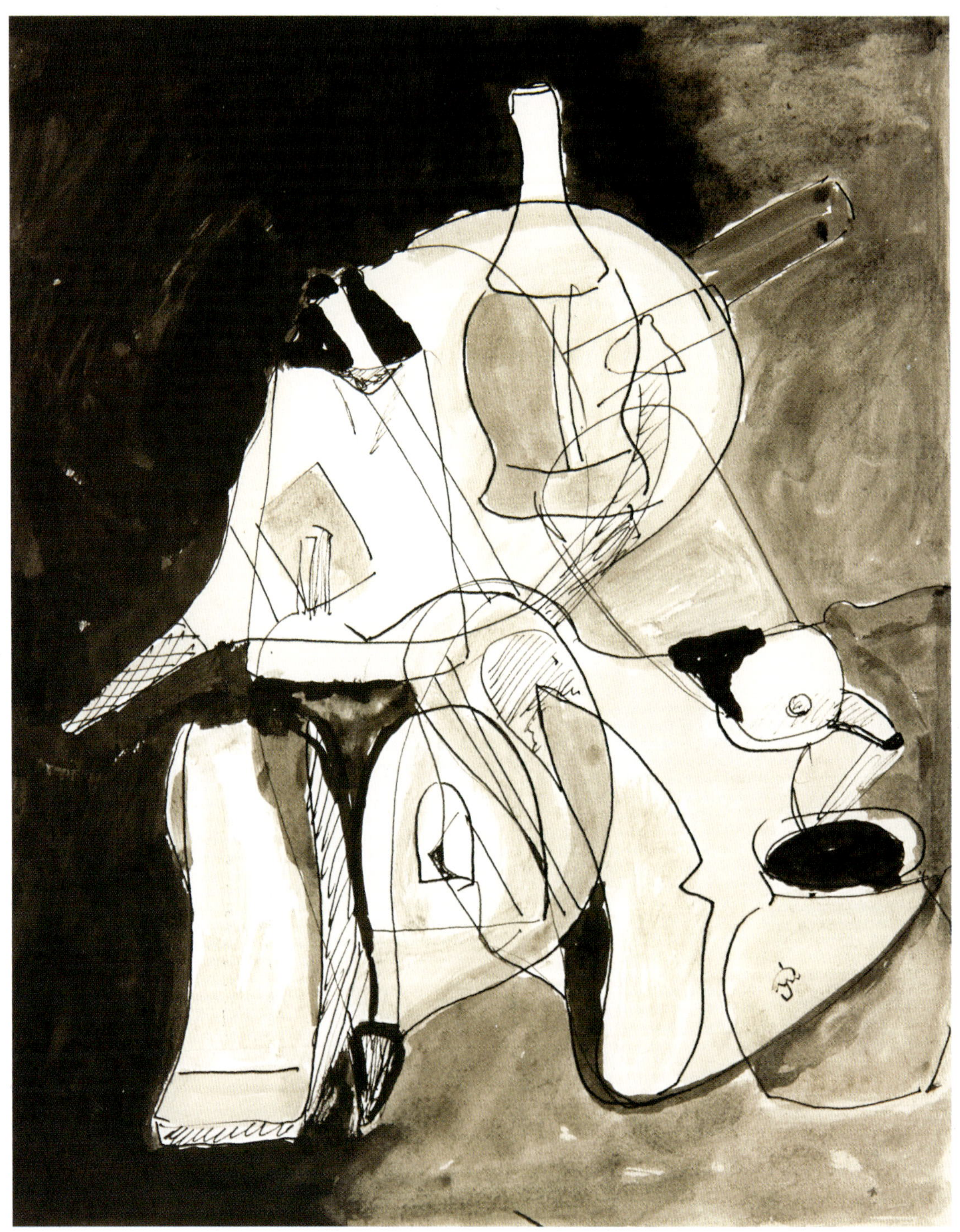

Music and Cooking

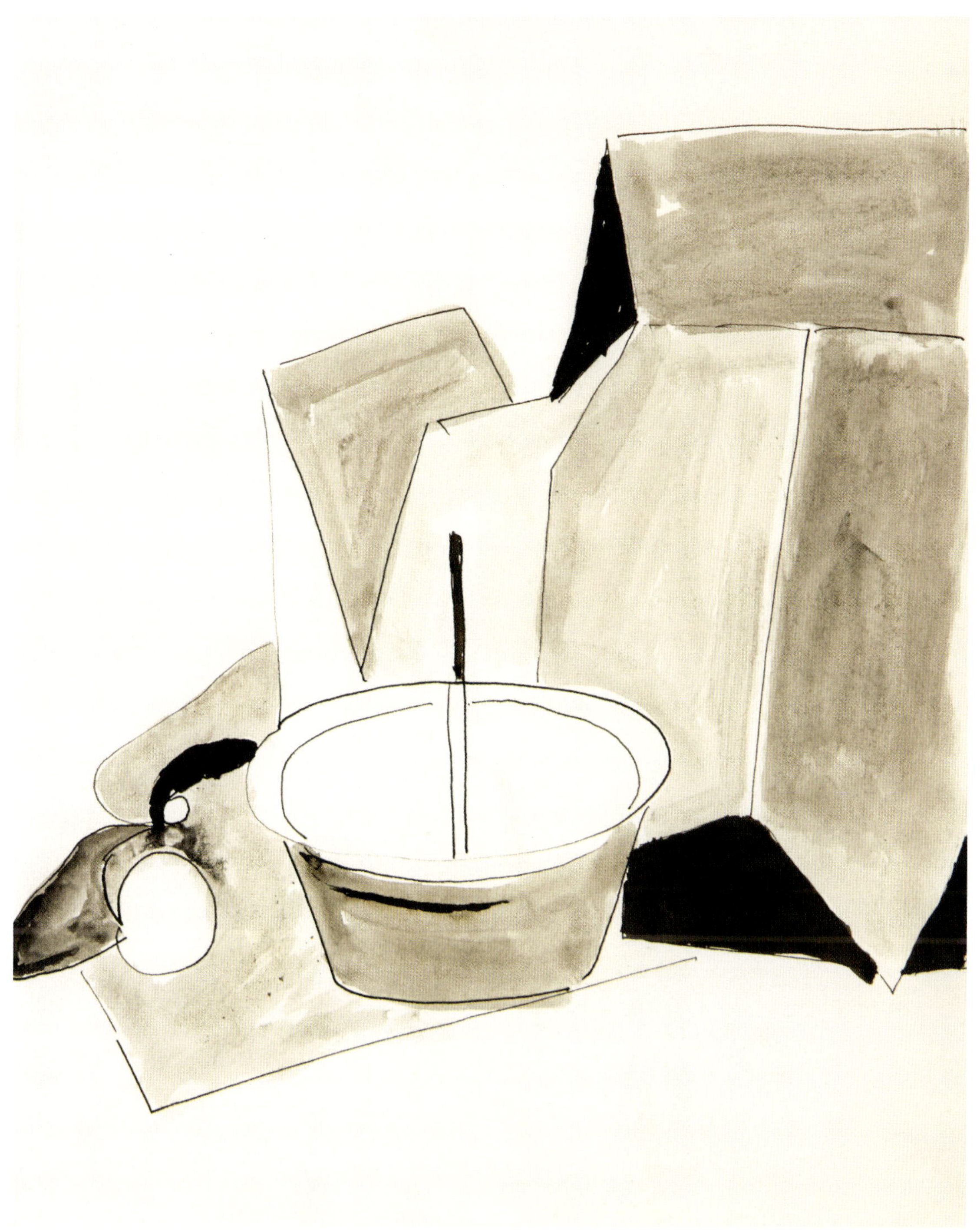

Stirring Pot

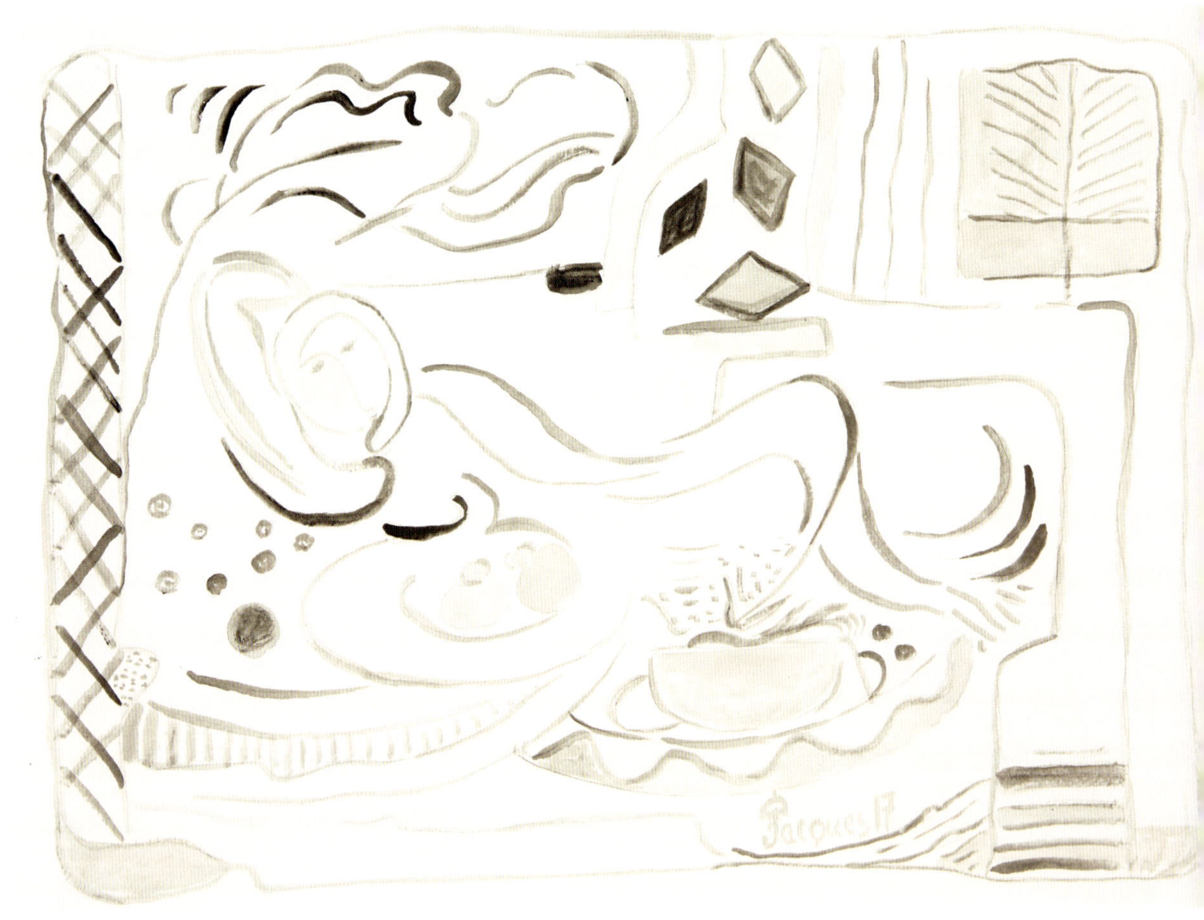

Relaxing, 2017

COLLARD GREENS & YELLOW GRITS SOUP

I thicken this soup with yellow grits, but you can use couscous or another type of grain, and kale could be substituted for collard greens if you prefer. If you make the soup ahead and find that it is too thick when reheated, add water to bring it to the desired consistency.

Serves 4 to 6

- 1 tablespoon olive oil
- 12 ounces collard greens, leaves cut into 1-inch pieces, stems into ½-inch pieces (7 cups, lightly packed)
- 2 carrots (5 ounces), peeled and cut into ½-inch pieces (1 cup)
- 7 cups chicken stock (or beef stock), preferably unsalted
- 1 teaspoon salt (or less, if using salted stock)
- ½ teaspoon freshly ground black pepper
- ⅓ cup yellow grits

▸ Heat the olive oil in a large pot. When it is hot, add the collard greens and sauté them over high heat for 4 to 5 minutes, stirring occasionally, until they are wilted.

▸ Add the carrots and stock to the pot. Bring to a boil, reduce the heat to low, cover, and boil gently for 15 minutes. Add the salt, pepper, and grits, cover, and continue to boil the mixture gently for 10 minutes longer. Serve immediately or cool, cover, refrigerate, and reheat at serving time.

TOMATO POTAGE

A tomato potage is a nice start to a meal, and this recipe couldn't be easier. Traditionally a *potage* is a thick soup made from vegetables. We start by sautéing onion pieces in olive oil, and a little flour is added as a thickener. Then water is stirred in along with quartered tomatoes, garlic, and seasonings, and the mixture is cooked for 15 minutes. I use water rather than stock in this soup and in many of my vegetable soups. Stock tends to overpower some vegetables, but water allows their taste to shine.

Serves 4

1 tablespoon olive oil

1 medium onion (4 ounces), peeled and cut into 1-inch pieces (1 cup)

2 teaspoons all-purpose flour

2 pounds ripe tomatoes, quartered

2 garlic cloves, peeled and crushed

1 teaspoon herbes de Provence

1 teaspoon sugar

¾ teaspoon salt

½ teaspoon freshly ground black pepper

3 tablespoons butter

12 basil leaves, cut into strips (julienne), for garnish

▸ Heat the olive oil in a large saucepan. When it is hot, add the onion and sauté it over medium to high heat for 3 to 4 minutes. Sprinkle the flour on top, mix well, and cook for 1 minute, then add 1½ cups of water. Mix well and bring to a boil.

▸ Add the tomatoes, garlic, herbes de Provence, sugar, salt, and pepper to the saucepan. Bring to a boil over high heat and stir well. Reduce the heat to low, cover, and cook for 15 minutes. Emulsify in a blender or with a handheld immersion blender. Add the butter and process again for a few seconds. Serve immediately, with the basil julienne on top.

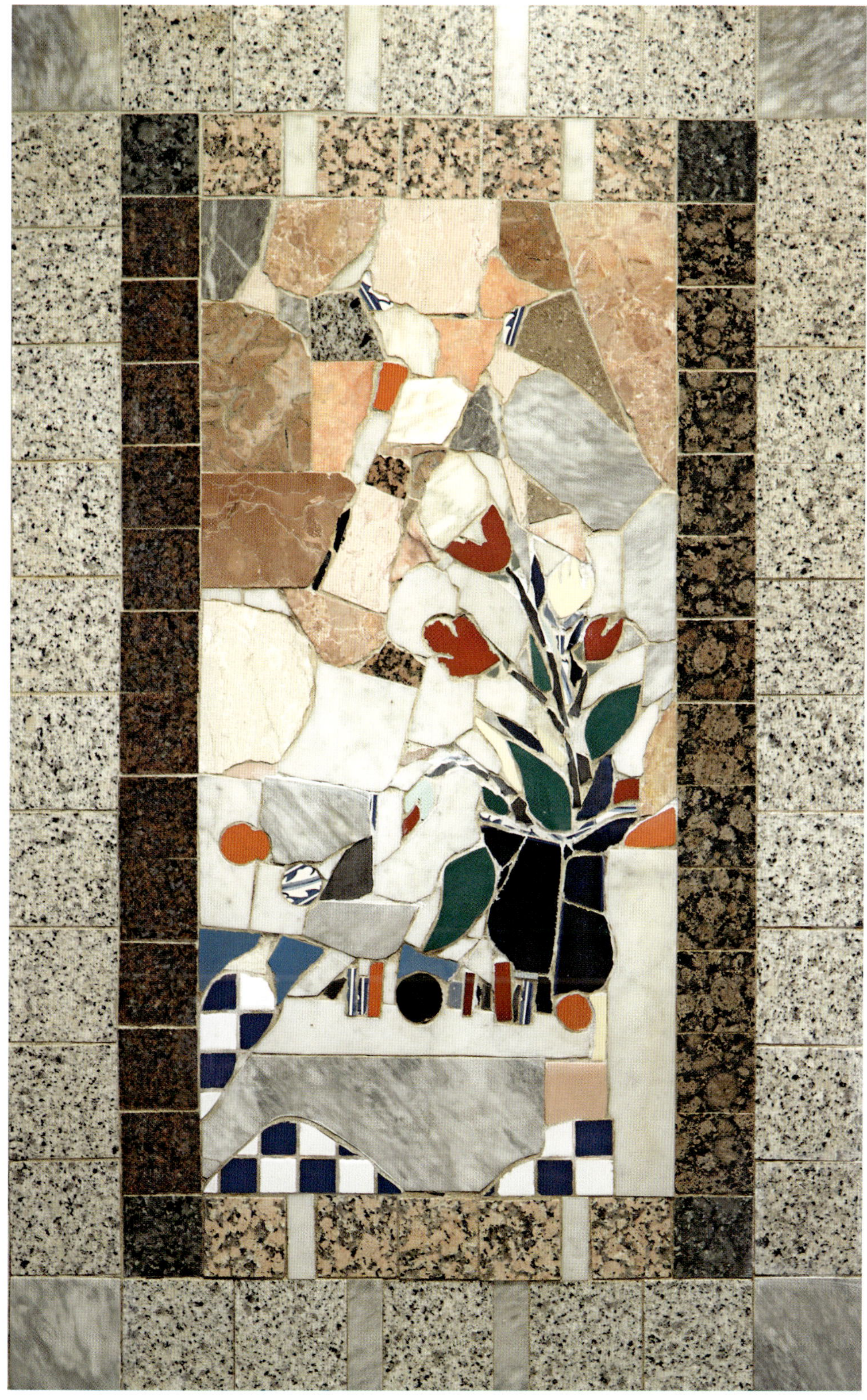

Still Life (mosaic)

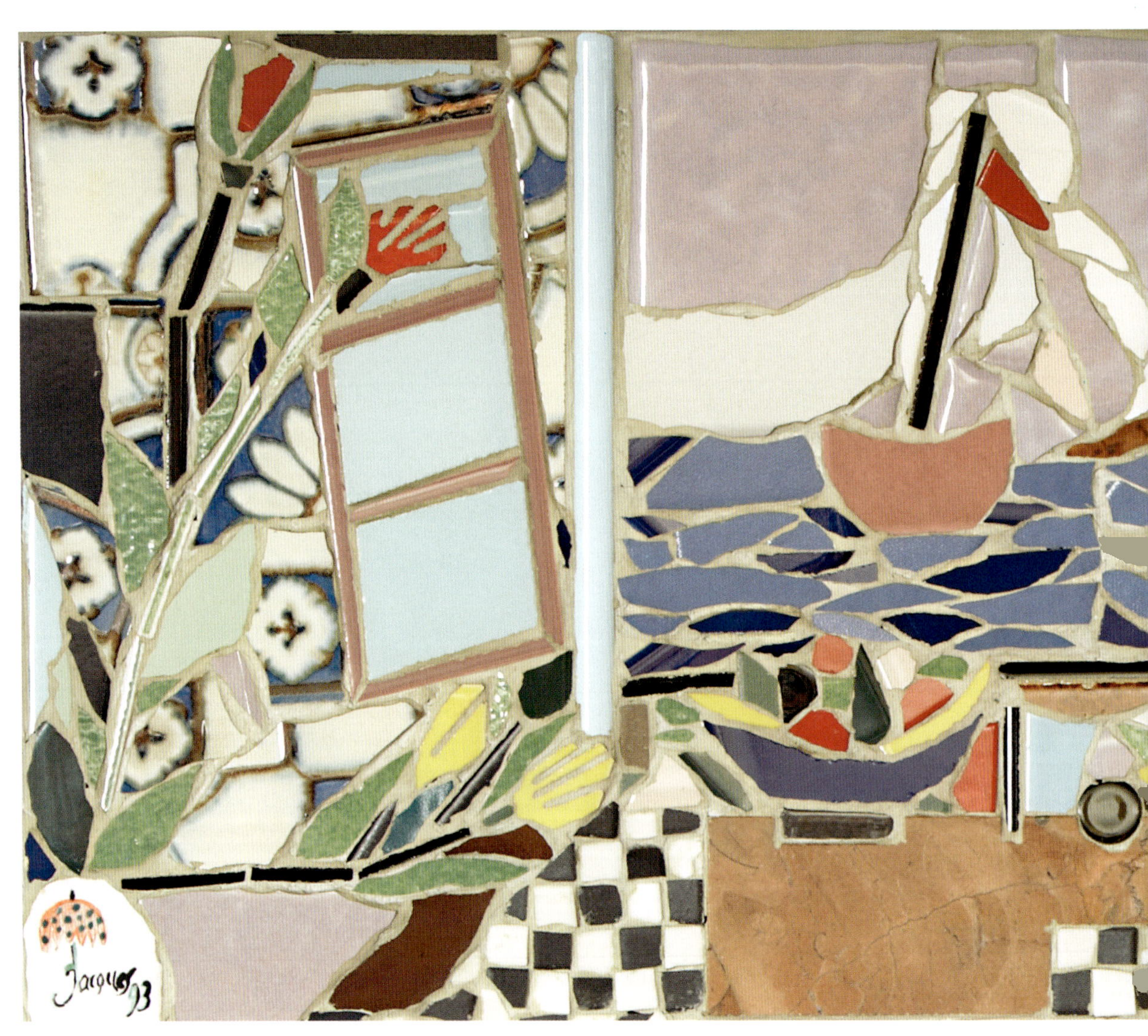
Jacques 93

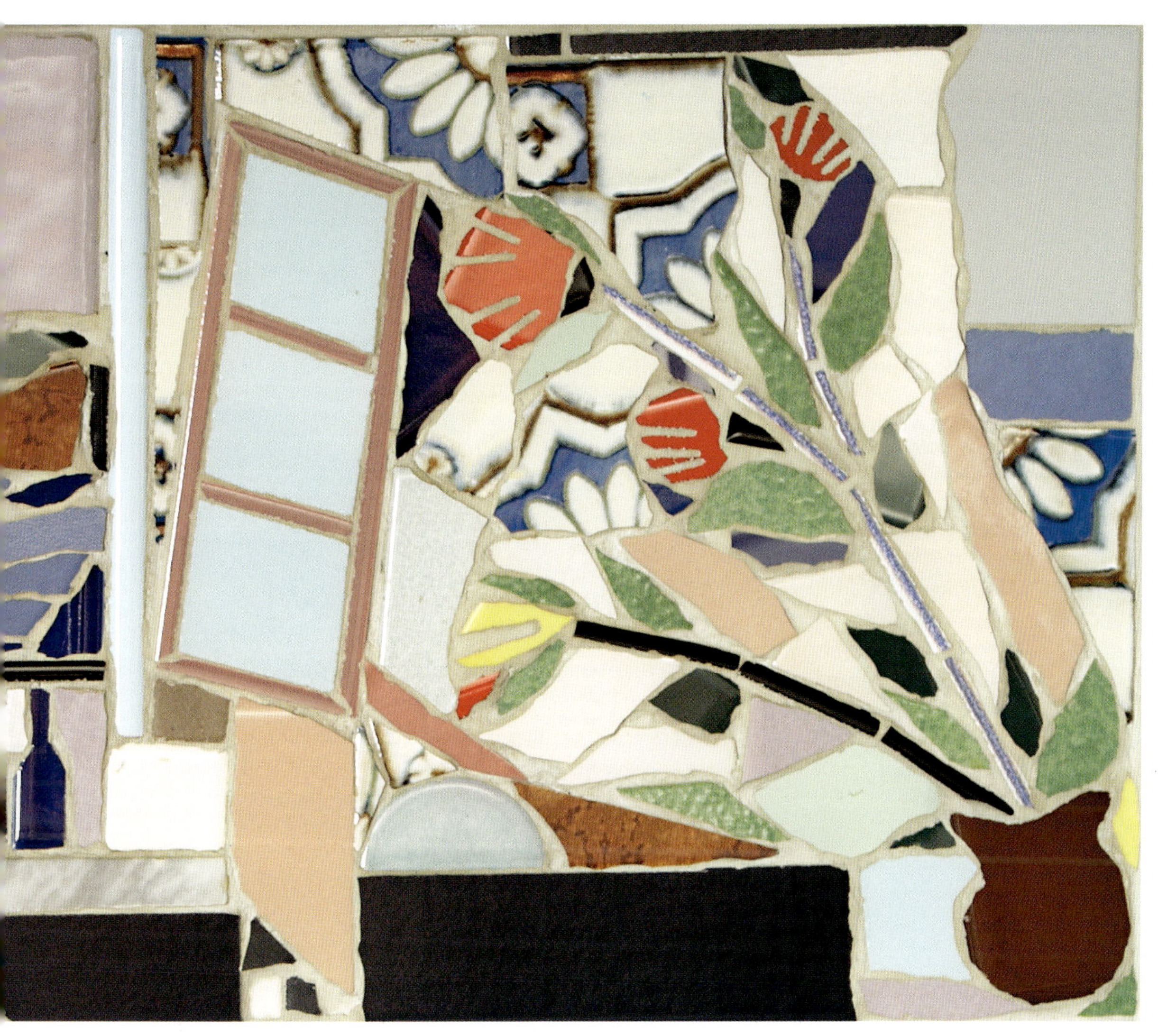

Window View (mosaic), 1993

BREAD & ONION SOUP

This soup is an ideal vehicle to use up leftover bread, which I cut up and brown in the oven first to improve its taste. Grated cheese, one of my favorite additions to the soup, is another great flavor enhancer. With so few ingredients this a good opportunity to use some homemade stock, but if you don't have any something from the store will work fine.

Serves 4

2 cups 1-inch-cubed leftover bread

1½ tablespoons peanut oil or other neutral oil

2 medium onions (10 ounces), peeled and thinly sliced (about 3 cups)

5 cups chicken stock, preferably unsalted

¼ teaspoon salt

½ teaspoon freshly ground black pepper

½ cup grated Gruyère cheese

1 tablespoon minced fresh chives

▸ Preheat the oven to 400°F. Place the cubed bread on a baking sheet and bake for 10 to 12 minutes, until nicely browned

▸ Place the oil and onions in a 12-inch saucepan and cook over high heat for 8 to 10 minutes, stirring occasionally, stirring occasionally, until the onions are nicely browned.

▸ Add the stock, salt, and pepper and bring the mixture to a strong boil, and keep it boiling for 5 minutes.

▸ Meanwhile, place the bread cubes in a large soup tureen and sprinkle the cheese on top. Pour the boiling stock and onion mixture into the tureen and mix well. Ladle into soup plates, sprinkle the chives on top, and serve immediately.

CREAM of MUSHROOM SOUP

A handful of simple ingredients are transformed into a delicate and tasty soup in a short amount of time. I always like serving something like this as an introduction to a dinner with multiple courses, but of course it can be served on its own as well. To save time, it can be made ahead. You could also freeze it, adding the cream just before serving.

Serves 6

7 cups chicken stock

2 cups coarsely chopped leek

1 cup ½-inch-diced onion

10 ounces white button or cremini mushrooms

¾ teaspoon salt

¾ teaspoon freshly ground black pepper

⅓ cup all-purpose flour

6 tablespoons butter, melted

½ cup heavy cream

▸ Place the stock, leek, and onion in a stockpot and bring to a boil over high heat. Meanwhile, cut some of the mushroom caps into thick slices, stack together, and cut into thin strips (julienne). You should have about 1½ cups—this will be cooked, then reserved for garnish. Cut the rest of the mushrooms into coarse pieces and add to the stockpot. Place the julienned mushroom caps in a strainer and set on top of the boiling liquid so the mushrooms boil in the stock for 2 minutes. Remove and set aside. Continue to boil the stock for 15 minutes. Add the salt and pepper, adjusting depending on the saltiness of your chicken stock and to your liking. Meanwhile, whisk together the flour and melted butter (this is a beurre manié). Whisk into the soup to thicken. Boil for 10 minutes. Using a handheld immersion blender, emulsify the mixture into a fine, smooth texture. Alternatively, transfer the soup to a blender or food processor and process until finely pureed. Stir in the cream and the mushroom garnish. Serve.

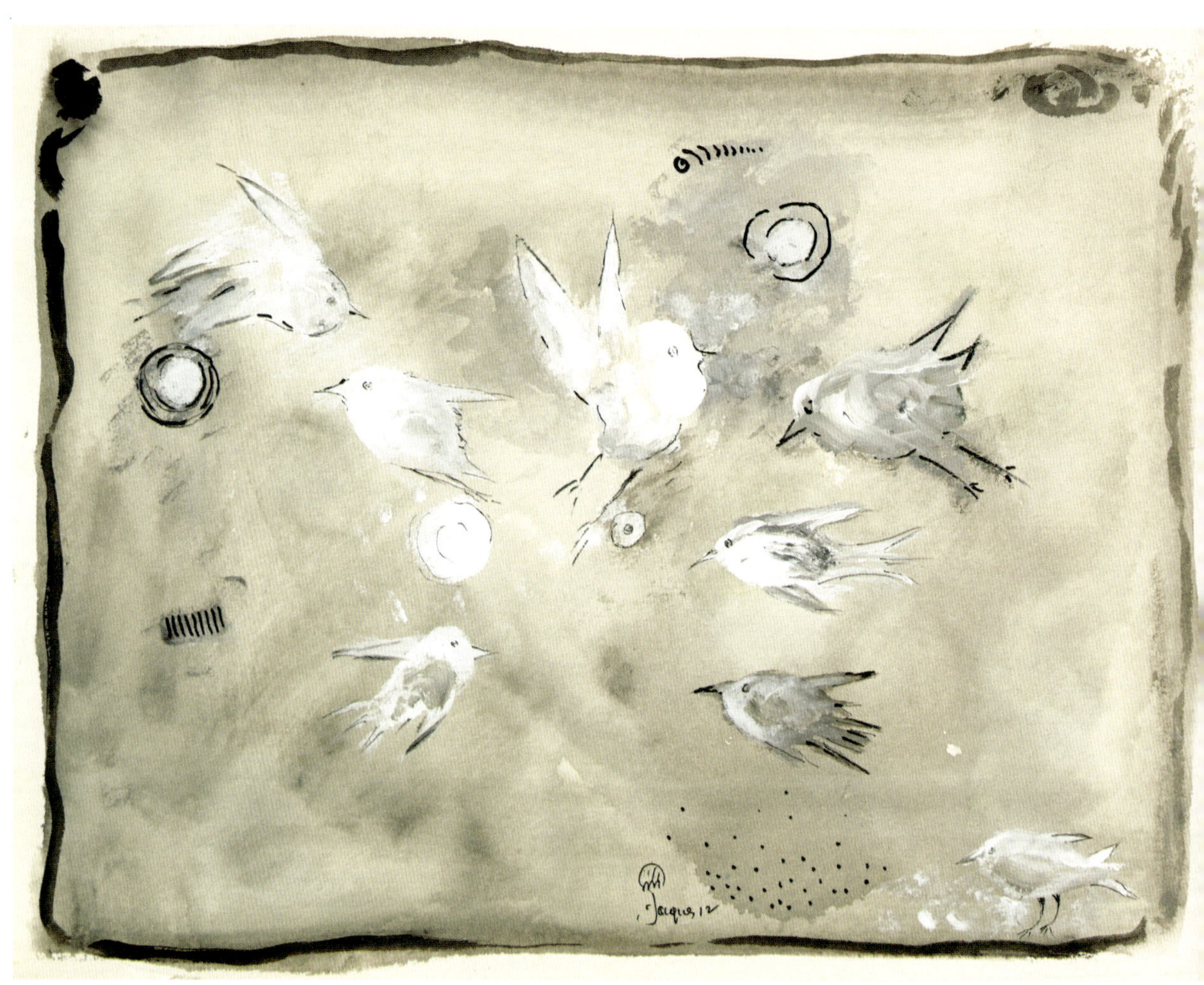

Les Oiseaux, 2012

WATERCRESS SOUP & SALAD

I love watercress. When I find it at a market, I like to buy two bunches and use them to make two different recipes—a soup and a salad. This makes use of the whole plant. It can be hard to find sometimes. You may need to visit an Asian specialty market. Watercress wilts very easily. You can make your dressing ahead if you like, but do not dress the salad until you're ready to eat.

Soup serves 6, salad serves 4

1½ cups cubed leftover bread

1½ tablespoons olive oil

SOUP

2 bunches watercress, stems and leaves separated

6 cups chicken stock

1¼ pounds potatoes, peeled and roughly chopped

1 leek, trimmed, washed, and coarsely chopped

¾ cup diced onion

½ teaspoon salt

½ teaspoon freshly ground black pepper

⅓ cup heavy cream

SALAD

1 teaspoon finely chopped garlic

1 teaspoon Dijon-style mustard

1 tablespoon lemon juice

3 tablespoons peanut, canola, or grapeseed oil

¼ teaspoon salt

¼ teaspoon freshly ground black pepper

▸ Preheat the oven to 350°F.

▸ Scatter the bread cubes on a baking sheet, drizzle with the olive oil, and toss. Bake for about 12 minutes, or until the croutons are nice and brown. Set aside.

▸ Separate the stems from the leaves of the watercress by cutting below the leaves. You should have about 3 ounces of leaves (about 6 cups)–reserve these for the salad. Place the stems, stock, potatoes, leek, onion, salt, and pepper in a stock-pot and bring to a boil. Lower the heat, partially cover, and boil gently for 40 minutes, or until the potatoes are cooked through. Emulsify with a handheld blender. Alternatively, transfer the soup to a blender or food processor and process until finely pureed. Stir in the cream. Serve as needed.

▸ Make the dressing in a jar if you're doing it ahead, or in a large bowl if you're ready to eat. Combine the garlic, mustard, lemon juice, and oil and season with the salt and pepper. Toss with the watercress leaves just before serving. Place on individual plates and garnish with the croutons.

SALADE JEANNETTE

This was a specialty of my mother's. She would whip a little bit of cream for a few seconds until it became foamy, then add some vinegar, which thickened the dressing. The irony here is people think cream is so caloric, but in fact, the salad could almost be considered low calorie because a tablespoon of cream is about 50 calories, which is certainly much less than the 120 calories in a tablespoon of oil—and it's delicious. This dressing is also good served with poached fish.

Serves 4

¼ cup heavy cream

¼ teaspoon salt

¼ teaspoon freshly ground black pepper

2 teaspoons white or red wine vinegar

6 cups mixed salad greens, washed and dried

▸ In a large salad bowl, lightly whisk the cream for about 15 seconds, until it is just foamy. Add the salt and pepper and stir in the vinegar. The dressing will thicken. Add the greens and toss together until the leaves are lightly coated. Serve immediately.

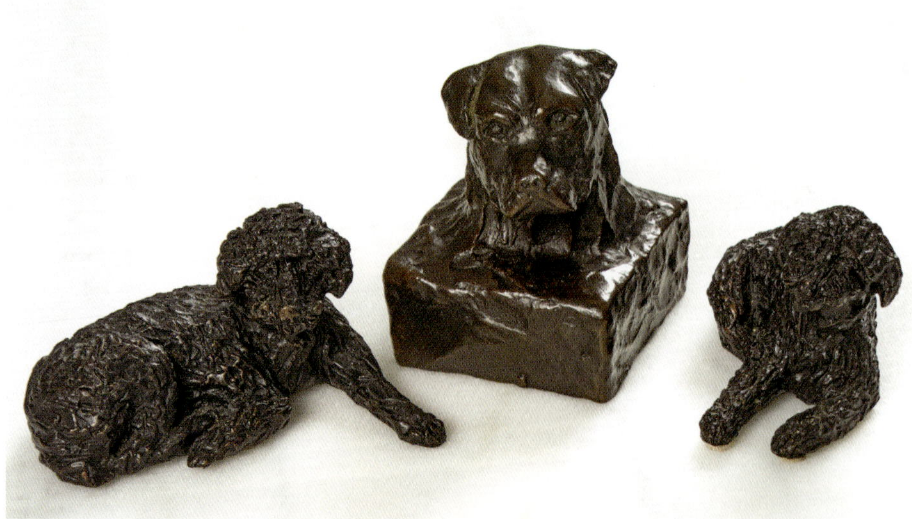

Three Dogs

GREENS & SARDINE SALAD

Use a variety of salad greens in this dish and wash them if necessary. After gently agitating the greens in a sink full of cold water, lift them from the water, drain them thoroughly, and dry—preferably in a salad spinner. Thorough drying is necessary because water will dilute the dressing and render the salad tasteless. I love the canned sardines, preferring the plump ones from Portugal or the southwest of France.

Serves 4

1 (4-ounce) can sardines in olive oil

½ cup chopped mild onion

3 ripe plum tomatoes, cut into 1-inch dice (1½ cups)

2½ tablespoons extra virgin olive oil

1½ tablespoons red wine vinegar

¼ teaspoon salt

¼ teaspoon freshly ground black pepper

5 cups salad greens (Boston lettuce, escarole, or other varieties), trimmed, rinsed, and thoroughly dried

▸ Reserving the juices and oil in the can, cut the sardines into 1-inch pieces. Place the pieces in a large salad bowl and add the reserved juices and oil. Add the onion, tomatoes, olive oil, vinegar, salt, and pepper and mix them together gently.

▸ At serving time, add the greens to the bowl, toss to coat them with the dressing, and divide among four plates for serving.

▸ Alternatively, arrange the greens on individual plates or on a large platter and spoon the sardine mixture on top.

FENNEL & OLIVE SALAD

In this salad, the fennel is blanched briefly. This prevents it from discoloring and makes it tender but still crunchy. You can prepare the fennel as a side dish by blanching it the same way and sautéing it in oil before serving. This is a great salad to prepare in the summer, as it keeps well in the refrigerator and does not rely on quick-wilting lettuces, though it should be brought to room temperature before serving.

Serves 4

1 bulb fennel (8 ounces)

1 large garlic clove, peeled, crushed, and finely chopped (1½ teaspoons)

½ teaspoon salt

½ teaspoon freshly ground black pepper

1 teaspoon poppy seeds

2 tablespoons olive oil

2 teaspoons cider vinegar

¾ cup finely diced red onion

¼ cup pitted kalamata olives (about 16)

▸ Using a vegetable peeler, peel and clean the fennel of any dark, tough, or damaged parts. Using a mandoline or a blade attachment for a food processor, slice it into very thin slices (about 3 cups lightly packed). Bring 3 cups of water to a boil in a medium-size pot. Add the fennel and return to a boil. Let boil for 10 seconds, then drain. Combine the garlic, salt, pepper, poppy seeds, olive oil, and vinegar in a shallow serving bowl and mix well. Add the drained fennel and diced onion to the dressing and toss to combine. Scatter the olives on top and serve.

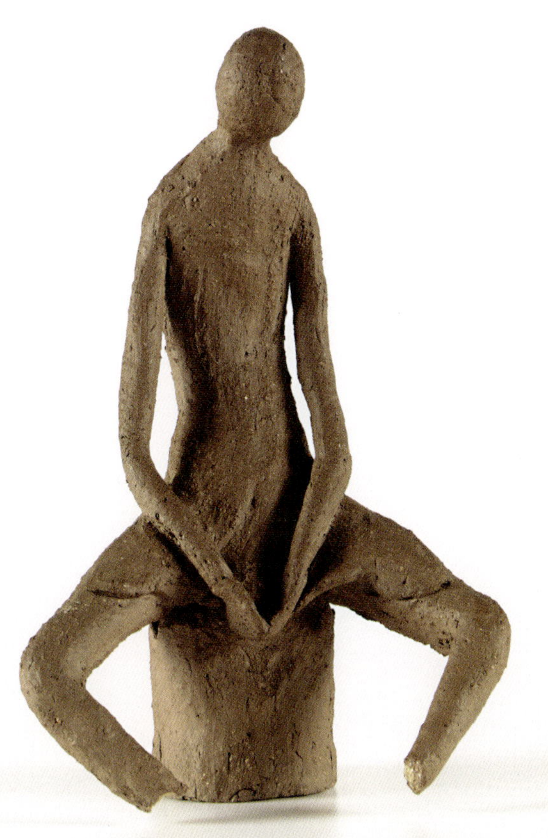

Sitting Nymph

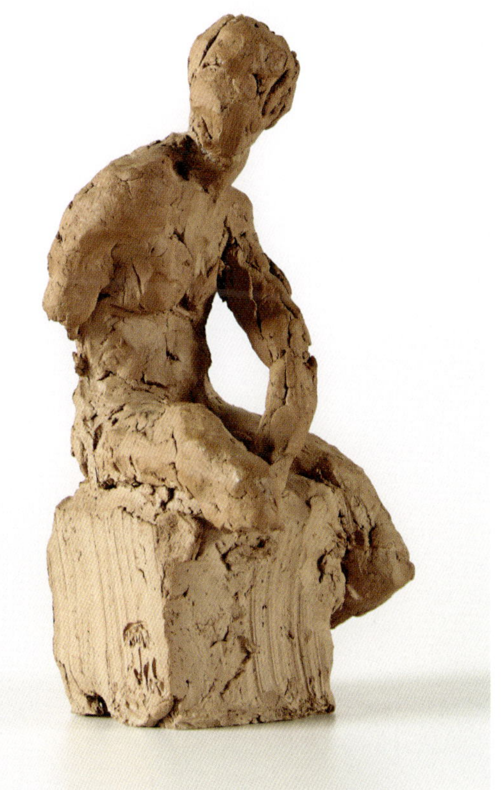

Sitting Man

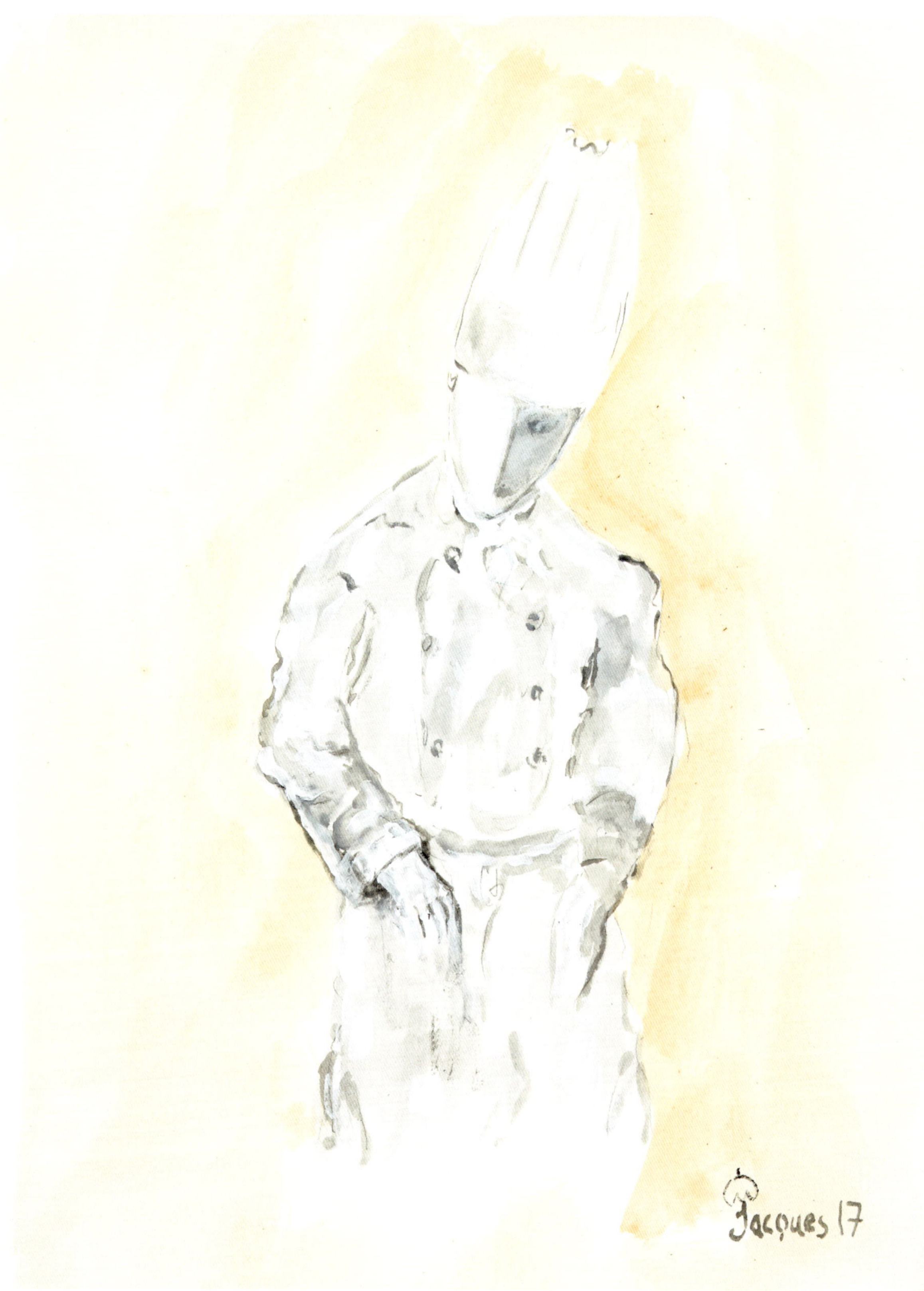

Chefs 1, 2017

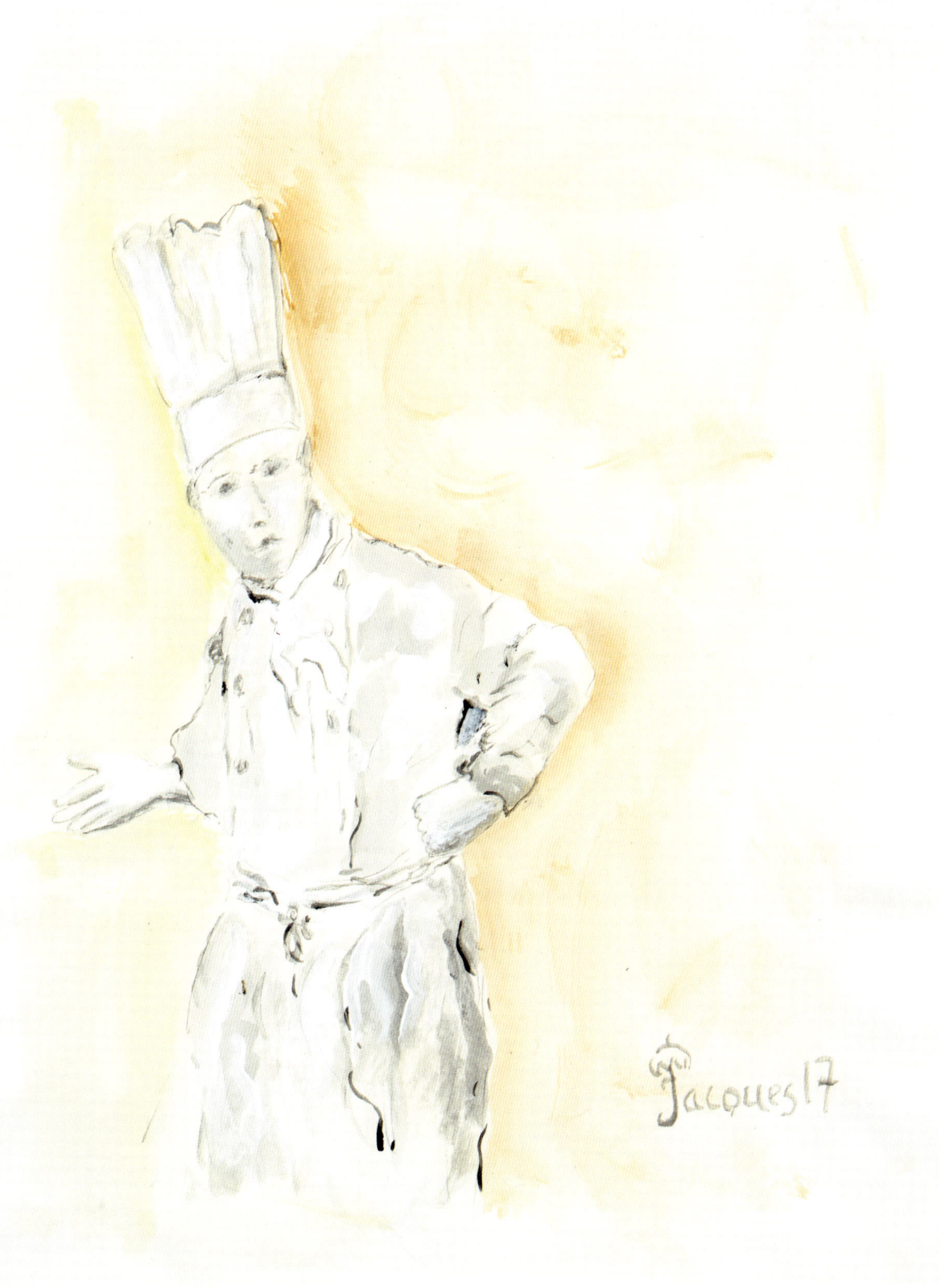

Chefs 3, 2017

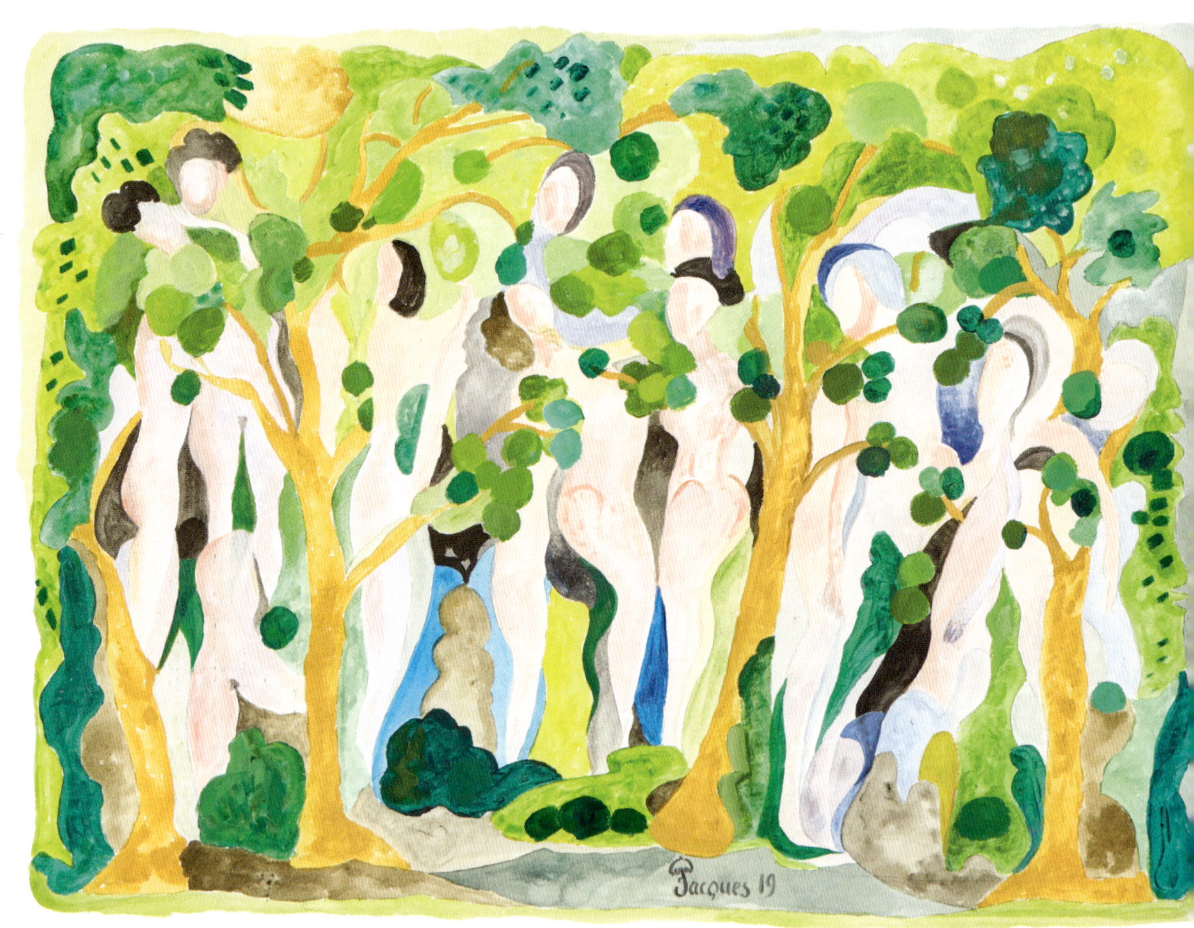

Nudes in the Forest, 2019

SALAD RIVIERA

This is a salad I always enjoy when I travel on Oceania cruise lines. Simple, classic, beautiful, and easy to put together, it makes an easy first course for a light dinner. The salad can be plated ahead, and the dressing added just before serving.

Serves 2

1 small head baby lettuce (about 1½ ounces)

3 tablespoons thinly sliced shallot

1 piece soft Gorgonzola cheese (about 1½-inch square)

DRESSING

1½ teaspoons Dijon-style mustard

2 teaspoons red wine vinegar

¼ teaspoon salt

¼ teaspoon freshly ground black pepper

2 tablespoons olive oil

▸ Separate the leaves of the lettuce and arrange them on two soup plates with bigger leaves outside and smaller leaves in the center so that it resembles a rose. Sprinkle the shallots on top and cut or break the Gorgonzola into ½-inch pieces to sprinkle on top.

▸ To make the dressing, place the mustard, vinegar, salt, and pepper in a bowl and whisk. Add the olive oil and mix well. At serving time, drizzle over the salad and serve immediately.

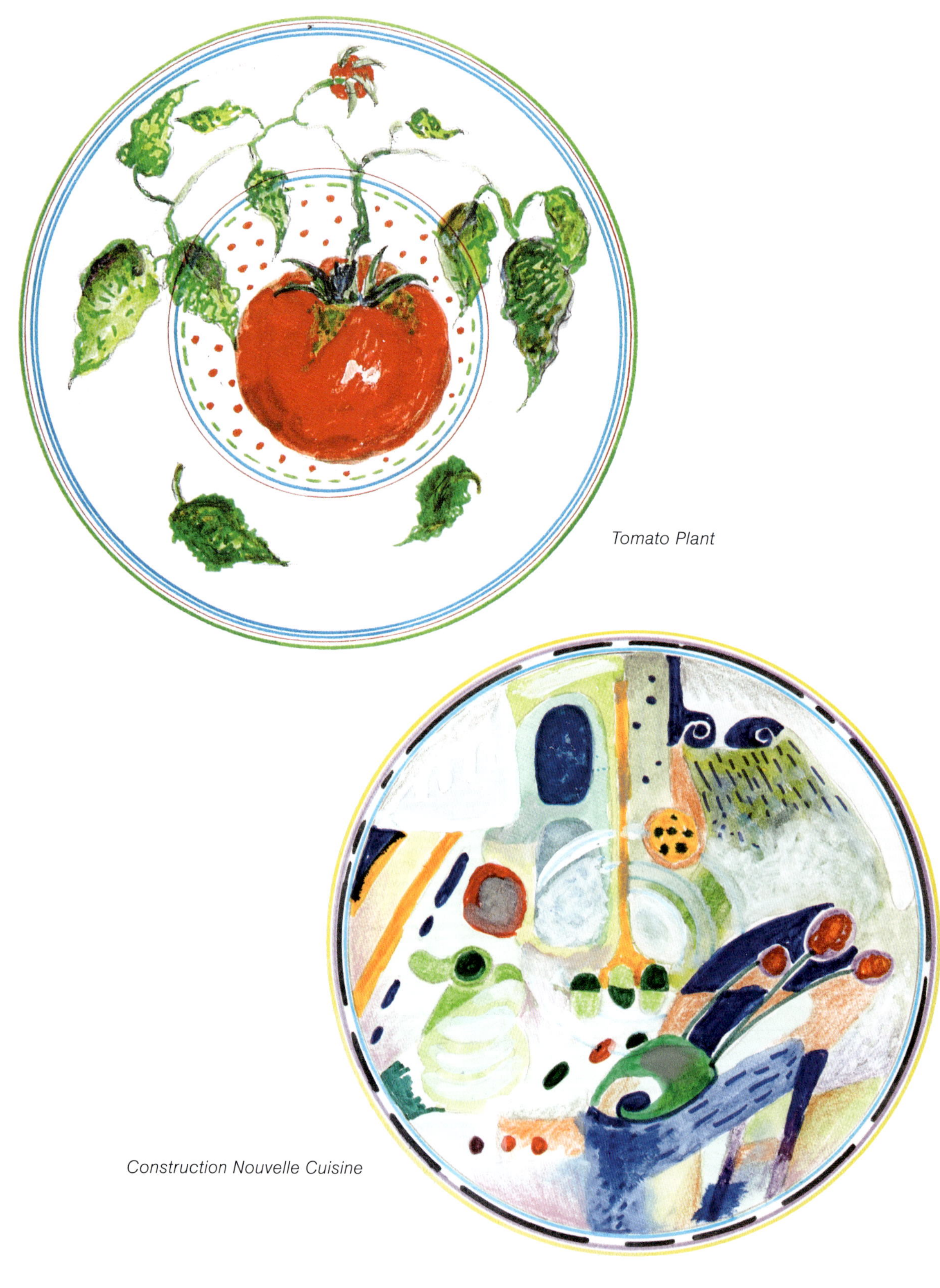

Tomato Plant

Construction Nouvelle Cuisine

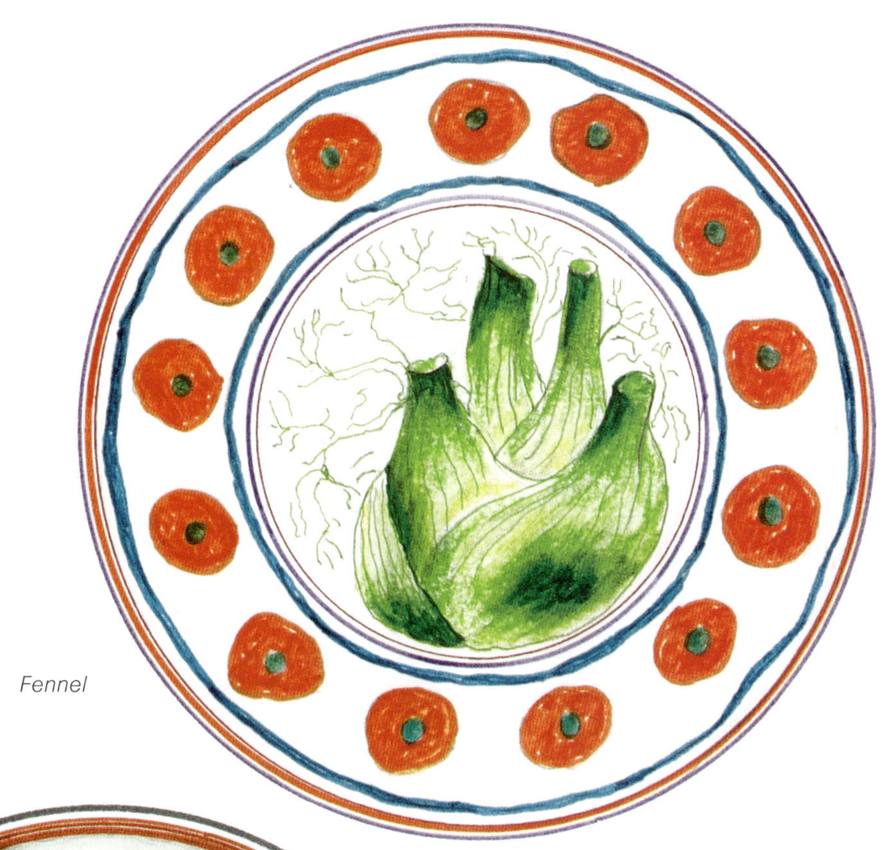

Fennel

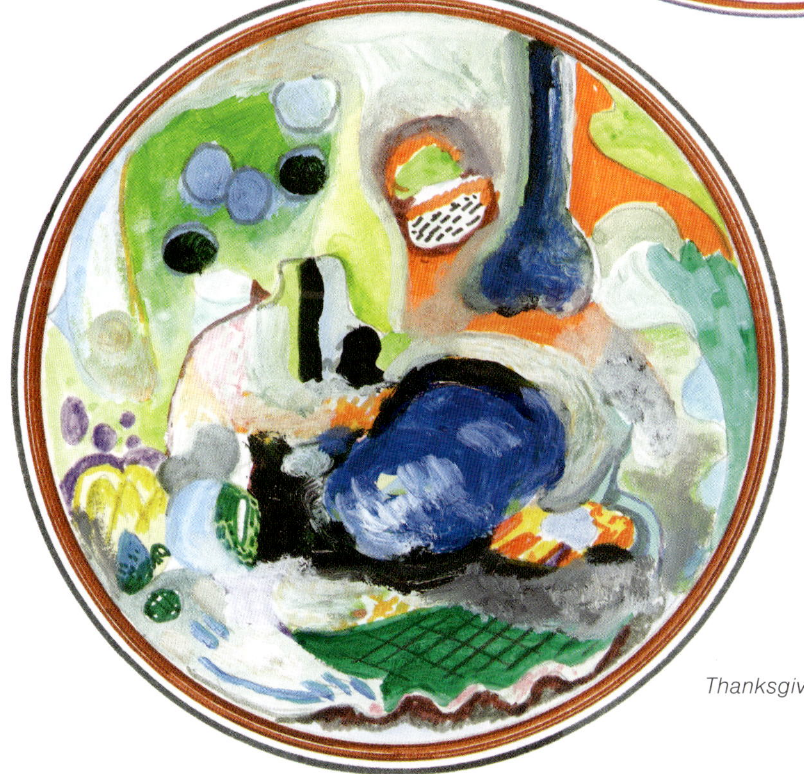

Thanksgiving

BEAN SPROUT SALAD

I often sauté bean sprouts for dishes I prepare at home and sometimes have extra raw sprouts. This versatile salad quickly and easily solves the problem of what to do with those leftover sprouts. It's become a family favorite.

Serves 4

2 teaspoons black sesame seeds

2 teaspoons white sesame seeds

1 pound bean sprouts

6 scallions, cut into ½-inch pieces (¾ cup)

2 tablespoons red wine vinegar

1½ teaspoons sugar

½ teaspoon salt

1 tablespoon sesame seed oil

1 tablespoon canola oil

▸ Preheat the oven to 375°F.

▸ Evenly distribute the black and white sesame seeds on a baking sheet. Bake for 6 to 8 minutes, until they are lightly toasted. Set aside.

▸ Bring 4 cups of water to a boil in a large saucepan. Add the bean sprouts and bring the water back to a boil, which will take 3 to 4 minutes. Boil the sprouts for 10 seconds, then drain.

▸ In a bowl large enough to hold the finished salad, mix the scallions, vinegar, sugar, salt, sesame seed oil, and canola oil. Add the sprouts and toasted sesame seeds and mix well. Serve at room temperature or refrigerate and serve cold. This dish will keep in an airtight container in the refrigerator for 3 to 4 days.

CARROT & PARSLEY SALAD

This carrot and parsley salad appears often on my table and is a mainstay in homes and bistros across France, where it's called *carottes râpées*. The carrots can be grated by hand or in a food processor fitted with the shredding insert. I use lots of parsley and some garlic, and I season the salad with a simple oil and vinegar dressing for a fresh flavor. It keeps well.

Serves 4

12 ounces carrots

1¼ cups fresh flat-leaf parsley leaves

2 large garlic cloves, peeled, crushed, and finely chopped

½ teaspoon salt

¼ teaspoon freshly ground black pepper

4 teaspoons red wine or cider vinegar

3 tablespoons extra virgin olive oil

▸ Peel and shred the carrots into small strands using the large holes of a box grater or in a food processor fitted with the shredding insert.

▸ Place the carrots, parsley, and garlic in a bowl. Stir in the salt, pepper, vinegar, and olive oil and mix well. Serve.

BULGUR & MINT SALAD

Bulgur is a form of whole wheat that has been cracked, cleaned, parboiled, and dried, and it only needs hot water and time to be ready to eat. I like hot sauce, especially sriracha, and have used it liberally in this salad because I think its hotness contrasts nicely with the coolness and pungency of the mint and other herbs. Light and delightful, this summer dish can be served as a first course or as an accompaniment to almost any meat or fish main course. It will keep, refrigerated, for 4 or 5 days.

Serves 4

1 cup bulgur wheat

1 cup lightly packed fresh mint leaves

1 cup lightly packed fresh flat-leaf parsley or other herbs

1 carrot (about 5 ounces), peeled and grated into strips using the large holes of a box grater (about ½ cup)

4 scallions, minced (about 1 cup)

2 to 3 garlic cloves, peeled, crushed, and minced (about 2 teaspoons)

1 teaspoon salt

1½ teaspoons sriracha or other hot pepper sauce (more or less depending on your taste)

¼ cup lemon juice

¼ cup corn or peanut oil

▸ Place the bulgur in a bowl and add about 3 cups of water. Soak for 3 to 4 hours, or as long as overnight.

▸ Meanwhile, coarsely chop the mint and parsley together.

▸ Drain the bulgur in a strainer for 10 to 20 minutes. Place the drained bulgur in a bowl and add the chopped herbs, carrot, scallions, garlic, salt, sriracha, lemon juice, and oil. Mix well.

▸ Serve at room temperature.

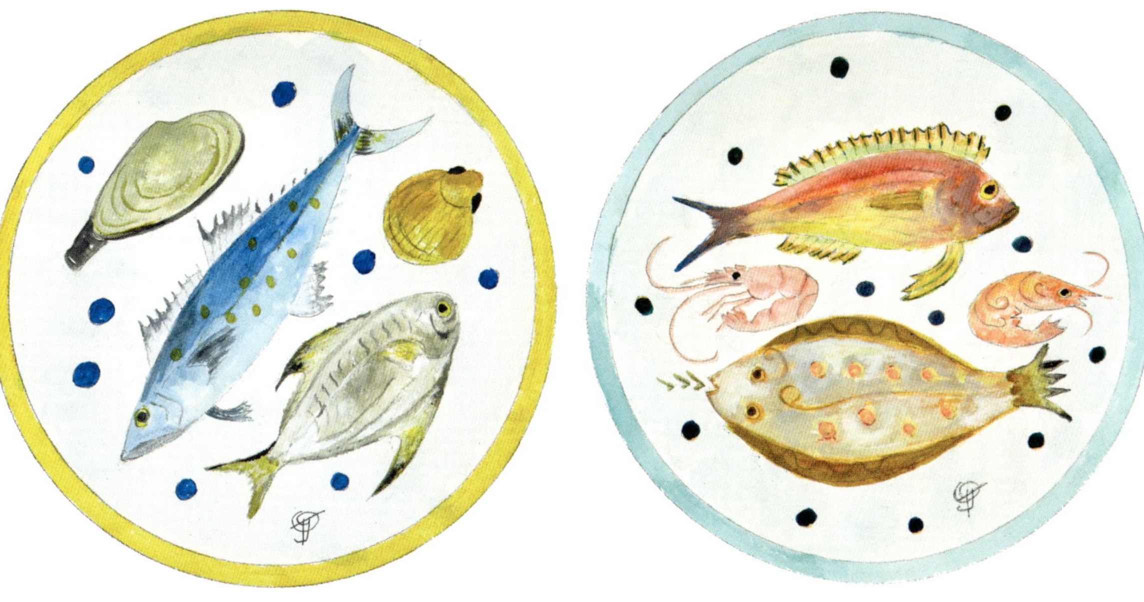

Fish 1

Fish 2

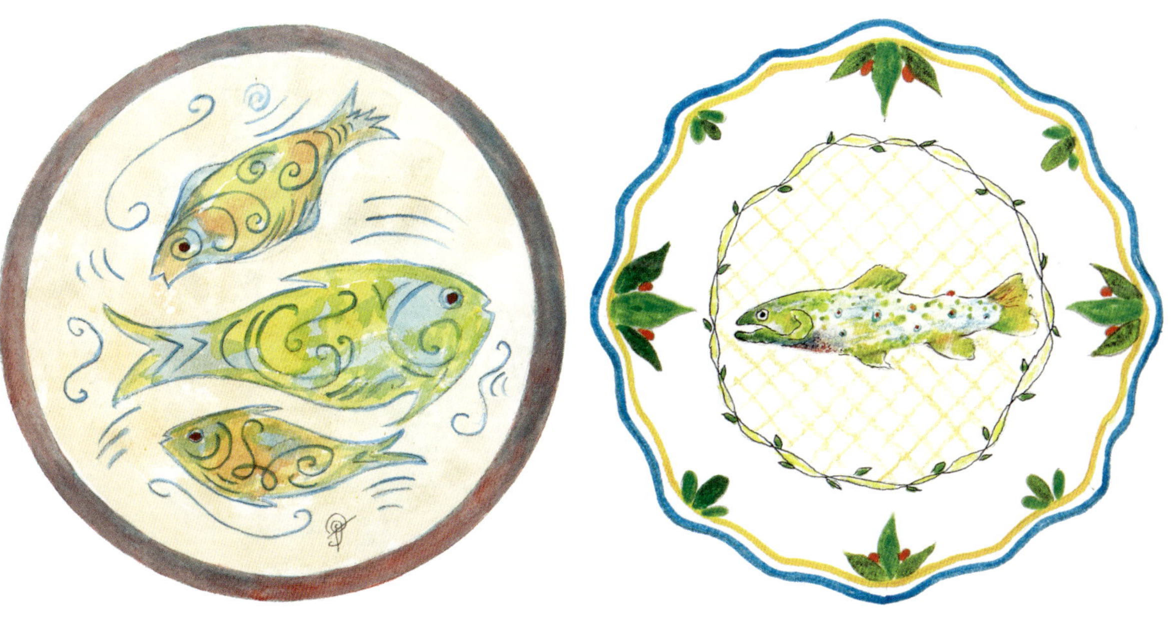

Fish 3

Fish 4

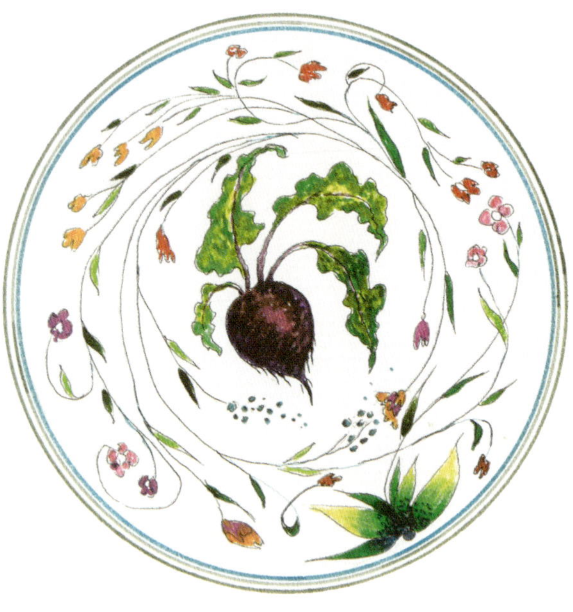

Beet

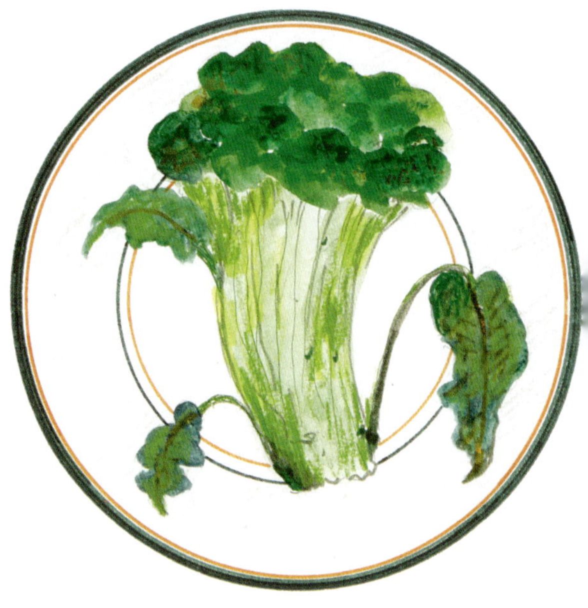

Broccoli

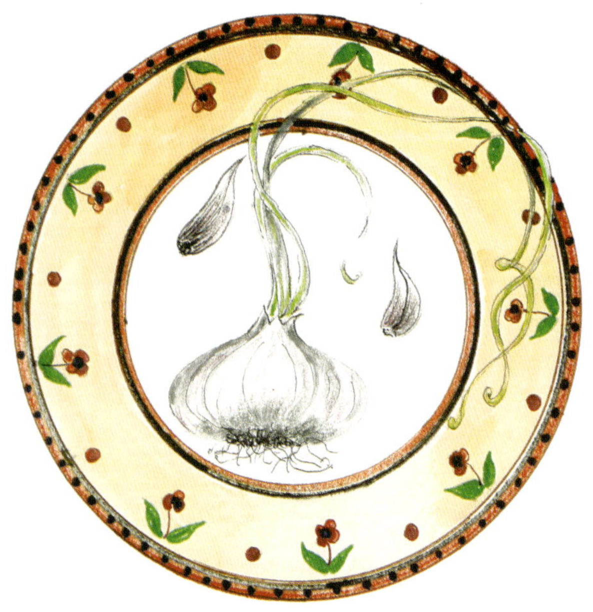

Garlic, 1998

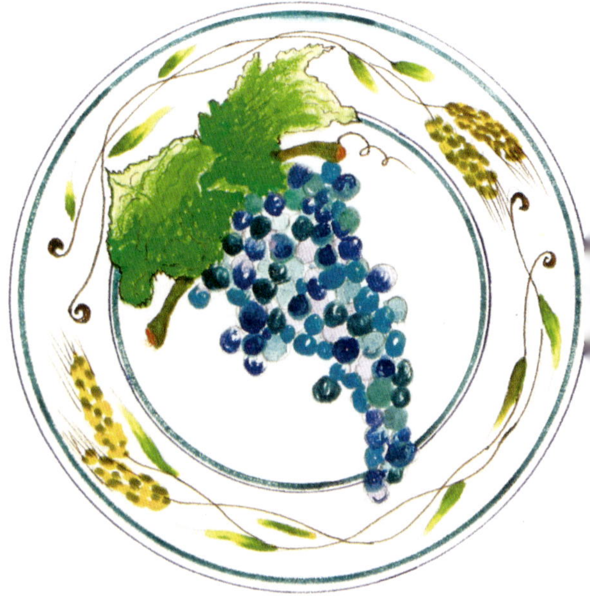

Grapes, 1997

MOCK CAESAR SALAD

This salad is an ideal first course. It's a great vehicle for leftover salad greens, bread—which we turn into croutons—and cheese. I love to use blue cheese here, but I also included some cheddar and Camembert that I had on hand.

Caesar salads are usually made with romaine lettuce, but I use escarole in my version, and you can substitute any other salad green varieties you have on hand. In keeping with tradition, lemon juice replaces vinegar in the dressing, which also includes garlic, olive or peanut oil, seasonings, and the crumbled cheese.

Serves 2

3 cups loosely packed escarole leaves

1 slice stale bread (about 1 ounce), cut into ½-inch pieces

1 teaspoon olive oil

DRESSING

1 small garlic clove, peeled

2 anchovy fillets in oil, coarsely chopped

1 tablespoon lemon juice

2 tablespoons extra virgin olive or peanut oil

Dash of salt

Dash of freshly ground black pepper

¼ cup crumbled blue cheese, or a combination of blue with pieces of cheddar, Camembert, and so on

▸ Preheat the oven to 400°F.

▸ Remove and discard any wilted or damaged areas from the salad leaves and tear the trimmed greens into 2-inch pieces. Wash the greens and dry them thoroughly in a salad spinner.

▸ Toss the bread cubes with the 1 teaspoon of olive oil and place them on a small baking sheet. Bake for 10 minutes, or until nicely browned on all sides.

▸ To make the dressing, mash and chop the garlic into a coarse puree. Combine it in a small bowl with the anchovy, lemon juice, olive oil, salt, and pepper.

▸ Right before serving time, add the salad greens to the dressing in the bowl and toss well. Sprinkle with the croutons and cheese and serve as needed.

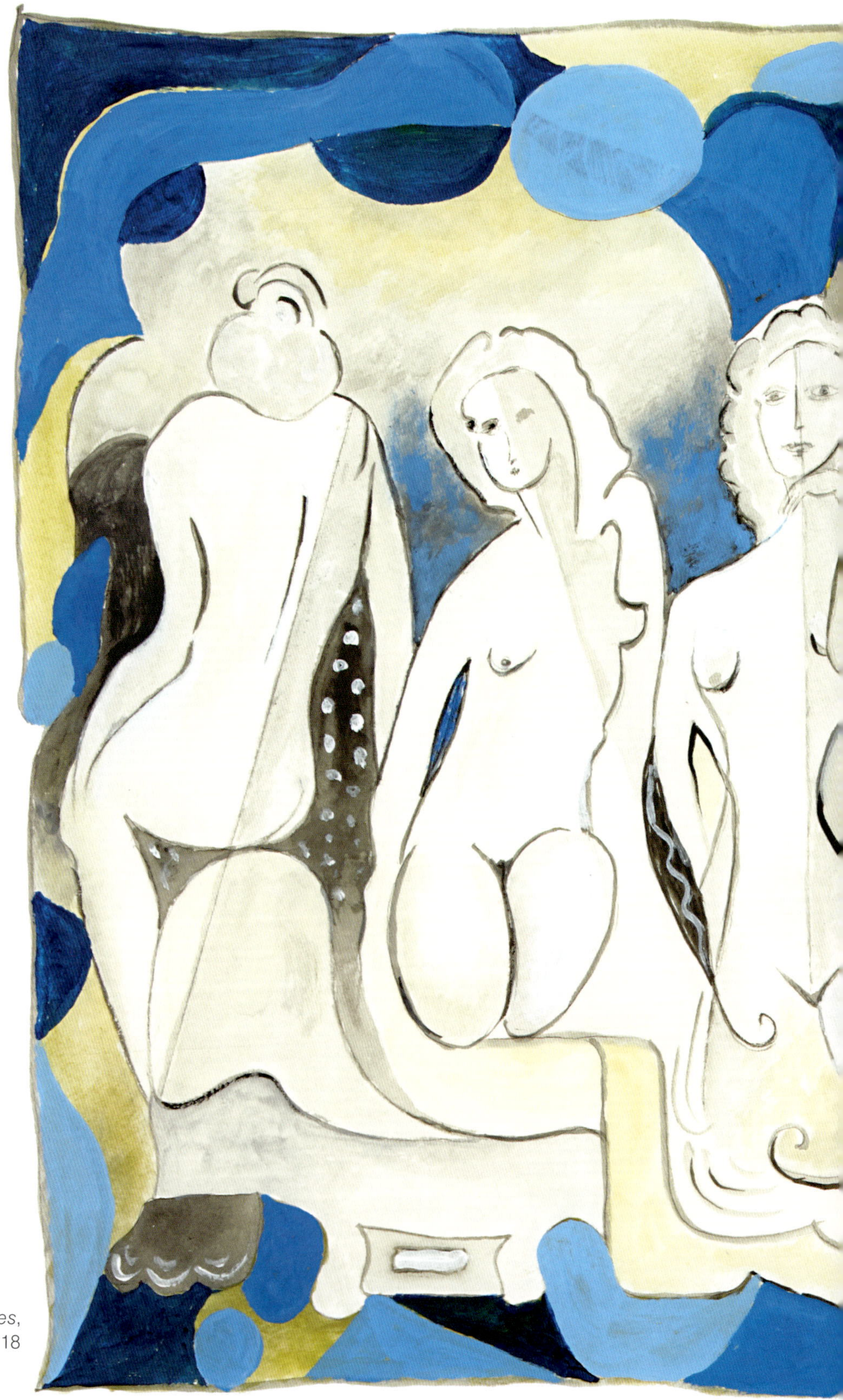

Les Demoiselles, 2018

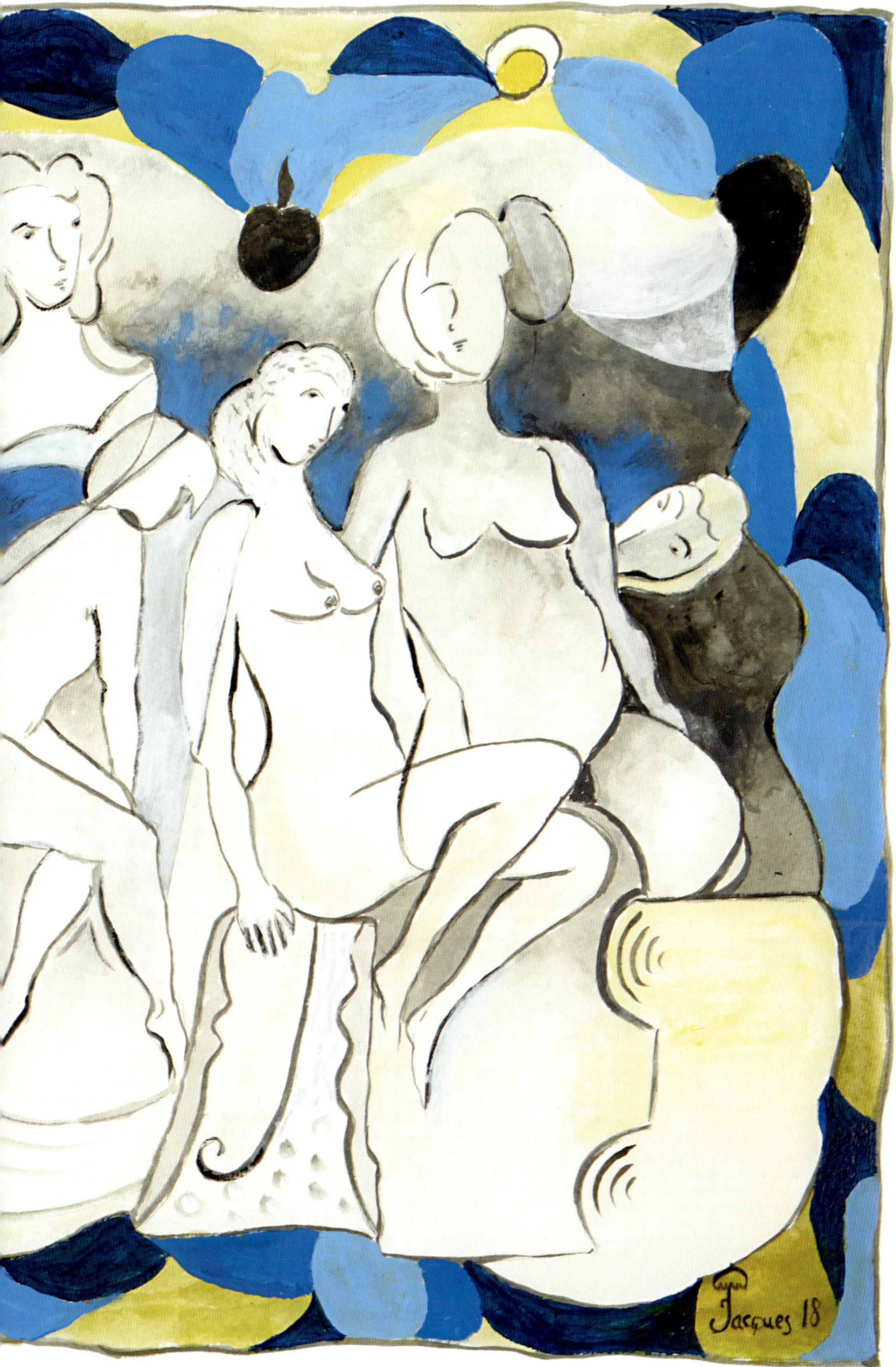
Jacques 18

CUCUMBER SUMMER SALAD

This salad of cucumber, onion, dill, and mint makes a refreshing addition to most any summer menu. Allow the ingredients to macerate in the refrigerator for at least 30 minutes in order for the cucumbers to absorb some additional flavor, but do let it sit on the counter a bit before serving so it isn't ice cold. Adding some baguette to the table will give you some more texture.

Serves 4

2 cucumbers (about 1¾ pounds), peeled, seeded, and thinly sliced (about 4 cups)

1 large mild onion (8 ounces), peeled and thinly sliced (about 2 cups)

⅓ cup shredded fresh dill

⅓ cup shredded fresh mint

1 teaspoon salt

3 tablespoons cider vinegar

3 tablespoons extra virgin olive oil

2 teaspoons sugar

½ teaspoon Tabasco sauce

▸ Combine all the ingredients in a large bowl. Mix well and refrigerate for at least 30 minutes but as long as 8 hours.

▸ Remove from the refrigerator a few minutes before serving. Serve cool with crunchy bread.

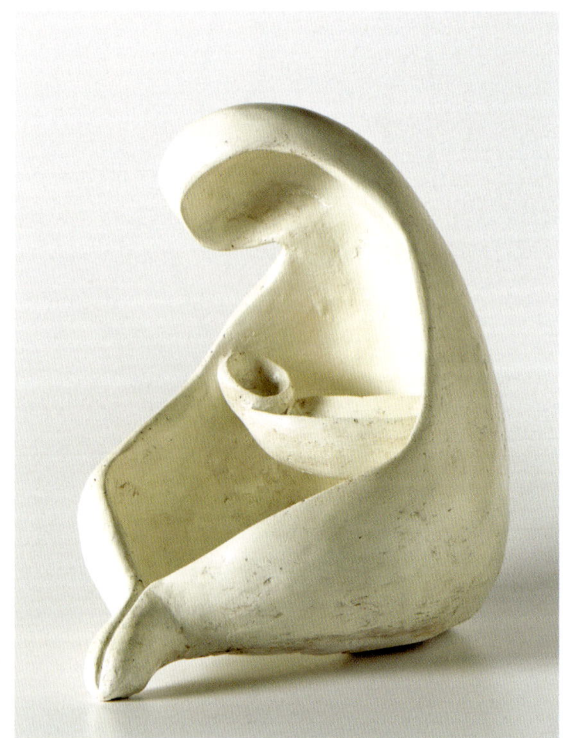

Virgin and Child

RADICCHIO SALAD with GARLIC DRESSING

October through January is peak radicchio season, so this is a hearty wintertime salad to serve along with a main dish. Cold weather makes radicchio sweeter and intensifies its natural color, which is nice to see on the table in wintertime. The bitterness of the salad is tempered by the garlicky dressing. While many people want their vinaigrette to be perfectly emulsified, I prefer to combine mine gently with a whisk so that it doesn't weight down the salad.

Serves 4

DRESSING

1 large garlic clove, peeled, crushed, and chopped (1 teaspoon)

1½ teaspoons Dijon-style mustard

1 tablespoon red wine vinegar

¼ cup extra virgin olive oil

¼ teaspoon salt

¼ teaspoon freshly ground black pepper

10 ounces radicchio, sliced (4 to 5 cups)

Flat-leaf parsley, for garnish

▸ To make the dressing, place the garlic, mustard, vinegar, and olive oil in a large bowl, then season with the salt and pepper and whisk to combine. Add the radicchio right to the same bowl, tossing to distribute the dressing. Garnish with parsley and serve.

Page 44: *Cuisiner, Cuisineière*, 2019
Page 45: *La Cuisinière*, 2018

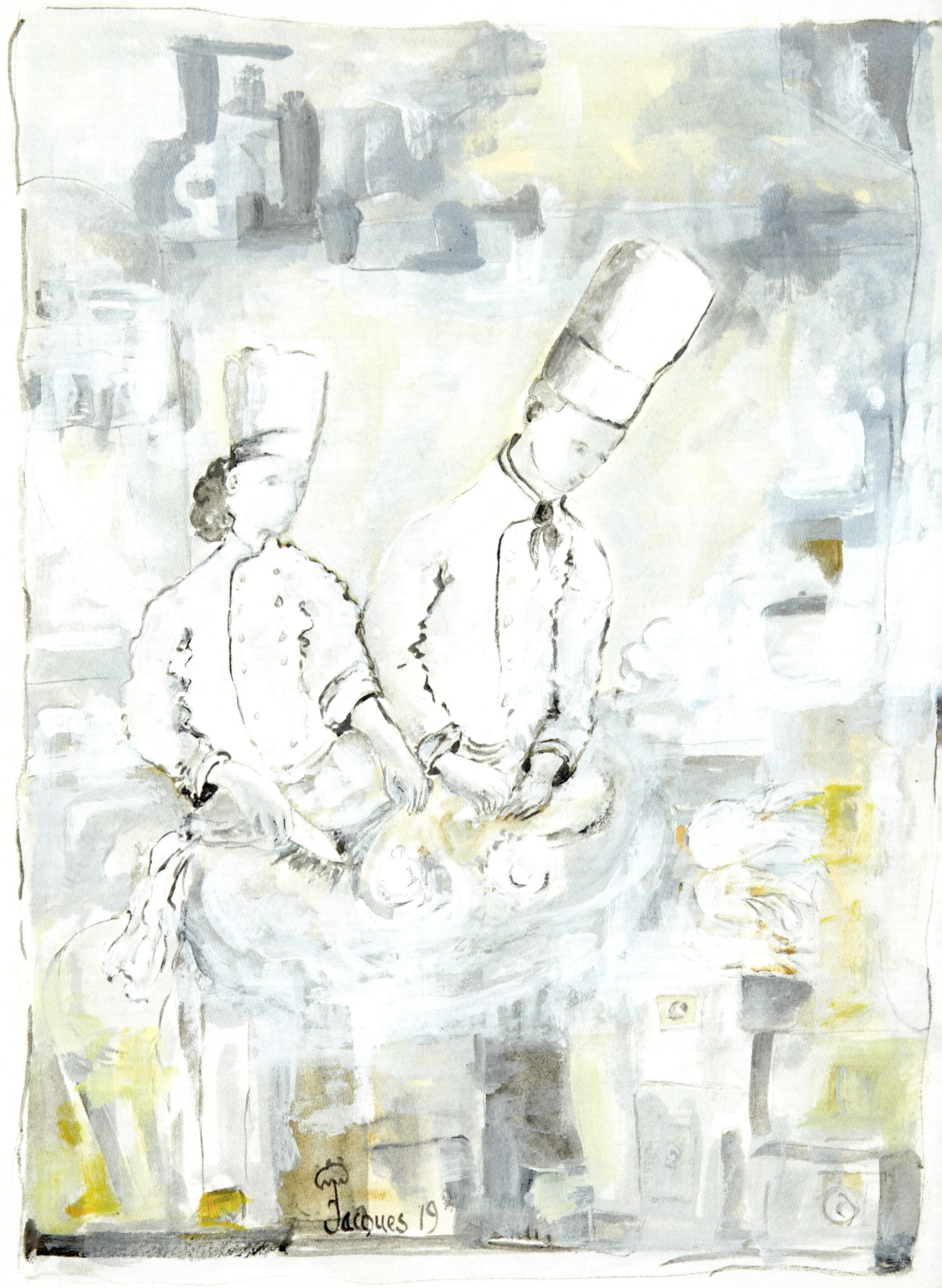
Jacques 19

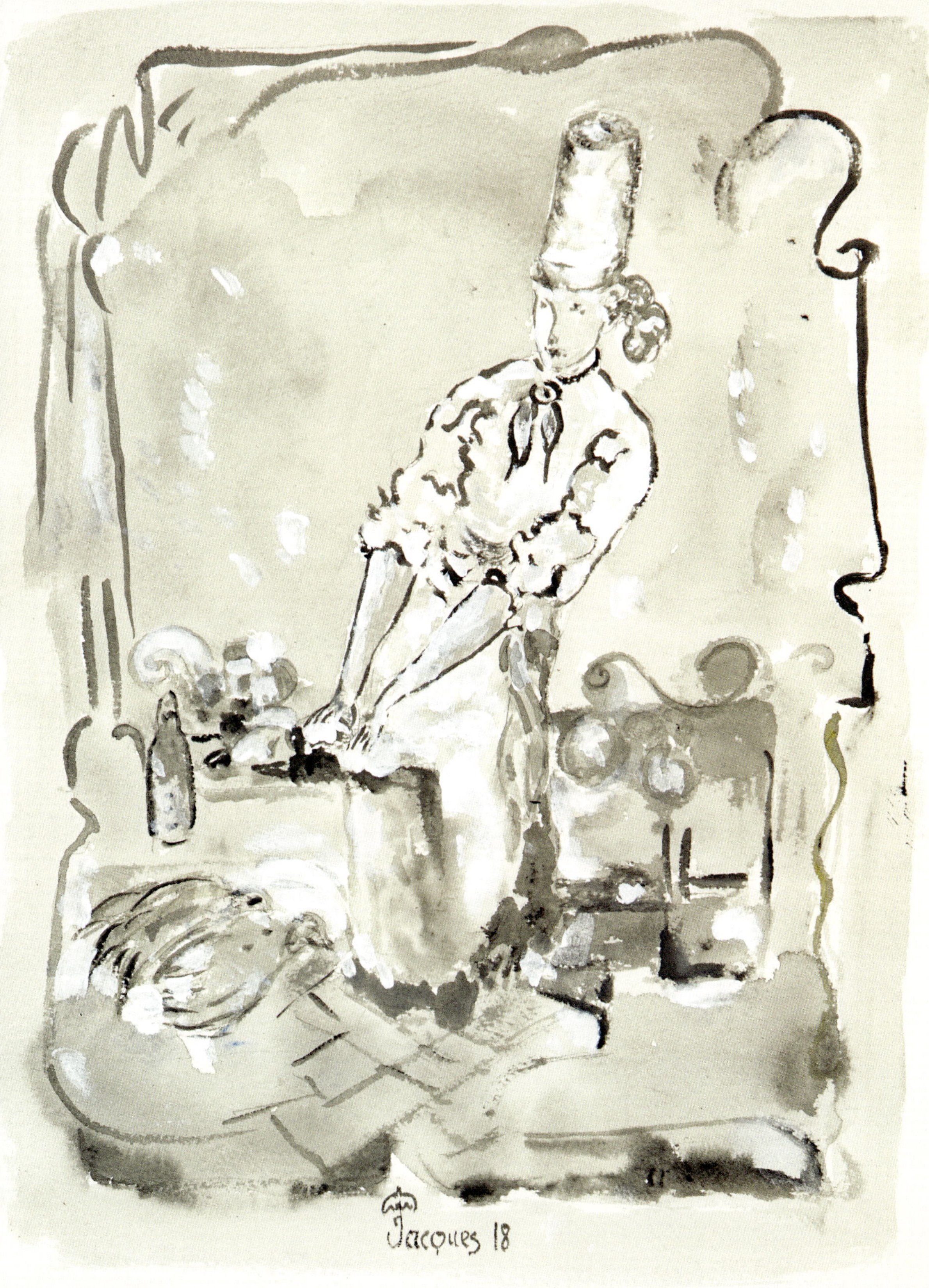
Jacques 18

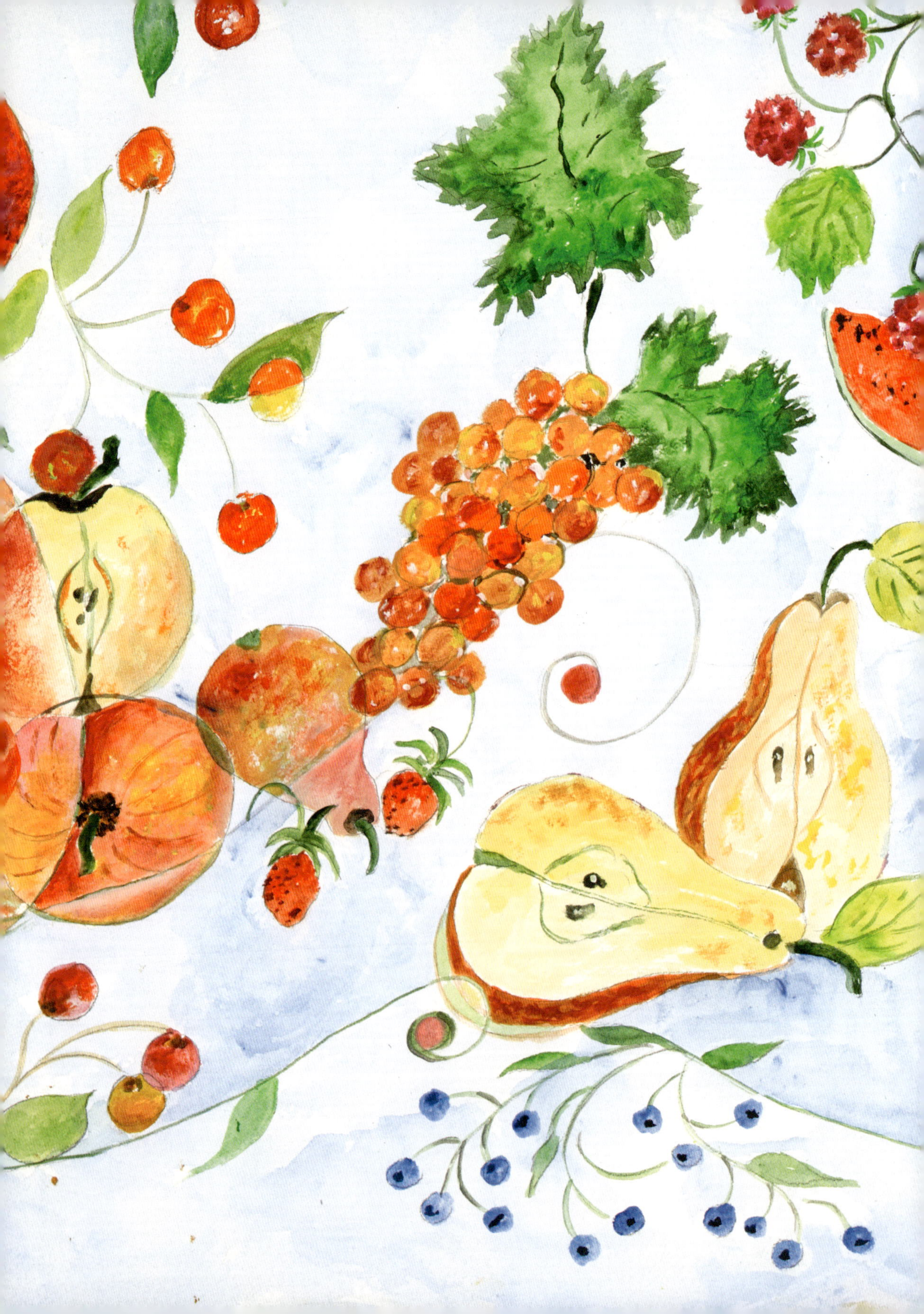

Eggs, Pasta & Vegetables

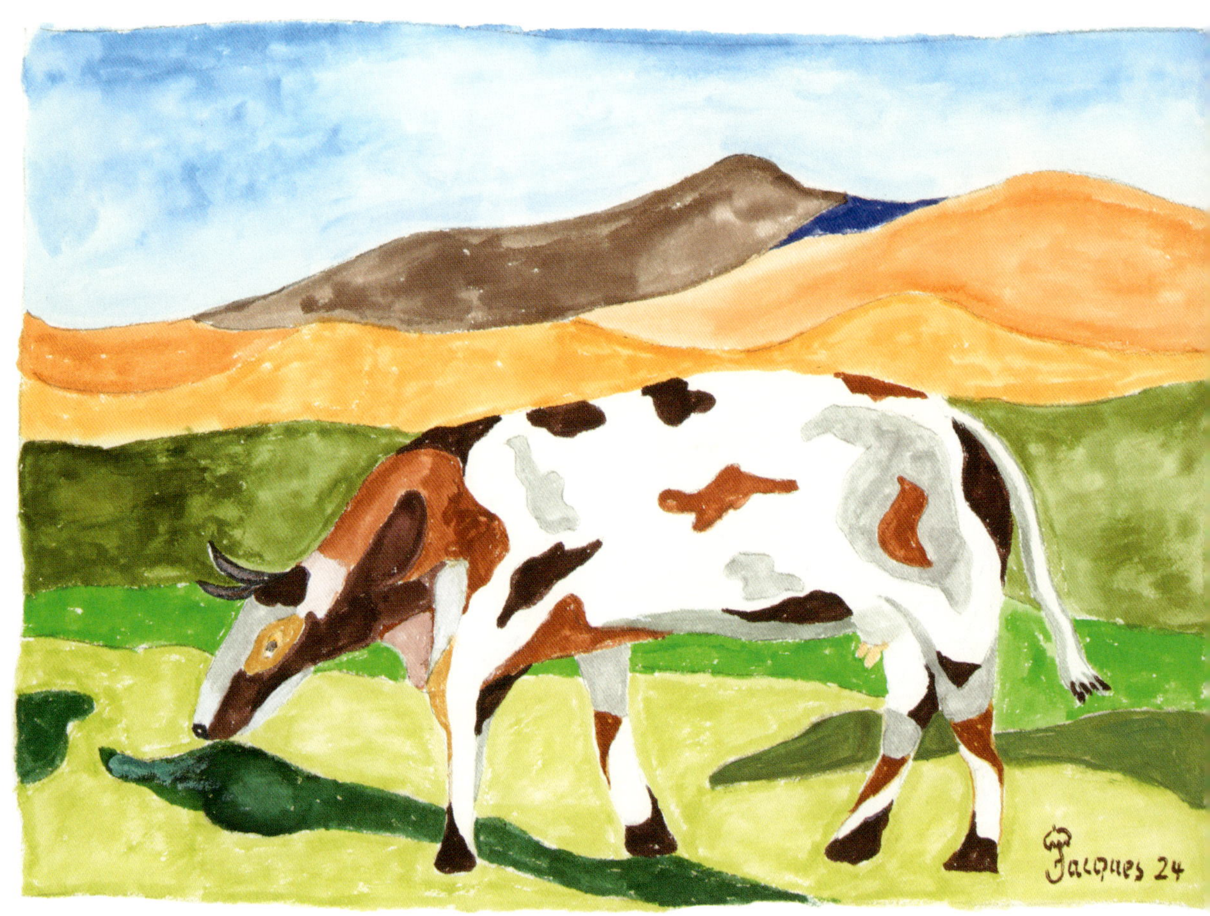

Cow in Pasture, 2024

HARD-COOKED EGGS in MUSTARD SAUCE

I am very finicky about my cooked eggs. I want them cooked very gently in barely boiling water to prevent the white—mostly albumen—from toughening, and then they should be refreshed immediately in ice water. I like the yolks yellow throughout, with their centers slightly soft.

The eggs should be left until completely cool in the ice water so that the sulfur in them—the element responsible for giving eggs an unappealing odor and turning the outer part of the yolks green—has enough time to be extracted and dissipate in the water. The sauce accompaniment is a vinaigrette containing a lot of mustard, a perfect combination with the eggs.

Serves 4

4 large eggs

MUSTARD SAUCE

1 large garlic clove, peeled, crushed, and chopped (1 teaspoon)

1 tablespoon Dijon-style mustard

1/8 teaspoon salt

1/8 teaspoon freshly ground black pepper

2 teaspoons red wine vinegar

3 tablespoons olive oil

8 Boston lettuce leaves

1 tablespoon chopped fresh chives

Crusty French bread

▸ Bring 2 cups of water to a boil in a saucepan. Using a thumbtack or pushpin, make a small hole in the rounded end of each egg. This will release the pressure in the air chamber and prevent the egg from cracking. Lower the eggs gently into the boiling water. Bring the water back to a very gentle boil and cook the eggs for 8 to 9 minutes. Drain off the water and shake the pan to crack the shells of the eggs. Then add ice to the pan and let the eggs cool completely.

▸ Meanwhile, to make the mustard sauce, combine the garlic, mustard, salt, pepper, and vinegar in a medium bowl. Add the olive oil slowly, mixing it in with a whisk or a spoon as it is added. Set aside at room temperature until ready to use. Do not worry if the sauce separates.

▸ Shell the eggs (it's easier to shell them under running water). Cut them in half lengthwise. The centers of the yolks should be slightly soft. Divide the lettuce leaves among four plates and place two egg halves cut side up on top of the lettuce on each plate. Coat the eggs with the mustard sauce, sprinkle with chives, and serve immediately with crusty French bread.

TOMATO, BASIL & CHEESE SOUFFLE

A soufflé always makes an elegant first course. For this particularly appealing one, tomato tops and insides are processed into a puree, which is first thickened, then combined with egg whites, and finally, spooned into tomato cavities and baked. A summery delight, this soufflé has a somewhat soft center because of the juice rendered by the tomatoes as they cook.

Serves 4

4 large ripe (but firm) tomatoes (about 2½ pounds)

1 teaspoon salt

2½ tablespoons olive oil

¼ cup all-purpose flour

¼ teaspoon freshly ground black pepper

3 large eggs

3 tablespoons chiffonade of basil

¼ cup grated Swiss cheese

1 tablespoon grated Parmesan cheese

▸ Preheat the oven to 375°F.

▸ Using a sharp knife, remove the top ½ inch from the smooth end of each tomato and reserve these "caps." Scoop out the insides of each tomato with a spoon, removing and reserving the center and ribs in a bowl, and leaving tomato shells that are about ½ inch thick.

▸ Sprinkle the shells with ½ teaspoon of the salt and place them hollow side down in a gratin dish. Bake the shells for 8 to 10 minutes to soften them.

▸ Meanwhile, place the reserved tomato caps and tomato insides in a food processor and process the mixture for 15 seconds.

▸ Heat the olive oil in a medium saucepan. Add the flour, mix it in with a whisk, and cook the mixture over medium to high heat for 30 seconds. Add the processed tomato insides, the remaining ½ teaspoon of salt, and the pepper, and bring the mixture to a boil, whisking continuously. Boil for about 30 seconds.

▸ Meanwhile, separate the eggs, placing the yolks in a small bowl and the whites in a larger bowl. Whisk the yolks, basil, and Swiss cheese into the tomato mixture in the saucepan. Beat the egg whites until they form soft peaks (they should not be too firm), then combine them well with the tomato mixture.

▸ Turn the tomato shells over so they are hollow side up in the gratin dish and fill them with the tomato soufflé mixture. Spoon any remaining soufflé mixture around the tomatoes and sprinkle them with the Parmesan. Place the tomatoes in the oven and bake for 25 minutes, until the soufflé mixture puffs up and browns nicely on top.

▸ Serve immediately, one tomato per person with some of the extra soufflé mixture alongside.

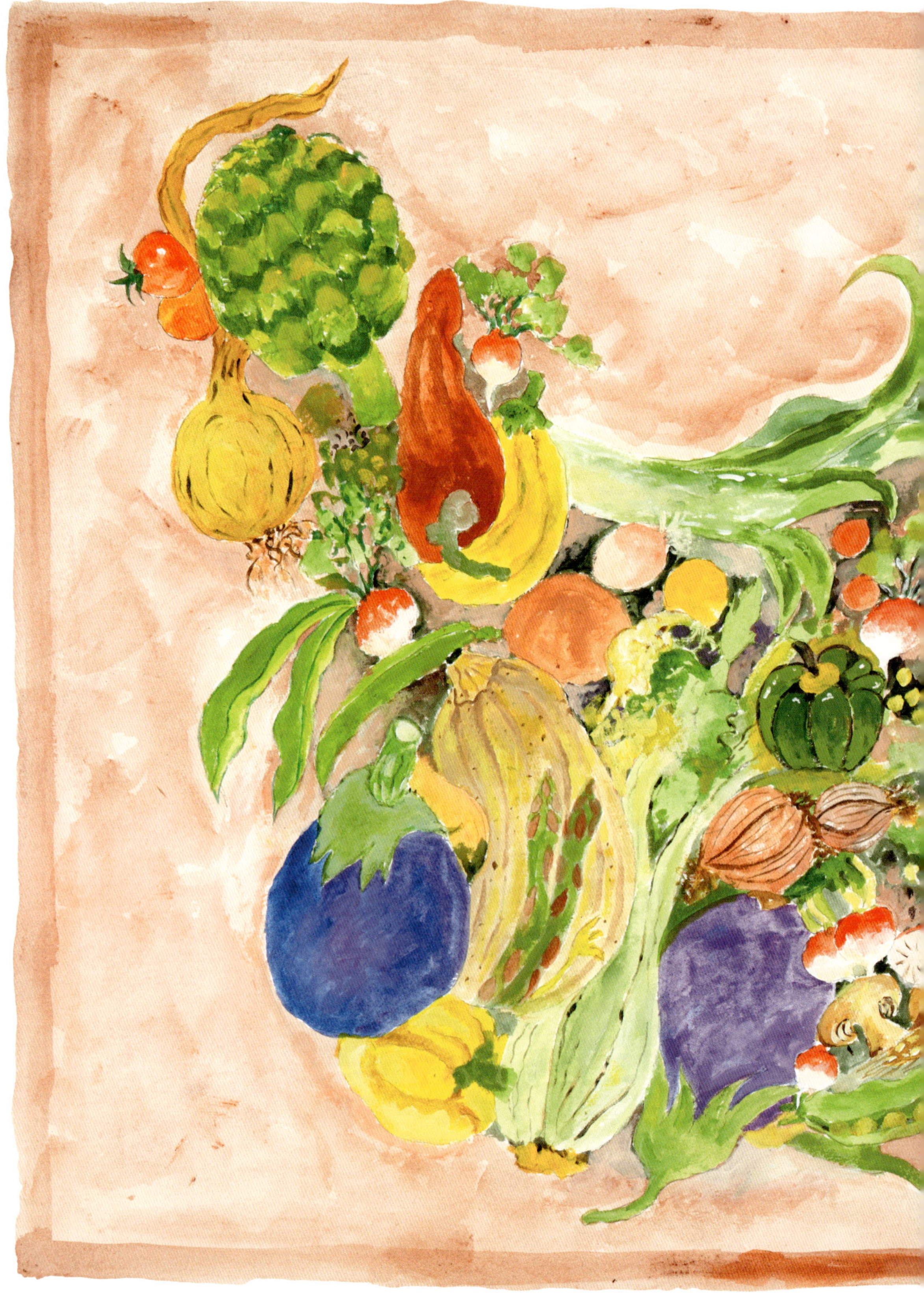

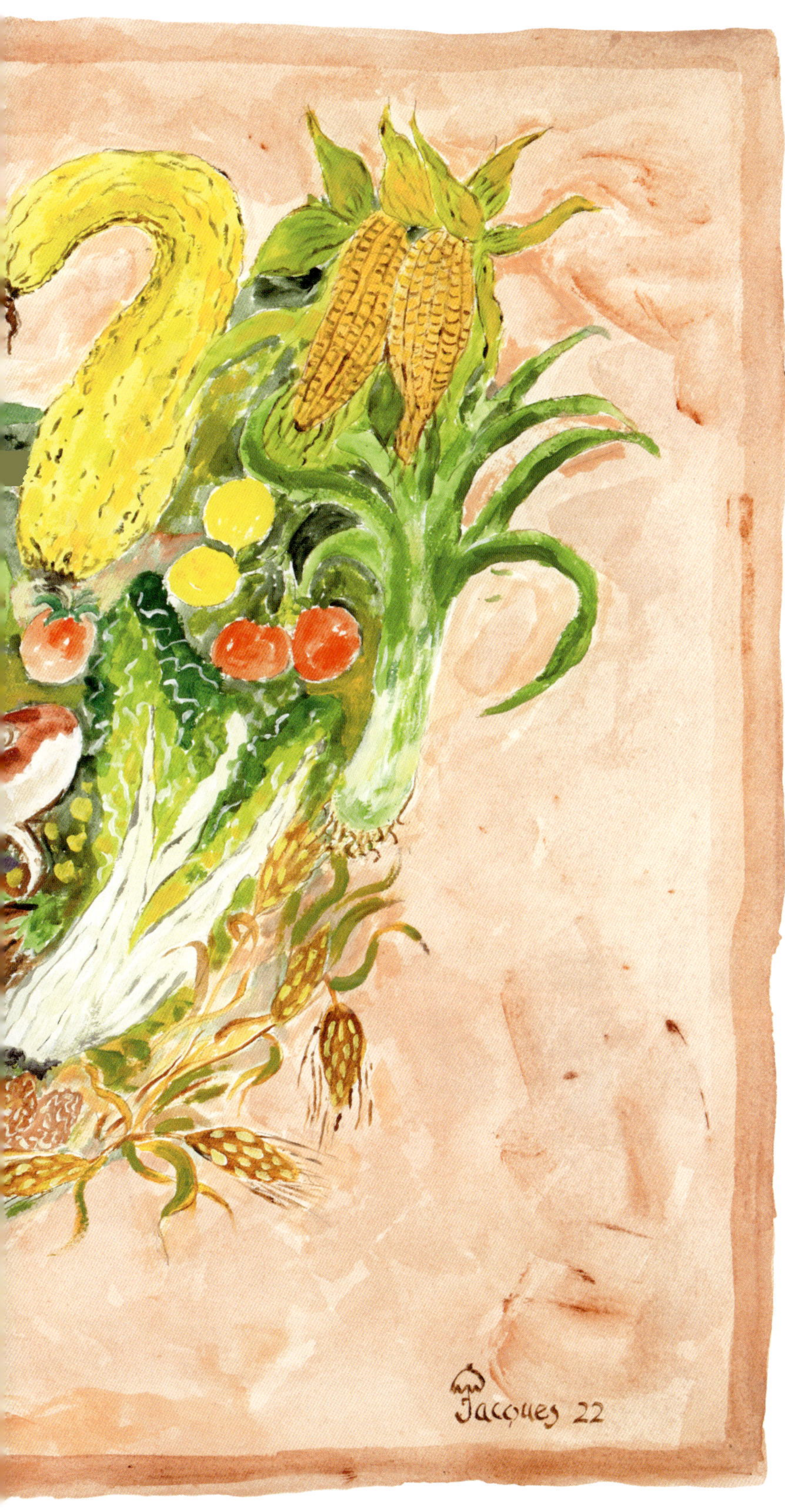

Vegetable Pot Pourri, 2022

EGG SALAD

Egg salad is a very simple, savory dish—but of course in order to make it, you have to first boil the eggs properly. Once that is done, you can combine them with a number of tasty garnishes.

I like olives, chives, and curry powder, but you can use what you have on hand and what you like. Serve presented on a bed of lettuce for a nice light lunch.

Serves 3

6 large eggs

1/3 cup scallions, finely sliced

1/4 cup mayonnaise

1 tablespoon Dijon-style mustard

1/2 teaspoon curry powder

1/2 teaspoon Tabasco sauce

1/4 teaspoon salt

FOR SERVING

6 lettuce leaves, for garnish

6 black olives, pitted and halved, for garnish

1 medium ripe tomato, cut into 6 wedges, for garnish

2 tablespoons chopped fresh chives, for garnish

▸ Bring water to a boil in a medium saucepan. There should be enough water to completely submerge the eggs. Using a thumbtack or pushpin, make a small hole in the rounded end of each egg. This will release the pressure in the air chamber and prevent the eggs from cracking. Lower the eggs gently one by one into the boiling water, making sure there is enough water to cover the eggs. The water will take about 2 minutes to come back to a boil. Lower the heat to a very gentle boil and cook for 9 to 10 minutes (including the 2 minutes it took for the water to come back to a boil), depending on how large your eggs are. When the time is up, immediately drain the eggs and submerge them in ice water. This will prevent the green tinge around the yolk. When they are cooled, break the shells with a spoon and peel under running water. The running water will help you remove the membrane that surrounds the egg, making them easier to peel. To cut the eggs, I like to use an egg slicer in both directions, but you can easily use a knife if you don't have one.

▸ Combine the scallions, mayonnaise, mustard, curry powder, Tabasco, and salt in a medium-size bowl. Add the chopped eggs and mix well.

▸ Arrange lettuce leaves on a platter. Spoon the egg salad in the center, garnish with the black olives, and place the tomato wedges around the outside. Scatter with chives and serve.

Facing page: The Champion Cock, 2023

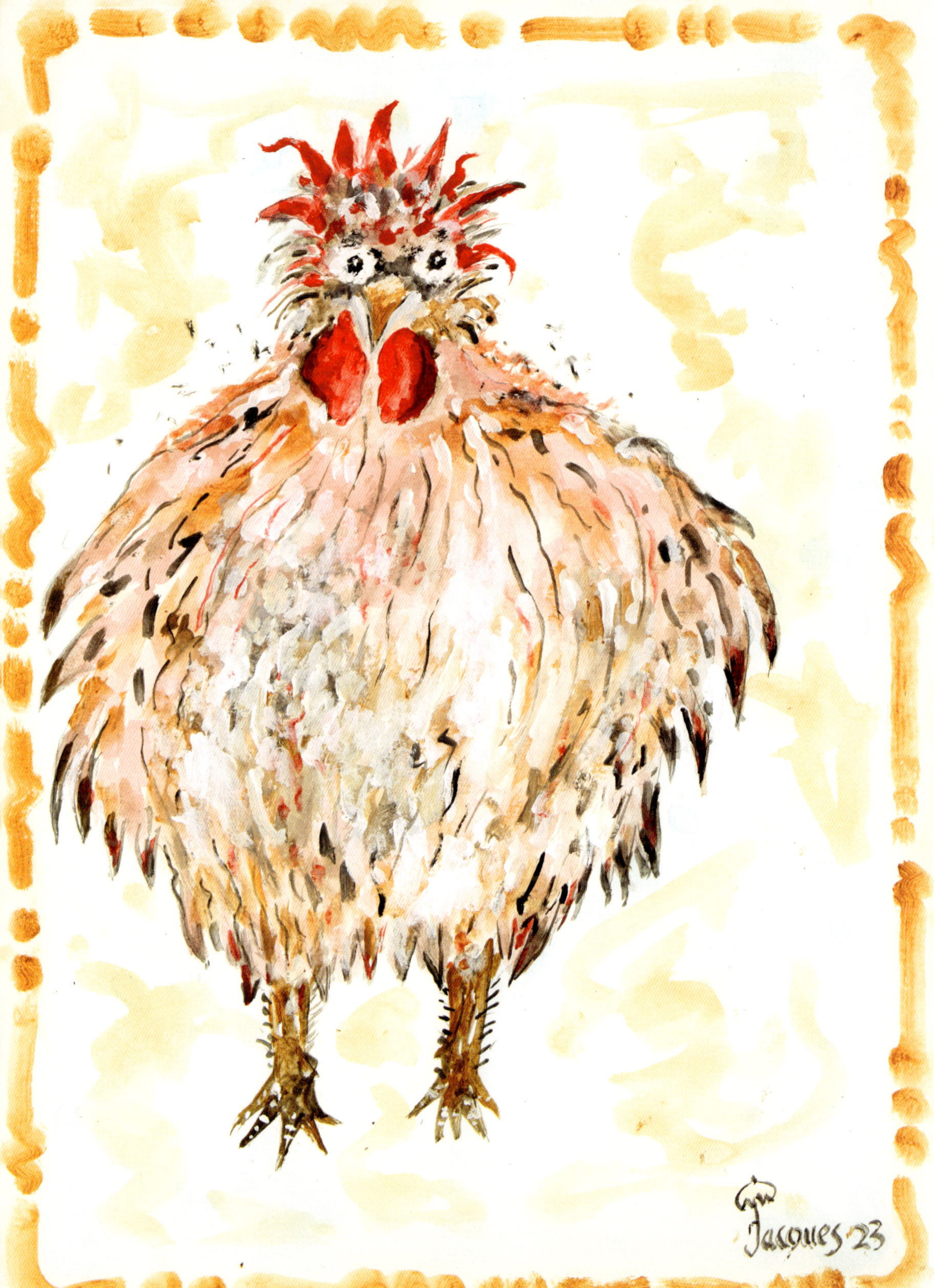
Jacques 23

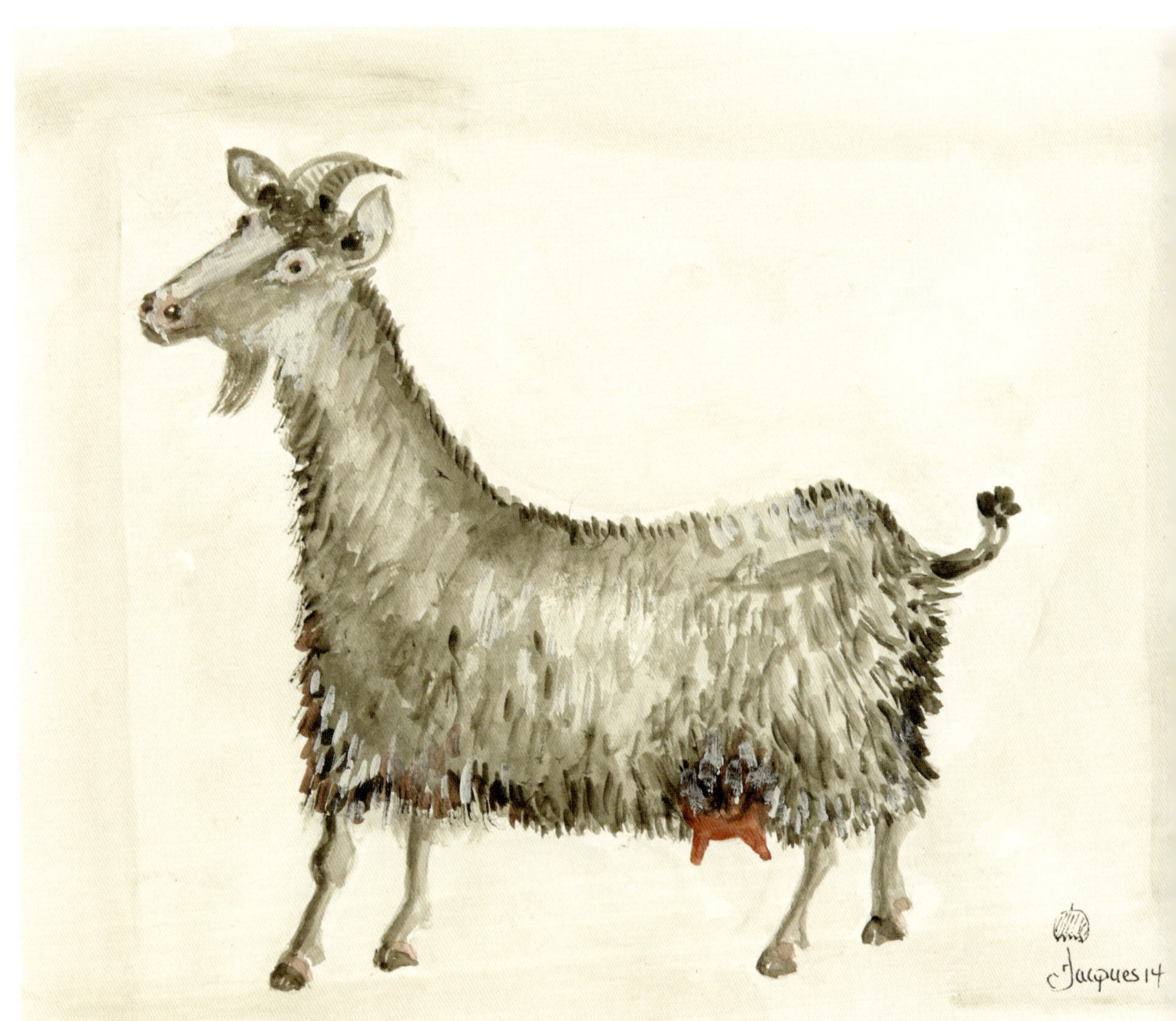

Goat 1, 2014

ZITI with SAUSAGE & VEGETABLES

Always take advantage of the market when cooking; if good-quality cauliflower is less expensive than broccoli, use that instead. Use cherry or regular tomatoes, whichever is more attractively priced—or riper. As for the Italian sausage, look for the best price; sometimes sausage links are less expensive, sometimes patties are cheaper, and sometimes it is more economical to buy sausage meat packaged in bulk.

Serves 4

6 ounces hot and/ or mild Italian-style sausage

2½ tablespoons olive oil

12 ounces ziti

2 stalks broccoli (1 pound total)

1 tablespoon chopped garlic

2 large ears sweet corn, husked and kernels removed (about 2 cups)

12 ounces cherry tomatoes

¾ teaspoon salt

¼ cup grated Parmesan cheese

▸ Break the sausage into ½-inch pieces and place it in a large saucepan with ½ tablespoon of the olive oil. Cook over medium heat for about 10 minutes, until most of the fat has emerged from the sausage and the pieces are nicely browned.

▸ Meanwhile, bring 3 quarts of salted water to a boil in a large saucepan or pot and add the pasta. Mix well, bring the water back to a boil, and boil the pasta, uncovered, until tender, about 12 minutes.

▸ While the pasta is cooking, separate the broccoli florets from the stalks and cut the florets into 1-inch pieces. Peel the fibrous skin from the exterior of the broccoli stalks and cut the stalks into 1-inch pieces. When the sausage has cooked for 10 minutes, add the broccoli to the saucepan and mix it in well. Then stir in the garlic, reduce the heat to medium, cover, and cook for about 6 minutes.

▸ When the pasta is cooked to your liking, remove ½ cup of the cooking liquid, then drain the pasta in a colander. Add the reserved cooking liquid to the sausage and broccoli mixture along with the corn, tomatoes, remaining 2 tablespoons of olive oil, and the salt. Cover, bring to a boil, and boil for 2 minutes.

▸ In a large serving bowl, combine the drained pasta with the sausage and vegetables, tossing the mixture together well. Serve with the grated Parmesan.

LINGUINE à la CARBONARA

Here is my take on a quick, satisfying pasta classic, carbonara. Some do not believe in adding cream to this dish, but I like what it adds and believe we should all cook according to our own tastes and preferences. Use whatever type of long pasta you happen to have.

Serves 2

1 cup ½-inch-diced pancetta (5 ounces)

1 tablespoon olive oil

8 ounces linguine

1½ tablespoons chopped garlic

1 large egg

⅓ cup heavy cream

½ teaspoon salt

½ teaspoon freshly ground black pepper

¼ cup grated Parmesan cheese

3 tablespoons chopped fresh chives and/or flat-leaf parsley

▸ Place the pancetta in a skillet with the olive oil. Cook over low heat, partially covered and stirring occasionally, until nicely browned and crisp, 8 to 10 minutes.

▸ Meanwhile, bring 2 quarts of salted water to a boil in a large stockpot and add the pasta. Cook to your liking and according to the package directions. Add the garlic to the pancetta. Cook for 1 minute over low heat. Beat the egg and cream together.

▸ When the pasta is cooked, remove ⅓ cup of the cooking liquid, then drain the pasta in a colander. Place the drained pasta in a bowl and combine with the pancetta-garlic mixture, salt, pepper, and cream-egg mixture. Add the reserved cooking liquid and mix well so the egg cooks from the residual heat. Divide between two plates and garnish with the Parmesan and herbs.

NOODLES & PEAS

I like to use imported fettucine or tagliatelle for this dish, cooking it at the last moment and combining it with the petite peas, Parmesan cheese, salt, pepper, and some of the cooking water from the pasta. This is an easy, satisfying, comforting dish that everyone in the family will enjoy.

Serves 4

12 ounces fettucine (including the large fettucine, called tagliatelle), preferably imported

1 cup frozen petite peas

3 tablespoons grated Parmesan cheese, or more to taste

2½ tablespoons olive oil

½ teaspoon salt

½ teaspoon freshly ground black pepper

▸ Bring 3 quarts of salted water to a boil in a large saucepan or pot and add the pasta. Mix well, bring the water back to a boil, and cook, uncovered, 10 to 12 minutes, depending on your preference.

▸ Meanwhile, place the frozen peas in a strainer, then run them under hot tap water until all the ice particles have melted and the peas are thawed. Place the peas in a large serving bowl with the cheese, olive oil, salt, and pepper.

▸ When the pasta is cooked, remove ⅔ cup of the cooking liquid and add it to the bowl with the peas. Drain the pasta and add it to the bowl. Toss well and serve immediately, with more cheese if desired.

Pages 60–61: *The Fishes,* 2024

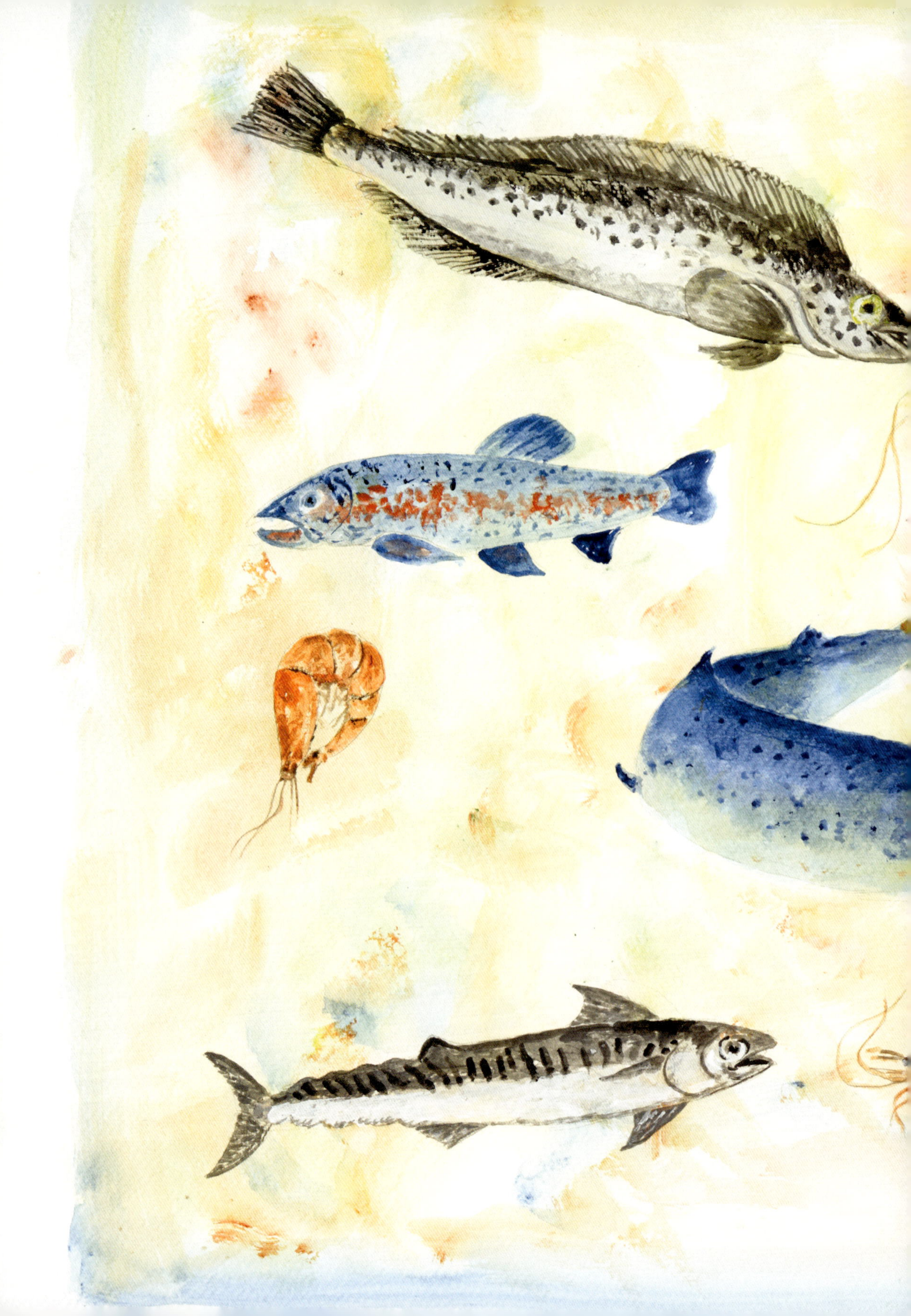

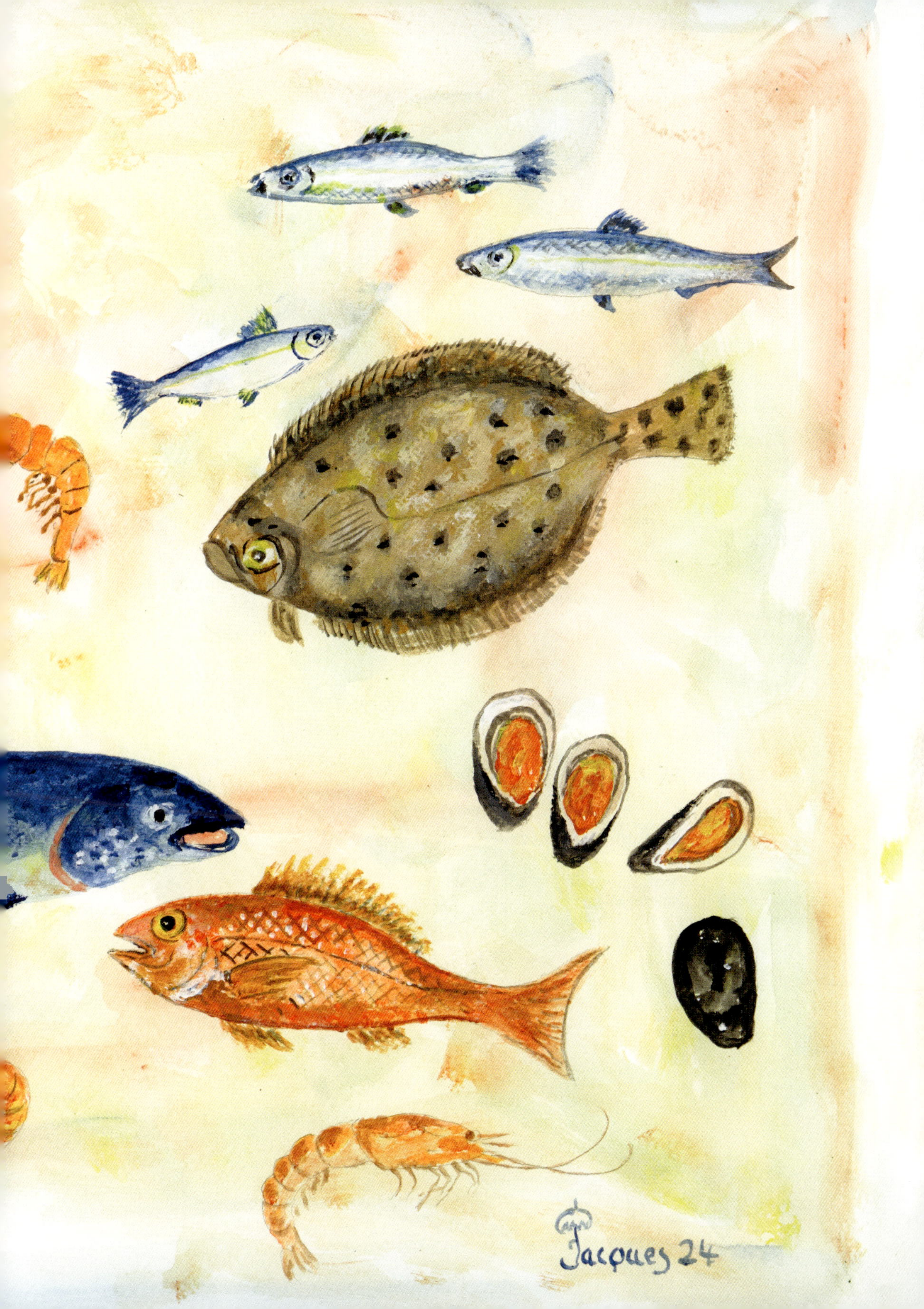
Jacques 24

FUSILLI with ESCAROLE, EGGPLANT & OLIVE SAUCE

Pasta is one of the most versatile ingredients available to the cook. I combine it here with a sauce made of olives, escarole, eggplant, pine nuts, garlic, and peas because that was what was available in my fridge the day I made it. On another day, depending on the contents of my refrigerator, red onion, zucchini, green pepper, tomato, and broccoli could find their way into this recipe along with capers or anchovy fillets. Feel free to experiment with the sauce ingredients for this dish and try some of the different pasta shapes the market offers as well.

Serves 4

SAUCE

1 eggplant (about 1 pound)

½ teaspoon salt

1 tablespoon canola or peanut oil

¼ cup extra virgin olive oil

2½ tablespoons pine nuts

3 garlic cloves, peeled and thinly sliced (2 tablespoons)

10 ounces escarole (about ½ head), cut into 2-inch pieces (about 6 cups loosely packed), washed and drained

½ cup petite peas (fresh or frozen)

24 kalamata olives, pitted

¼ teaspoon freshly ground black pepper

‣ Preheat the oven to 400°F.

‣ Trim and discard the ends of the eggplant and cut it lengthwise into 5 slices of about equal thickness. Sprinkle the slices with ¼ teaspoon of the salt. Line a baking sheet with aluminum foil and coat the foil with the canola oil.

‣ Press the slices of eggplant into the oil on the baking sheet, then turn them over (so they are lightly oiled on both sides) and arrange them in a single layer. Place the eggplant in the oven for 40 minutes, until the slices are tender and slightly browned. When they are cool enough to handle, cut them into 1½-inch pieces.

‣ Heat the olive oil in a large skillet. Add the pine nuts and garlic and sauté for about 20 seconds. Add the escarole, still wet from the washing, cover, and cook over medium to high heat for 3 to 4 minutes, until wilted and starting to brown. Add the peas, olives, eggplant, the remaining ¼ teaspoon of salt, and the ¼ teaspoon pepper. Mix well and set aside. (This can be done up to 1 hour ahead.)

12 ounces fusilli

½ teaspoon salt

½ teaspoon freshly ground black pepper

Grated Parmesan cheese, for garnish

▸ At serving time, bring 3 quarts of salted water to a boil in a large saucepan or pot and add the pasta. Mix well, bring the water back to a boil, and cook the pasta, uncovered, 10 to 12 minutes, depending on your preference. Remove ½ cup of the cooking liquid and add it to the sauce mixture. Drain the pasta.

▸ Combine the pasta with the sauce and the ½ teaspoon each salt and pepper. Mix well. Divide among four plates, sprinkle with Parmesan, and serve immediately.

ORZO with ARUGULA SAUCE

Orzo, sometimes called *risoni*, is a pasta shaped like kernels of rice. Since each small kernel releases starch as it cooks, orzo should be cooked in a lot of water—otherwise, it tends to stick together or doesn't cook sufficiently throughout. Although I like my pasta cooked slightly al dente, I prefer orzo cooked for 10 to 12 minutes to develop its full volume and texture.

Serves 6

- **2 tablespoons olive oil**
- **½ cup pine nuts**
- **1 small onion (about 3 ounces), peeled and finely chopped (½ cup)**
- **5 to 6 scallions, coarsely minced (½ cup)**
- **1 (2-ounce) can anchovy fillets in oil, cut into ½-inch pieces**
- **8 cups loosely packed arugula (8 to 10 ounces), washed and cut into 2-inch pieces**
- **1 teaspoon salt**
- **½ teaspoon freshly ground black pepper**
- **2 large ripe tomatoes (about 1 pound total), peeled, halved, seeded, and cut into 1-inch pieces (about 2 cups)**
- **1 pound orzo**
- **4 tablespoons shaved or grated Parmesan cheese**

▸ Heat the olive oil in a large saucepan. When it is hot, add the pine nuts and onion. Cook over medium heat for 5 minutes, until the nuts are lightly browned and the onion is soft and translucent.

▸ Add the scallions, anchovies (along with the oil from the can), and the arugula. Mix well and cook for about 4 minutes, uncovered, until the arugula is wilted. Add ½ teaspoon of the salt, the pepper, and the tomatoes, bring to a boil, and cook for 1 minute. The recipe can be made ahead up to this point.

▸ Near serving time, bring 8 cups of water to a boil and add the remaining ½ teaspoon of salt. Add the orzo, bring the water back to a boil, and boil, uncovered, stirring occasionally, for 10 to 12 minutes, or until cooked to your liking.

▸ Meanwhile, reheat the sauce mixture. Drain the orzo in a colander. (You will have about 6 cups, although some brands swell up more, and the yield could be a bit more.) Add the orzo to the sauce and mix well.

▸ Divide the mixture among four plates and sprinkle each serving with 1 tablespoon of the Parmesan. Serve immediately.

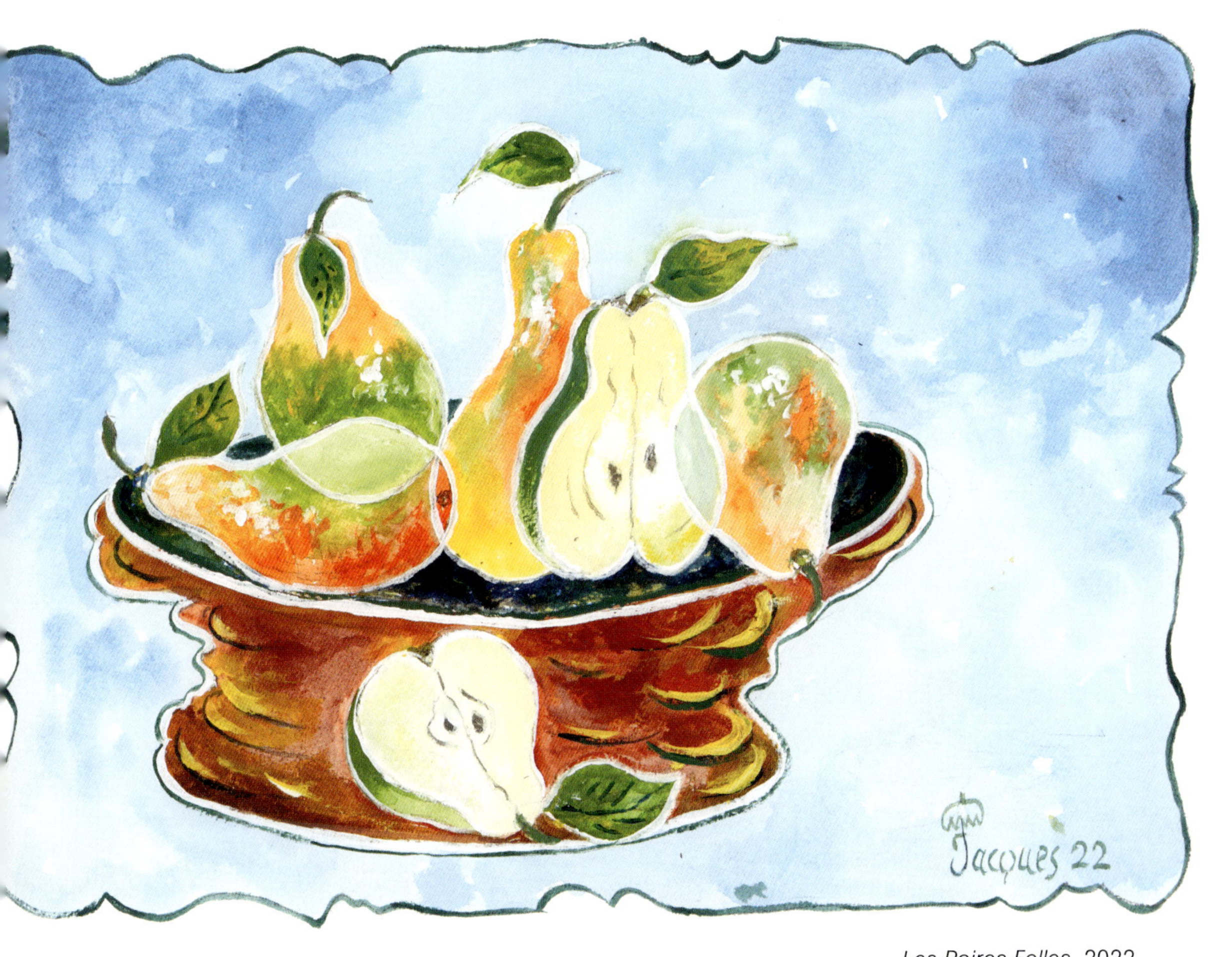

Les Poires Folles, 2022

RICE with CUMIN

I like my rice cooked in chicken stock, preferably homemade when possible. An ancient spice, cumin is the aromatic dried fruit of a plant in the parsley family. Its assertive, nutty taste lends a distinctive flavor to this rice dish.

Serves 4

2 tablespoons olive oil

1 medium onion (5 ounces), peeled and chopped (about 1 cup)

1½ cups long-grain converted rice

1 tablespoon ground cumin

3 cups unsalted homemade chicken stock or canned low-salt chicken broth

Salt to taste, depending on the saltiness of your stock

▸ Heat the oil in a large, heavy saucepan with a lid. When the oil is hot but not smoking, add the onion and sauté for 30 seconds.

▸ Add the rice and cumin and stir well to coat the grains of rice with the oil. Add the chicken stock and salt, if needed, and bring to a boil, uncovered, stirring occasionally, over high heat. Then reduce the heat to low, cover, and cook for 20 minutes. The liquid should be completely absorbed by the rice, which should be tender.

▸ Fluff the rice with a fork and serve as needed.

BROCCOLI & RICE ETUVEE

This dish can be served as an accompaniment to meat or fish, but it also makes a good meatless main course. *Etuvée* translates to "braised," and can also refer to the act of cooking vegetables in their own juices. I use brown rice, cooking it slowly, covered, until soupy; then I place the broccoli on top of the rice, cover it again, and cook it until both the rice and broccoli are tender. This combination is delicious, and with only one pan involved, the cooking and cleanup are simplified. Other green vegetables could be substituted here; if you don't like broccoli, cook squash, asparagus, or green beans with the rice in the same manner.

Serves 1

1 tablespoon olive oil

3 tablespoons chopped onion

⅓ cup short-grain brown rice

1 cup chicken or beef stock, preferably homemade and unsalted

Salt to taste, depending on the saltiness of your stock

Dash of red pepper flakes

1 stalk broccoli (3 to 4 ounces)

2 tablespoons grated Swiss cheese

▸ Heat the oil in a small, sturdy saucepan. When it is hot, add the onion and cook over medium heat for 2 minutes, stirring occasionally, until lightly browned.

▸ Add the rice, stir well, then add the stock, salt, and red pepper flakes. Bring the mixture to a boil, cover, reduce the heat to very low, and cook for 30 minutes.

▸ Meanwhile, peel the broccoli stem to remove the fibrous skin. Cut the peeled stem into ½-inch pieces and the florets into 1-inch pieces.

▸ When the rice has cooked for 30 minutes (it will still be soupy), place the broccoli on top of the rice (don't stir it in). Cover and cook over low heat for 10 to 15 more minutes, until the rice and broccoli are tender. Add the cheese, stir, and serve immediately.

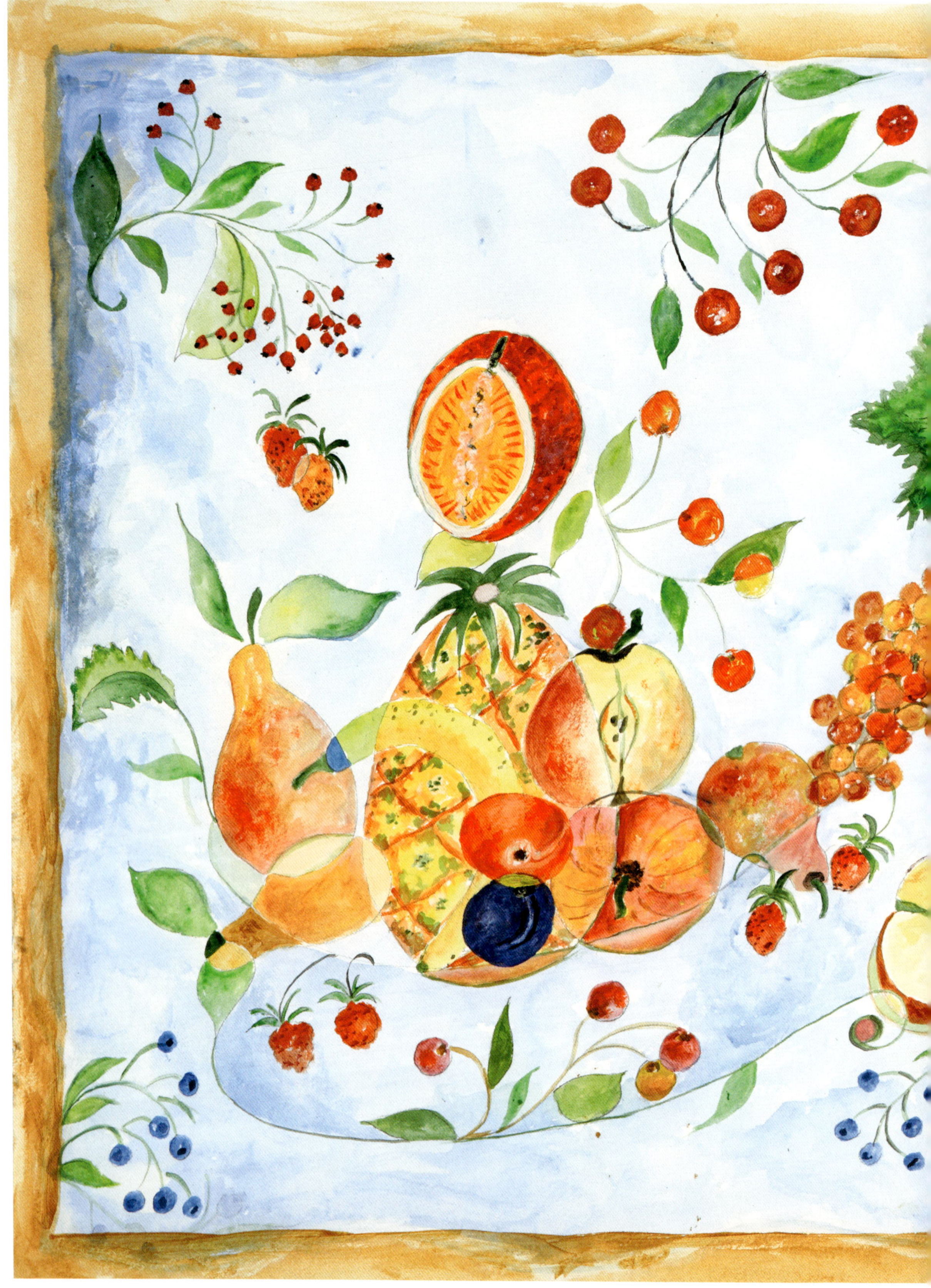

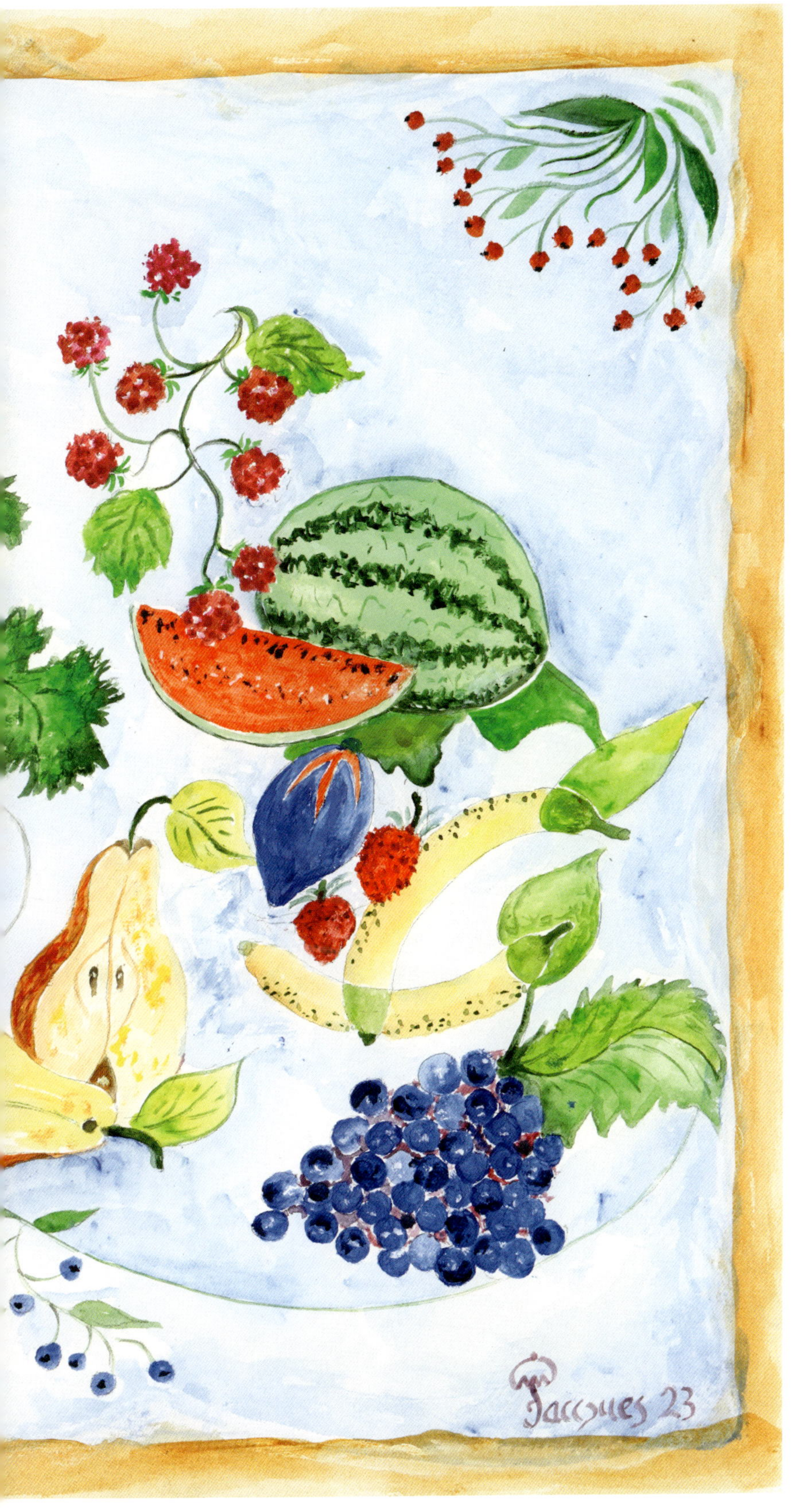

Fruit Galore, 2023

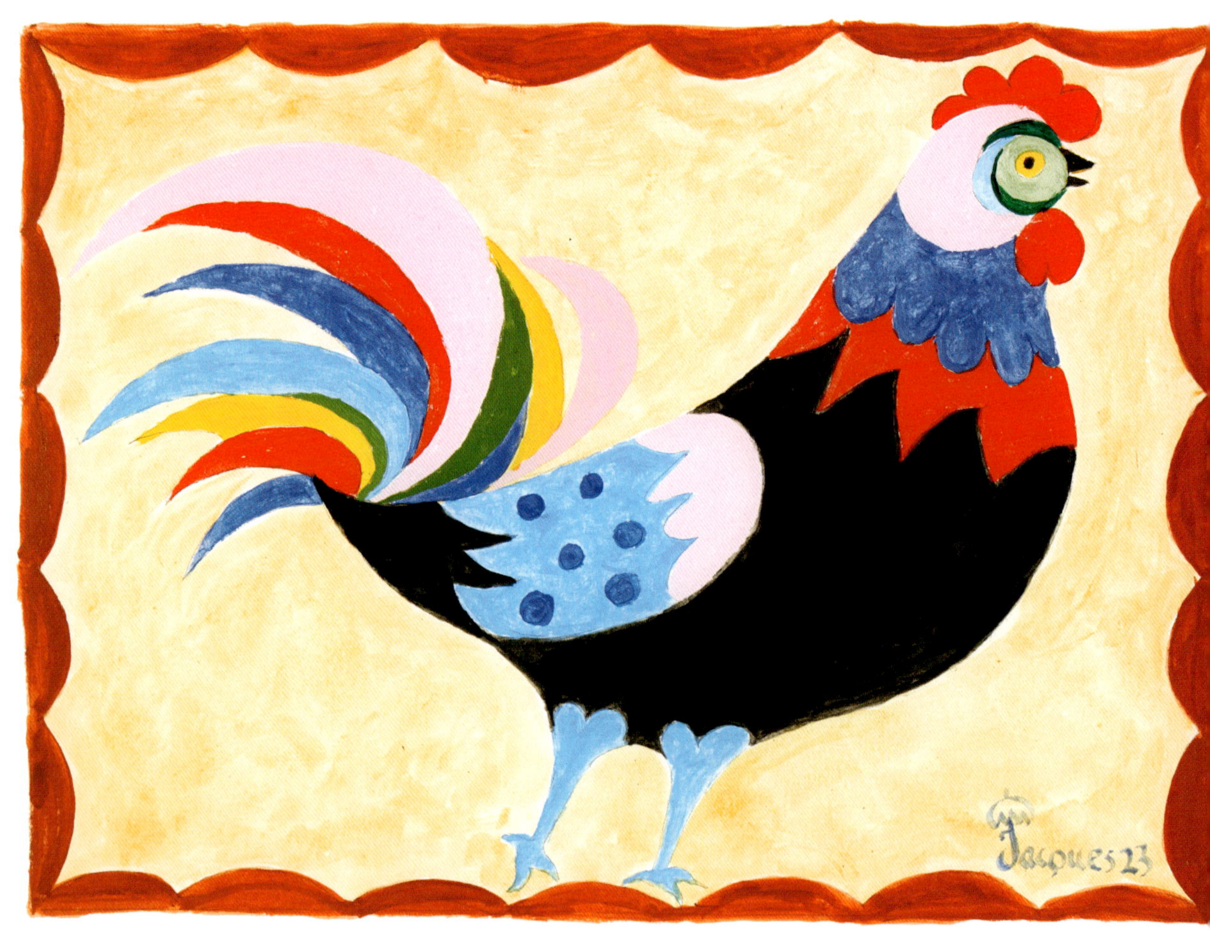

Royal Rooster, 2023

ARTICHOKE & TOMATO STEW

In peak condition, artichokes can be costly. When they begin to wilt or the leaves yellow a little, five or six of them are usually packaged together at my market and sold at a very reasonable price. This is when I buy artichokes for artichoke bottom recipes or for stews, such as this one.

Serves 4

4 medium artichokes (6 to 8 ounces each)

2 tablespoons olive oil

2 medium ripe tomatoes (12 ounces total), cut into 1-inch pieces (3 cups)

1 medium onion (4 ounces), peeled and thinly sliced (3/4 cup)

3 large garlic cloves, peeled and thinly sliced (1 tablespoon)

1/2 teaspoon salt

1/2 teaspoon freshly ground black pepper

▸ With a sharp knife, cut 1½ inches from the top of each artichoke. Then trim off the tough outer leaves with the knife, taking care that you don't cut into the tender inner leaves or the white heart inside. If your artichokes have stems, peel off the outer layer of these to make them edible. Quarter the trimmed artichokes and artichoke bottoms and remove and discard the bristly choke from each piece.

▸ Place the artichokes in a medium saucepan (preferably stainless steel) and add the olive oil, tomatoes, onions, garlic, salt, pepper, and ½ cup of water (or more as needed). Bring to a strong boil over high heat, then lower the heat to medium-low, cover, and cook for 20 minutes. Serve as needed.

CARROTS with ORANGE & DILL

I like to season carrots with different herbs. Here, I cook carrots in orange juice, which sweetens them and imparts a mild orange taste, and serve them with fresh dill. The carrots can be cooked up to a day ahead, but don't add the dill until the last moment, as it tends to lose its flavor and darken if added too soon.

Serves 4

1 pound carrots, peeled and cut into 1-inch dice (3 cups)

¾ cup freshly squeezed orange juice

1 tablespoon butter

½ teaspoon salt

½ teaspoon freshly ground black pepper

¼ cup loosely packed fresh dill leaves

▸ Place the carrots, orange juice, butter, salt, and pepper in a medium stainless steel saucepan.

▸ Bring the mixture to a boil and boil, uncovered, over medium to low heat for about 15 minutes, until the carrots are tender, all the liquid has evaporated, and the carrots are beginning to glaze in the butter.

▸ Sprinkle with the dill and serve immediately.

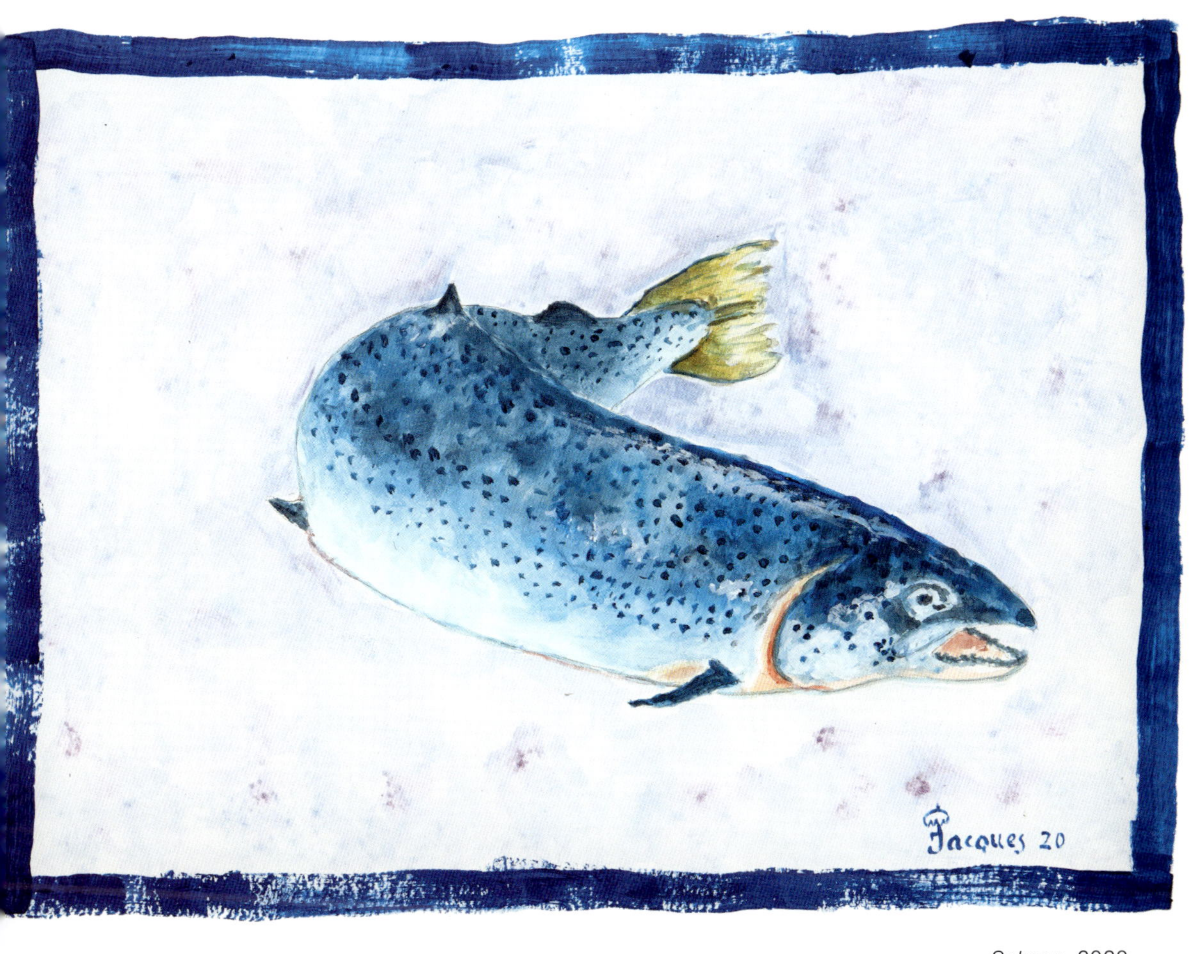

Salmon, 2020

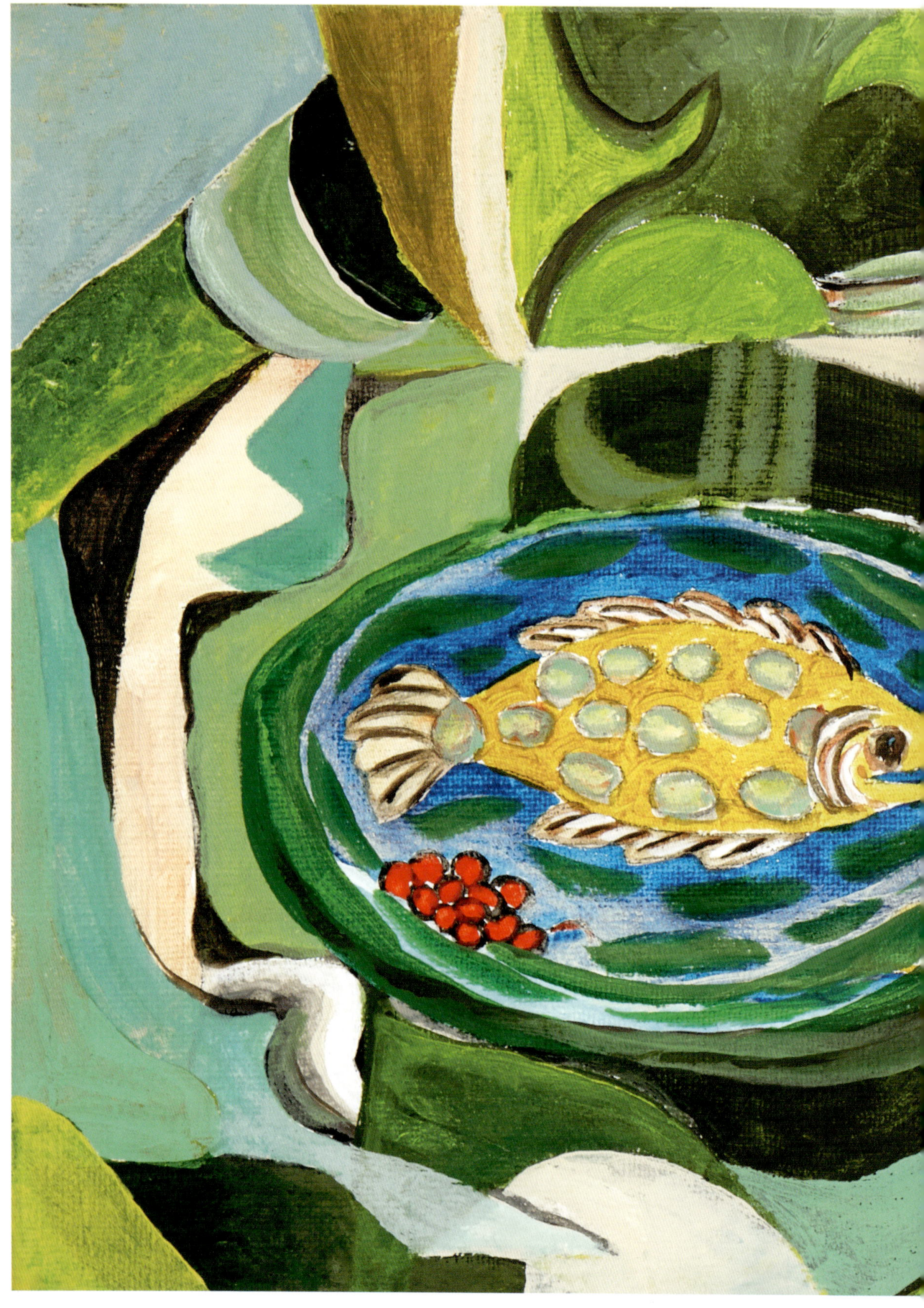

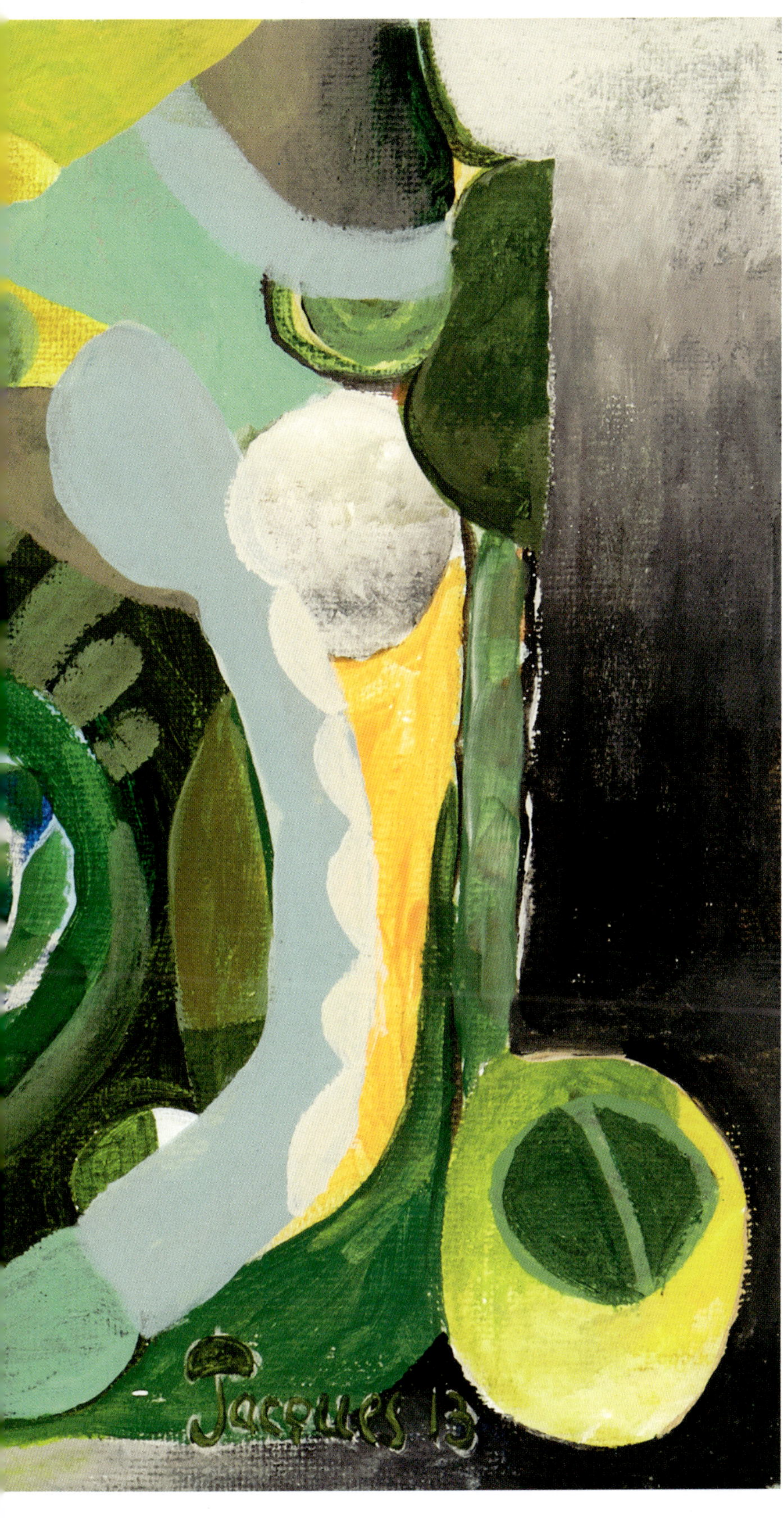

Poisson Jaune, 2013

STEW of SPRING VEGETABLES

These spring vegetables are prepared in the "old style": onion and garlic are sautéed first in a little butter, flour is added along with seasonings and water to create a slightly thickened base, and the vegetables are cooked in this base. The dish can be prepared ahead, but don't add the peas until the last minute as they tend to yellow if cooked ahead and rewarmed. Of course, if it is not springtime, you can always use frozen petite peas, which are of excellent quality.

4 to 6 servings

2 tablespoons butter

1 medium onion (4 to 5 ounces), peeled and coarsely chopped (1 cup)

3 to 4 large garlic cloves, peeled and coarsely chopped (1 tablespoon)

1 tablespoon all-purpose flour

1 teaspoon herbes de Provence, or a mixture of your favorite dried herbs (like thyme, oregano, savory, and marjoram)

1 teaspoon salt

½ teaspoon freshly ground black pepper

3 Yukon Gold potatoes, peeled and cut into 1-inch pieces (2 cups)

12 ounces carrots, peeled and cut into 1-inch pieces (2 cups)

2 pounds fresh peas, shelled (about 1 pound shelled; 2 cups), or 2 cups frozen petite peas, rinsed well under warm water in a colander

1 tablespoon chopped fresh flat-leaf parsley (optional)

If preparing this dish ahead, complete through step 2, then set aside. At serving time, bring the mixture to a boil, add the peas, and cook as indicated.

▸ Heat the butter until melted in a large, sturdy saucepan. Add the onion and garlic and sauté over medium heat, stirring occasionally, for 1½ minutes. Add the flour, stir well, then mix in the herbes de Provence, salt, pepper, and 1½ cups of water, and bring to a boil.

▸ Add the potatoes and carrots, bring back to a boil, and cook, covered, for 12 minutes.

▸ Add the peas, bring back to a boil, reduce the heat to low, and cook, covered, until the peas are just tender, 4 to 5 minutes if using fresh peas, or 1½ to 2 minutes if using frozen petite peas. Garnish with parsley, if desired, and serve.

BRAISED ENDIVE

I love Belgian endive. In Belgium they call it *chicon*. I like to braise them briefly with butter and a little lemon zest and juice for a delicious side dish.

Serves 2

2 large Belgian endive (4 to 5 ounces each)

¼ teaspoon salt

½ teaspoon sugar

2 tablespoons butter

1 teaspoon grated lemon zest

2 teaspoons lemon juice

Minced fresh chives, for garnish (optional)

▸ Trim off any damaged leaves and cut each endive in half lengthwise. Set them in a medium saucepan and add ⅓ cup of water, the salt, sugar, butter, lemon zest, and lemon juice. Bring to a boil over medium-high to high heat, cover, reduce the heat to low, and cook, uncovered, until they are tender, 8 to 10 minutes. If there is still too much liquid, remove the lid, increase the heat, and cook until most has evaporated, leaving a buttery sauce. Arrange the endive on a platter and pour the sauce over them. Sprinkle with chives, if desired, and serve immediately.

ROASTED CORN PUREE

This recipe, a combination of cooked cornmeal and caramelized corn kernels, is perfect for corn aficionados. Intense in flavor and chewy, the caramelized kernels can be served on their own. Do be aware of the cooking time of your cornmeal. It can vary widely and you may need to adjust your liquid according to the package instructions.

Serves 4

3 tablespoons corn or peanut oil

2 ears sweet corn, husked and kernels removed (about 1½ cups)

2½ cups water

¾ teaspoon salt

2 large scallions, minced (¼ cup)

½ cup instant yellow cornmeal

▸ Heat the oil in a large saucepan and add the corn kernels. Cook over medium to high heat, covered (to prevent splattering), for about 8 minutes, shaking the pan occasionally and stirring the kernels, until they are nicely browned on all sides. Set aside.

▸ Meanwhile, place the water, salt, and scallions in a saucepan, and bring the mixture to a boil over high heat. Add the cornmeal, sprinkling it on top of the boiling liquid and stirring at the same time to avoid lumps, and cook, partially covered, over medium to low heat for 10 minutes, stirring occasionally to prevent the mixture form sticking. (The puree should have a smooth consistency.) Add the roasted corn kernels and mix them in well.

▸ Serve as needed.

Pages 80–81: *Peaches,* 2019

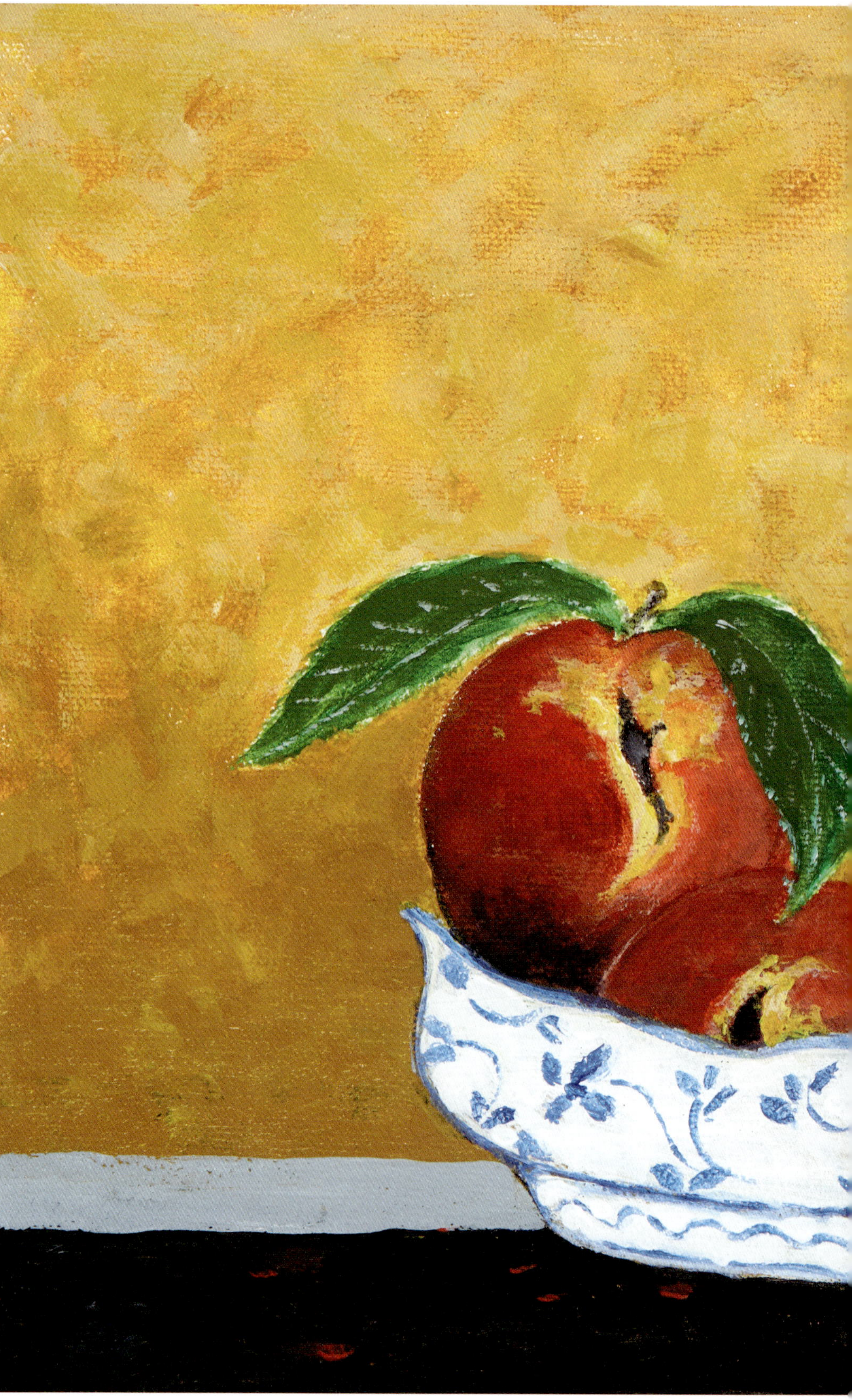

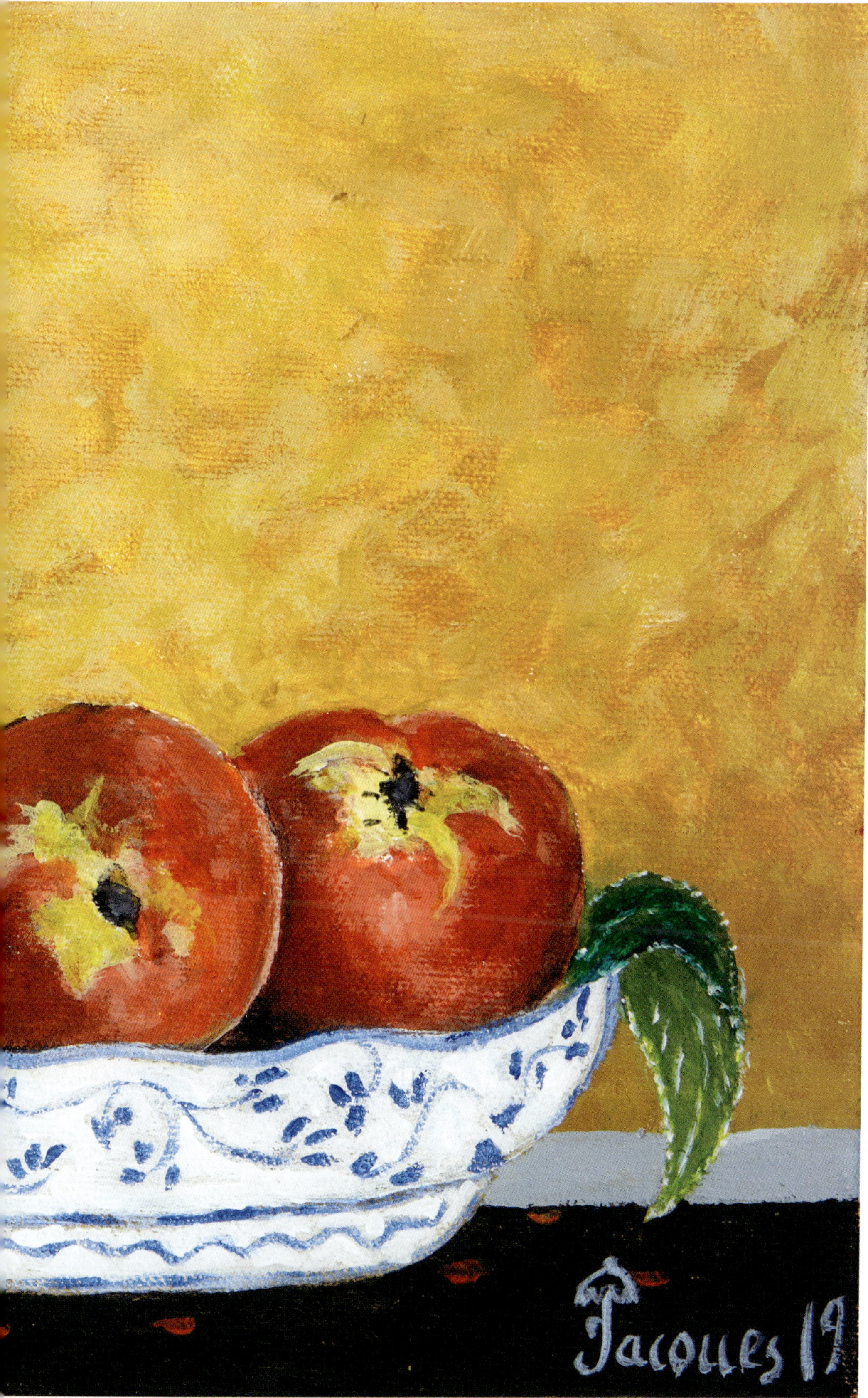
Jacques 19

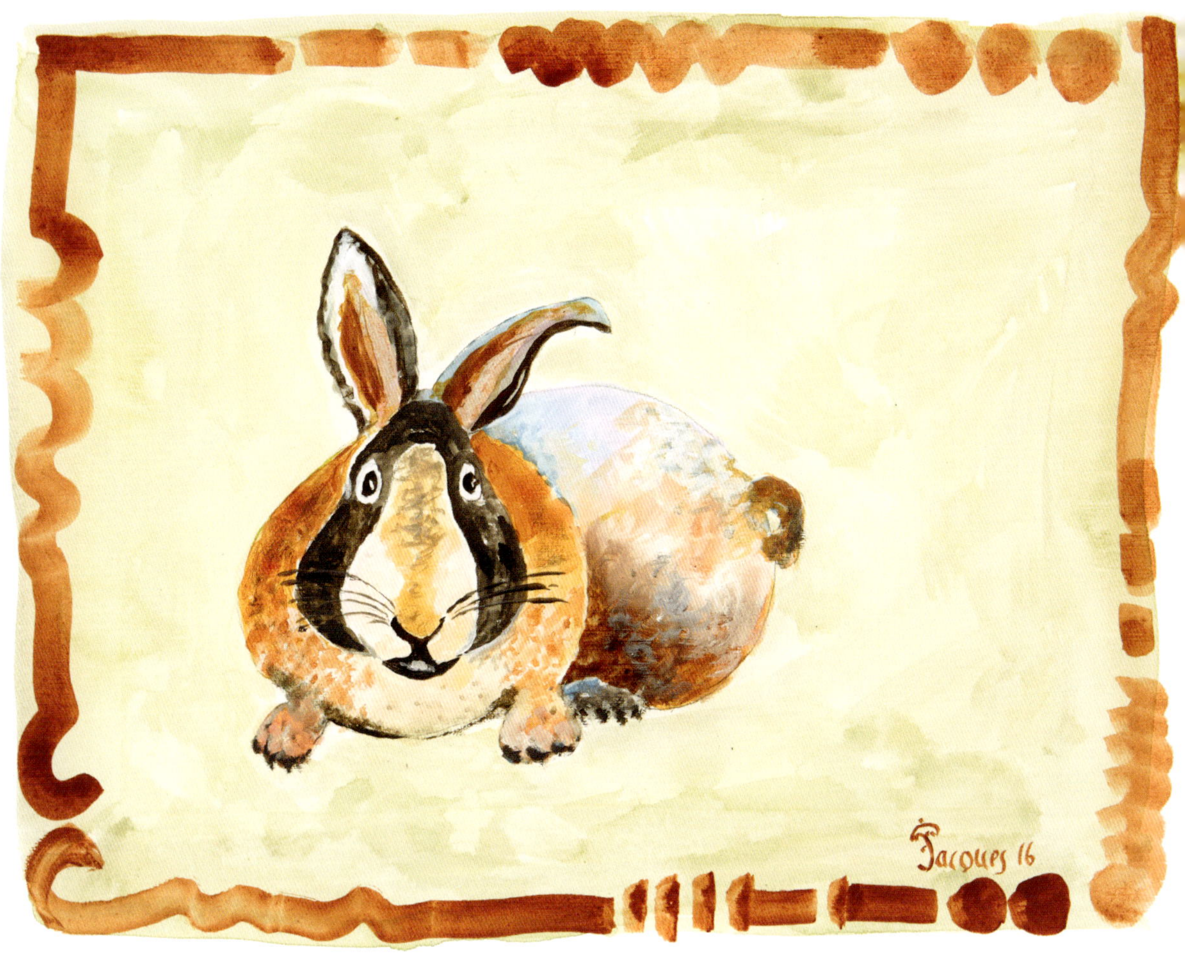

Curious Rabbit, 2016

MUSHROOMS en PAPILLOTE

This recipe couldn't be simpler or tastier. When food is prepared *en papillote*, the French term for "in paper," it generally is baked inside parchment paper. I get the same effect with aluminum foil here; the mushrooms cook and steam in a foil package, retaining all their flavor and moisture.

Serves 6

1 pound small- or medium-size white or cremini mushrooms, left whole

½ teaspoon salt

½ teaspoon freshly ground black pepper

6 garlic cloves, peeled and thinly sliced (2 tablespoons)

2 tablespoons butter

1 tablespoon olive oil

1 tablespoon chopped fresh flat-leaf parsley

▸ Preheat the oven to 400°F. Arrange a 16- to 18-inch square of aluminum foil on a flat work surface.

▸ Wash the mushrooms, drain them well, and pile them in the center of the foil. Sprinkle them with the salt, pepper, and garlic. Dot with the butter, then sprinkle with the oil. Gather up the edges of the foil and fold the edges together securely to encase the mushrooms in a square package. The mushrooms should not be packed tightly; there should be some space between the mushrooms and the foil so it develops some steam inside the bag.

▸ Place the foil package seam side up on a baking sheet and bake for 30 minutes.

▸ Unwrap the mushroom package and serve the mushrooms in their own juices with a sprinkling of parsley on top.

ROASTED POTATOES & ONIONS

To save on cleaning time, line a baking sheet with aluminum foil. Baked cut side down in a minimal amount of oil (much of the oil remains in the pan afterward), the potatoes emerge brown, moist, and very delicious.

Serves 4

4 baking or all-purpose potatoes (about 8 ounces each), unpeeled, but washed and any dark or damaged spots removed

4 medium onions (about 5 ounces each), unpeeled (Vidalia or Maui onions are a good choice)

3 tablespoons peanut or safflower oil

½ teaspoon salt

▸ Preheat the oven to 400°F. Line a baking sheet with aluminum foil.

▸ Split the potatoes in half lengthwise and cut the onions in half crosswise.

▸ Rub the oil on the lined baking sheet. Sprinkle the salt over the potatoes and onions and place them cut side down in one layer on the oiled baking sheet.

▸ Place the baking sheet on the bottom rack of the oven. Bake for 40 minutes, until the potatoes and onions are tender when pierced with a fork, lightly browned on top, and dark brown on the underside.

▸ Set aside to rest for 10 minutes before serving.

CAULIFLOWER GRATIN

When I was a child, my mother often made gratin. Potatoes, spinach, mushrooms, eggs, and Swiss chard were all turned into tasty gratin with some béchamel sauce and grated cheese sprinkled on top. A gratin is a great accompaniment for a roast chicken or roast pork, as well as lamb. If the gratin is prepared ahead, it is reheated and browned in a 350°F oven for 30 to 40 minutes. If the gratin is prepared at the last moment, while the cauliflower and the sauce are hot, it is finished for a few minutes under the broiler before serving.

Serves 4

1 head cauliflower (about 1 pound)

2 tablespoons butter

2 tablespoons all-purpose flour

1¾ cups half-and-half

½ teaspoon salt

½ teaspoon freshly ground black pepper

½ cup grated mozzarella

1 tablespoon grated Parmesan cheese

▸ Separate the cauliflower into florets of similar size. In a large saucepan, bring 3 cups of salted water to a boil over high heat. Add the florets and return the water to a boil. Cover and cook until the florets are just firm-tender and still a bit crunchy, about 6 minutes. Drain and arrange the florets in a gratin dish in a single layer.

▸ Set the rack about 4 inches from the broiler heating element and preheat the broiler. To make the sauce, melt the butter in a medium saucepan over medium heat and add the flour, whisking until combined to make a roux. Cook for 1 minute and then add the half-and-half, whisking until smooth. Bring the sauce to a boil, whisking occasionally. Add ¼ teaspoon of the salt and the pepper and boil for 1 to 2 minutes. Season the cauliflower with the remaining ¼ teaspoon of salt and sprinkle with half of the mozzarella. Pour the sauce over the top and sprinkle with the rest of the mozzarella and the Parmesan. Broil until the top is bubbling and golden brown, about 3 minutes or, if made ahead, place the gratin in the oven preheated to 350°F for 30 to 40 minutes, until warmed through and nicely browned on top. Serve as needed.

MINI PEPPER TREAT

This is a great summer dish to serve at room temperature with a chilled rosé. Mini peppers are colorful, abundant, and inexpensive in the summertime. Use grape tomatoes if available as they fit well in the half of the mini pepper.

Serves 4

8 mini peppers (about 8 ounces total)

8 grape tomatoes (about 4 ounces total)

1½ tablespoons chopped garlic

6 anchovy fillets, chopped (about 1½ tablespoons)

3 tablespoons olive oil

¼ teaspoon salt

½ teaspoon freshly ground black pepper

½ teaspoon herbes de Provence

1½ tablespoons grated Parmesan cheese

1 tablespoon chopped fresh chives

▸ Preheat the oven to 375°F.

▸ Split the peppers in half lengthwise and remove the ribs and seeds. Cut the tomatoes in half and place one half in each of the halves of pepper and set them in a gratin dish. Mix the garlic, anchovies, olive oil, salt, pepper, and herbes de Provence in a small bowl. Divide the mixture on top of and around the tomatoes. Sprinkle with the Parmesan and bake for 25 minutes, until the peppers soften and the cheese looks toasted. Cool to room temperature, sprinkle with chives, and enjoy.

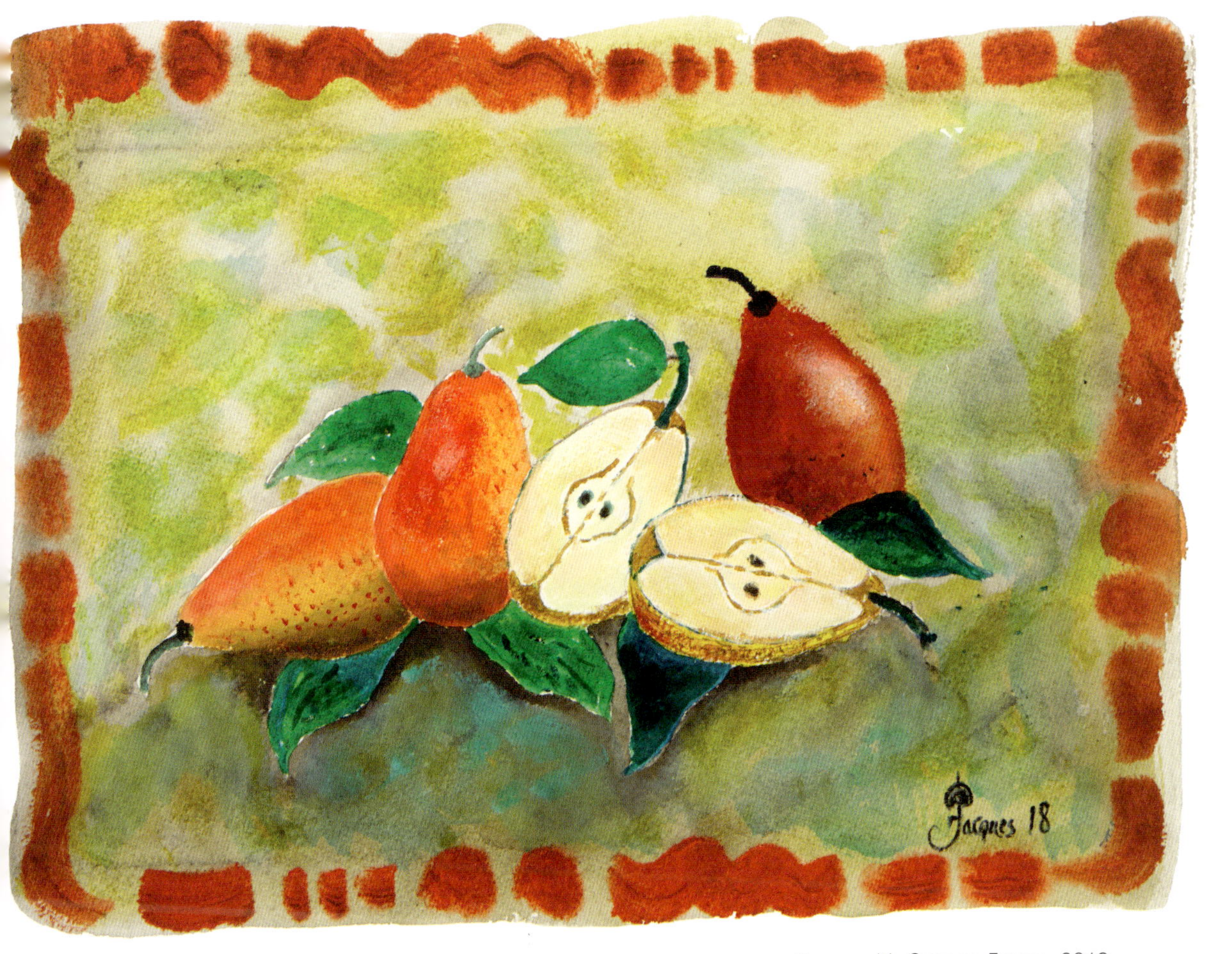

Pears with Orange Frame, 2018

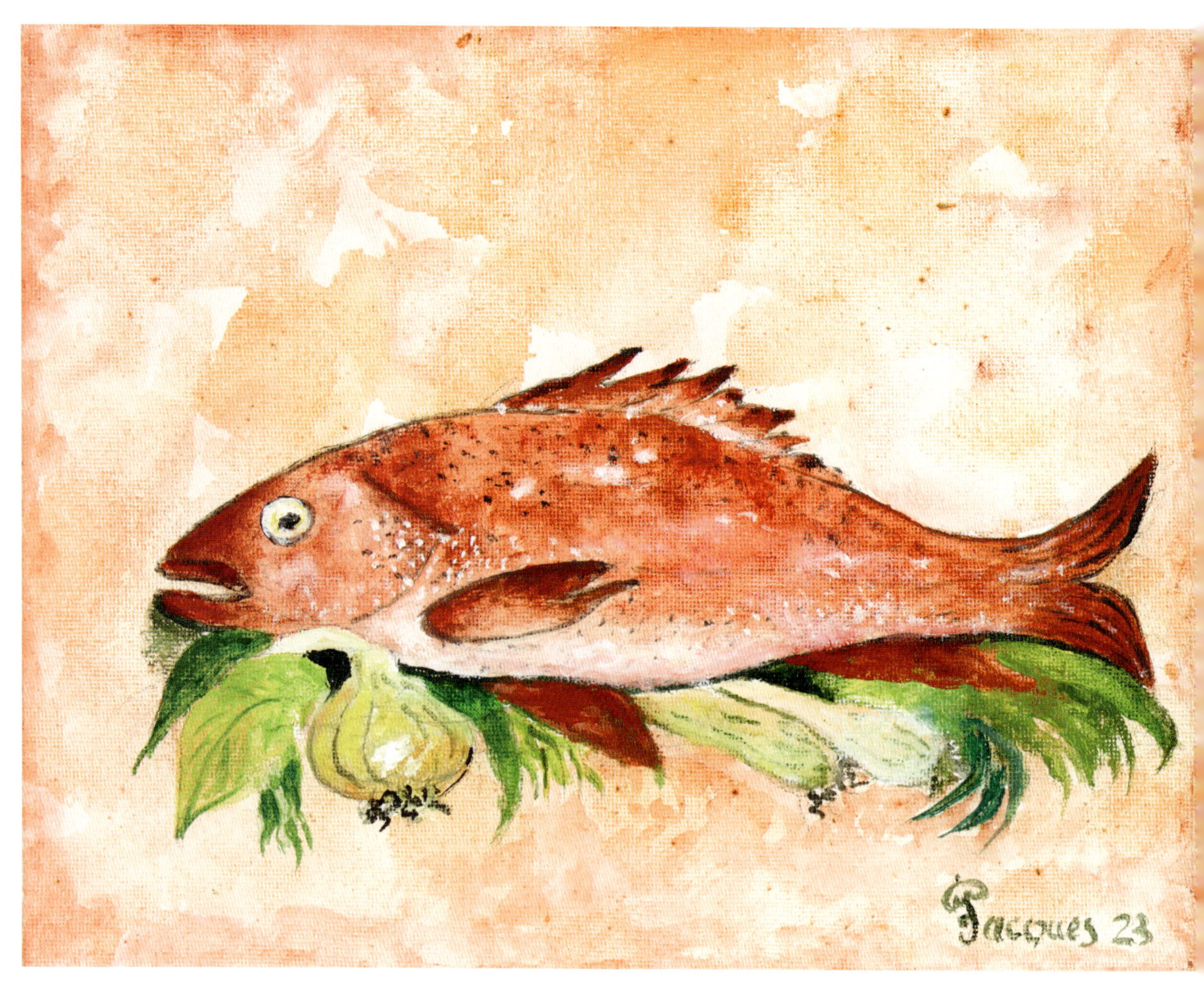

Red Snapper, 2023

MUSHROOMS à la CREME

I like mushrooms, adding them to a wide range of dishes. This simple preparation of thinly sliced white button mushrooms finished with cream is a classic side dish. You can use any mushroom variety, or a mixture: regular white button, cremini, oyster, or chanterelles, adding herbs such as chives, tarragon, thyme, or flat-leaf parsley at the end of the cooking time.

Serves 2 to 3

1 tablespoon olive oil

1 tablespoon butter

12 ounces white button or cremini mushrooms, thinly sliced

½ teaspoon salt

½ teaspoon freshly ground black pepper

2 shallots, peeled and coarsely chopped (¼ cup)

1 teaspoon all-purpose flour

½ cup heavy cream

Minced fresh chives or other chopped herbs, for garnish

▸ Heat the oil and butter in a medium skillet over medium-high to high heat. Add the mushrooms and cook until most of the moisture has evaporated and they begin to sizzle, 5 to 6 minutes. Season with the salt and pepper, add the shallots, and cook for about 2 minutes. Sprinkle the flour over the mushrooms and stir well. Pour in the cream and bring to a boil, stirring, and cook gently over low heat for 2 to 3 minutes. Taste and adjust the seasoning. Transfer to a serving dish and sprinkle with the herbs. Serve as needed.

CELERIAC PUREE

In this recipe, celeriac—the knobby root of a celery cultivated for its root—is cooked until tender in water seasoned with a little salt and sugar. The small amount of liquid remaining in the pan is then thickened and blended with the cooked celeriac into a smooth puree with a wonderfully intense flavor.

Serves 4

1 large celeriac (celery root; about 1½ pounds)

¾ teaspoon salt

1 teaspoon sugar

⅓ cup Cream of Wheat

2 tablespoons butter

▸ Using a sharp paring knife, remove the skin and any damaged areas from the celeriac, then cut it into 2-inch pieces.

▸ Place the celeriac pieces in a large saucepan with the salt, sugar, and 2¼ cups of water. Bring to a boil, reduce the heat to low, cover, and boil gently for 20 minutes, until the celeriac is very tender.

▸ Using a skimmer, remove the celeriac pieces and place them in a bowl so the liquid in the pan is more visible. Gradually add the Cream of Wheat to the liquid in the pan, whisking it in as you add it so that it doesn't lump. Return the celeriac pieces to the saucepan and bring the mixture back to a boil, stirring occasionally. Reduce the heat to low, cover, and boil gently for 5 minutes.

▸ Place the contents of the saucepan in a food processor and add the butter. Process for 20 to 30 seconds, until the mixture is smooth and creamy. Serve as needed.

Facing page: *Rabbits on Yellow,* 2016

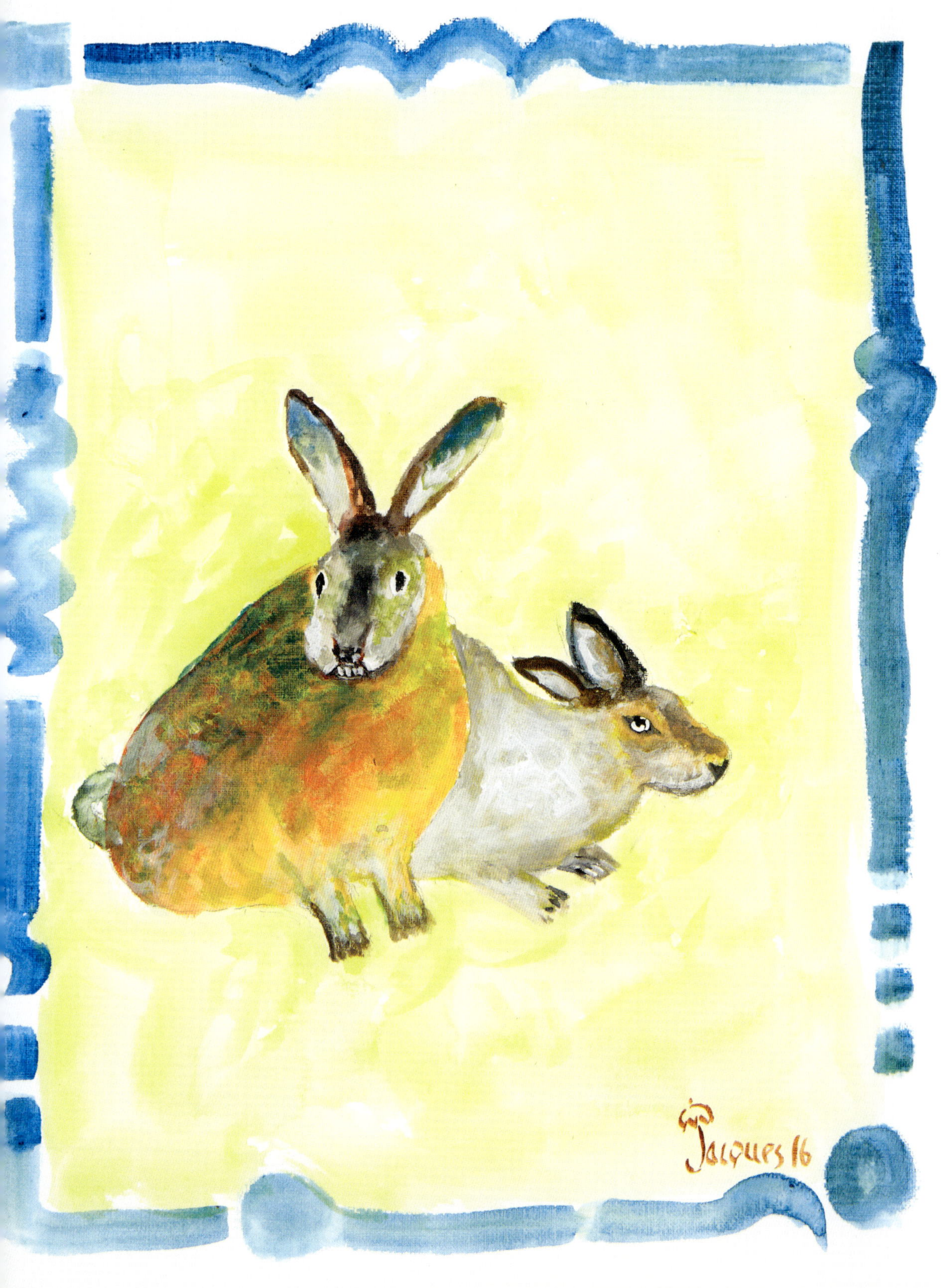
Jacques 16

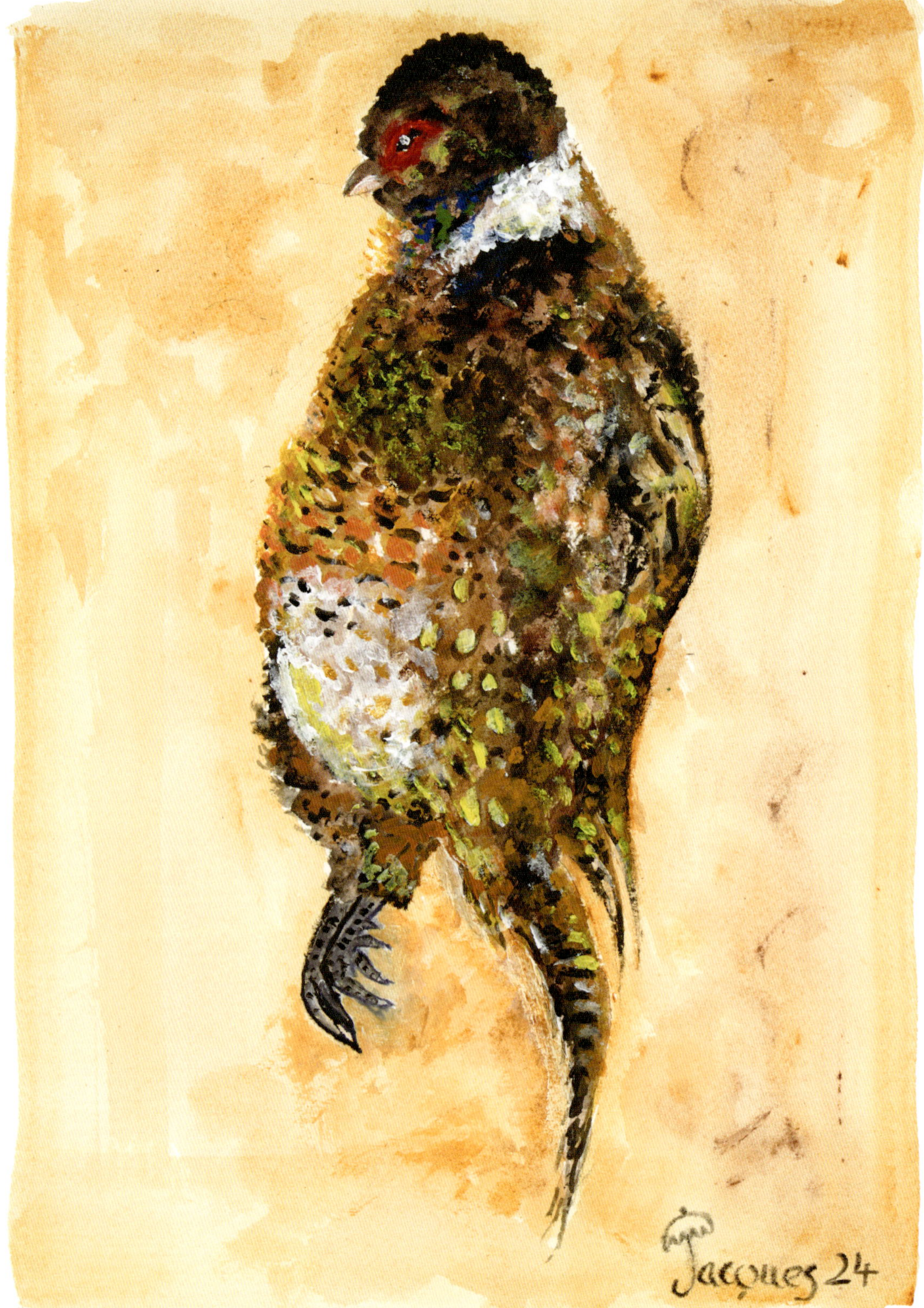
Jacques 24

POTATO LATKES

I love potatoes in any form—pureed, fried, in soup, or roasted. I also like to prepare these latkes for lunch. They are always best when eaten right away, but if you do want to make them ahead, set a wire rack over a baking sheet in a low oven so that they stay crispy on both sides.

Makes 6 pancakes, serves 3 as a garnish

1 large potato (about 8 ounces), peeled

2 to 3 tablespoons grated onion

1 large garlic clove

1 large egg

2 tablespoons chopped fresh flat-leaf parsley

1 tablespoon all-purpose flour

½ teaspoon salt

¼ teaspoon freshly ground black pepper

¼ cup peanut oil, for frying

▸ Shred the potato on the large holes of a box grater. Using your hands, press as much of the excess liquid out of the shredded potato as you can. Then shred the onion and the garlic, using the box grater again.

▸ In a medium bowl, whisk the egg until smooth, then add the potato, onion, garlic, parsley, flour, salt, and pepper. Mix well to combine.

▸ Heat the oil in a large, nonstick skillet over medium-high heat. Place about ¼ cup of the potato mixture in the hot oil and press it down to make a 4- to 5-inch latke; you should be able to fit about 3 in the pan at a time. Cook each latke, flipping once, for 2 to 3 minutes on each side, until golden brown. Repeat to make another batch. Serve immediately or keep warm on a wire rack set over a baking sheet in a low oven.

Facing page: *Pheasant,* 2024

CAULIFLOWER "SALMIS"

A *salmis* is, by definition, a kind of stew or ragout of different types of precooked meats. I use the word loosely here, applying it to a stew of small pieces of cooked cauliflower combined with shallots, scallions, garlic, ketchup, and some hot sauce. This makes a great side dish that is particularly complementary to poultry, meat, and fish.

Serves 4

1 head cauliflower (about 2 pounds), leaves and root end removed, and remainder (about 1¼ pounds) divided into florets

2 tablespoons olive oil

2 to 3 shallots, peeled and finely chopped (⅓ cup)

2 to 3 scallions, minced (¼ cup)

2 large garlic cloves, peeled, crushed, and chopped (2 teaspoons)

2 tablespoons ketchup

½ teaspoon salt

1 teaspoon hot sauce (such as sriracha or Chinese hot garlic sauce, or ½ teaspoon Tabasco)

1 tablespoon minced fresh flat-leaf parsley

▸ Bring 2 cups of water to a boil in a large saucepan. Add the florets, bring the water back to a boil, cover, and cook over high heat for about 7 minutes, until the cauliflower is tender. Drain and cool to lukewarm. Cut into 1-inch pieces.

▸ Heat the olive oil in a large skillet over medium heat. Add the shallots, scallions, and garlic and cook for 1 minute. Add the cauliflower along with the ketchup, salt, and hot sauce. Mix well and cook for 1 to 2 additional minutes, until hot. Serve the cauliflower with parsley sprinkled on top.

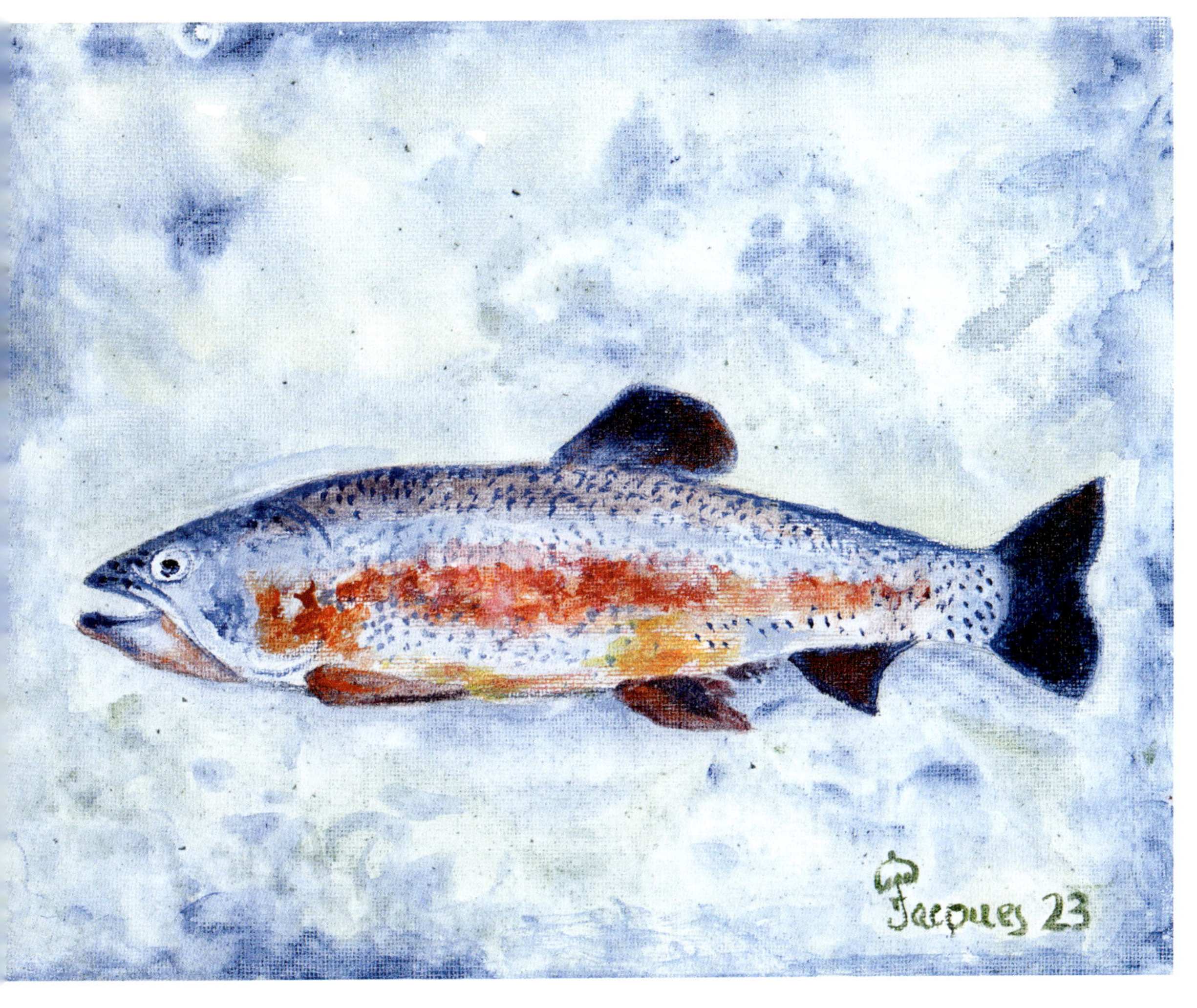

Rainbow Trout, 2023

Pages 96–97: Flower Shrimps, 2022

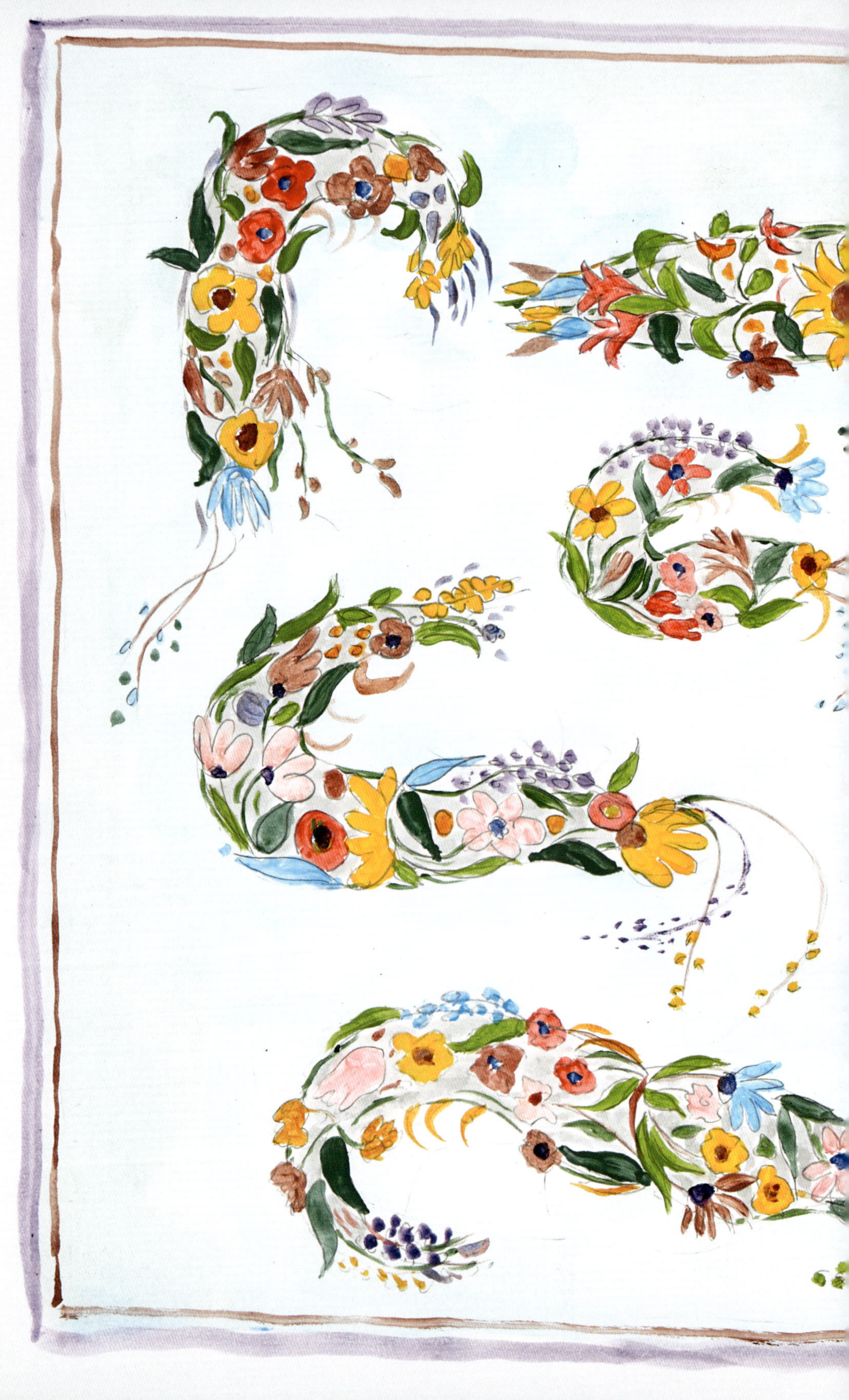

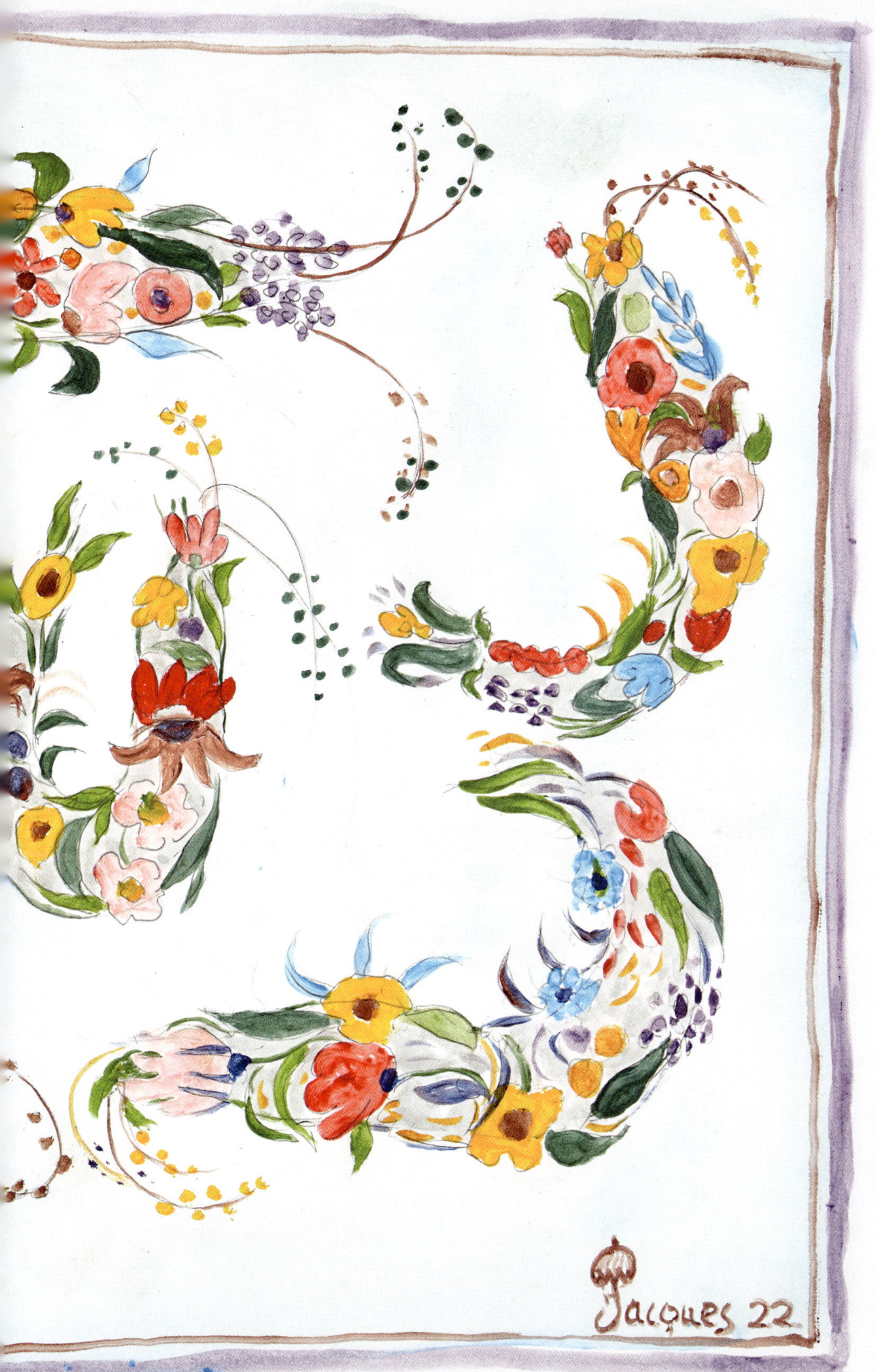
Jacques 22

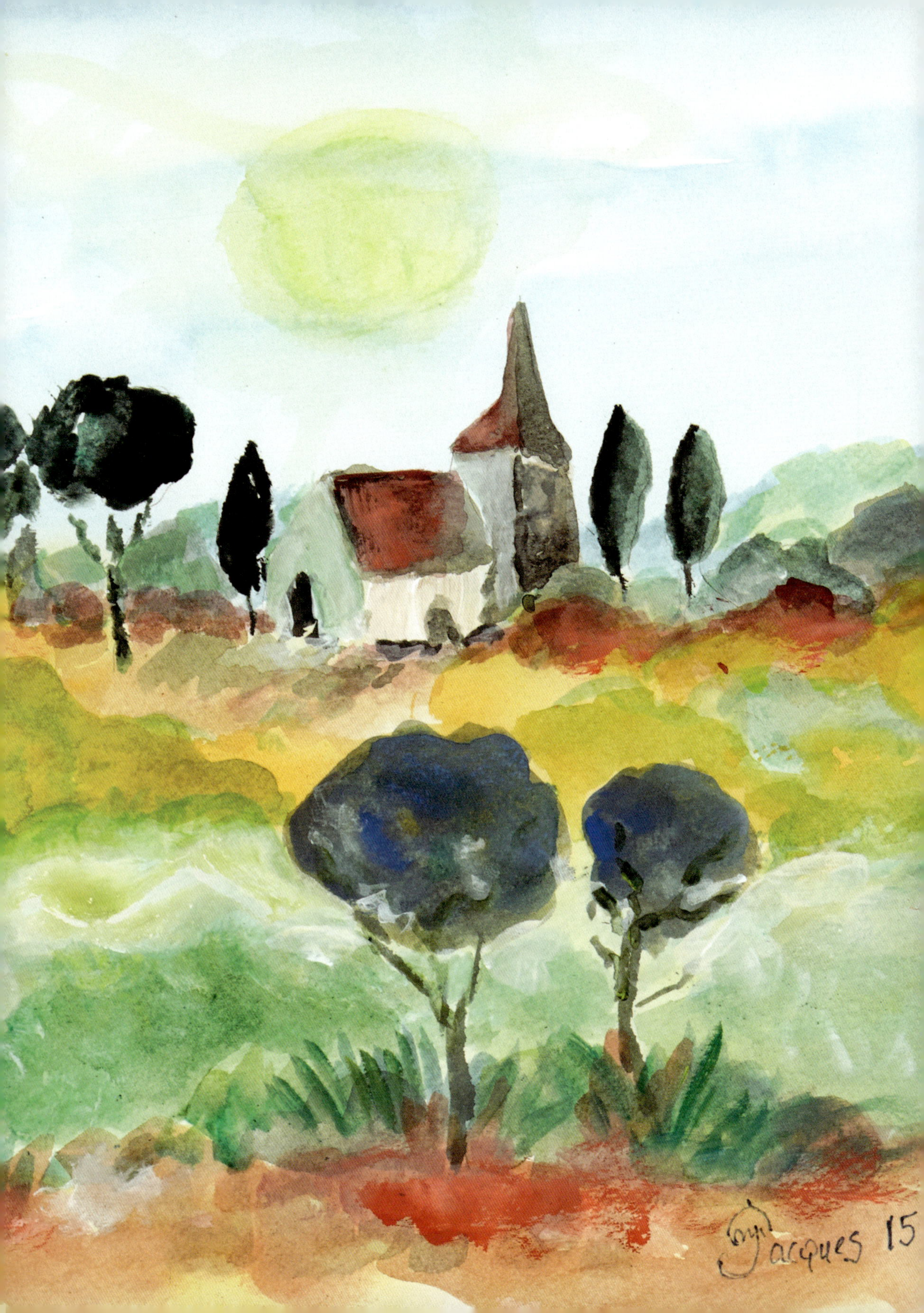
Jacques 15

Fish & Shellfish

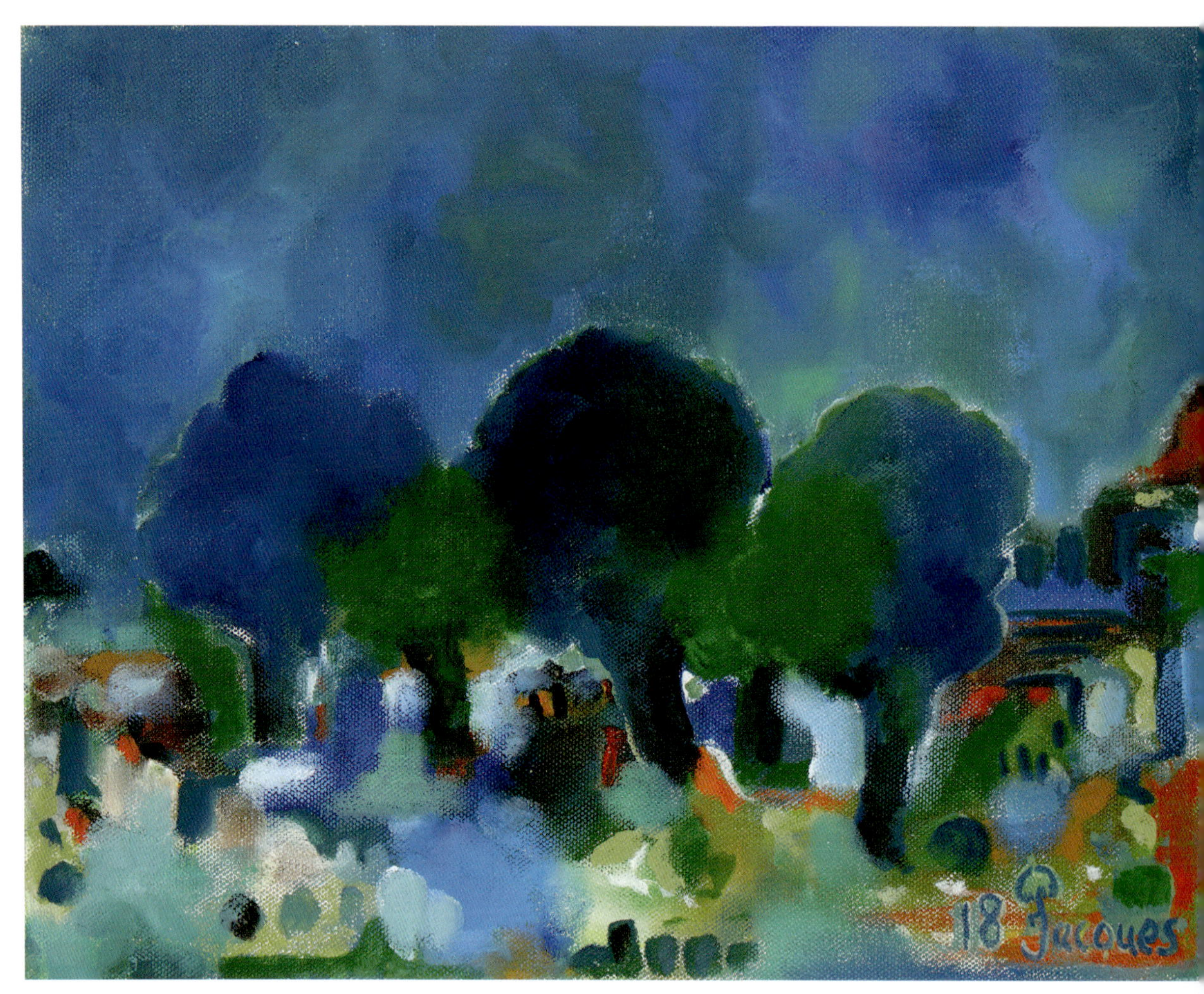

Backyard, 2018

SEAFOOD COMBO SHORELINE

This is one of those excellent seafood dishes that includes a colorful assortment of vegetables along with the fish and shellfish—in this instance, scallops, shrimp, and monkfish, although another firm-textured fish can be substituted if monkfish is not available. It takes awhile to cut up all the vegetables and fish, but the dish takes only 5 to 6 minutes to cook from beginning to end.

Serves 4

½ cup dry white wine

1½ tablespoons olive oil

1½ tablespoons butter

1 teaspoon salt

1 teaspoon freshly ground black pepper

4 ounces cremini mushrooms, washed and cut into ½-inch slices

1 large ripe tomato (10 ounces), halved, seeded, and cut into 1-inch pieces (about 1 cup)

1 small stalk broccoli (6 ounces), stem peeled and cut into 1½-inch pieces (about 1½ cups)

1 zucchini (6 ounces), cut into sticks 2 inches long and ½ inch thick (about 1⅓ cups)

¼ cup chopped onion

3 large garlic cloves, finely chopped

10 ounces scallops, washed and cut into 1-inch pieces (1¼ cups)

8 ounces medium shrimp, shelled and each cut into 3 pieces (1 cup)

1 piece monkfish (9 ounces), with black skin removed (about 8 ounces trimmed) and cut into ¾-inch pieces (1 cup)

▸ Place the wine, oil, butter, salt, pepper, mushrooms, tomato, broccoli, zucchini, onion, and garlic in a stainless steel saucepan. Bring the mixture to a strong boil over high heat and cook for 1 minute (this can be done ahead of time). When ready to serve, add the scallops, shrimp, and monkfish to the mixture in the pan, cover, and cook over high heat for 4 to 5 minutes, stirring once or twice. Set the pan aside, covered, off the heat for 5 minutes before ladling it into soup plates. Serve immediately.

ROASTED RED SNAPPER

Red snapper was commonly prepared and served like this years ago, and hopefully, roasting the whole fish and carving it in the dining room just before serving will become popular again. The advantages: it is an easy dish to prepare, fish cooked on the bone is more flavorful, the presentation of the whole fish at the table is impressive, and carving it in view of guests is a convivial activity that encourages everyone's participation in the dining experience.

Serves 6

1 large red snapper (about 4 pounds) scaled, gutted, and head and tail removed (about 2¼ pounds ready-to-cook weight)

1 small onion (3 ounces), peeled and finely chopped (½ cup)

4 scallions, finely minced (⅓ cup)

1 large ripe tomato (9 ounces), halved, seeded, and cut into ½-inch pieces (1¼ cups)

1 tablespoon coarsely chopped fresh oregano

¾ teaspoon salt

½ teaspoon freshly ground black pepper

¾ cup dry, fruity white wine

2 tablespoons olive oil

2 tablespoons butter

▸ Preheat the oven to 400°F.

▸ Cut 3 evenly spaced slits, each about ¼ inch deep, across the surface of one side of the fish. Place the onion, scallions, tomato, oregano, salt, pepper, wine, oil, and butter in a medium saucepan, bring the mixture to a boil, and boil it for 30 seconds. Distribute half of the mixture in the bottom of a sturdy gratin dish large enough to accommodate the fish. Then place the fish on top and pour the rest of the mixture over the fish.

▸ Place the fish in the oven for 25 to 30 minutes, just until it is cooked through and the flesh separates from the center bone when lifted with a fork. Bring the gratin dish to the table. Carve the fish, beginning with the side that is facing up, and serve it with some of the surrounding juices and vegetable garnish.

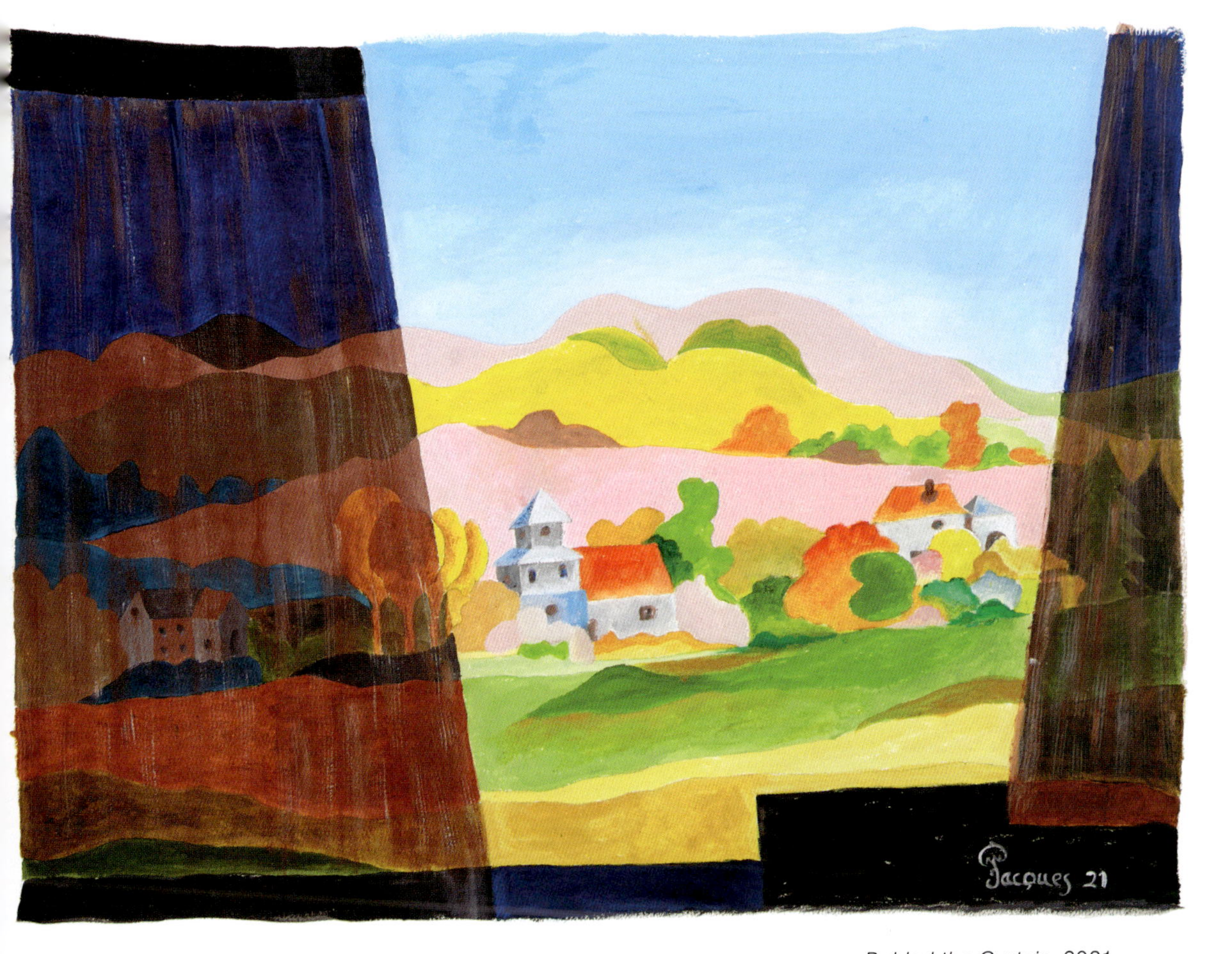

Behind the Curtain, 2021

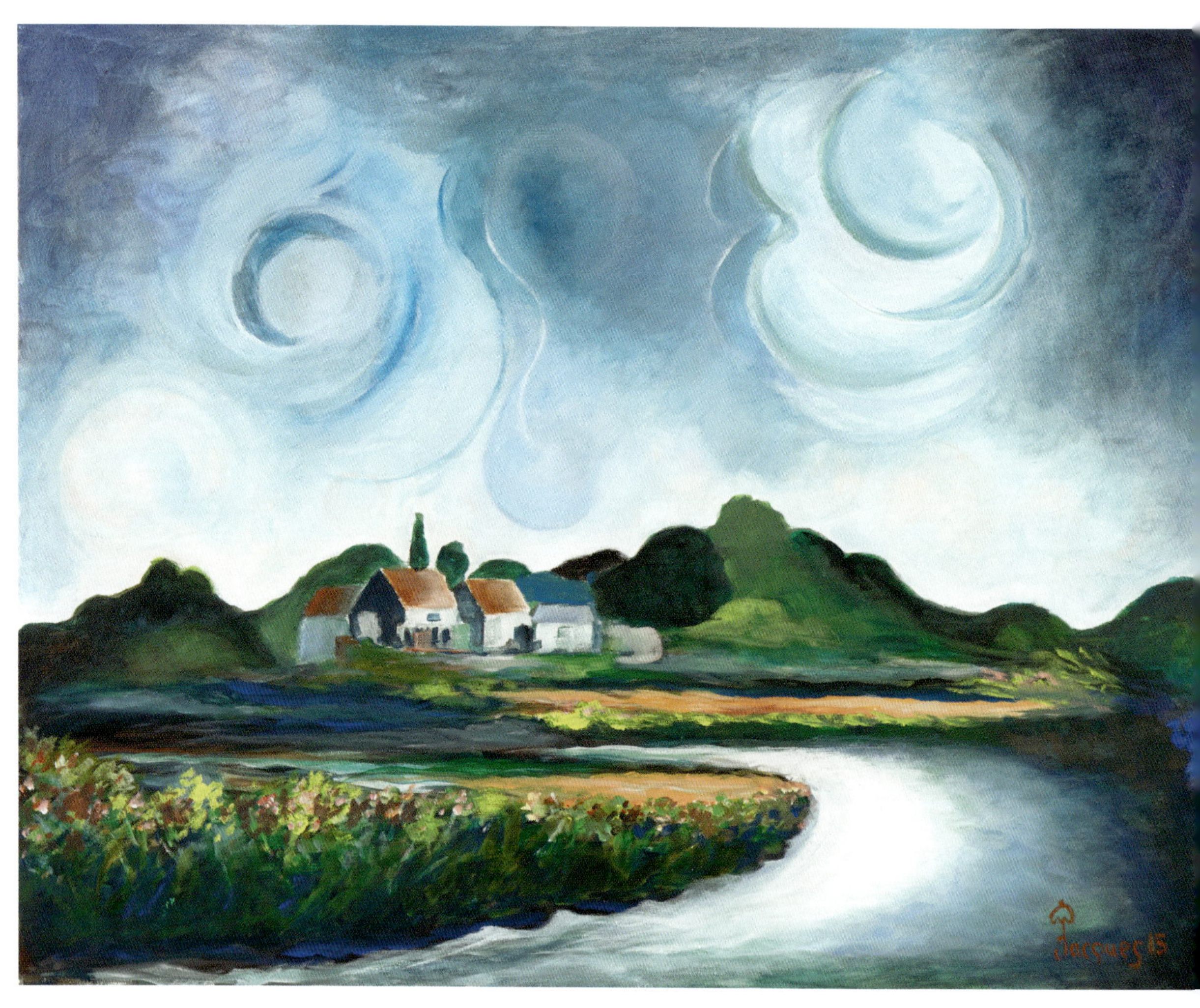

River at Night, 2015

CATFISH with FRESH PEAS in ZUCCHINI "BOATS"

Farmed catfish are now available all over the country, and the quality is much better than what I remember in my youth, when they came from muddy ponds. Today, catfish have a mild, nutty taste, especially if you remove any black flesh from the surface of the fillets. The black part tends to be a bit stronger in taste. In this fast, easy recipe, the fish are prepared with zucchini, shelled peas, and mushrooms.

Serves 4

1½ tablespoons olive oil

1 tablespoon butter

1 zucchini (about 6 ounces), quartered lengthwise

1 pound fresh peas, shelled (9 ounces shelled; about 1⅓ cups), or the same amount of frozen petite peas

5 ounces white mushrooms, washed and cut into ½-inch dice (about 1¾ cups)

1 teaspoon salt

½ teaspoon freshly ground black pepper

4 catfish fillets (about 6 ounces each, 1½ pounds total), cleaned of all fat, skin, and sinews

4 slices lemon

Flat-leaf parsley sprigs, for garnish

▸ Heat the oil and butter in a large skillet. Add the zucchini, peas, mushrooms, and half of the salt and pepper. Cover and cook over high heat for 4 minutes. Using a slotted spoon, remove the vegetables from the skillet and place them on a plate.

▸ Sprinkle the remaining salt and pepper on the catfish fillets and place them in a single layer in the hot drippings in the skillet. Cook them over high heat for 2½ minutes, then turn them over, reduce the heat to medium, and cook them for 2½ minutes on the second side.

▸ Meanwhile, using a knife, make a slit lengthwise down the fleshy center of each zucchini quarter (without cutting through the surrounding skin at the edges) to create small receptacles or "boats." Arrange one zucchini boat on each of four dinner plates and fill the center cavity of the boats with the mushroom and pea mixture.

▸ Place a fish fillet alongside the zucchini boat on each plate. Garnish the fillets with the lemon slices and parsley and serve.

BAKED MACKEREL MARIE-LOUISE

This recipe involves layering and baking sliced potatoes, onions, and tomatoes in a gratin dish until they are tender, then arranging fish on top and finishing the dish under the broiler. If fresh mackerel is not available, substitute another fish of about the same weight—whiting, small sea bass, small red snapper, or catfish, for example.

Serves 4

1¼ pounds red bliss or Yukon Gold potatoes, peeled and thinly sliced (about 3 cups)

2 medium onions (8 ounces total), peeled and thinly sliced

1 tablespoon chopped fresh savory, or 1 teaspoon dried

1½ tablespoons olive oil

¼ teaspoon freshly ground black pepper

¾ teaspoon salt

⅓ cup chicken stock, preferably unsalted homemade

2 large ripe tomatoes (1 pound), cut into ½-inch slices

⅓ cup dry white wine

4 mackerel (12 to 15 ounces each), gutted and heads and tails removed (about 8 ounces each ready-to-cook weight)

½ teaspoon herbes de Provence

2 tablespoons chopped fresh flat-leaf parsley

▸ Preheat the oven to 400°F.

▸ Rinse the potato slices in cool water, then drain them in a colander. Place the drained potato slices in a bowl with the onion, savory, olive oil, pepper, and ½ teaspoon of the salt. Mix well and transfer to a gratin dish. Add the stock and arrange the sliced tomatoes over the potato and onion mixture.

▸ Place the gratin dish in the oven for 45 minutes, until the potatoes are tender. Remove and add the wine. Preheat the broiler.

The potato-onion-tomato mixture can be prepared up to 1 hour ahead. Bake for 45 minutes, as indicated in the recipe, then set aside until about 10 minutes before serving time. Arrange the mackerel on top and finish under the broiler according to the recipe instructions.

▸ Meanwhile, make three horizontal slits, each about ¼ inch deep, through the skin on both sides of each mackerel. Sprinkle the fish with the remaining salt and the herbes de Provence and arrange them in one layer, pushing them into the tomatoes in the gratin dish.

▸ Place the dish under the broiler so it is about 10 inches from the heat and broil for 10 minutes, until the fish is just cooked.

▸ Sprinkle with parsley and serve as needed.

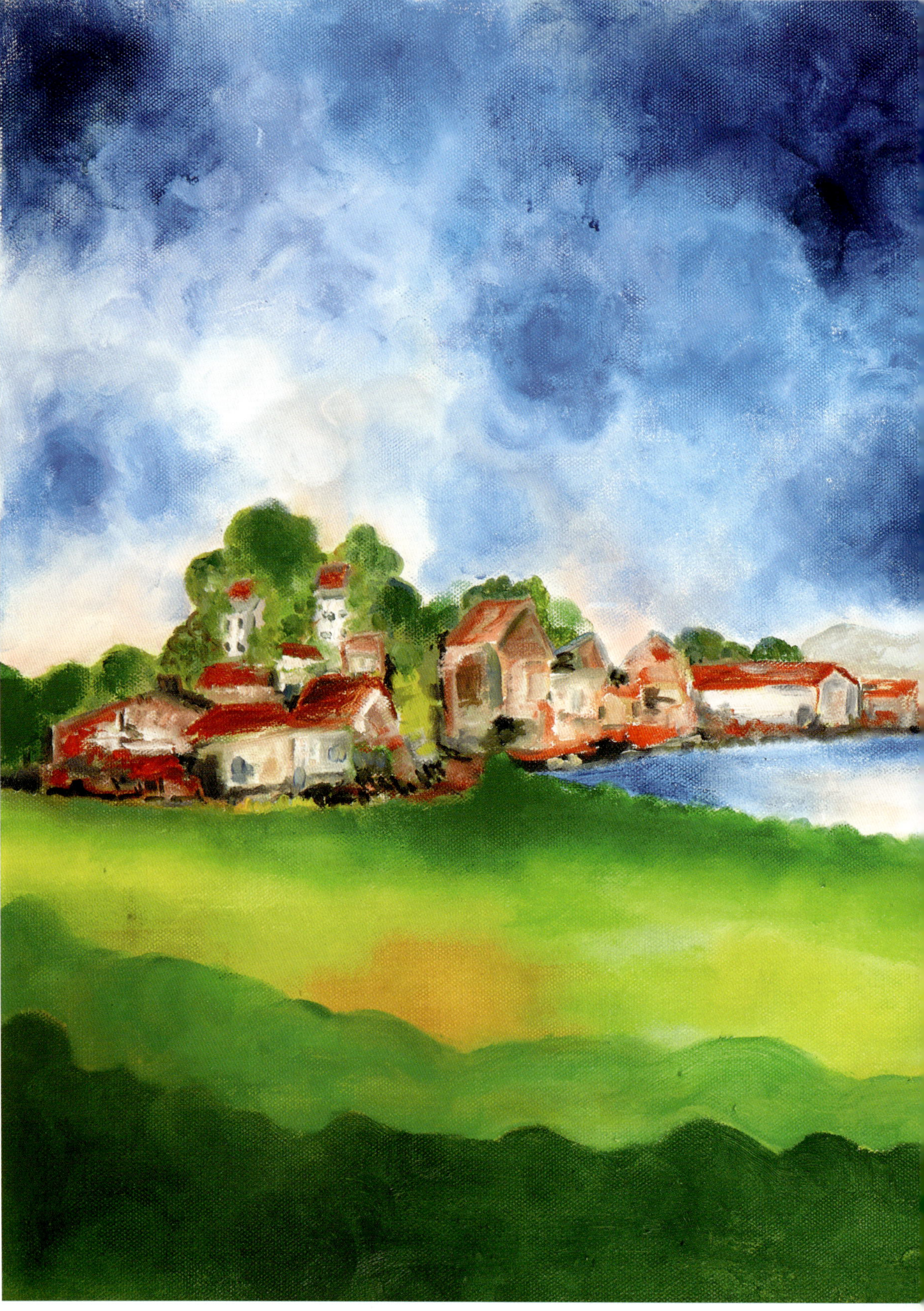

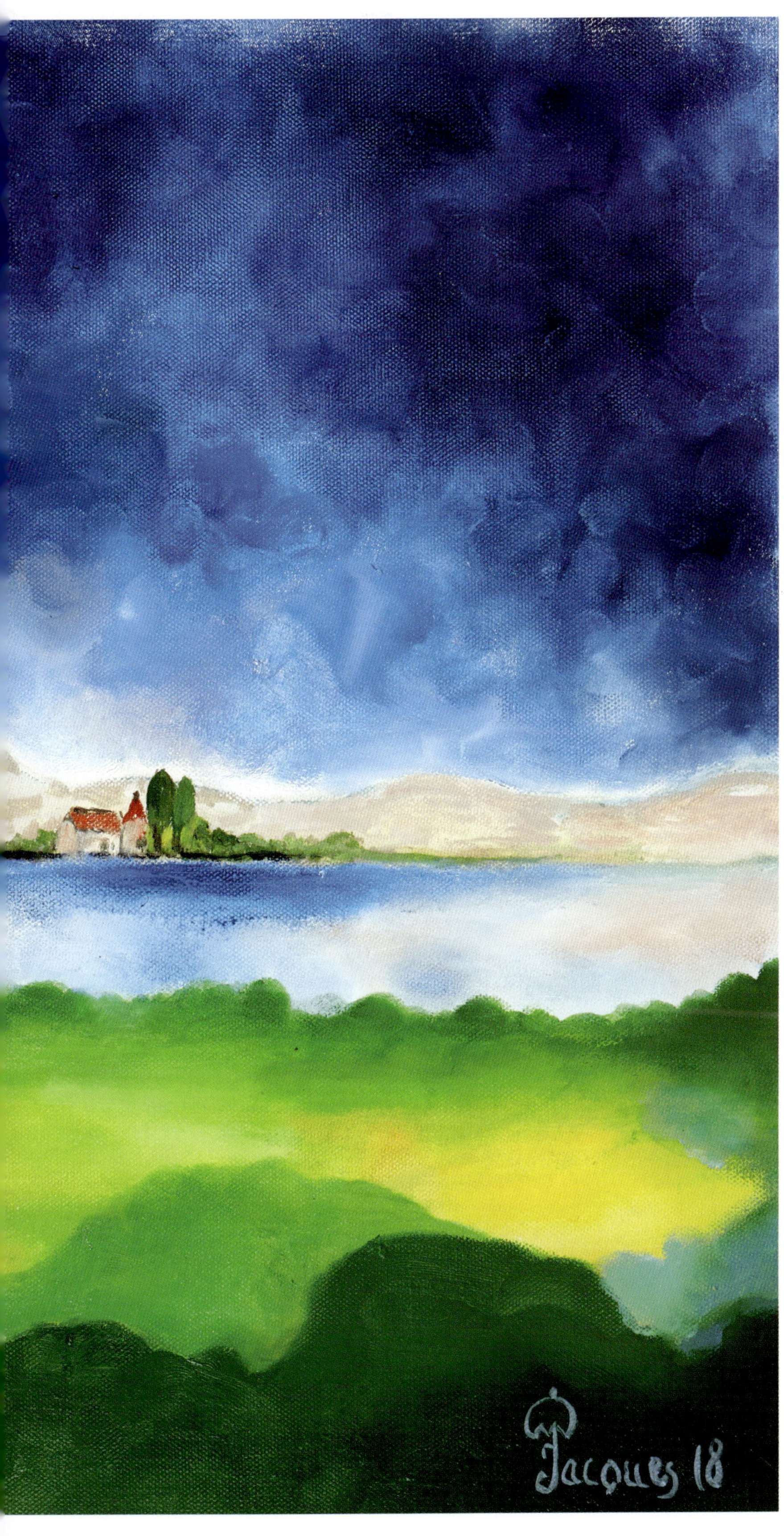

Village on a Lake, 2018

BROILED LOBSTER with BREAD STUFFING

I am very fond of broiled as well as grilled lobster and always prepare it both ways a few times every summer. I like to blanch lobsters in boiling water for a few minutes before broiling or grilling them; I find that their meat retains its moistness and is more tender as a result. When possible, I like the female lobsters, which have savory eggs in the cavity of their body.

Serves 4

4 lobsters, preferably female (about 1¼ pounds each)

4 slices bread from a large country loaf (8 ounces total)

2 tablespoons butter

2 tablespoons olive oil

4 shallots, peeled and finely minced (1 cup)

8 scallions, finely minced (1 cup)

¼ teaspoon freshly ground black pepper

Tabasco sauce to taste

½ cup dry, fruity white wine

▸ Bring 4 quarts of water to a boil in a large pot. When it is boiling, drop in the lobsters and cover the pot. Cook for about 5 minutes, just until the water returns to a boil. Remove the lobsters and set them aside until they are cool enough to handle.

▸ Meanwhile, toast the bread, then let it cool to room temperature. Break the toast into a food processor and process it into coarse crumbs.

▸ Melt the butter in a medium saucepan, add the olive oil, shallots, and scallions, and cook for 2 minutes. Add the breadcrumbs, pepper, and Tabasco and toss lightly. Remove from the heat.

▸ When the lobsters are cool enough to handle, remove the claws from each and place them in a plastic bag to prevent splattering as you proceed. Pound the claws with a meat pounder to crack the shells, then either place them as they are on a large jelly roll pan lined with aluminum foil, or remove the claw meat intact from the shells and place it on the foil-lined pans.

▸ Preheat the broiler.

▸ Split each lobster in half and remove and discard the stomachs and intestinal tracts from each. Reserve the juices emerging from the lobsters and combine them with the wine in a bowl.

▸ Arrange the lobster body halves side by side and flesh side up next to the cracked claws or claw meat. Lightly fill the body cavities with the stuffing mixture and sprinkle some of the stuffing on the flesh of the tails. Pour the wine and juice mixture around the lobsters.

▸ Place the pan under the hot broiler on the lowest oven shelf (10 to 11 inches from the heat). Cook for 10 minutes, until the stuffing is nicely browned and the lobsters are cooked through and hot inside.

▸ Arrange two stuffed lobster body halves on each of four plates and place two lobster claws, or the meat from two claws, alongside. Spoon some pan juices over the lobsters and serve as needed.

Pages 112–113: *Abstract Landscape,* 2024

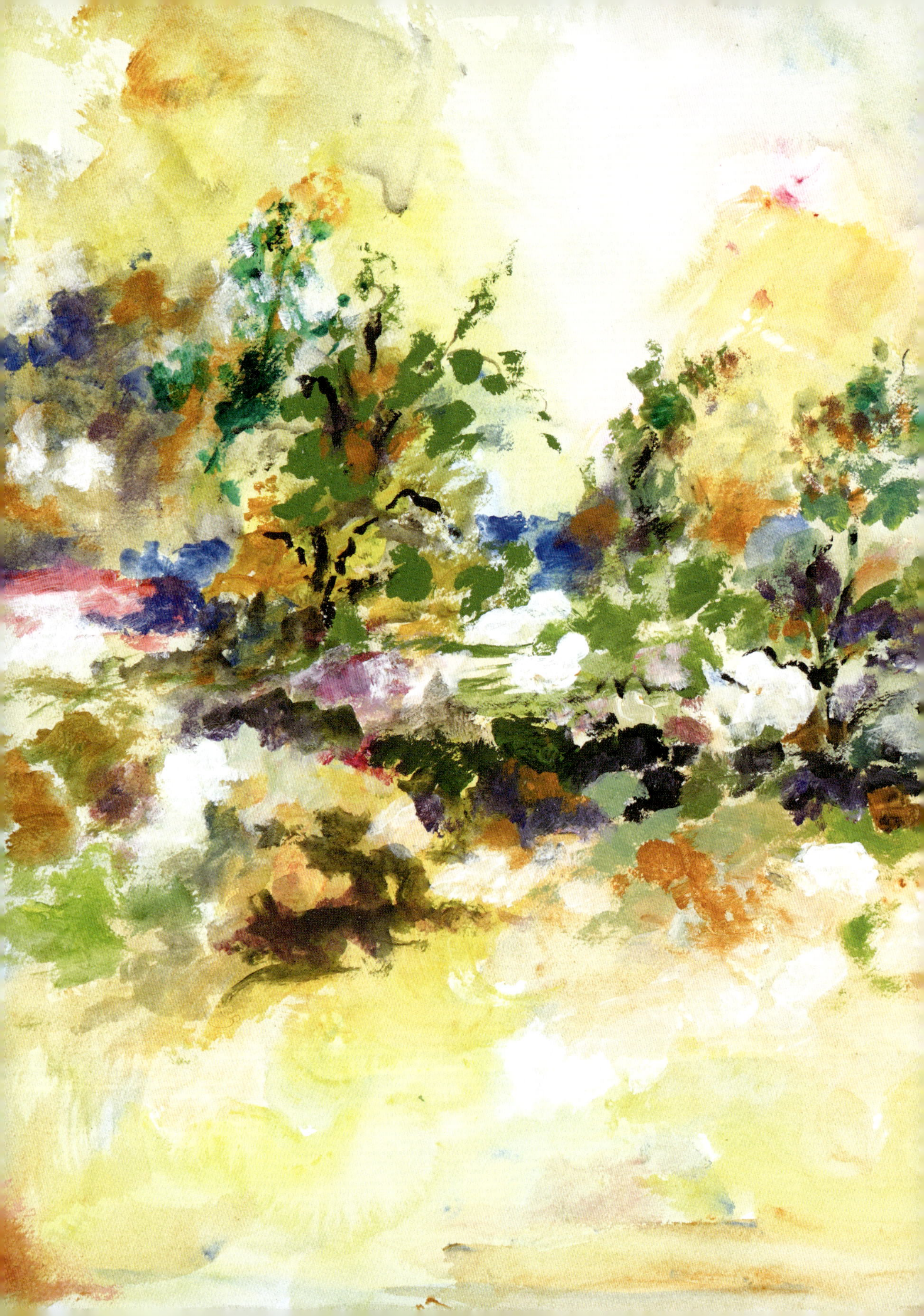

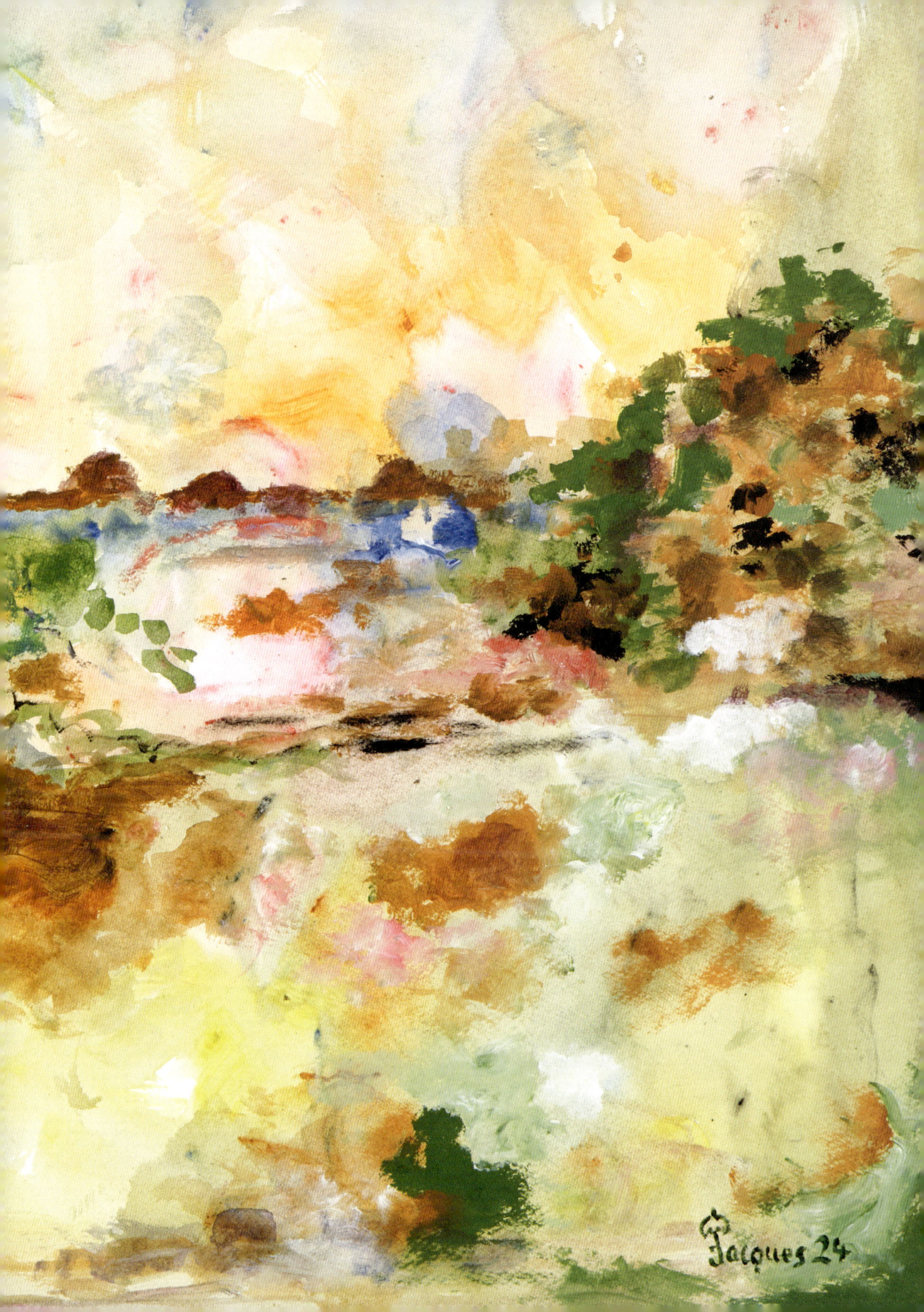
Jacques 24

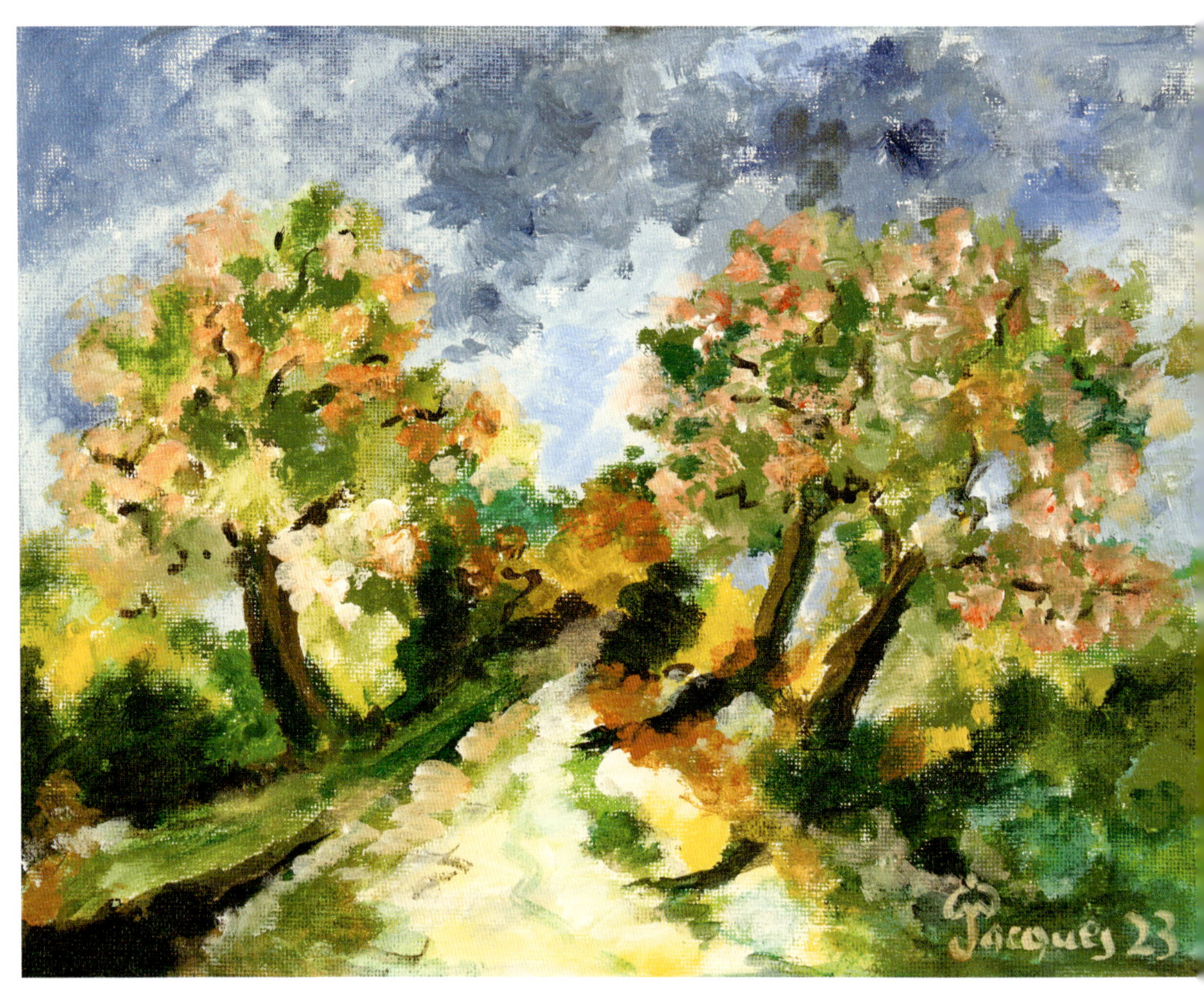

Road in the Sun, 2023

CRAB CAKES with HOT SAUCE

Crab cakes are one of the glories of New England. I have made them with eggs, sometimes with cream, or with potatoes or corn flour, and they are a favorite for a summer menu. They are not economical—as good-quality lump crabmeat is very expensive—but they make an excellent treat worth the occasional splurge.

Serves 2 as a main course or 4 as an appetizer

8 ounces lump crabmeat

¼ cup mayonnaise

¼ teaspoon salt

2 large scallions, finely sliced (¼ cup)

1 tablespoon chopped fresh flat-leaf parsley

¾ cup fresh breadcrumbs, about 1½ slices white bread processed in the food processor

2 tablespoons olive oil

1 tablespoon butter

SAUCE

⅓ cup mayonnaise

1 teaspoon horseradish, fresh or from a jar

¼ cup tomato juice, such as V8

½ teaspoon sriracha or other hot sauce

1 teaspoon lemon juice

1 to 2 tablespoons minced fresh chives

▸ In a large bowl, combine the crabmeat, mayonnaise, salt, scallions, parsley, and breadcrumbs and gently stir together. Divide the mixture into four and shape into patties about 1¼ inches thick. The crab cakes can be prepared up to this point, covered, and refrigerated for a few hours until you are ready to cook them.

▸ Heat the olive oil and butter in a large skillet, preferably nonstick. Add the crab cakes and cook over medium heat for about 2 minutes on each side, until golden brown.

▸ To make the sauce, in a small bowl, whisk together the mayonnaise, horseradish, tomato juice, sriracha, lemon juice, and chives.

▸ To serve, spread the sauce over the base of a platter or individual plates and top with the crab cakes.

SEARED SHRIMP in THEIR SHELLS

I would often make this for myself and Gloria when we visited Amelia Island off the coast of Florida, buying the shrimp directly from the fishermen on their boats. Be prepared to eat these with your fingers and chew on the shells. The recipe easily scales up and can be enjoyed in the company of good friends.

Serves 2

8 jumbo shrimp (fewer than 15 per pound), deveined, shell-on (about 8 ounces)

1 tablespoon extra virgin olive oil, plus more for drizzling

¼ teaspoon Tabasco sauce

¼ teaspoon dried minced garlic

1 teaspoon smoked paprika

⅛ teaspoon salt

Chopped fresh chives or flat-leaf parsley, for garnish

▸ Place the shrimp in a medium bowl and add the olive oil, Tabasco, garlic, paprika, and salt. Stir to combine, cover and let sit for 30 minutes or refrigerate if marinating longer, up to 12 hours.

▸ Heat a heavy skillet or cast-iron pan over high heat for 3 to 4 minutes until very hot. Add the shrimp in an even layer and cook for about 1½ minutes on each side, until firm but barely cooked. Immediately transfer the shrimp to a plate, drizzle with olive oil, and top with chives. Enjoy, making sure you chew and suck on the shells.

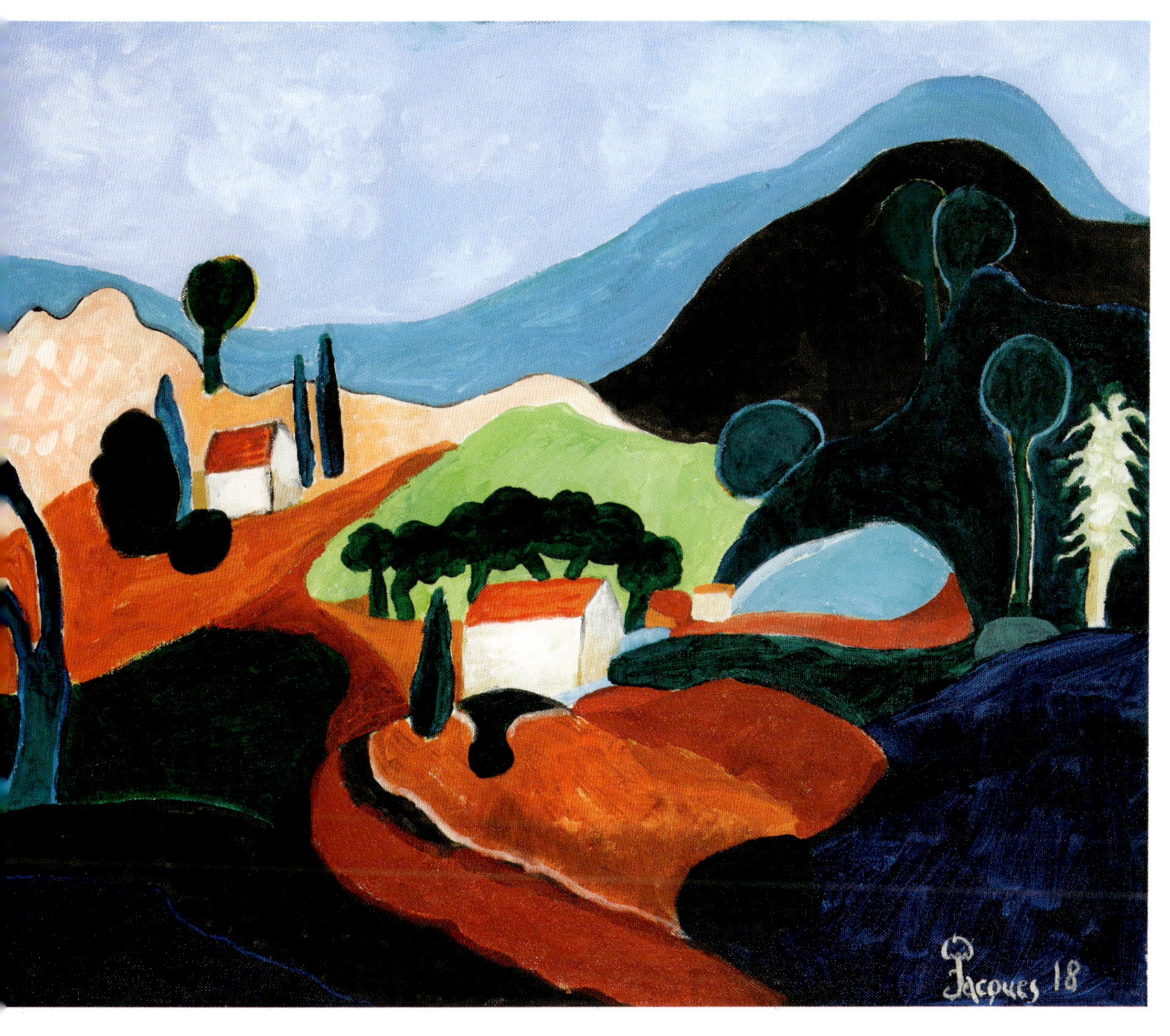

Poetic Landscape, 2018

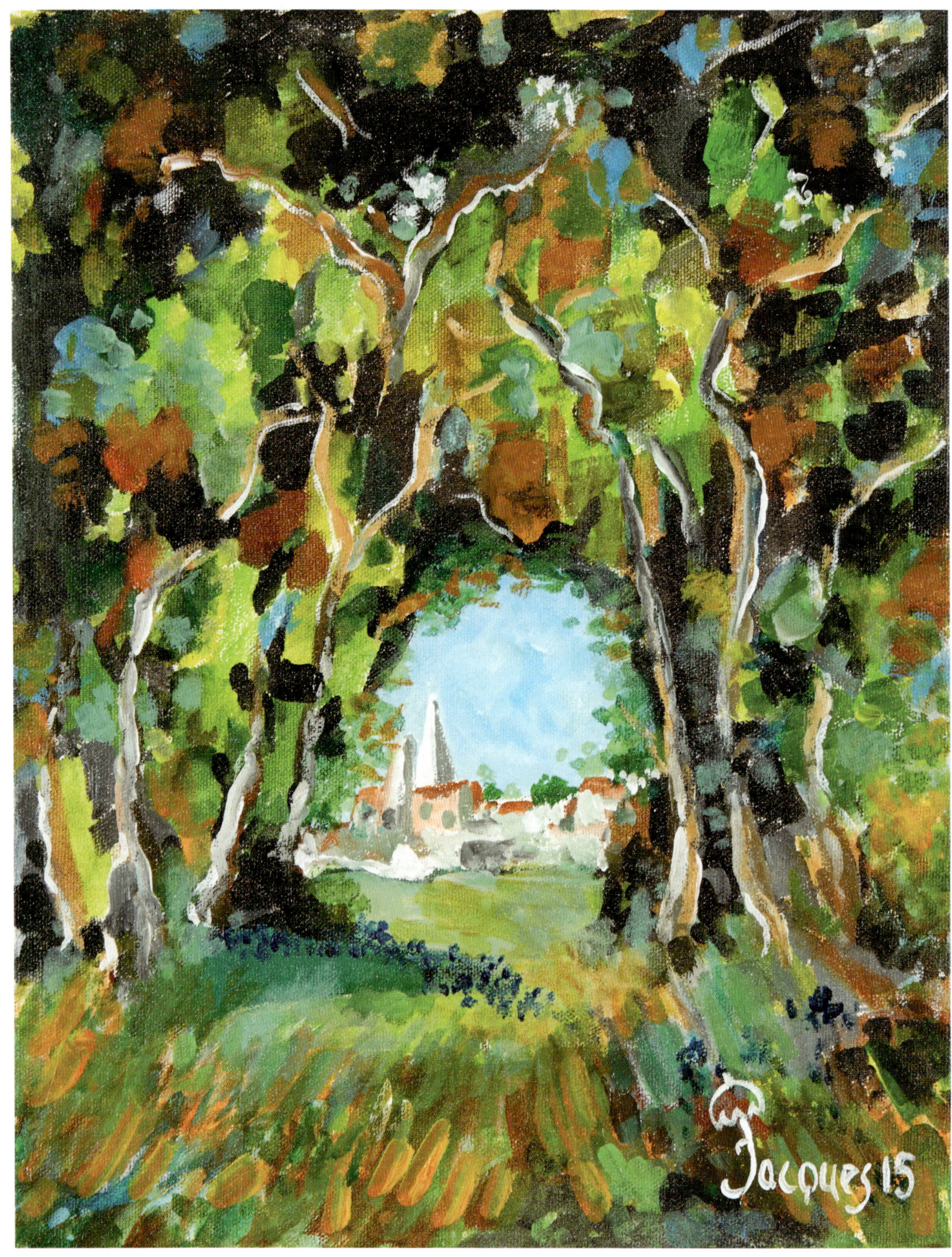

Village Through the Wood, 2015

SHRIMP PATTIES with MUSHROOMS

This dish is a classic mousse of shrimp served on mushrooms. The combination of pureed shrimp and chopped shrimp pieces will make two large patties for a main course, or four as a first course. The same method could be used with scallops or fish.

Serves 2 as a main course, 4 as an appetizer

SHRIMP PATTIES

8 ounces peeled shrimp

¼ teaspoon smoked paprika

¼ teaspoon salt

½ teaspoon freshly ground black pepper

¼ cup heavy cream

½ cup panko

2 tablespoons peanut oil

MUSHROOM GARNISH

1 tablespoon butter

1 tablespoon olive oil

¼ cup sliced shallots

1½ cups sliced white mushrooms

¼ teaspoon salt

¼ teaspoon freshly ground black pepper

1 tablespoon chopped fresh chives

▸ To make the mousse, cut the large ends of the shrimp in ½-inch pieces (about ½ cup) and set aside. Place the rest of the shrimp (about 1½ cups) in a food processor. Add the paprika, salt, pepper, and cream and process until very smooth, about 30 seconds. Combine the reserved shrimp pieces with the mousse. Spread the panko on a plate. Divide the shrimp mixture into two large patties, about 1 inch thick and about 4 inches in diameter. Alternatively, divide the shrimp mixture into 4 smaller patties. Place on the panko. Press more panko on top. Heat the peanut oil in a saucepan and sauté the patties over medium heat for about 2½ minutes on each side, until nicely browned. Transfer to a plate.

▸ To make the mushroom garnish, in the same skillet, heat the butter and olive oil until the butter is melted and add the shallots. Cook for about 1 minute, then add the mushrooms, salt, and pepper. Cook for a few minutes, until the mushrooms release their water and start sizzling. Stir in the chives. Place on a platter with the shrimp patties on top. Serve as needed.

STEAMED SCALLOPS on SPINACH with HAZELNUT DRESSING

This recipe is done on the stovetop in a skillet and comes together very quickly. The spinach goes in first, still wet from washing to help it steam, and the scallops are added on top. Everything is topped with a delicious dressing made using toasted hazelnuts that provides excellent taste and texture.

Serves 2

¼ cup hazelnuts

1 tablespoon lemon juice

1 teaspoon chopped garlic

4 tablespoons olive oil

½ teaspoon salt

½ teaspoon freshly ground black pepper

4 ounces spinach (about 4 cups, lightly packed)

8 ounces sea scallops (about 8)

▸ Preheat the oven to 350°F.

▸ Place the hazelnuts on a baking sheet and roast for 10 to 12 minutes, until nicely browned. Cool and remove some of the skins by rubbing the nuts, then crush with a small skillet into ¼-inch pieces. Mix the lemon juice, garlic, and 3 tablespoons of the olive oil in a small bowl and add the hazelnuts. Season with half of the salt and pepper. Heat the remaining 1 tablespoon of olive oil in a medium skillet and add the spinach, still wet from washing. Cover and cook over high heat for about 2 minutes, until wilted. Season the scallops with the remaining salt and pepper and place on top of the spinach. Cover and cook for about 3 minutes, until the scallops are cooked but still soft inside. There should be almost no liquid left in the skillet. If you have a bit, add it to the dressing. Divide the spinach onto two plates, arrange the scallops on the spinach, and drizzle the hazelnut dressing on top. Serve as needed.

SAUTEED SCALLOPS & ENDIVE

Scallops and Belgian endive work so well together that I often make this dish. If you're making this as a first course for company, you can prepare the endive ahead of time and reheat at the last moment.

Serves 2

2 tablespoons butter

2 Belgian endive (about 8 ounces), cut lengthwise into thin strips (julienne)

½ teaspoon salt

¼ teaspoon sugar

6 large sea scallops (about 6 ounces)

¼ teaspoon freshly ground black pepper

2 teaspoons olive oil, plus more for drizzling

1 tablespoon chopped fresh chives, for garnish

▸ Melt the butter in a medium, nonstick skillet over medium heat and add the endive, ¼ teaspoon of the salt, sugar, and 2 tablespoons of water. Cover and cook until they are wilted, about 2 minutes. Remove the lid and cook until tender and the liquid has evaporated. Transfer the cooked endive to a plate and wipe out the pan.

▸ To prepare the scallops, sprinkle with the remaining ¼ teaspoon of salt and the pepper and drizzle with the olive oil.

▸ Return the pan to high heat. Once hot, add the scallops and cook for about 1½ minutes on each side for a soft center, or to your liking. To serve, divide the endive between two plates and sprinkle with chives. Arrange three scallops on top of each, drizzle with olive oil, and serve immediately.

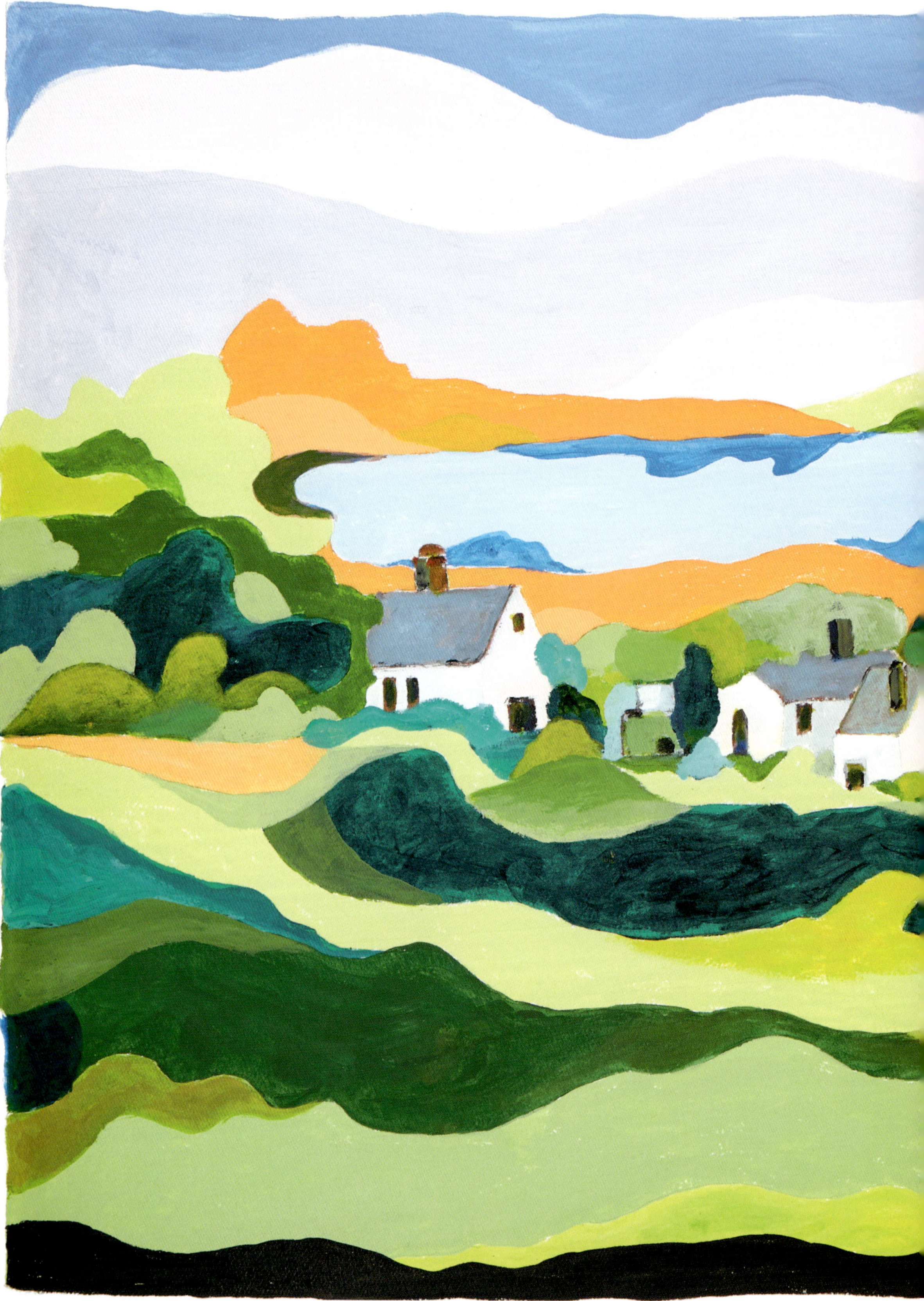

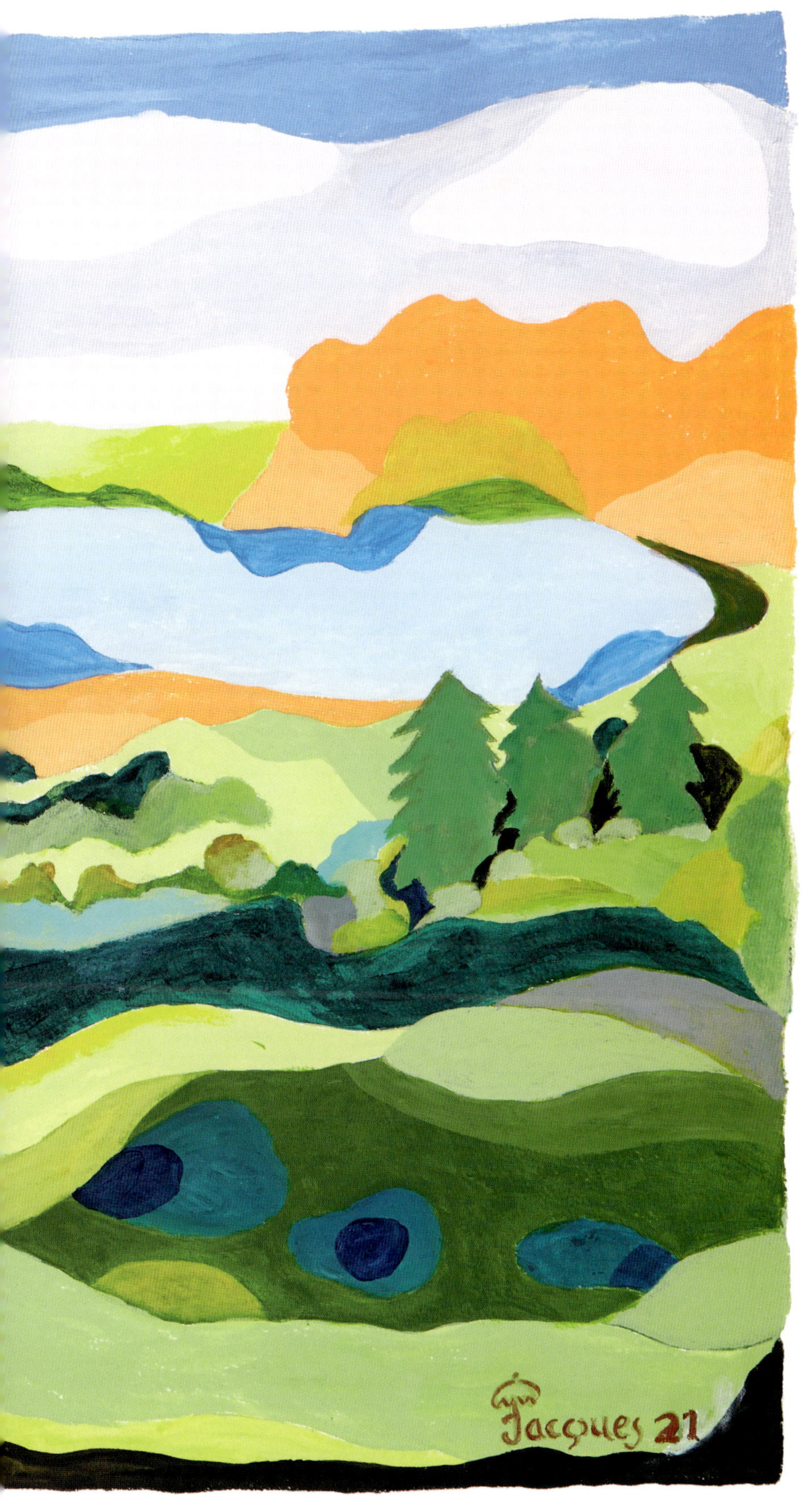

Lake in the Valley, 2021

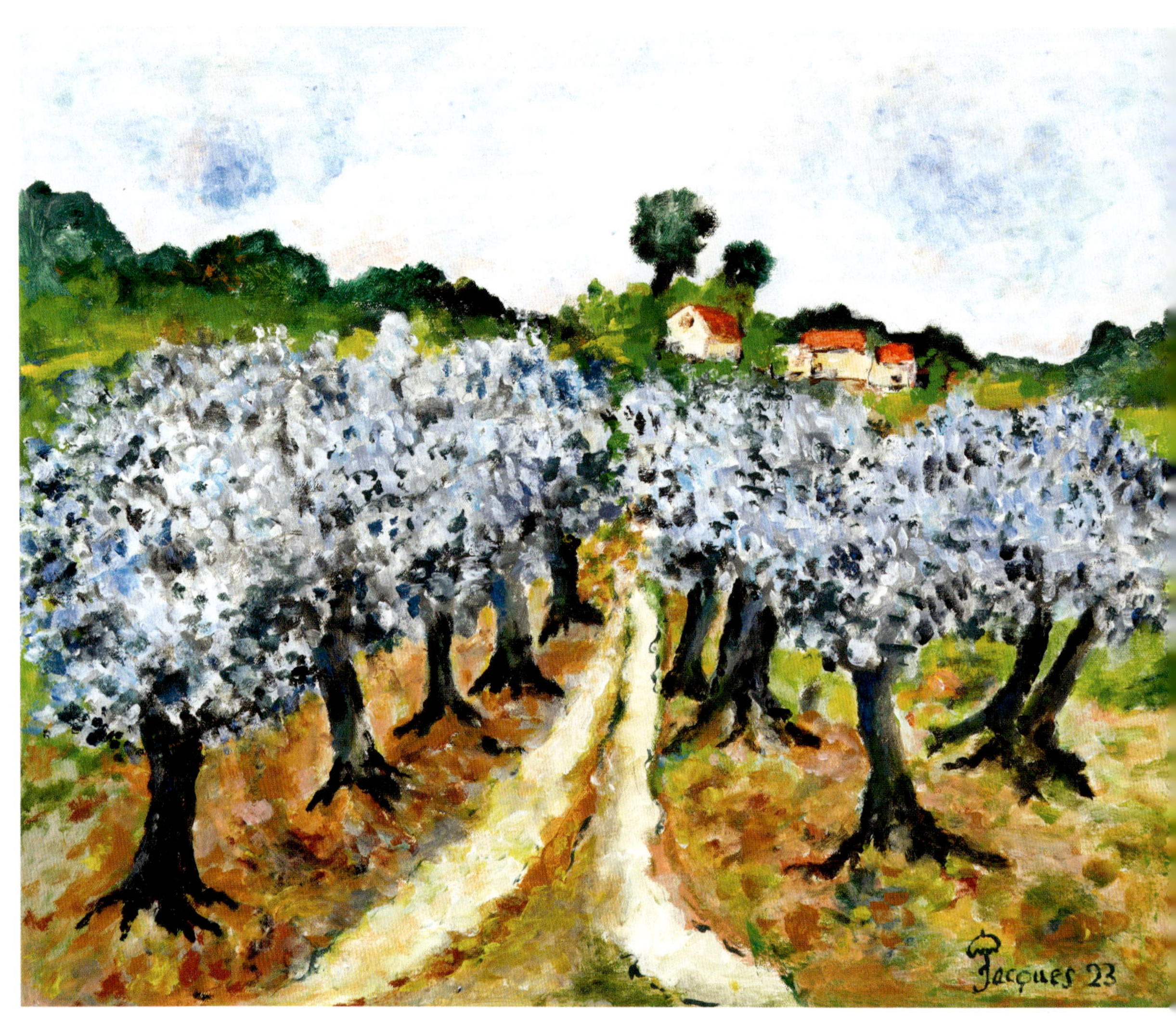

Olive Field, 2023

SCALLOP CEVICHE

Scallops arranged on top of a garnish of long cucumber strips makes a light and beautiful first course. In this recipe, we use large scallops and cut them into about ¾-inch pieces, but if you use bay scallops, you can leave them whole. Adjust the seasonings and garnishes according to your taste and what you have on hand. Allow time for the scallops to marinate for a bit in the refrigerator and serve chilled but not ice cold.

Serves 3

6 ounces sea scallops (about 6 large)

1 tablespoon mayonnaise

1 teaspoon grated lemon zest

1 tablespoon lemon juice

¼ teaspoon salt, plus a dash

¼ teaspoon freshly ground black pepper

1 teaspoon diced jalapeño, or more to taste

2 to 3 tablespoons sliced scallions

3 tablespoons chopped sweet onion

2 tablespoons diced black olives

3 tablespoons extra virgin olive oil

1 teaspoon sriracha hot sauce, or to taste (optional)

1 cucumber

Dash of sugar

Chopped fresh chives, for garnish

▸ Remove the small abduction muscles from the scallops. Cut each scallop into 6 pieces.

▸ In a medium bowl, whisk together the mayonnaise, lemon zest, and lemon juice. Then add the salt, pepper, jalapeño, scallion, onion, olives, 2 tablespoons of the olive oil, and the scallops. Season with sriracha, if desired. Refrigerate to marinate and serve chilled, about 30 minutes.

▸ Using a vegetable peeler, make long strips of cucumber, stopping short of the seeds. Sprinkle with a dash of salt and sugar. Let sit for 5 to 10 minutes.

▸ Arrange the cucumbers on 3 plates and place the scallop ceviche in a mound in the center. Sprinkle with chives and drizzle the cucumbers with the remaining tablespoon of olive oil. Serve as needed.

VIETNAMESE-INSPIRED SALMON CUBES

This is a recipe I made for my granddaughter, who loves raw salmon. If you can get the belly of the salmon, it's the most tender, a bit fatty, and very good raw. This is an impressive-looking but easy to execute hors d'oeuvre to serve with an aperitif when your friends come over.

Serves 4 as an hors d'oeuvre

1 skinless salmon belly fillet (about 5 ounces)

¼ teaspoon salt

¼ teaspoon sugar

2 teaspoons toasted sesame oil

2 teaspoons oyster sauce

1 teaspoon sriracha or other hot sauce

2 tablespoons chopped fresh chives, plus more for garnish

2 teaspoons sesame seeds, for garnish

▸ Using a sharp knife, cut the fish into 1-inch cubes. You should have around 16 cubes. Place in a bowl, and sprinkle the cubes with the salt and sugar and toss them well. Let sit, covered, for 10 minutes.

▸ In a small bowl, combine the sesame oil, oyster sauce, and sriracha. Add the salmon and chives and stir well to coat the cubes with sauce. Arrange the cubes on a serving dish and sprinkle with the additional chives and the sesame seeds. Place a toothpick in each cube and serve immediately.

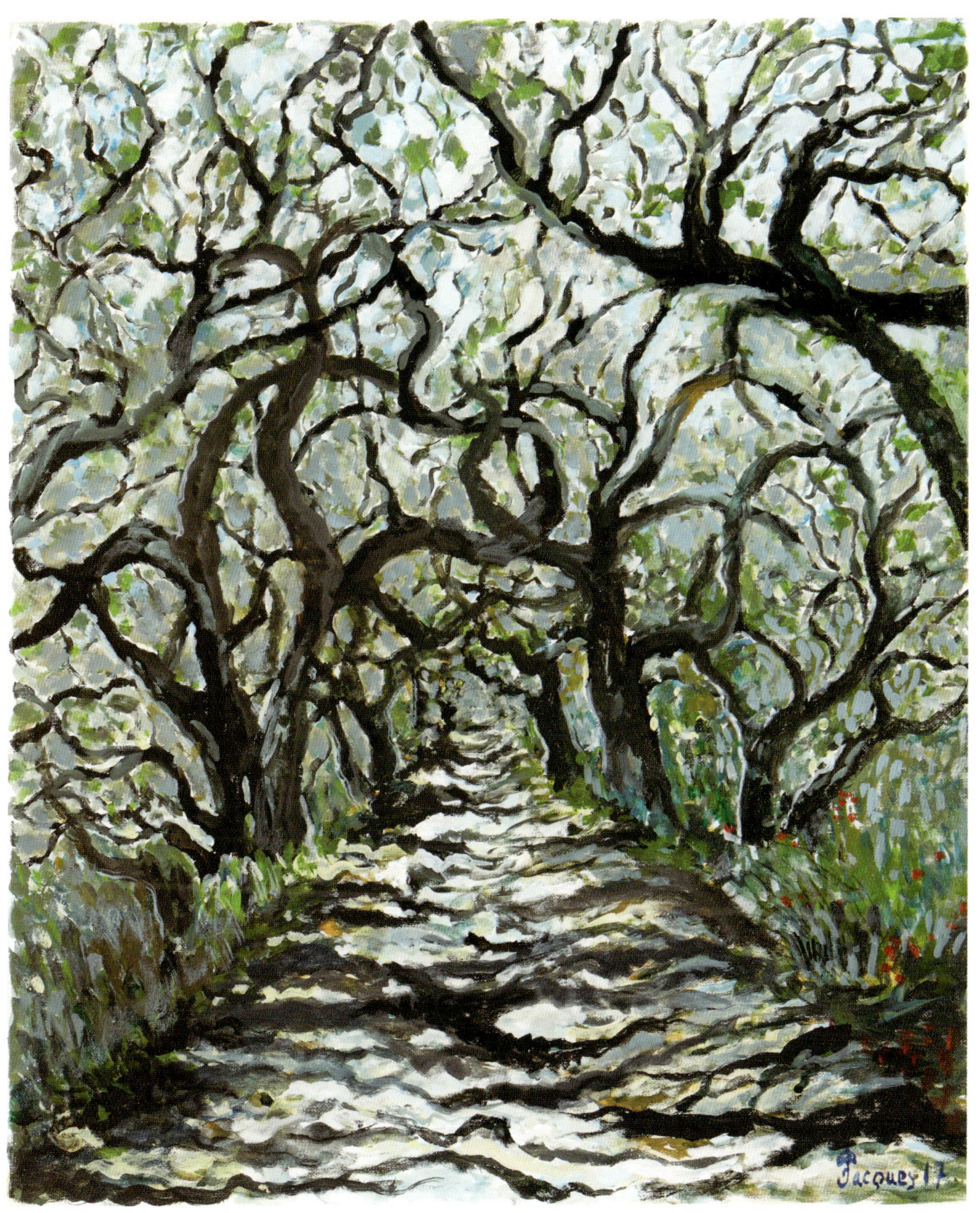

Cumberland, 2017

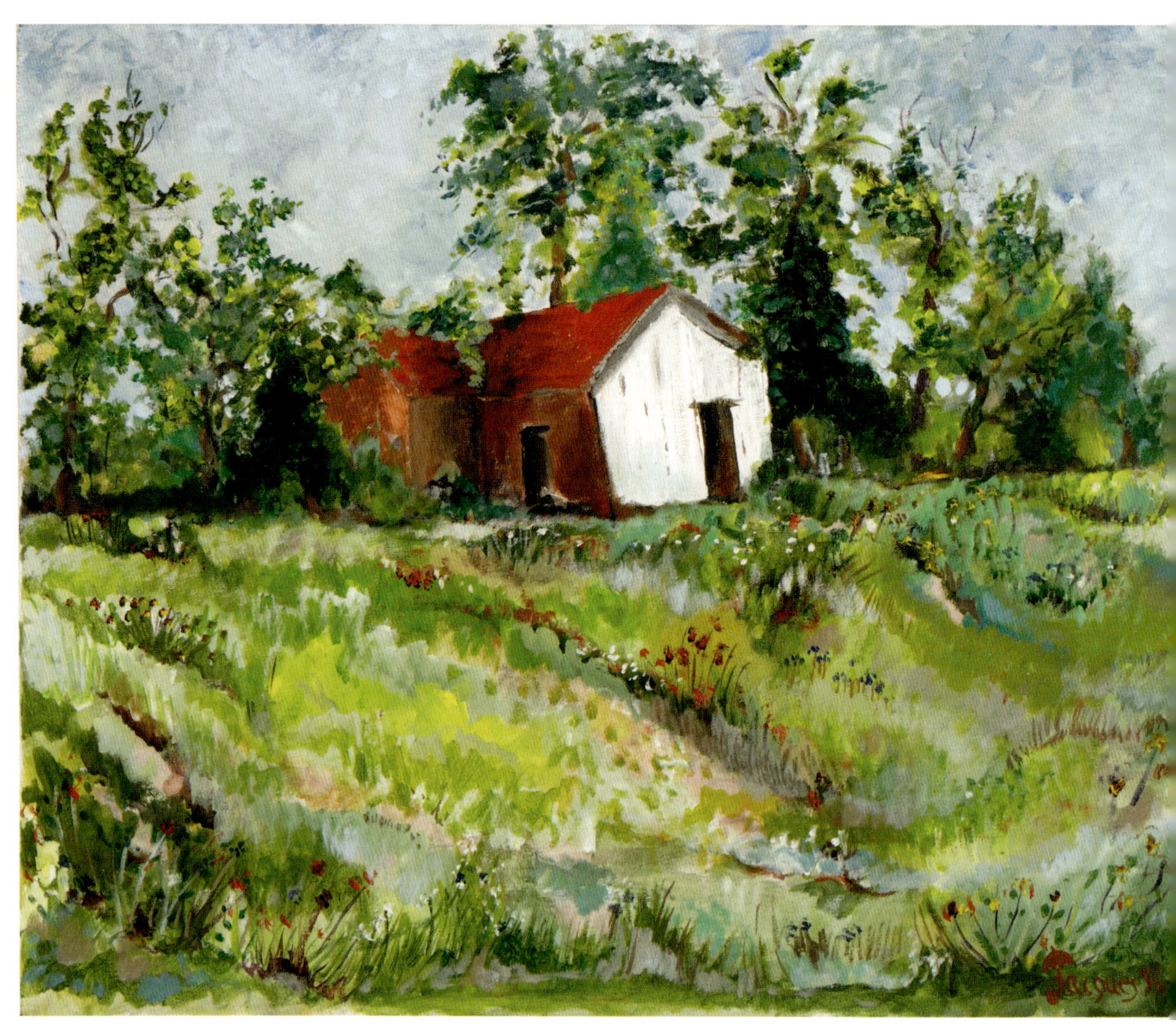

Red Barn, 1996

BAKED SALMON with PESTO BUTTER SAUCE

This simple dish using pesto from the supermarket as the base for the sauce is quick, simple, and tasty. Other fish fillets can be substituted for the salmon. It's something to keep in your back pocket for a busy weeknight.

Serves 2

2 skinless salmon fillets (about 5 ounces each)

¼ teaspoon salt

¼ teaspoon freshly ground black pepper

1 teaspoon olive oil

1 tablespoon butter, melted

2 tablespoons basil pesto

Basil sprigs, for garnish

▸ Preheat the oven to 350°F. Line a small baking sheet with aluminum foil.

▸ Place the salmon on the lined baking sheet. If the salmon is thicker at one end than the other, tuck the thinner belly portion underneath so the salmon steaks are about the same thickness. Sprinkle with the salt and pepper and drizzle with the olive oil. Bake until cooked to your liking, 6 to 8 minutes for my taste, which leaves it slightly rare in the center.

▸ In a small bowl, stir the butter and pesto together to make the sauce. Place the salmon on a platter or individual plates, spoon the sauce over the salmon, and serve immediately, garnished with basil sprigs.

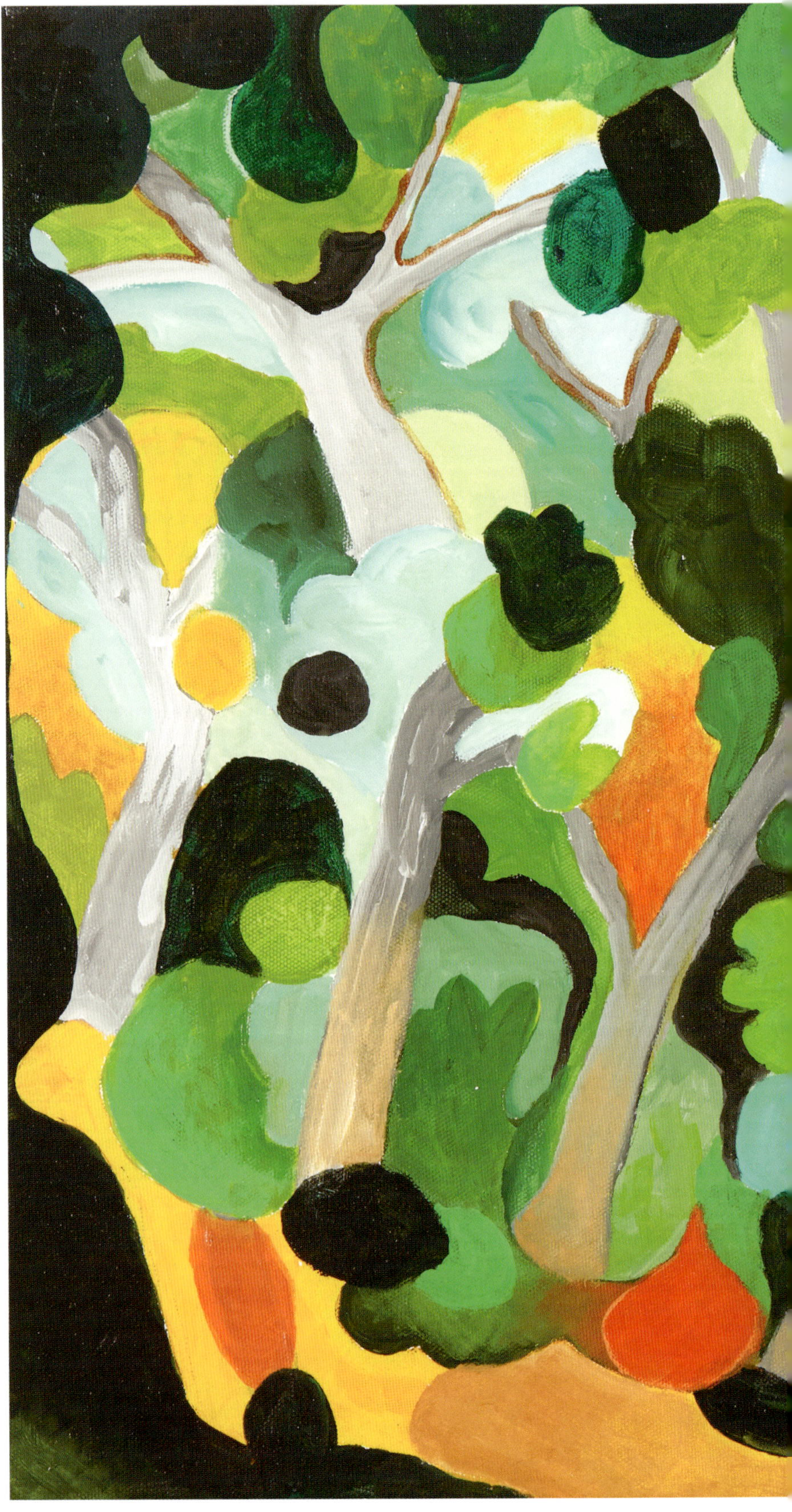

Dream Forest, 2015

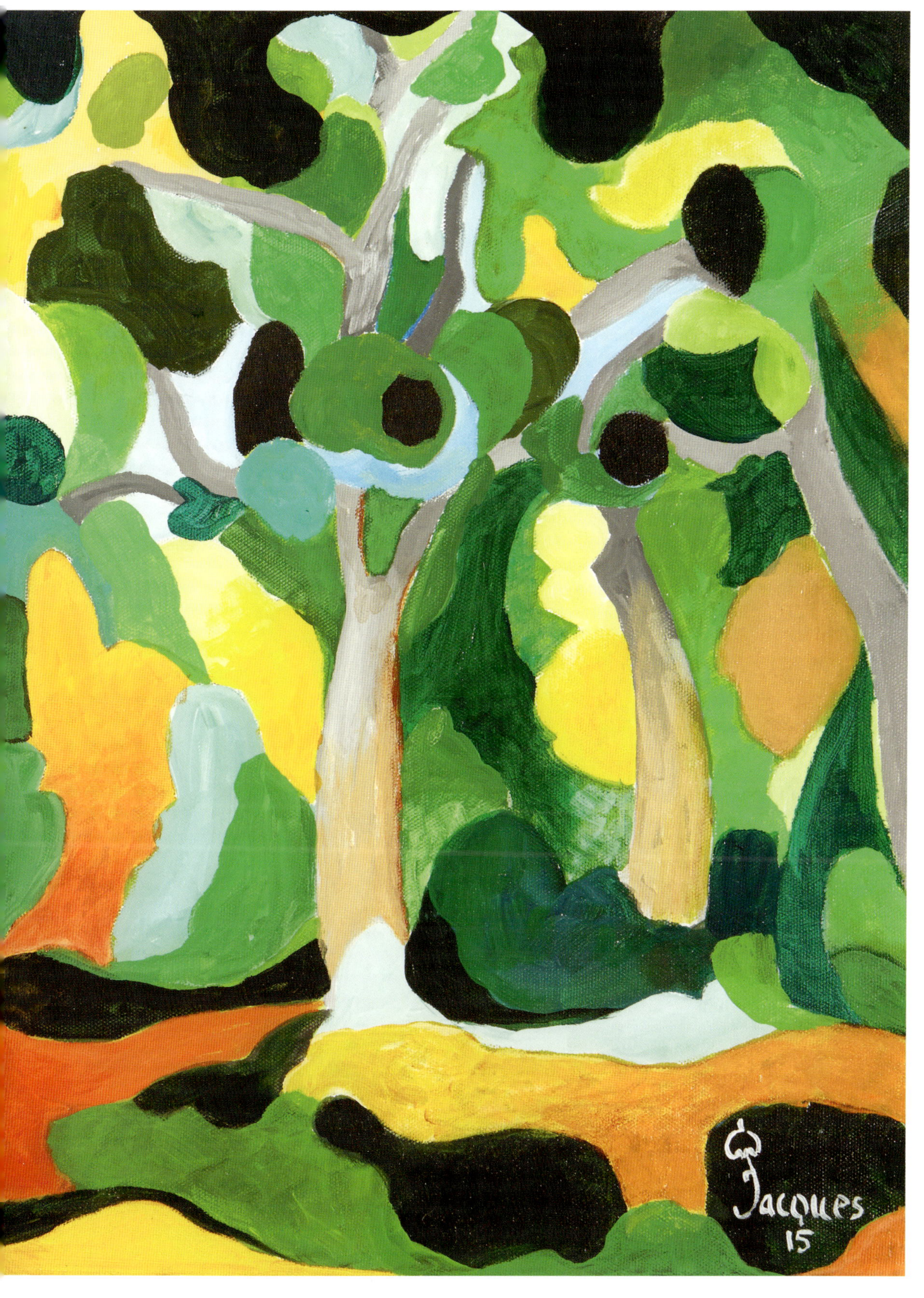
Jacques
15

CHILI-GARLIC BAKED COD

I love Asian flavors with fish—sesame, chili-garlic sauce, wasabi—and this is a nice way of preparing cod that keeps it moist and delicious. The broccoli garnish adds color, and of course you could substitute whatever vegetable you have on hand. Served with some rice, this makes a perfect dinner.

Serves 3

1 tablespoon chili-garlic sauce

1½ teaspoons toasted sesame oil

1½ teaspoons wasabi paste

1½ tablespoons olive oil

¾ teaspoon salt

3 cups broccoli florets

¼ teaspoon freshly ground black pepper

3 pieces skinless cod fillet (1¼ inches thick; 6 ounces each)

2 tablespoons butter

▸ Preheat the oven to 350°F. Line a baking sheet with aluminum foil.

▸ Mix the chili-garlic sauce, sesame oil, wasabi paste, olive oil, ½ teaspoon of the salt, and the pepper in a small bowl. Rub the mixture all over the fish. Place the fish on the lined baking sheet and bake for 8 to 10 minutes, depending on the thickness of your fish and how you like it cooked.

▸ Meanwhile, place the broccoli florets in a microwavable dish and microwave for 2½ minutes. Season with the remaining ¼ teaspoon of salt, top with the butter, mix well, and serve alongside the fish.

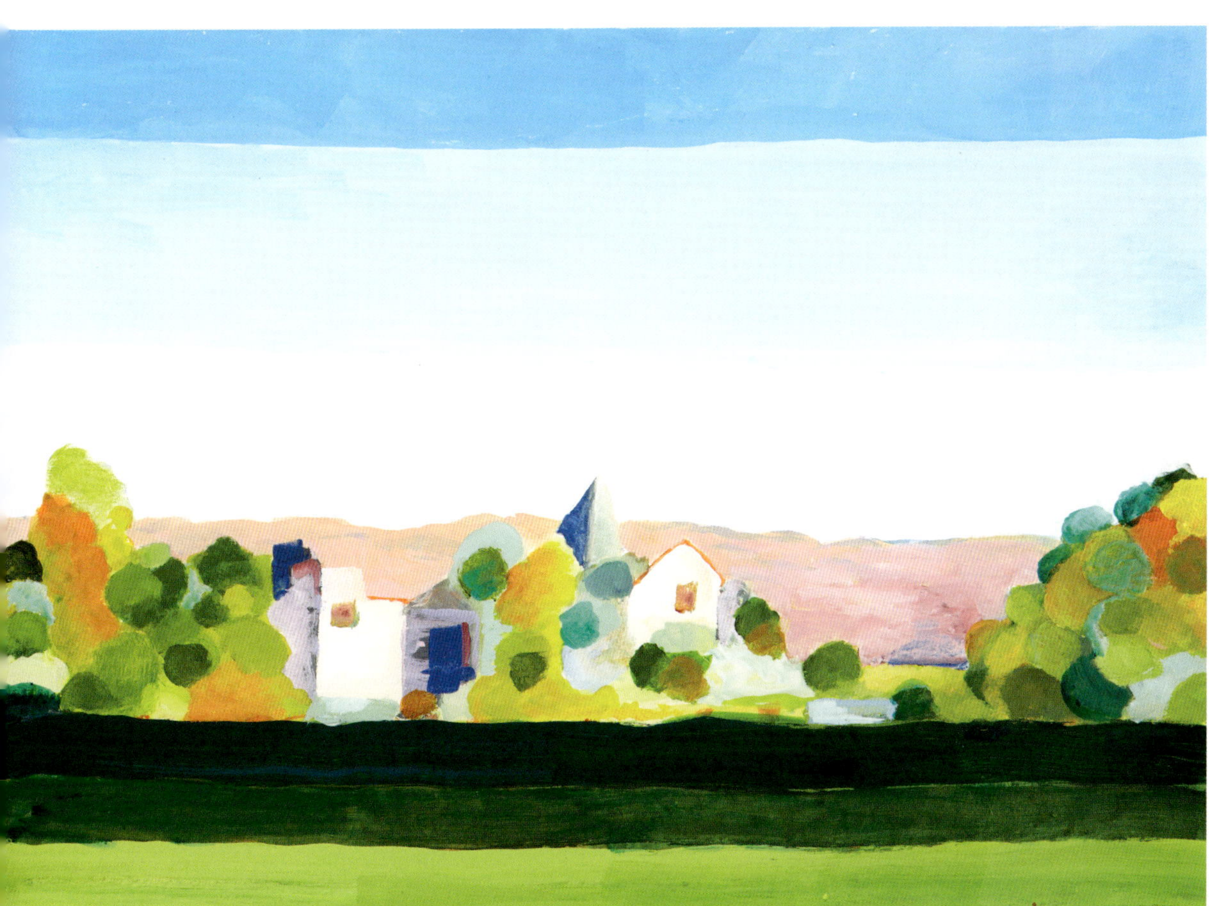

Serenity Landscape, 2016

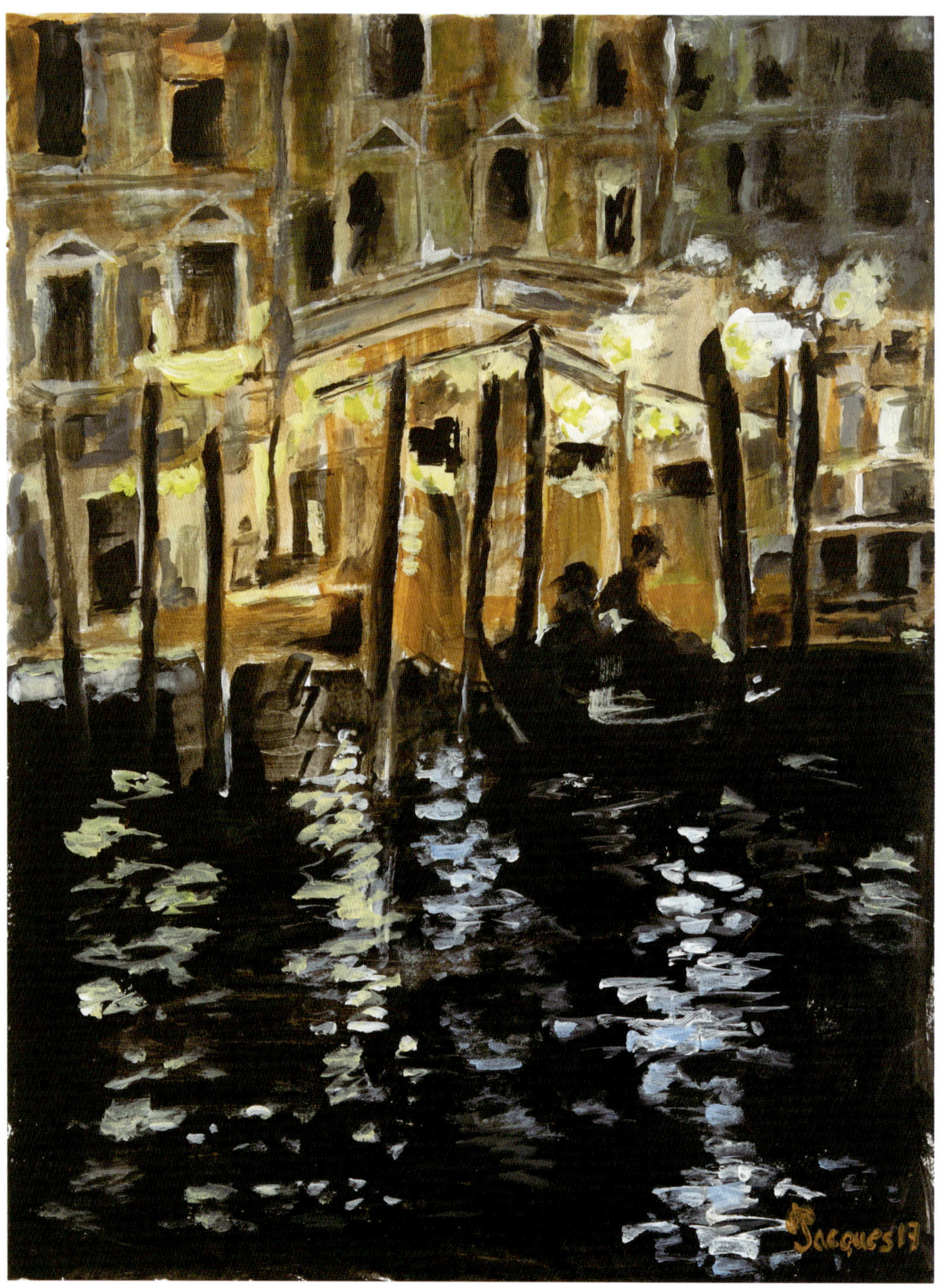

Venice at Night, 2017

GRILLED SWORDFISH with OLIVES, TOMATOES & ZUCCHINI

Swordfish is a delicious, firm fish that I often keep in my freezer. Make sure you thaw it slowly in the refrigerator and pat it dry before cooking. The cooking time, as with all fish, will depend on its thickness and your liking. I like to brown the fillets on one side, then cover them with a metal bowl to create steam and cook the fish through. Serving the fillets with the golden brown, marked side up, garnished with fresh vegetables warmed in the microwave, makes a great summer dish.

Serves 2

2 swordfish steaks (about 1¼ inches thick; 6 ounces each)

¼ teaspoon salt

¼ teaspoon freshly ground black pepper

1½ teaspoons peanut or other neutral oil

TOPPING

½ cup ½-inch-diced tomato

12 kalamata olives, pitted

2 tablespoons chopped sweet onion, such as Vidalia

1 tablespoon minced fresh flat-leaf parsley

¼ cup ½-inch diced zucchini

¼ teaspoon salt

¼ teaspoon freshly ground black pepper

2 tablespoons extra virgin olive oil

▸ Sprinkle the fish lightly with the salt and pepper and drizzle with the peanut oil. Heat a grill or cast-iron grill pan over high heat. When it is hot, add the fish and cook for 1½ minutes, then rotate it one half turn to create grill marks. Cover the fish with a metal bowl and cook for another 1½ minutes, or to your liking, so the steam created by covering the fish cooks the top. Remove from the heat and let sit in the hot pan for 4 to 5 minutes.

▸ To make the topping, in a medium glass or microwavable bowl, combine the tomato, olives, onion, parsley, and zucchini. Season with the salt and pepper and add the olive oil. Stir together, place in the microwave, and heat on full power for about 1 minute, until warm.

▸ To serve, place the fish on a platter or individual plates and spoon the warm garnish around. Serve immediately.

MISO BLACK COD with ZUCCHINI

I like miso (a Japanese fermented soybean paste) as a flavoring for fish. You can marinate the fish in this recipe 24 hours or more ahead of time, and you can use red or white miso paste, noting that white tends to be milder. I like to use black cod, also known as sablefish, when available, but any other fillet about 1 to 1¼ inches thick, from cod to bass or grouper, can be used. Make sure you adjust the cooking time according to the thickness of the fish and your own preference. I bake the fish and zucchini together for an easy preparation.

Serves 2

1 tablespoon miso paste

½ teaspoon chili-garlic sauce

2 teaspoons soy sauce

2 teaspoons mirin (rice wine)

2 pieces black cod (1¼ inches thick; about 6 ounces each)

1 zucchini (about 8 ounces)

⅛ teaspoon salt

⅛ teaspoon freshly ground black pepper

1 tablespoon extra virgin olive oil

Chopped fresh chives, for garnish

▸ On a dinner plate, mix the miso, chili-garlic sauce, soy sauce, and mirin together. Roll the fish in the marinade so that it is completely coated. Let the fish marinate for at least an hour at room temperature, or refrigerate overnight.

▸ Preheat the oven to 350°F. Line a quarter sheet pan with aluminum foil.

▸ Cut the zucchini into 4-inch lengths, then into ¼-inch slices lengthwise. Pile the slices together and cut into long, thin julienned strips. Toss the zucchini with the salt, pepper, and olive oil in a bowl.

▸ Spread the zucchini in one layer on the lined sheet pan, leaving room in the center for the fish. Place the fish in the center and drizzle with any remaining marinade. Bake for about 10 minutes, depending on the thickness of the fish, until the fish is just opaque in the center and flakes easily, or to your liking. To serve, arrange the fish on warm plates, scatter the zucchini around, and drizzle with any juices from the pan. Serve immediately.

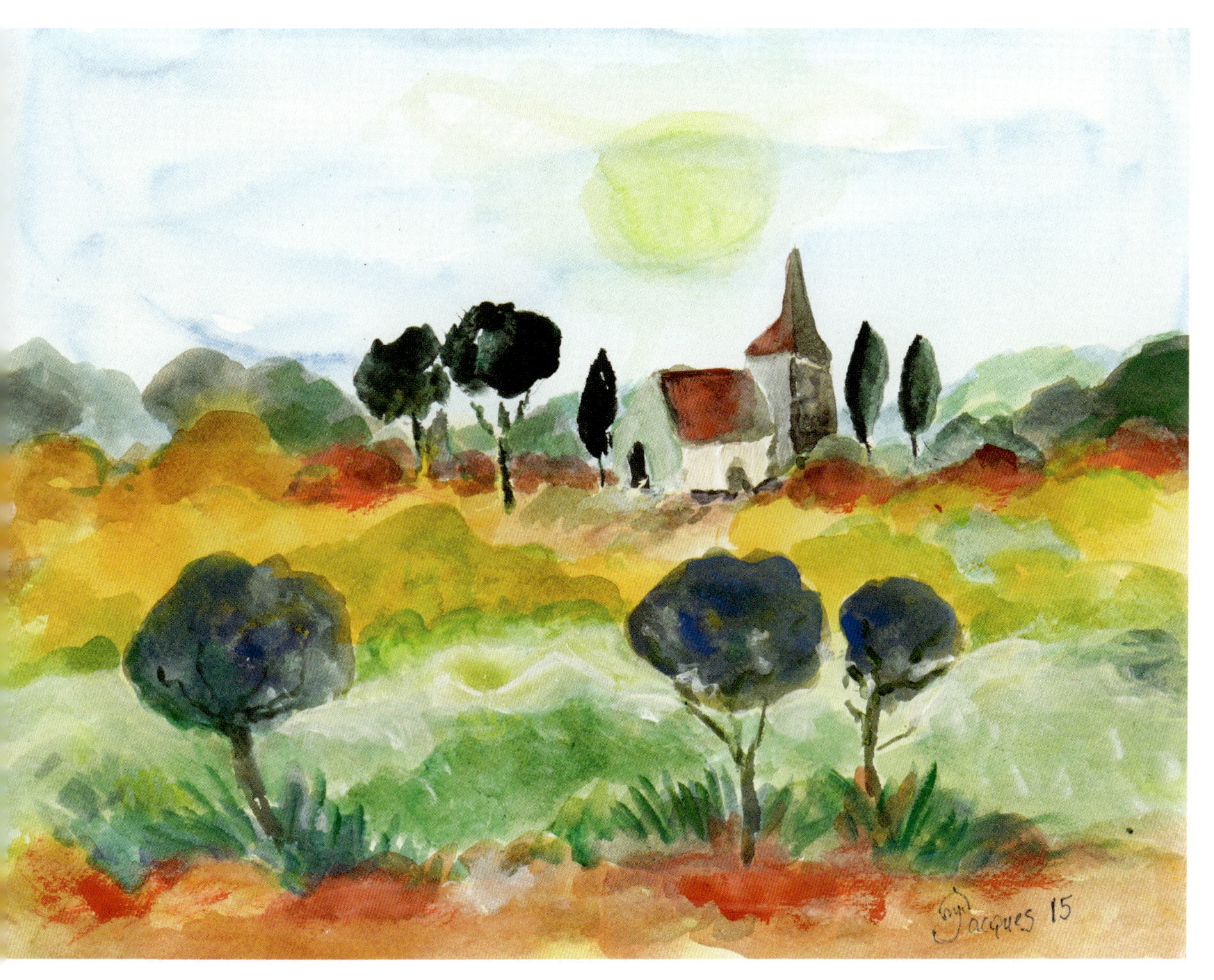

Paysage du Midi, 2015

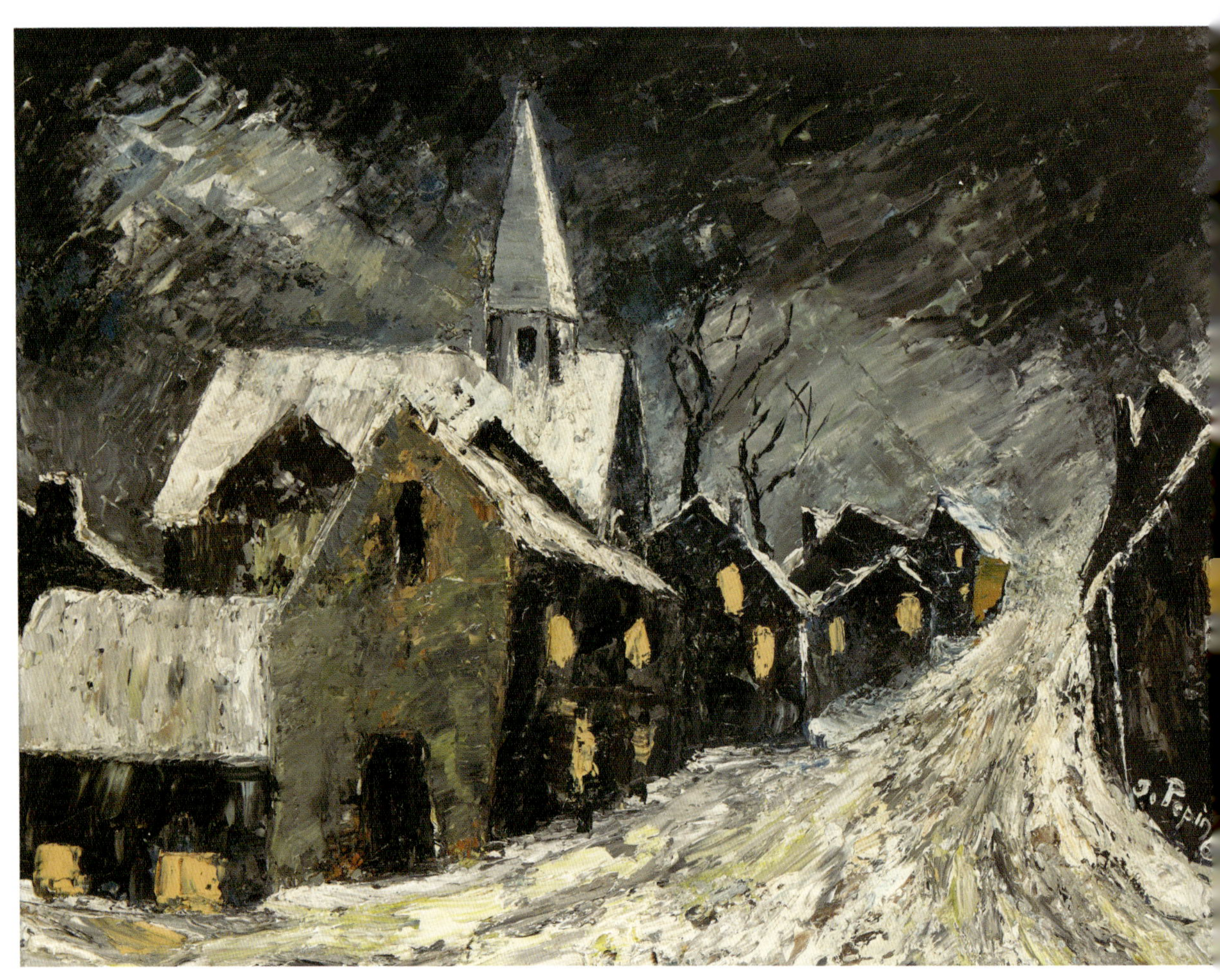

Village Winter, 1963

THREE FISH CRUDO

Crudo simply means "raw," and that's what this is, a selection of the freshest, most delicious raw fish you can find, along with some garnishes. Visit a local fish market, or talk with the person behind the fish counter at your local grocery store and tell them what you're planning to make. They will help guide you. I like to serve this as a first course for a dinner party or perhaps as an hors d'oeuvre with an aperitif. I chose tuna, salmon, and cod here, but you should use the freshest fish available, including scallops.

Serves 6

1 piece tuna (about 6 ounces)

1 piece salmon (about 6 ounces)

1 piece cod (about 6 ounces)

½ cup julienned fennel bulb

¾ cup chopped mild onion

2½ tablespoons extra virgin olive oil

1½ tablespoons toasted sesame oil

1¼ teaspoons salt

1 teaspoon freshly ground black pepper

¾ teaspoon Tabasco sauce

GARNISH

3 tablespoons capers

1½ teaspoons black sesame seeds

1½ teaspoons white sesame seeds

About ¼ cup fennel leaves

12 croutons (see note)

1 lemon, cut into wedges

▸ Cut all of the fish into ½-inch slices and then into ½-inch dice. Place in different bowls. Divide the fennel, onions, olive oil, sesame oil, salt, pepper, and Tabasco evenly among the bowls. Mix well and set aside. This can be done a few hours ahead. Arrange the fish on a large platter one next to the other and garnish with the capers, sesame seeds, and fennel leaves. Arrange the croutons and lemon wedges around the fish. Serve and enjoy.

To make croutons:
Cut 12 slices of baguette about ⅜ inch thick. Spread melted butter, oil, or a combination (2 tablespoons total) on a baking sheet. Press the slices of bread into the liquid and turn over so it is buttered or oiled on both sides. Bake in a 400°F oven for 10 to 12 minutes, until nicely brown. Serve as needed.

TUNA TARTARE

When I find a beautiful piece of tuna at my market, I like to make this tuna tartare. I cut the fish into small dice with a sharp knife; I do not use a food processor, as it tends to make the fish mushy. Spending a little time on the presentation transforms this simple dish into an elegant first course.

Serves 3

2 tablespoons butter, softened

5 thin slices dark rye bread

8 ounces ahi tuna, cut into ¼-inch dice

½ teaspoon salt

Tabasco sauce to taste

1 tablespoon extra virgin olive oil, plus more for drizzling

3 tablespoons finely chopped sweet onion, such as Vidalia

1 minced scallion (3 tablespoons)

⅓ cup ½-inch-diced cucumber

Dash of sugar

6 black olives, pitted and halved, for garnish

Fresh chives, for garnish

Lemon juice, for garnish

▸ Butter 4 of the slices of bread and stack them together, then add the final unbuttered slice on top. Set aside in the refrigerator so that the butter can harden. This should be prepared ahead.

▸ In a medium bowl, combine the tuna, most of the salt (reserving a dash for the cucumber), the Tabasco, olive oil, onion, and scallion. In a small bowl, combine the cucumber and dashes of salt and sugar. Let both sit for 15 minutes.

▸ To serve, spoon the tartare into three small glass custard cups and press lightly to pack into shape. Carefully unmold the tartare onto three plates and garnish with the diced cucumber, olive halves, and a drizzle of olive oil. Sprinkle some chives on top. Slice the bread vertically into thin slices to reveal the layers of bread and butter and arrange on the plate. Squeeze lemon juice on top just before serving.

ALBACORE TUNA SALAD

We all think of tuna as something to have on a sandwich for lunch, but this is an elevated presentation that makes a nice first course before a simple but elegant dinner. You can make and refrigerate the salad ahead of time, but let it sit at room temperature for a bit to take the chill off before serving.

Serves 2

2 tablespoons whipped cream cheese

2 tablespoons mayonnaise

1 (5-ounce) can albacore tuna, in oil

2 tablespoons chopped onion

3 tablespoons chopped fresh chives

1 tablespoon diced red pimientos

1 tablespoon capers

2 teaspoons horseradish

1 teaspoon chili-garlic sauce

½ teaspoon salt

6 leaves romaine lettuce

▸ Place the cream cheese and mayonnaise in a medium bowl and combine. Break the tuna into ½-inch pieces and add it with the liquid. Add the onion, 2 tablespoons of the chives, the pimientos, capers, horseradish, chili-garlic sauce, and salt and mix well. Arrange the lettuce leaves in martini glasses so the edges of the leaves hang outside the glass, scoop the fish in the centers, garnish with the remaining tablespoon of chives, and serve.

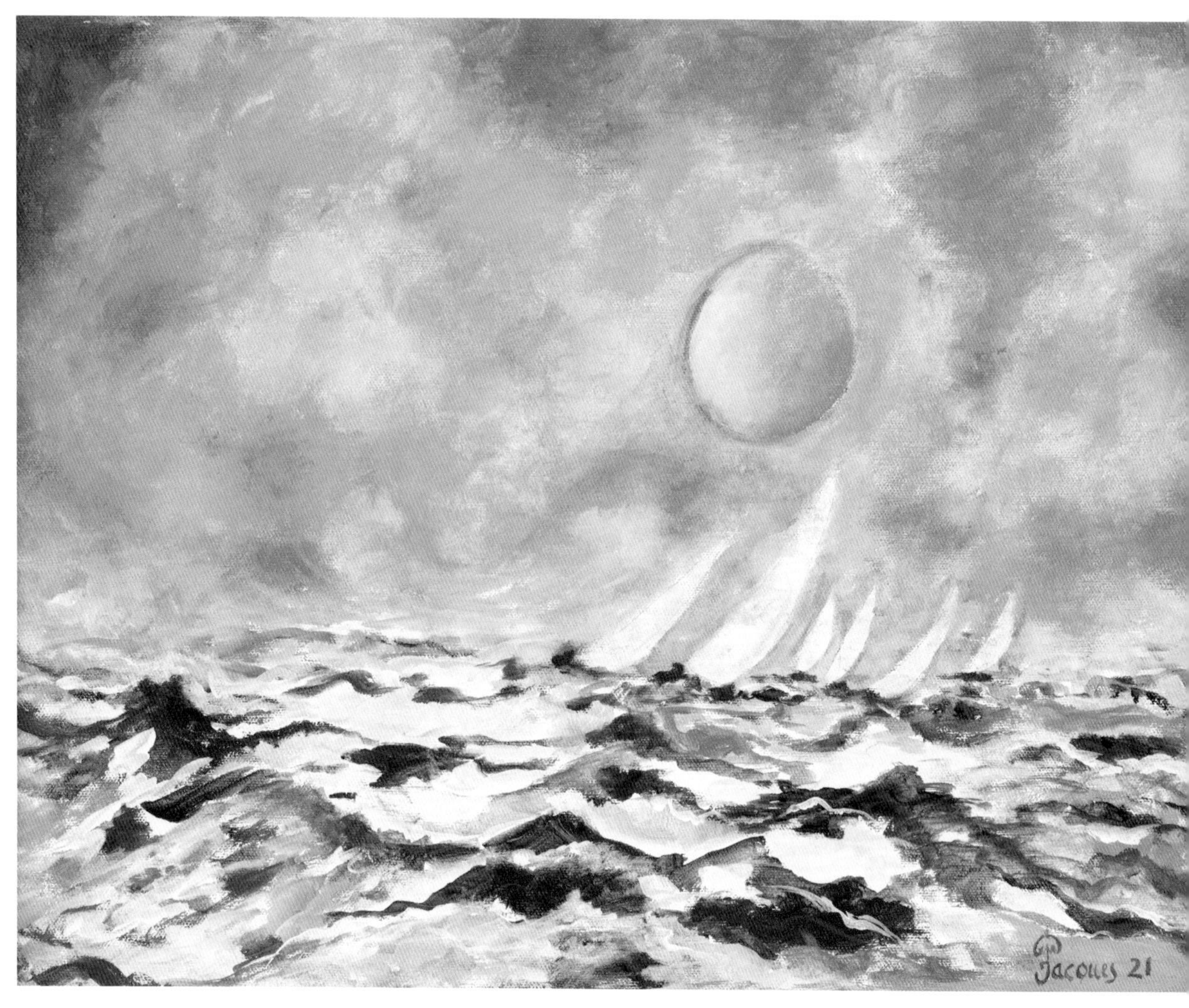

Sailboat Race, 2021

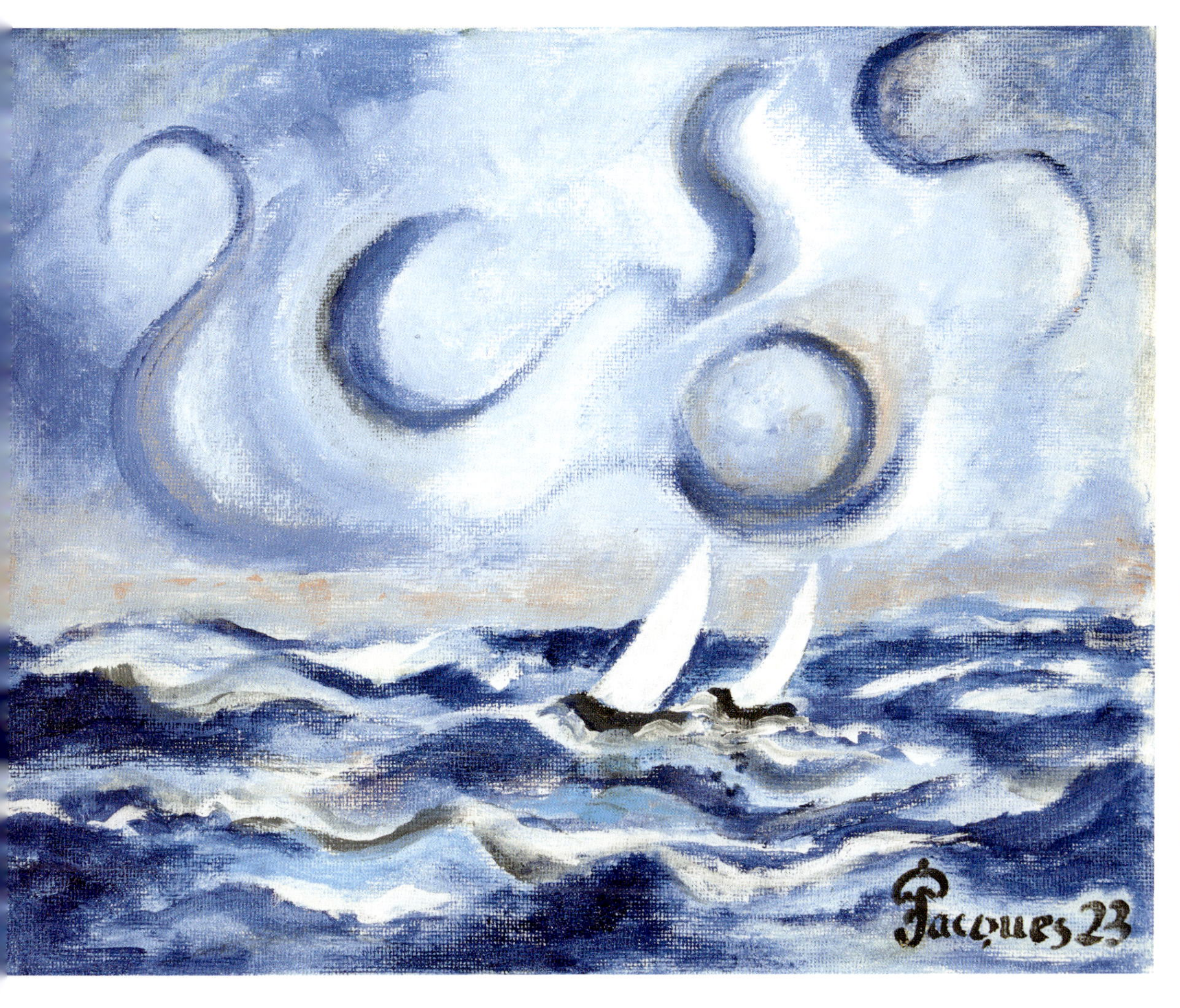

Stormy Sea, 2023

POACHED BLACK COD with CREAMY DRESSING

I love black cod, also called sablefish. That being said, if it's not available, you can certainly use regular cod instead. This is a simple presentation that brings out the best in the fish, keeping it moist, and with a delicious creamy dressing that adds extra flavor. The dressing makes a nice garnish for vegetables and potatoes as well.

Serves 4

DRESSING

¼ cup whipped cream cheese

¼ cup mayonnaise

1 tablespoon grated horseradish

2 tablespoons Dijon-style mustard

2 teaspoons hot sauce, like sriracha

¼ cup chopped scallions

4 small black cod steaks (about 1¼ inches thick; 1 pound total)

GARNISH

8 kalamata olives, halved

1 tablespoon chopped fresh flat-leaf parsley

▸ Combine the cream cheese, mayonnaise, horseradish, mustard, hot sauce, and scallions in a small bowl and set aside. Bring 1 quart of salted water to a boil over high heat. Close to serving time, add the cod steaks to the water and return to a boil. As soon as it reaches a boil, turn off the heat and let the fish poach in the hot water for about 5 minutes, depending on their thickness. Drain and dry the fish with a paper towel. Coat each fish piece with some of the dressing, sprinkle with olives and parsley, and serve with additional dressing on the side.

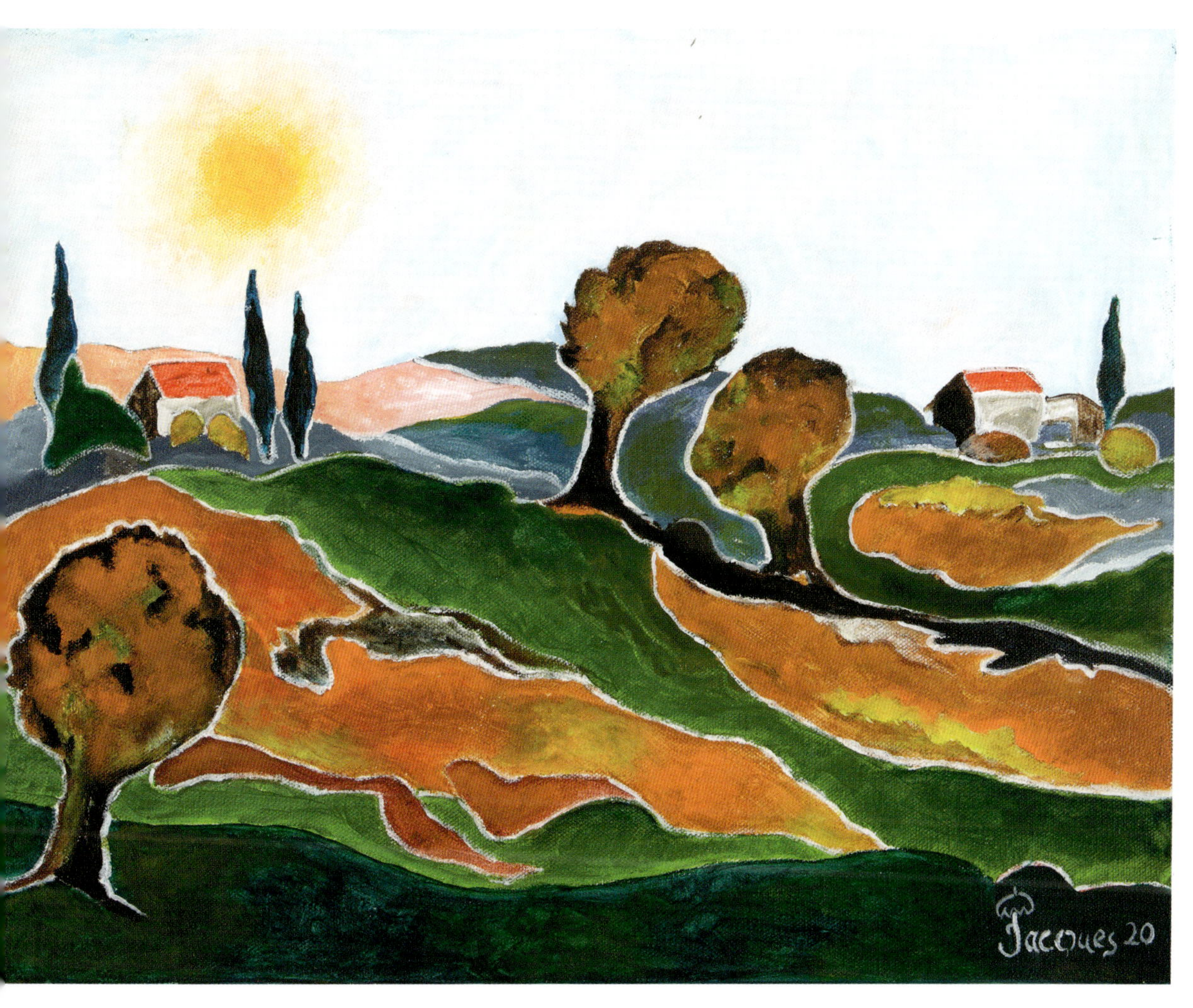

Allegorical Landscape, 2020

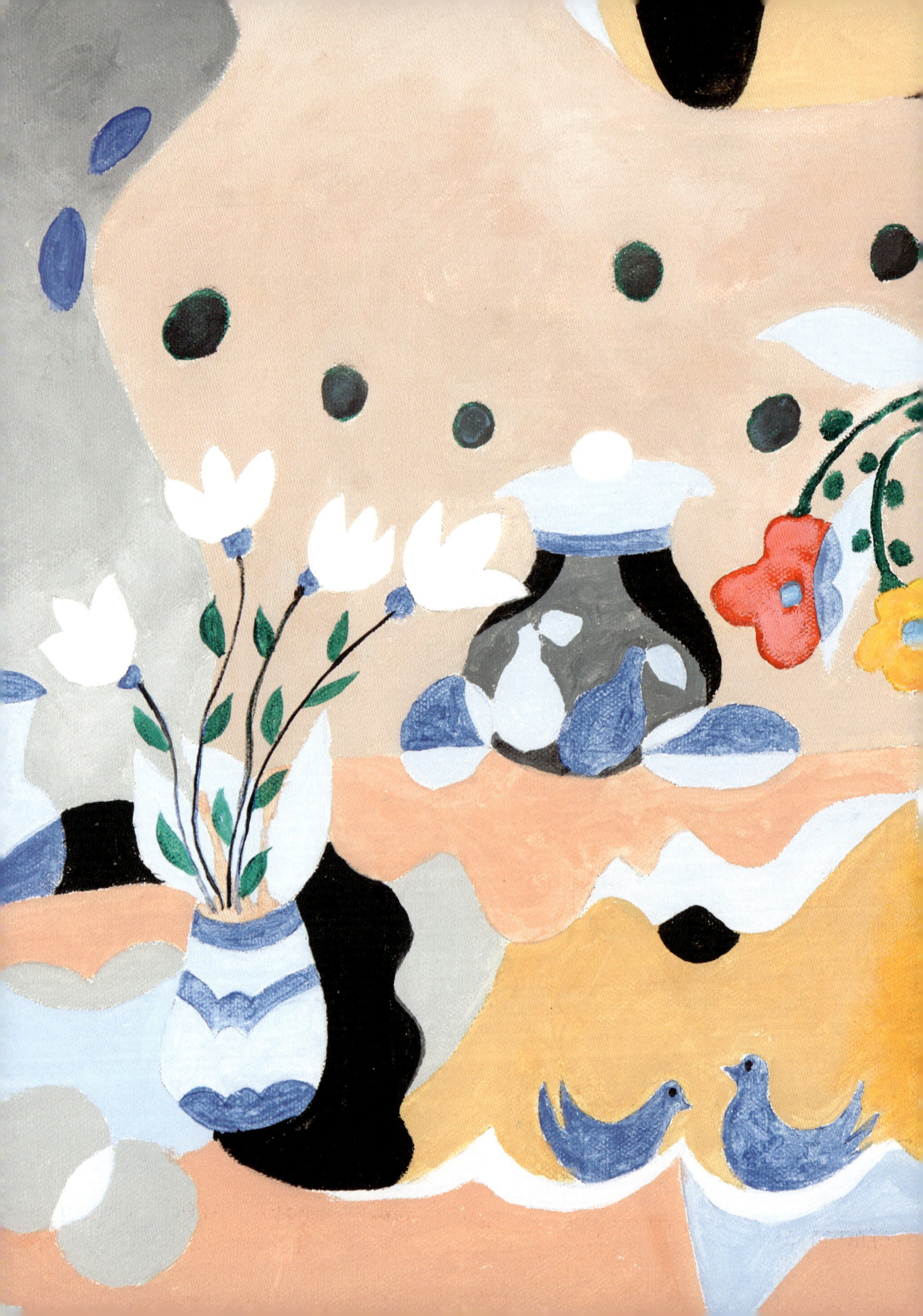

Poultry & Meat

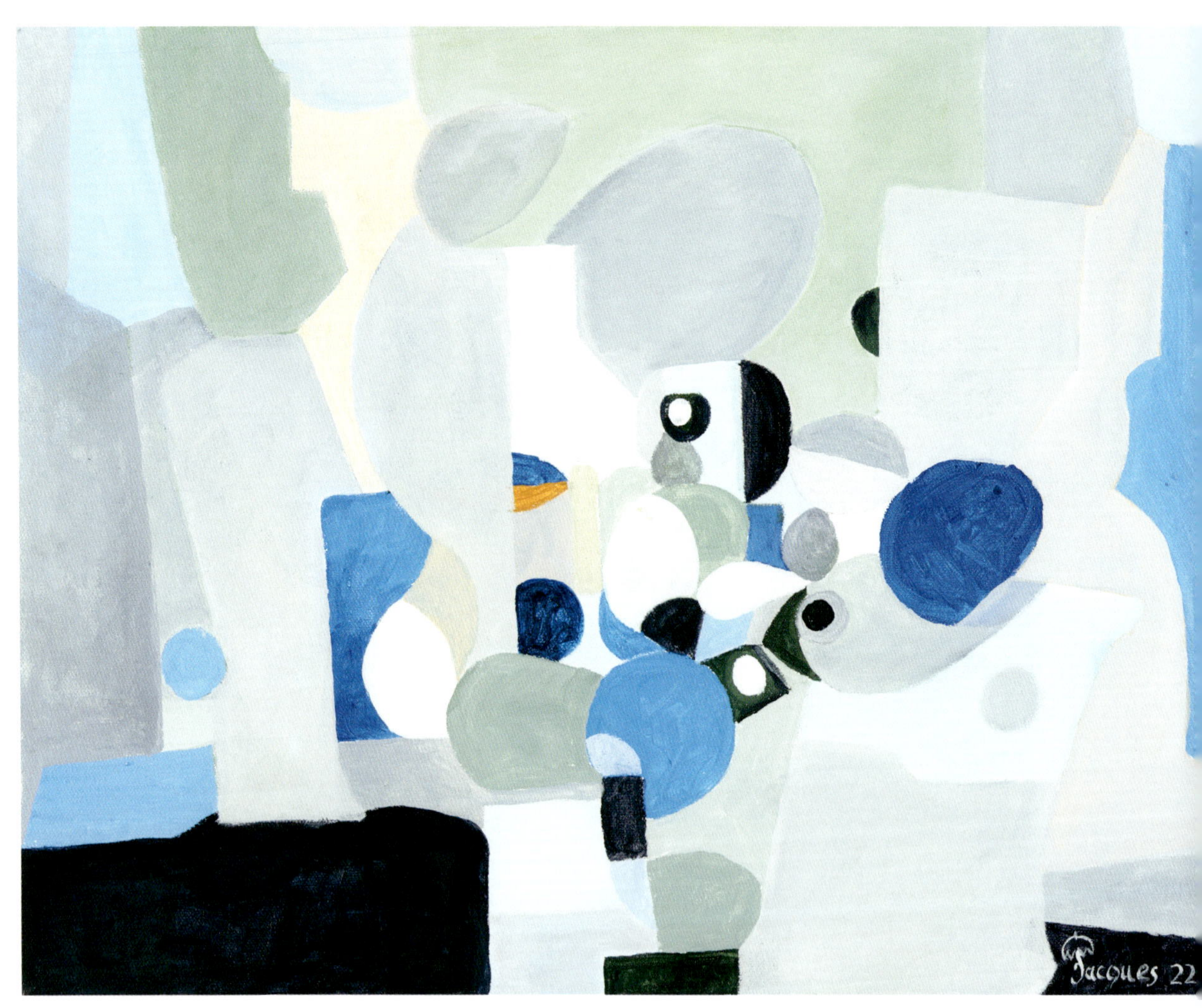

Grey Symphony, 2022

CHICKEN BREAST SAUTE with TOMATO & CHIVES

Here is an easy, fast way to prepare chicken breasts, sautéed with tomatoes. Be sure to dredge the chicken in flour just before cooking; it cannot be done ahead of time or it will get sticky. Served with a side of potatoes or pasta, this makes an inexpensive but satisfying meal that comes together quickly.

Serves 2

2 boneless, skinless chicken breasts (about 1 pound)

½ teaspoon salt

¼ teaspoon freshly ground black pepper

2 tablespoons olive oil

1½ tablespoons Wondra flour

½ teaspoon Tabasco sauce

1 teaspoon chopped garlic

2 tablespoons chopped fresh chives

1 tablespoon butter

¼ teaspoon Italian seasoning

1 tablespoon ketchup

¾ cup ½-inch-diced tomato

½ cup ½-inch-diced mushrooms

▸ Pat the chicken breasts dry with a paper towel and cut into 1½-inch chunks. Sprinkle with the salt and pepper. Heat the olive oil in a large nonstick skillet. Sprinkle the flour over the chicken chunks and be sure to coat each side. Place the chicken in the hot oil in one layer so that everything browns. Cook for about 3 minutes on one side, then turn to the other and cook an additional 3 minutes, stirring the pieces of chicken to cook them on all sides. Add the Tabasco, garlic, chives, butter, Italian seasoning, ketchup, tomato, and mushrooms and bring to a boil. Cook gently for 2 minutes. Divide onto plates and serve.

CHICKEN à la CLAUDINE

Once I had dinner at my daughter Claudine's and she made a dish of chicken, similar to this recipe. It inspired me to create a new and very easy way of cooking rice and chicken together.

Serves 4

4 large chicken drumsticks (about 1¼ pounds)
¼ teaspoon ground cumin
½ teaspoon paprika
¼ teaspoon salt
1 tablespoon olive oil
2 teaspoons chili-garlic sauce or sriracha
¾ cup Carolina rice
¾ cup canned chickpeas, drained
¾ cup chopped onion
½ cup minced scallions
1 cup ½-inch-diced zucchini
¾ teaspoon salt
1 cup spicy tomato juice, such as V8
1 cup chicken stock
Minced fresh chives or flat-leaf parsley, for garnish

▸ Preheat the oven to 350°F.

▸ Place the drumsticks in a large bowl and sprinkle with the cumin, paprika, salt, olive oil, and 1 teaspoon of the chili-garlic sauce. Roll them around to make sure they are coated, cover, and let sit for a few hours or refrigerate overnight.

▸ In a shallow 6-cup gratin dish, combine the rice, chickpeas, onion, scallions, zucchini, salt, remaining 1 teaspoon of chili-garlic sauce, the tomato juice, and stock. Cover with aluminum foil. Place the marinated pieces of chicken on top of the aluminum foil and bake for 45 minutes to 1 hour. Carefully remove the cooked chicken from the foil, making sure to reserve any juices that have accumulated. Remove the foil and pour the chicken juices over the rice before stirring gently. Set the chicken on top of the rice, garnish with chives, and serve family style.

Facing page: *Geometric Contour,* 2023

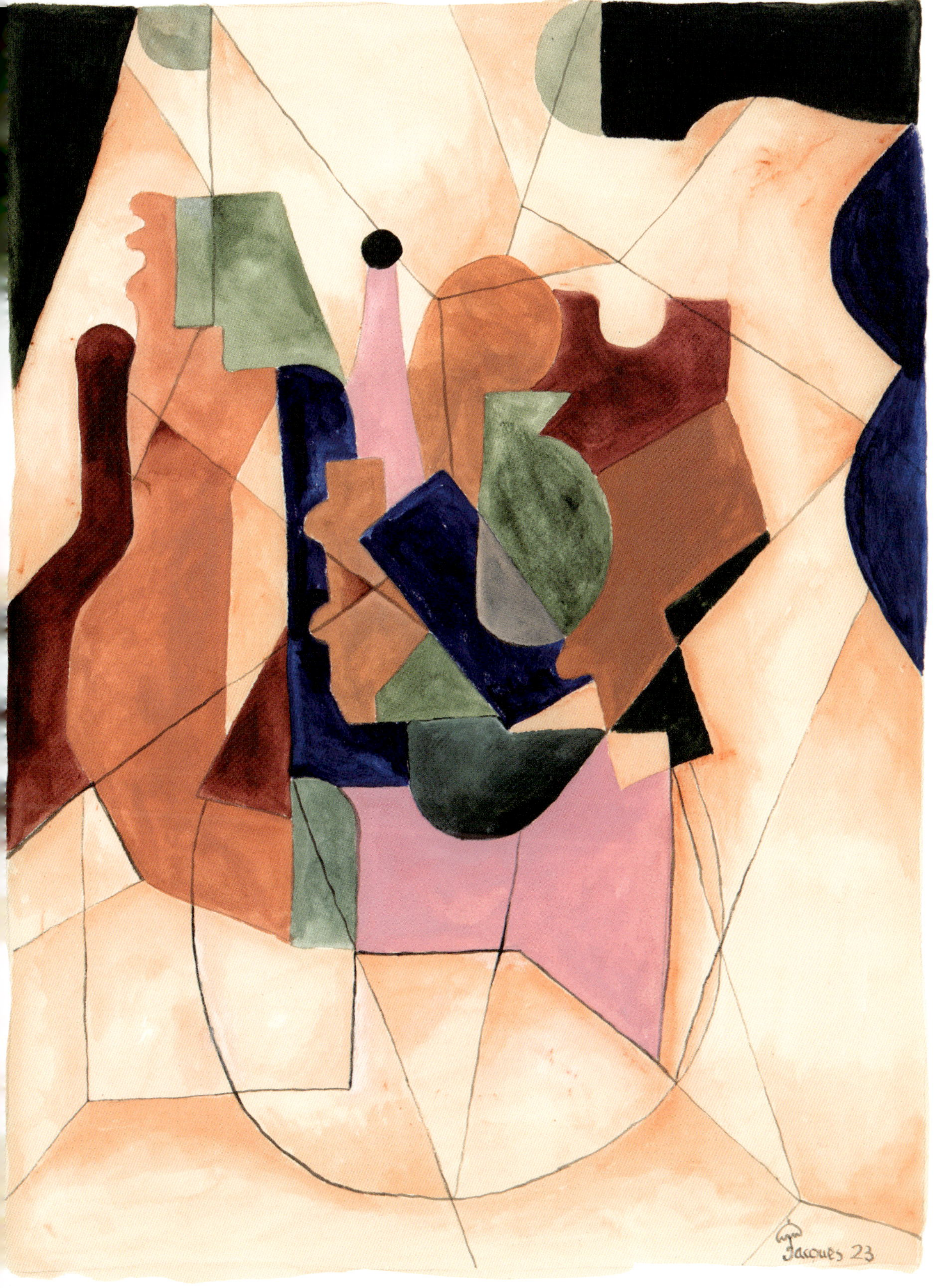
Jacques 23

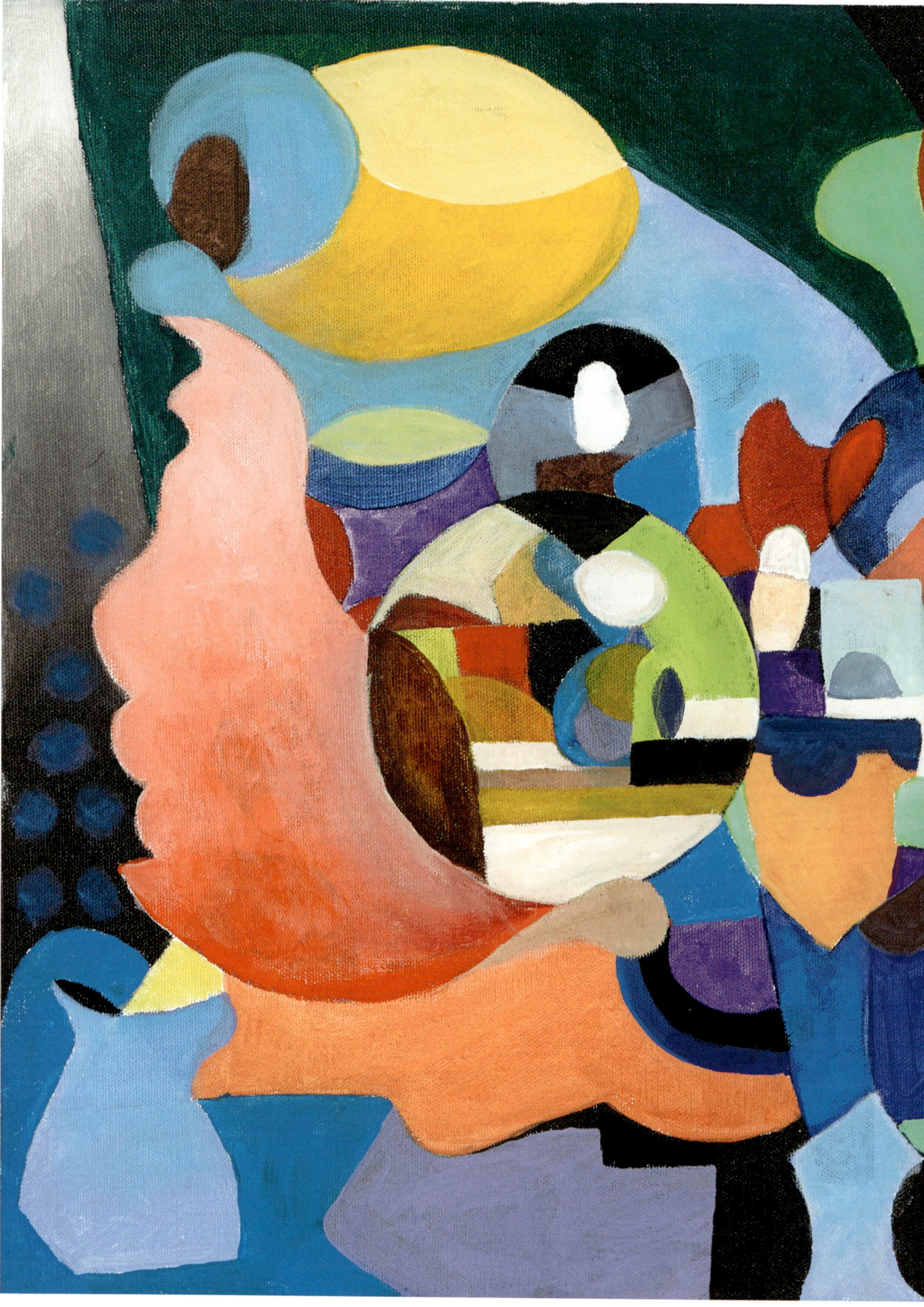

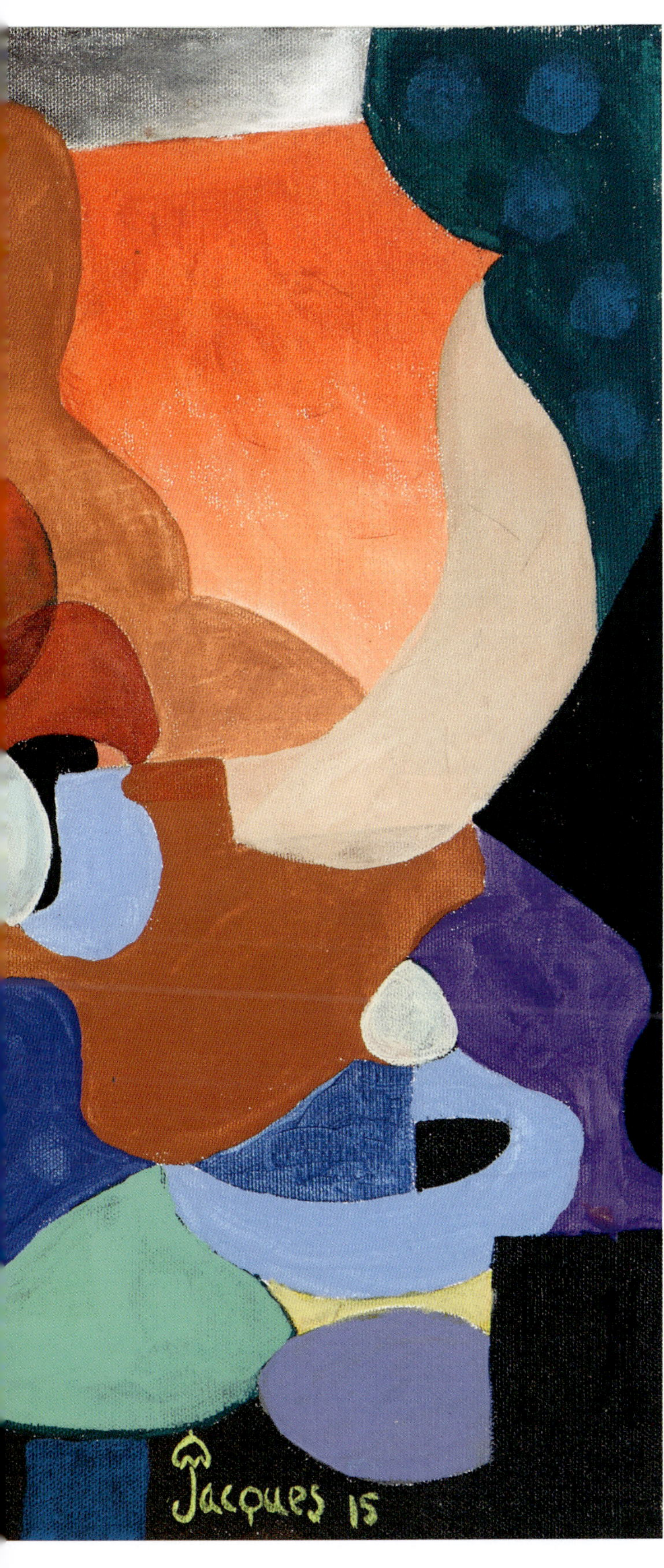

Assemblage 2, 2015

CHICKEN LEGS with YAMS, MUSHROOMS & PEARL ONIONS

This simple stew can be made with yams, sweet potatoes, yellow turnips (rutabagas), or potatoes. I have made it every way and like it because it can be made ahead and reheats well in its tasty juices.

Serves 2

2 chicken legs (10 to 12 ounces total)

1 yam or sweet potato (about 10 ounces)

1 tablespoon olive oil

1 tablespoon butter

1 teaspoon salt

½ teaspoon freshly ground black pepper

½ cup coarsely chopped onion

3 garlic cloves, peeled and chopped (1 tablespoon)

½ cup white wine

8 small cremini or white button mushrooms

12 frozen pearl onions

2 tablespoons chopped fresh flat-leaf parsley leaves, for garnish

▸ Remove the skin from the chicken and cut off the end of the drumstick. Separate the thigh from the drumstick. Peel the yam and cut it into 1-inch-thick slices.

▸ Heat the oil and butter in a medium skillet or shallow saucepan. Add the chicken, sprinkle with the salt and pepper, and brown over medium heat on all sides, 6 to 8 minutes. Add the onion and garlic. Deglaze the pan with the wine and 2 tablespoons of water. Add the mushrooms, yams, and pearl onions and bring to a boil. Lower the heat, cover, and simmer gently until the chicken is cooked through and the yams are tender, about 25 minutes. Taste and adjust the seasoning to your liking. Arrange the chicken, yams, mushrooms, and onions on a warm platter, spoon over the sauce, and sprinkle with parsley. Serve immediately or allow to cool if making ahead. The stew can be refrigerated for up to 2 days and reheated.

CHICKEN SCALLOPINI with CREAM SAUCE

This is a classic recipe, usually made with veal, but it works just as well using a chicken breast, which is much easier to find and less expensive. The chicken breast done this way is moist, flavorful, elegant, and simple. Here I prepare it with mushrooms, and to complete the meal I would serve some rice, pasta, or roasted potatoes and a nice green salad as well.

Serves 2

1 boneless, skinless chicken breasts (about 8 ounces)

2 tablespoons peanut oil

1 tablespoon butter

¾ teaspoon salt

¾ teaspoon freshly ground black pepper

1½ tablespoons Wondra flour

2 tablespoons chopped shallot

1 cup ½-inch-diced mushrooms (about 3 ounces)

¼ cup white wine

⅓ cup heavy cream

¼ teaspoon potato starch dissolved in 1 tablespoon water (you could also use cornstarch or rice flour)

▸ Cut the chicken breast into four slices lengthwise to get four scallopini, about ⅜ inch thick. Heat the oil and butter in a large skillet. Sprinkle the chicken with half of the salt and pepper and dredge in the flour. Place the chicken in the hot butter and oil and cook over high heat for about 1½ minutes on each side. Transfer to a platter and keep warm. Add the shallot and mushrooms to the skillet and cook for about 1 minute. Deglaze with the wine and cook for about 1 minute. Add the cream and remaining salt and pepper and bring to a boil. Add the diluted starch and boil gently for 15 seconds. Pour over the chicken and serve.

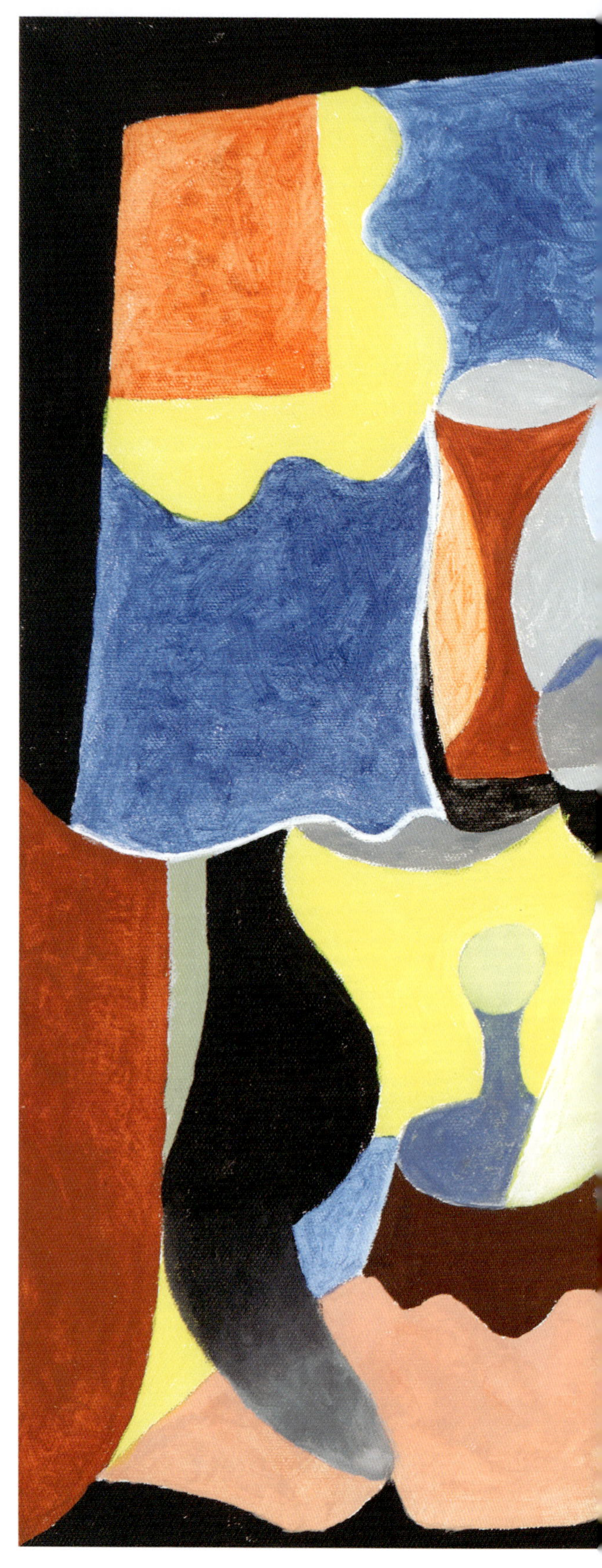

Hodgepodge Buffet, 2023

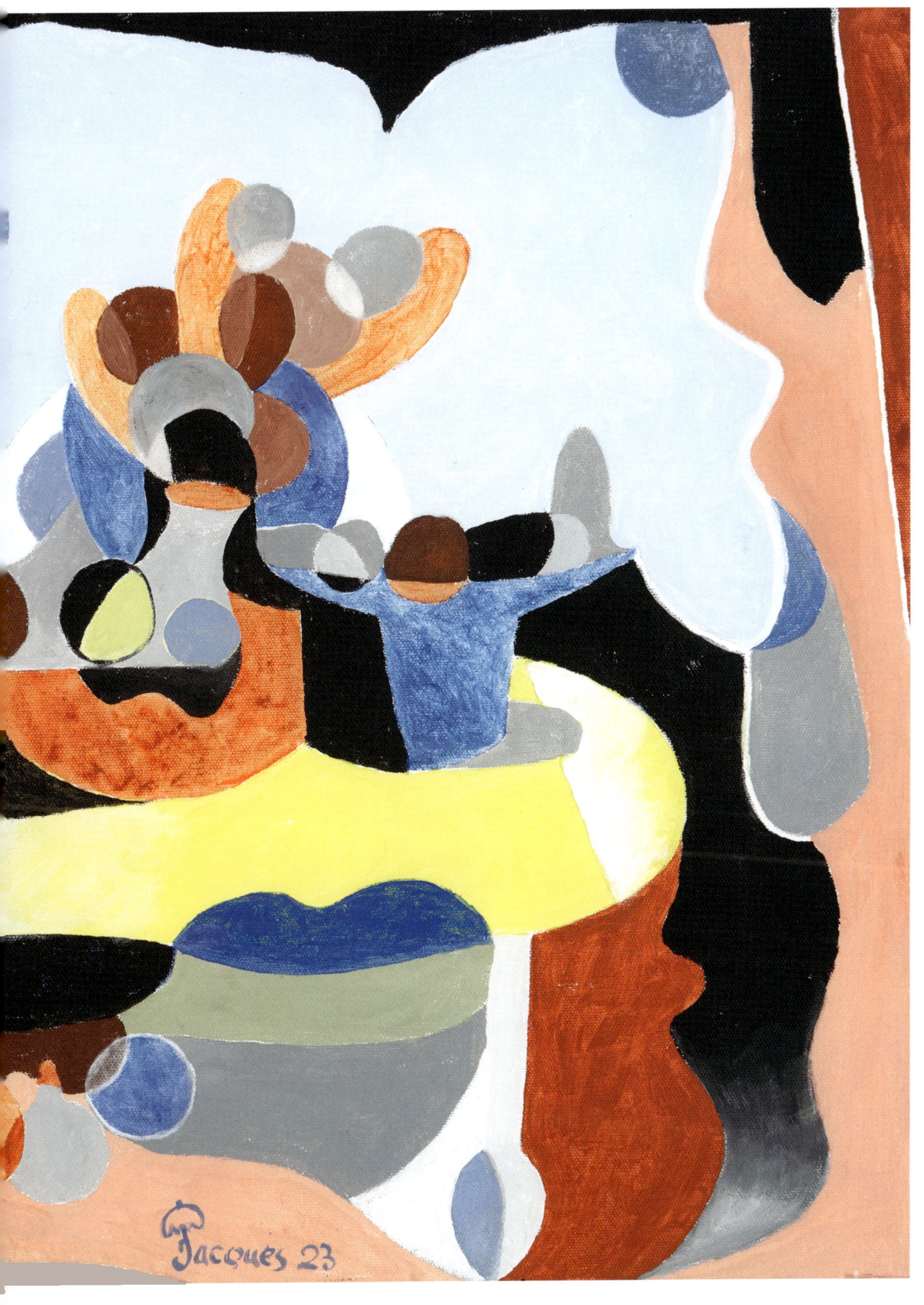
Jacques 23

CHICKEN THIGHS with SPINACH

In this recipe, two large chicken thighs are cooked, skin side down only, in a nonstick skillet for 20 to 25 minutes—no need to add any fat. Cutting along the bone of the thigh helps the chicken cook faster, and covering the skillet allows the steam to circulate and cook the top of the chicken. This way of cooking chicken makes the skin very crispy. Then, in the drippings of the chicken, which renders a fair amount of fat, sauté the garlic and the spinach and serve the whole thing together.

Serves 2

2 large chicken thighs (about 8 ounces each)

1/2 teaspoon salt

1/2 teaspoon freshly ground black pepper

1 teaspoon chopped garlic

4 ounces baby spinach (about 6 cups)

▸ Place the chicken thighs skin side down on a cutting board. Using a sharp knife, cut a slit in the flesh on each side of the bone about 1/2 inch deep; this will help the chicken cook faster. Sprinkle both sides of the chicken with half of the salt and pepper. Place them, skin side down, in a cold nonstick skillet, about 9 inches in diameter. Cook on high heat, uncovered, for about 3 minutes, until some of the fat begins to render and the skillet is hot, cover the pan and reduce the heat to very low. Let the chicken cook uninterrupted until the skin is golden and the top is cooked, 20 to 25 minutes. Transfer the chicken to a plate with the crispy skin facing up.

▸ Add the garlic to the pan with the rendered chicken fat and cook for about 10 seconds, shaking the pan. Add the spinach, season with the remaining salt and pepper, and add 2 tablespoons of water. Cook until wilted, turning the spinach with tongs, 2 to 3 minutes—most of the water should be evaporated. Spread the spinach on a platter and top with the chicken. Serve immediately.

POULET à la CREME

Chicken in a cream sauce is a specialty of the town where I was born, Bourg-en-Bresse. My mother's simple recipe included a whole cut-up chicken with water, a dash of flour, and a bit of cream to finish. I have added white wine and mushrooms to make the dish a bit more sophisticated, and used chicken thighs, which I consider to be the best part of the chicken. A sprinkling of chopped tarragon at the end makes it more special. I often serve this dish with rice.

Serves 4

1½ tablespoons butter

4 skinless chicken thighs (about 1½ pounds)

½ teaspoon salt

½ teaspoon freshly ground black pepper

½ cup chopped onion

1 tablespoon all-purpose flour

¼ cup white wine

1 cup sliced white mushrooms

¾ cup chicken stock

¼ cup heavy cream

1 tablespoon chopped fresh tarragon

▸ Heat the butter in a heavy skillet. Season the chicken with the salt and pepper on both sides. Brown the chicken in the butter over high heat for 2 minutes on each side. Add the onion and cook for another minute. Sprinkle with the flour and make sure it is evenly distributed, turning the chicken. Add the wine, mushrooms, and stock. Bring to a boil, lower the heat, cover, and boil gently for 30 minutes. Transfer the chicken to a serving dish, add the cream to the skillet, and return to a boil for another minute. Sprinkle the sauce with the tarragon, spoon over the chicken, and serve.

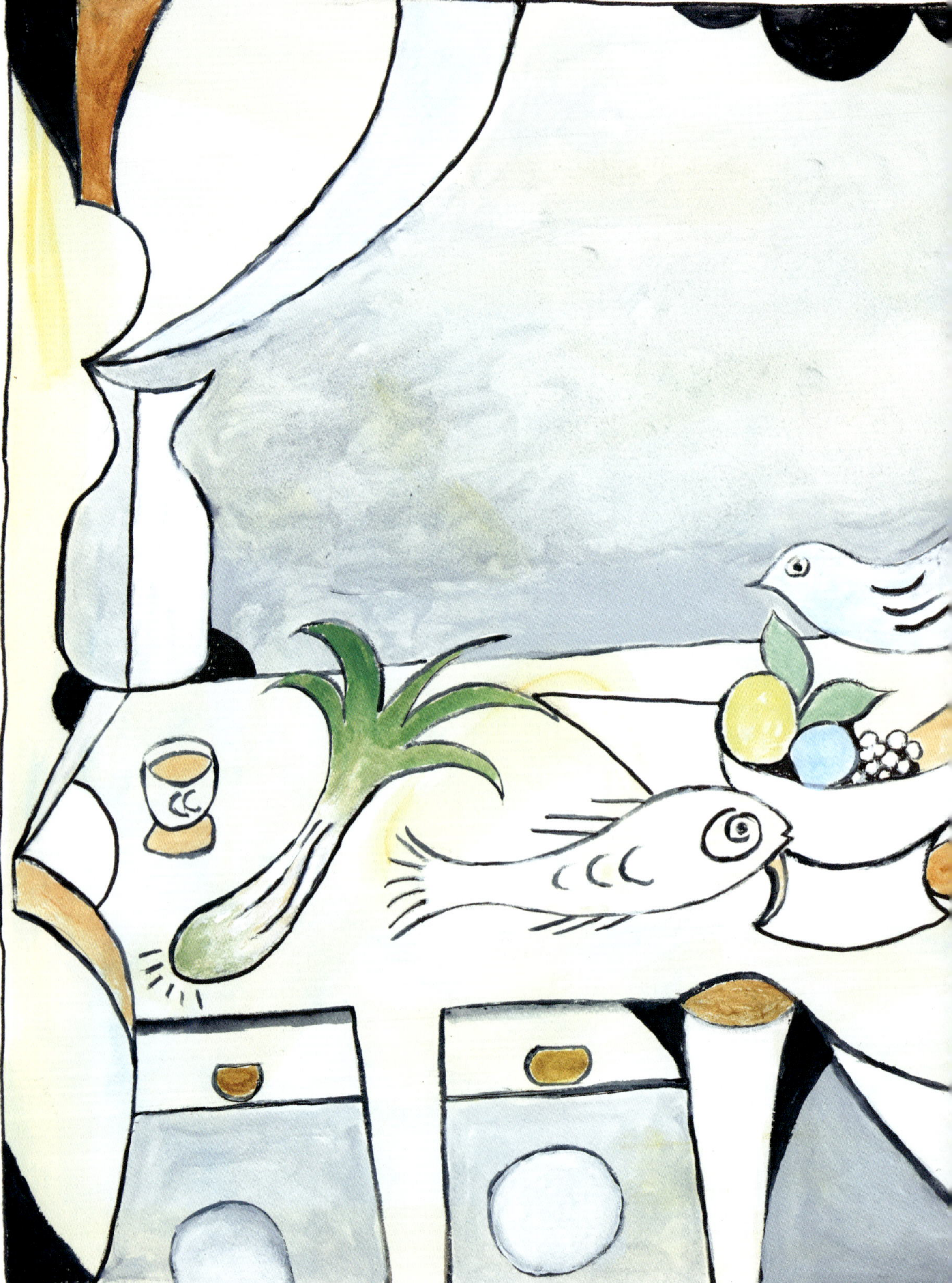

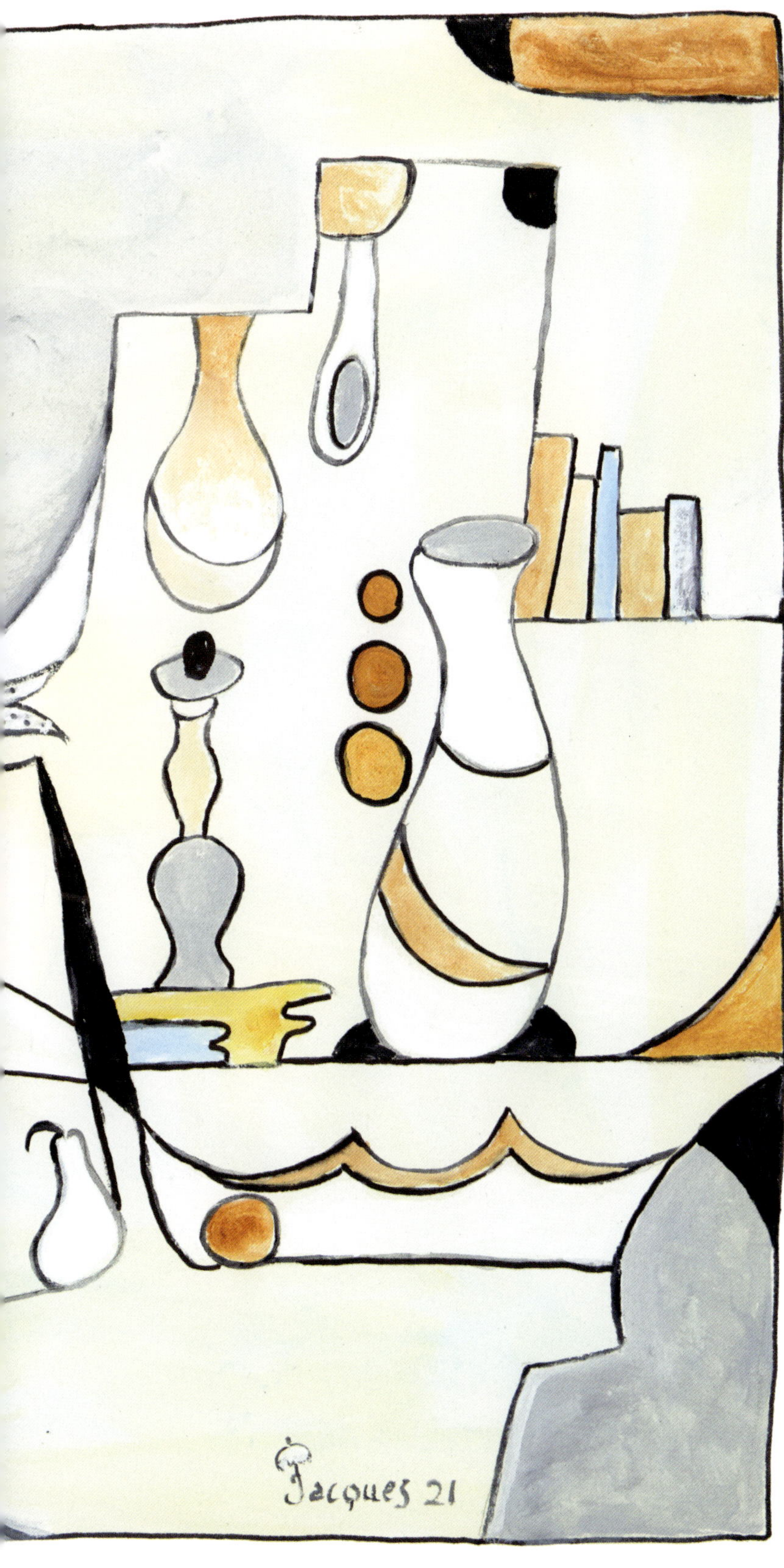

In My Kitchen, 2021

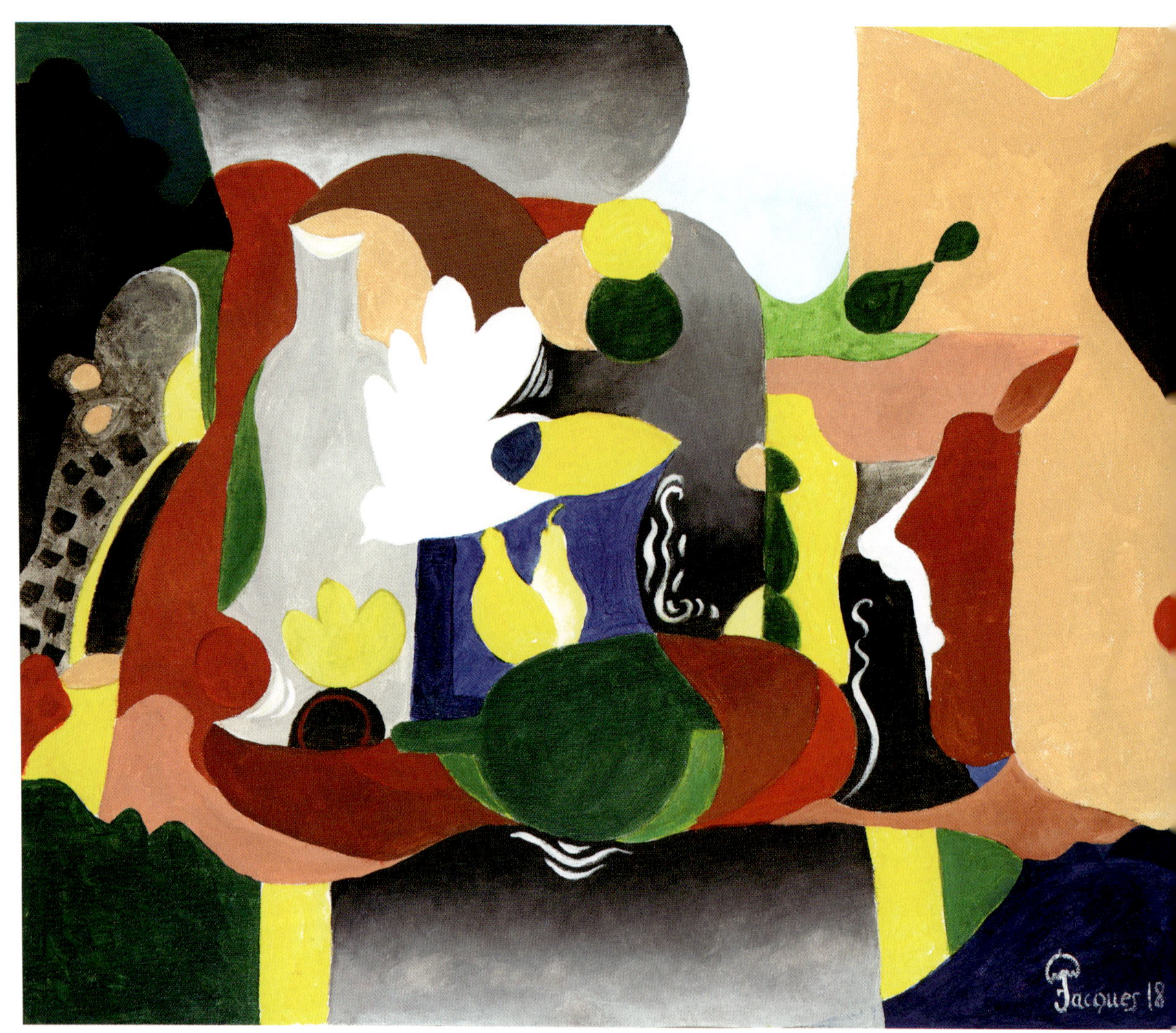

Salmagundi, 2018

ROASTED POUSSIN with GARLIC SAUCE

A poussin is a young chicken, very tender and succulent, similar to a Cornish hen, although the Cornish hen is usually slightly bigger. They can be found in some more specialty grocery stores or ordered online, but you could also substitute a Cornish hen if that is easier. In this recipe, one poussin, approximately 20 ounces, is served for two people.

Serves 2

1 poussin or Cornish hen (about 1¼ pounds)

1 tablespoon soy sauce

1 teaspoon hot sauce, such as sriracha

1 tablespoon oil

2 garlic cloves, peeled and thinly sliced

1 tablespoon white wine vinegar

⅓ cup diced canned tomato

1 tablespoon chopped fresh flat-leaf parsley or chives

▸ Preheat the oven to 375°F.

▸ Split the poussin into halves by cutting between the breast lengthwise. Cut about ½ inch deep in the joint between the drumstick and thigh to help ensure an even cooking process. Combine the soy sauce and hot sauce and spread the mixture on all sides of the chicken (this can be done hours ahead of cooking). At cooking time, heat the oil in a large nonstick, ovenproof skillet. Place the poussin skin side down in the skillet. Cover and cook over medium heat for 5 minutes. Uncover, place in the oven, and bake for 30 minutes. Remove the poussin and place on a platter. Return the pan to the stovetop over medium heat. Add the garlic to the drippings and cook for about 1 minute. Add the vinegar and boil for 30 seconds. Add the tomato and bring back to a boil. Taste for seasoning and adjust as needed. Spoon the sauce over the poussin and garnish with parsley. Enjoy.

STUFFED QUAIL with GRAPE SAUCE

This is a classic dish that takes a little more effort to prepare, but for a special dinner it is worth the extra attention. The quail are boned, and a stock is made from the bones. Stuffed with a vegetable mixture, the boned birds are roasted, then finished under the broiler. A delicious sauce is created from their cooking juices, the previously made stock, a little thickening agent, and white grapes.

Serves 4

1 leek (6 ounces), cut into 1-inch pieces and washed

2 carrots (4 ounces), peeled and cut into 1-inch pieces

2 stalks celery (5 ounces), cut into 1-inch pieces

1 tablespoon plus 1 teaspoon butter

2 garlic cloves, peeled, crushed, and finely chopped (1 teaspoon)

1 teaspoon salt

¼ teaspoon freshly ground black pepper

4 large quail (7 ounces each)

2 teaspoons peanut or corn oil

1½ tablespoons dark soy sauce

1 teaspoon honey

1 cup white seedless grapes (6 ounces)

½ teaspoon potato starch dissolved in 1 tablespoon water

1 tablespoon minced fresh flat-leaf parsley or chives, for garnish

▸ Place the leek, carrots, and celery in a food processor and pulse a few times to chop them coarsely.

▸ Melt the 1 tablespoon of butter in a large skillet. Add the vegetables and garlic along with ¼ cup of water. Cook the mixture, covered, over medium heat for 10 minutes, or until the vegetables are soft and tender and the water is gone. Add the salt and pepper, mix well, and set aside to cool.

▸ Bone the quail by cutting through the joint of the shoulders of each and pulling the carcass out without cutting open the skin. Cut off the ends of the drumsticks and remove the wing tips, leaving the first and second joint of the wings attached to the shoulder. Remove the thigh bones. (All the bones together should weigh about 8 ounces.) The only bones remaining in the quail should be those in the drumsticks and attached wings.

▸ Place the bones in a skillet with the remaining teaspoon of butter and the oil and brown them over low heat, covered, turning them occasionally, for 12 minutes. Add 4 cups of water and 1 tablespoon of the soy sauce to the skillet and bring the mixture to a boil. Reduce the heat, cover, and boil gently for 30 minutes, maintaining the gentle boil throughout. Strain the mixture through a fine-mesh strainer set over a saucepan and discard the bones. Boil the strained liquid in the saucepan to reduce it to 1 cup, then set this stock aside in the pan.

▸ Preheat the oven to 425°F.

▸ Using a pastry bag, stuff the quail with the cooked vegetable mixture. Arrange the stuffed quail on a plate and place them in a steamer set over boiling water. Steam, covered, for 5 minutes.

▸ Mix the remaining ½ tablespoon of soy sauce with the honey in a small bowl. Transfer the quail to a small ovenproof skillet and brush them with the soy mixture. Place them in the oven and cook for 10 minutes, then baste them with the liquid that has accumulated in the skillet. Preheat the broiler and broil the quail 6 to 8 inches from the heat source for 5 minutes, until they are nicely browned.

▸ Meanwhile, add the grapes to the cup of reserved stock in the saucepan, bring the mixture to a boil, and boil for 1 minute. Add the dissolved potato starch and stir to thicken the mixture. Boil for 1 minute.

▸ When the quail are cooked, remove them from the skillet and arrange them on a serving plate. Strain any accumulated juices in the skillet into the sauce containing the grapes. Pour the sauce over the quail on the serving plate. Sprinkle with parsley and serve one quail per person.

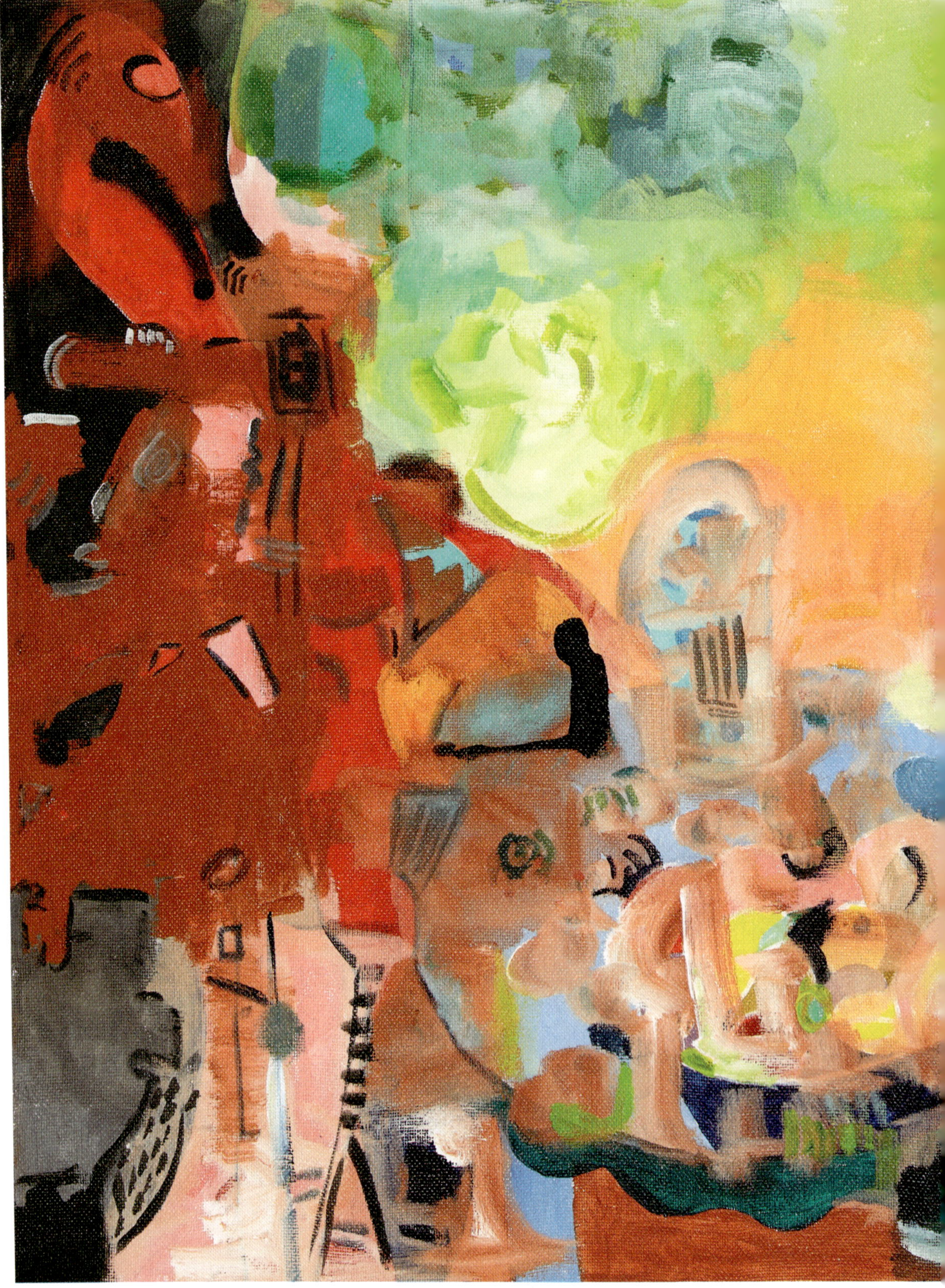

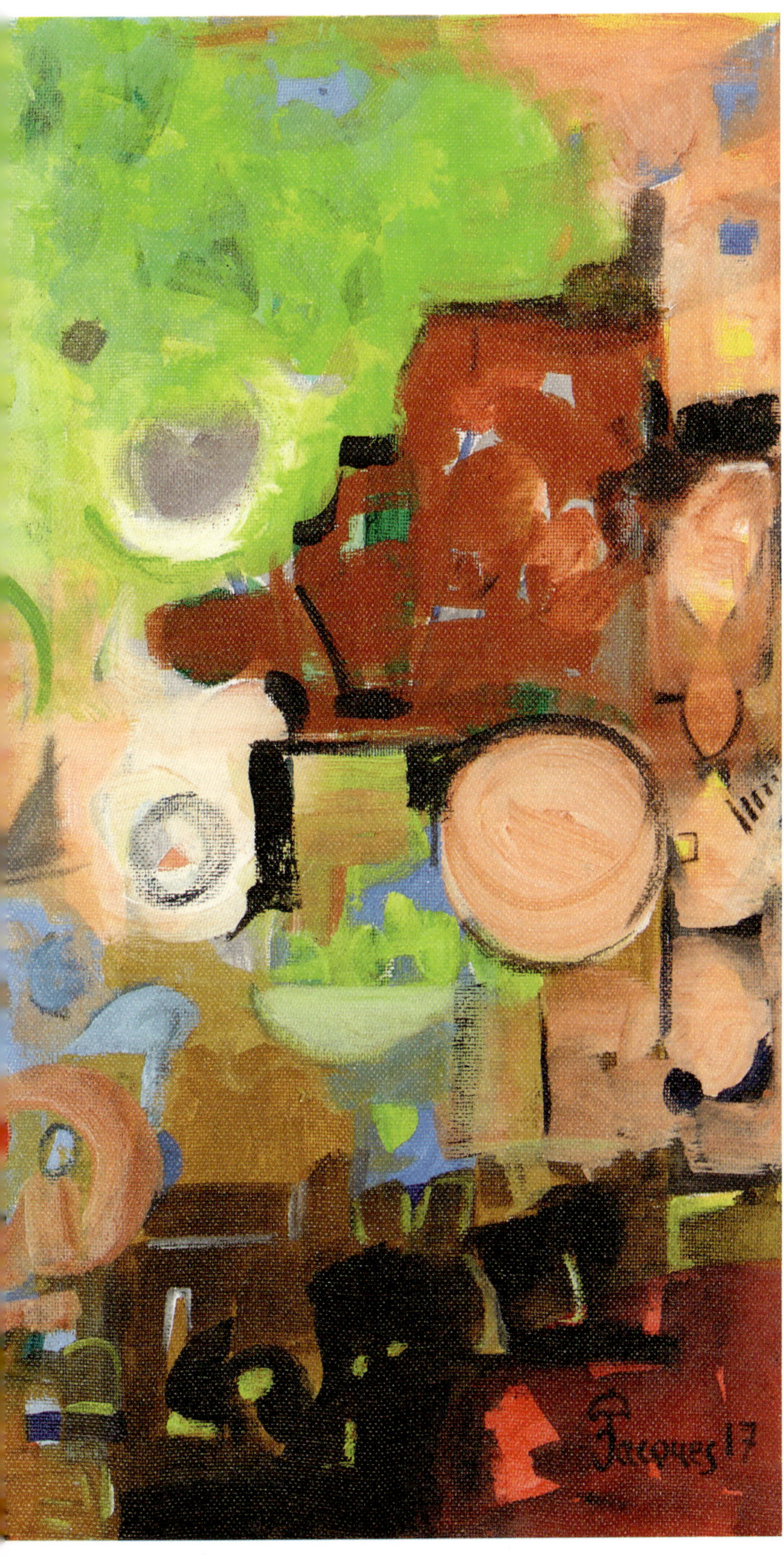

Green Abstraction, 2017

BRAISED DUCK with FENNEL & OLIVES

I like to use a little bit of duck fat in place of olive oil or butter to brown the duck pieces. Then, in the pan drippings, I cook fennel, flavoring it with red wine, wine vinegar, and a dash of sugar to caramelize it a little. I finish cooking the duck in the same mixture, at the end adding the olives and duck liver. This is a delicious stew that turns one duck into plenty of food for four people. I always choose Long Island duck, which is the most readily available variety. It has a mild flavor that adapts well to many cuisines.

Serves 4

1 Long Island duck (about 5¼ pounds)

½ teaspoon salt

½ teaspoon freshly ground black pepper

1 bulb fennel (1 pound)

¼ cup red wine

¼ cup red wine vinegar

1 tablespoon sugar

20 large black or green olives, or a mixture of both, pitted (8 ounces)

2 tablespoons minced fresh flat-leaf parsley, for garnish

▸ Cut the duck into four pieces: two legs and two breasts. Using a towel, grab hold of the skin and peel it off. (The skin is not used in this recipe. It can be kept to make crackling or discarded.) Remove the breast from the carcass and cut each wing into two segments. Cut off the tips of each drumstick. Use of the gizzard is optional but, if using it, cut off and discard the silver skin surrounding it. Cut enough duck fat into ¼-inch pieces so that you have 3 tablespoons.

▸ Heat the 3 tablespoons of duck fat until melted and hot in a large, sturdy saucepan. Add the wings and gizzard and cook them over medium heat for 10 minutes, turning the duck pieces occasionally. Add the breasts and legs and sprinkle the duck pieces with ¼ teaspoon each of the salt and pepper. Brown the duck pieces on all sides, still over medium heat, for 15 minutes. Transfer the duck to a plate.

▸ Meanwhile, slice the fennel bulb in half and cut each half into ¼-inch slices. Place the fennel in the same saucepan you used to cook the duck and add ½ cup of water. Bring the water to a boil over high heat, then reduce the heat to low, cover, and cook gently for 3 to 5 minutes, until all the water has evaporated and the fennel is starting to brown.

▸ Add the duck heart and liver to the pan along with the remaining ¼ teaspoon each salt and pepper, the wine, vinegar, and sugar. Cook over medium heat for 3 minutes. Remove the heart and liver and set aside.

▸ Return the duck pieces to the pan, arranging them on top of the fennel. Bring to a boil, reduce the heat to very low, cover, and cook for about 20 minutes. (The recipe can be prepared to this point a few hours ahead.)

▸ At serving time, add the olives and duck liver and bring the mixture to a boil. Reduce the heat to low, cover, and warm for a few minutes. Serve, sprinkled with parsley.

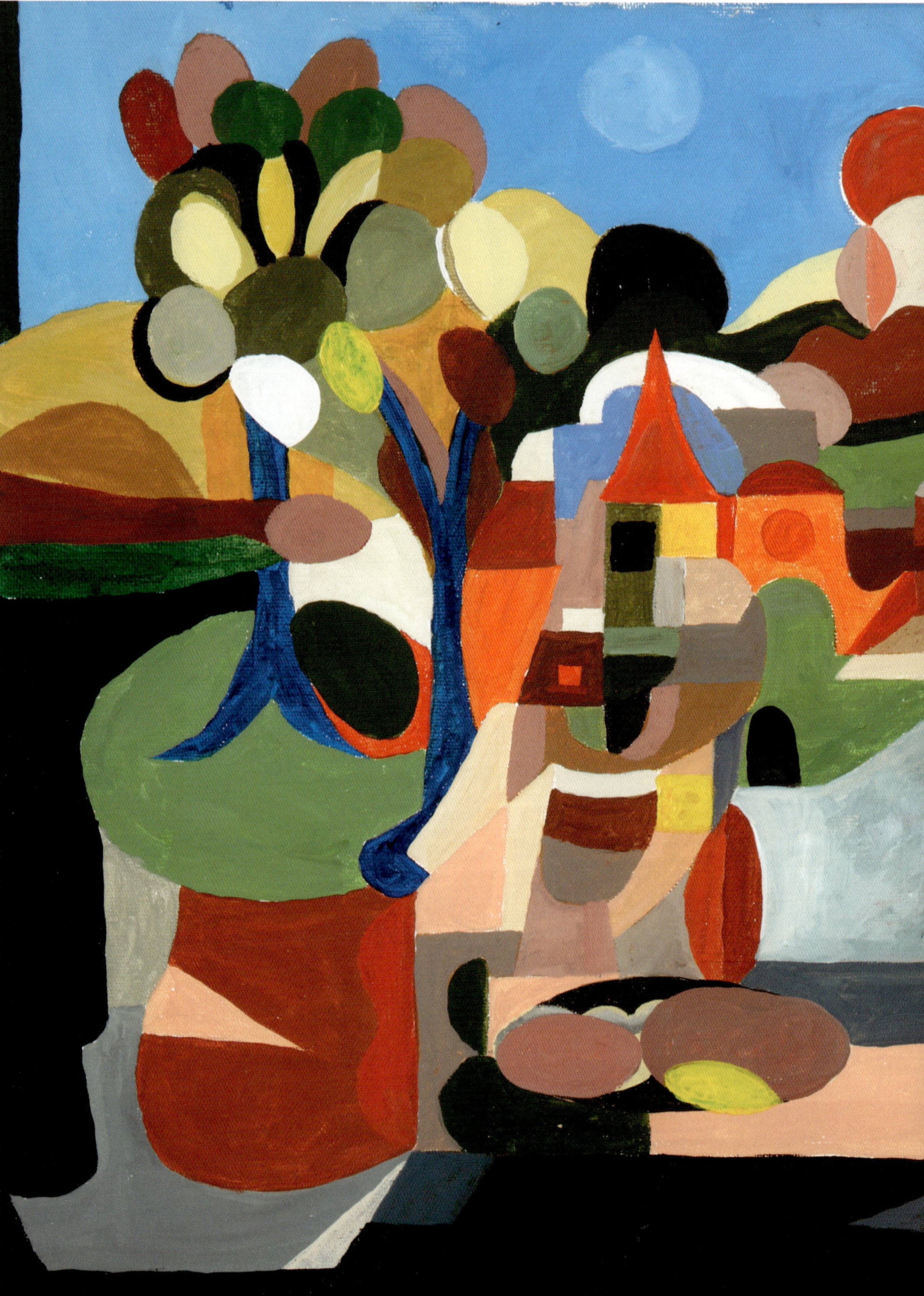

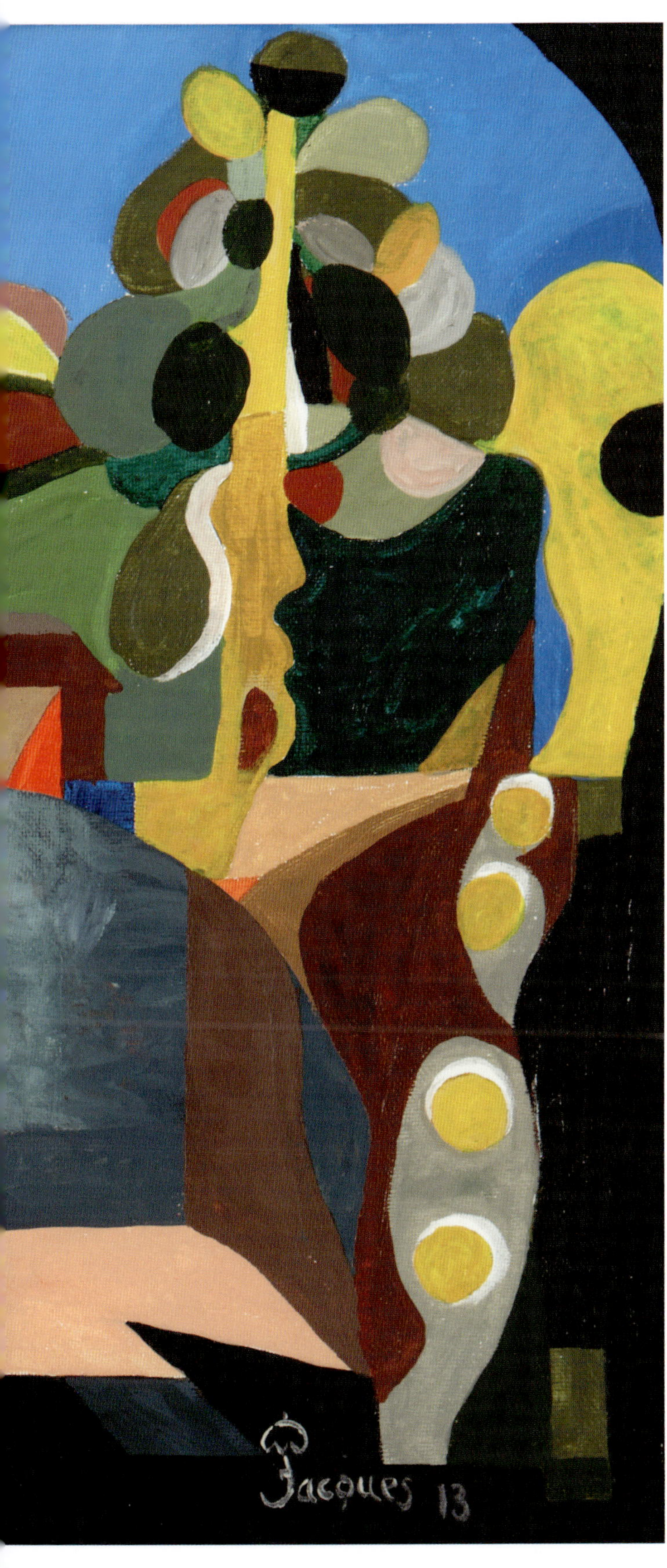

Starlight Landscape, 2013

VEAL SHANK PRINTANIERE

The shank is a sinewy muscle from the leg of a calf. Although this muscle can be removed from the attached bone by sliding a sharp knife along the bone, the shank is most often found at supermarkets already sliced crosswise with the round bone in the center for use in osso buco, the classic Italian dish. Here, however, the boneless shank is cut lengthwise into elongated pieces, which are sautéed, flavored with wine, then finished with an abundance of vegetables—spring vegetables specifically, as *printanière* simply means relating to spring.

Serves 6

2¼ pounds boneless veal shank

2 tablespoons butter

¾ pound whole shallots, peeled

8 ounces small, peeled carrots

½ cup chopped onion

2 teaspoons peeled, crushed, and chopped garlic

1 tablespoon all-purpose flour

1 teaspoon herbes de Provence

½ cup dry white wine

1 teaspoon salt

½ teaspoon freshly ground black pepper

4 ounces sugar snap peas, any strings removed (1 cup)

4 ounces fresh shelled peas (8 ounces unshelled) or equivalent frozen peas (1 cup)

▸ Cut the shank meat lengthwise into about twelve pieces, each about 5 inches long and 1½ inches thick. (Note: Do not remove the silver skin visible in the pieces; it is not fat and becomes moist, chewy, and delicate in texture as it cooks.)

▸ Melt the butter in a large saucepan over medium heat. When it begins to brown, add the meat strips in one layer and cook over medium to high heat for about 15 minutes, turning them occasionally, until they are nicely browned on all sides.

▸ Meanwhile, place the shallots and carrots in a medium saucepan with 2 cups of water. Bring the water to a boil, reduce the heat to low, cover, and boil the vegetables gently for about 8 minutes, until they are tender but still firm. Drain, reserving the cooking liquid. (You should have about 1 cup; adjust the yield accordingly, adding water, if necessary, to bring to 1 cup.) Set the shallots and carrots aside in a small bowl.

▸ When the veal is nicely browned, transfer it to a plate. Add the onion and garlic to the meat drippings in the pan and cook them for 1 minute. Add the flour and herbes de Provence, mix well, and cook for 10 to 20 seconds longer.

▸ Add the cup of reserved cooking liquid from the carrots and shallots to the pan along with the wine, salt, and pepper and bring the mixture to a boil. Return the meat to the pan, bring back to a boil, reduce the heat to very low, cover, and cook gently for 1 hour, until the meat is tender. (The recipe can be made to this point a few hours ahead.)

▸ At serving time, add the reserved shallots and carrots to the stew along with the sugar snap and shelled peas. Bring the stew back to a boil, reduce the heat to low, cover, and boil gently for 5 minutes. Serve.

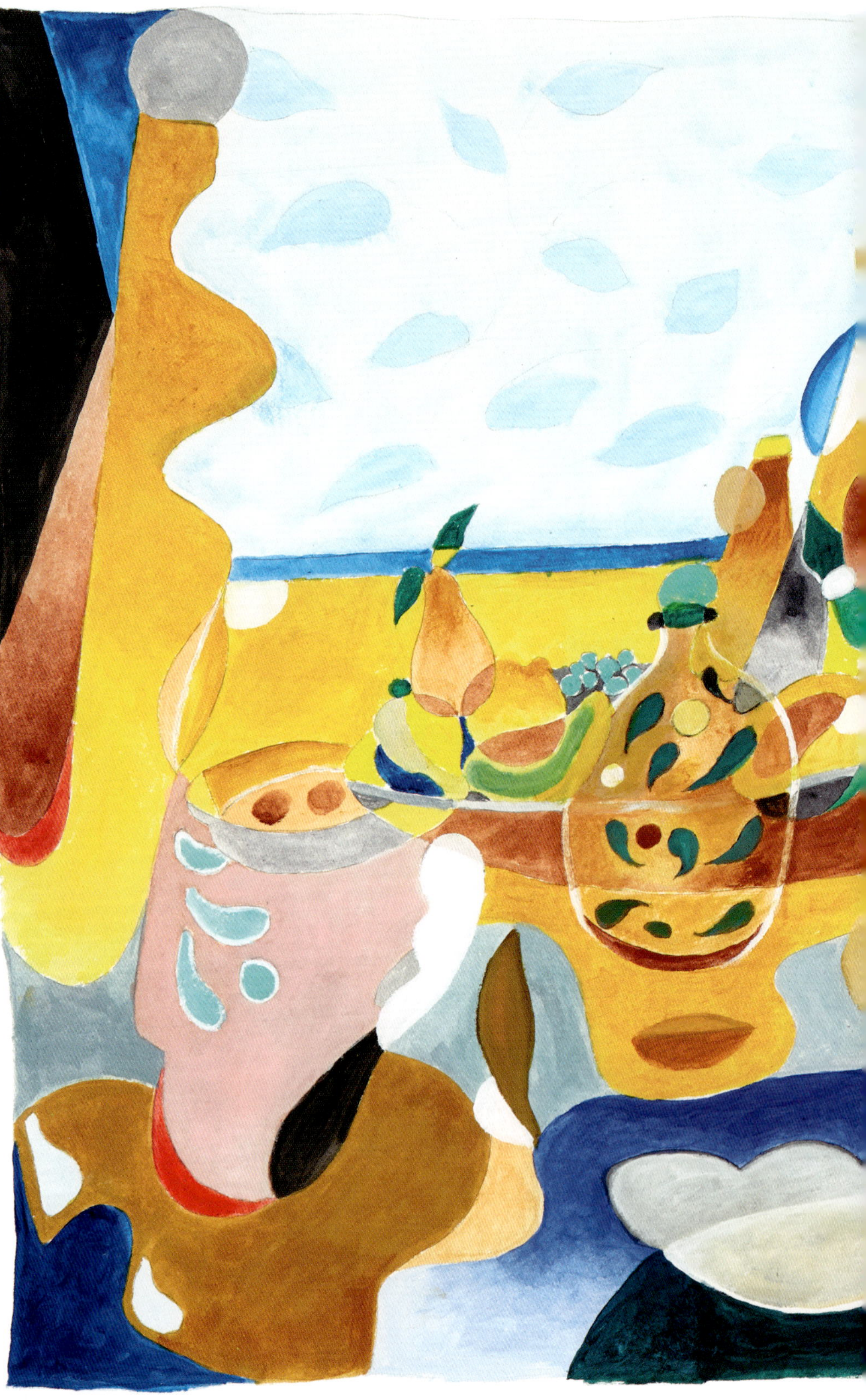

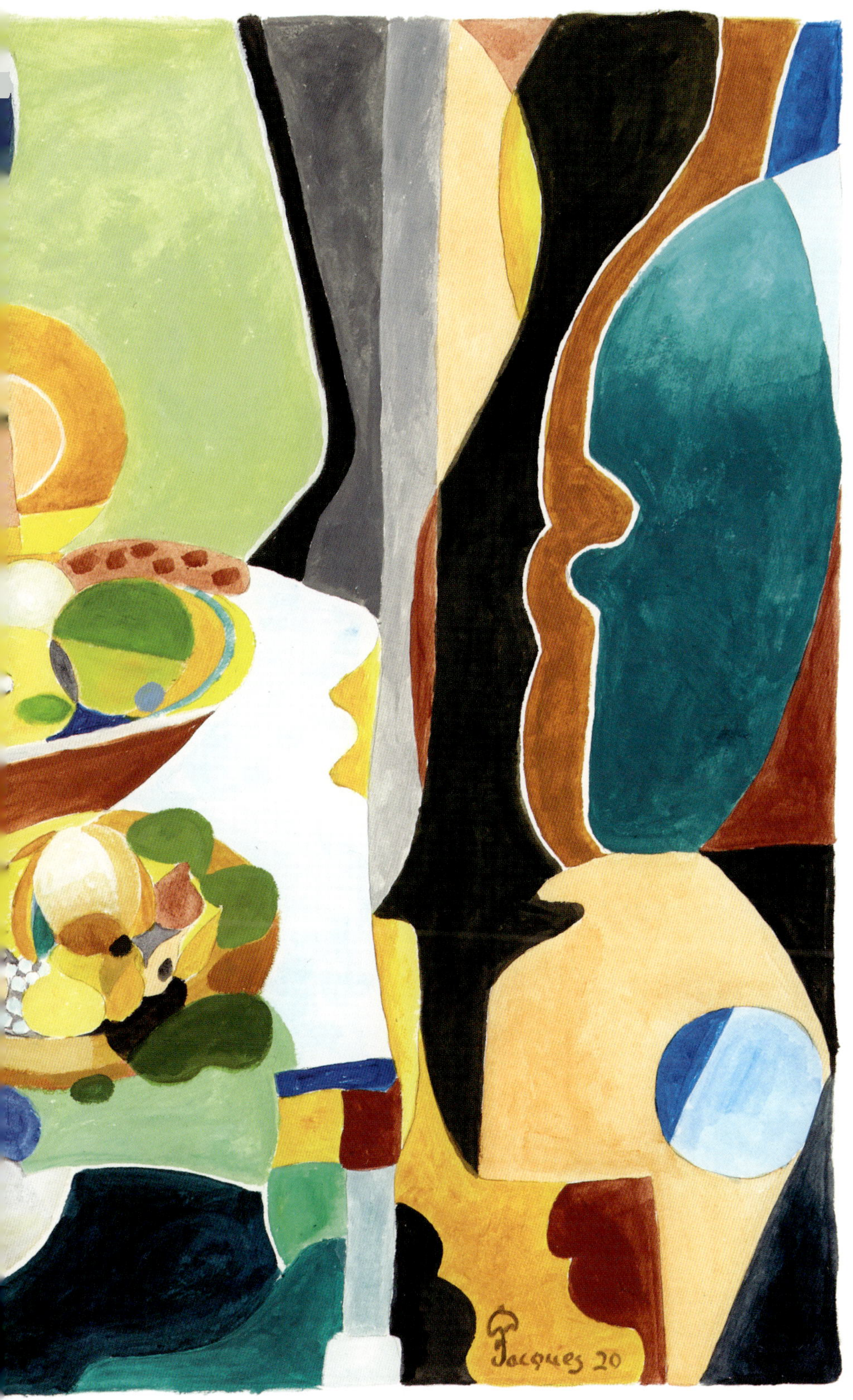

Yellow Buffet, 2020

VEAL FRICASSEE in CREAM SAUCE

Veal is one of the most delicate of meats and is the best to prepare in sauces. The shoulder, flank, breast, and shank are excellent cuts and not too expensive. This is a comforting, delicious meal, rounded out with some simple vegetable garnishes and a side such as rice, potatoes, polenta, or pasta.

Serves 4

2 tablespoons butter

1½ pounds veal (from the shoulder, shank, or osso buco), cut into 2-inch cubes

⅔ cup chopped onion

1 tablespoon chopped garlic

1 tablespoon all-purpose flour

½ cup white wine

¼ teaspoon salt

¾ teaspoon freshly ground black pepper

1 thyme sprig

12 pearl onions, peeled (about 6 ounces)

12 small button mushrooms, washed (about 5 ounces)

⅓ cup heavy cream

▸ Heat the butter in a heavy saucepan and add the veal in one layer. Cook over high heat, stirring occasionally, to ensure the meat browns on all sides, for about 12 minutes. Add the onion and garlic and cook for 1 minute. Sprinkle the flour on top and mix well. Cook for another minute, then stir in the wine, 1¼ cups of water, the salt, and pepper. Bring to a boil, cover, and cook on very low heat for 35 minutes, stirring occasionally to prevent sticking. Stir in the thyme, pearl onions, and mushrooms, cover, and cook for another 15 minutes, continuing to stir occasionally. The meat should be tender. Stir in the cream, bring to a final boil for 1 more minute, and serve as needed.

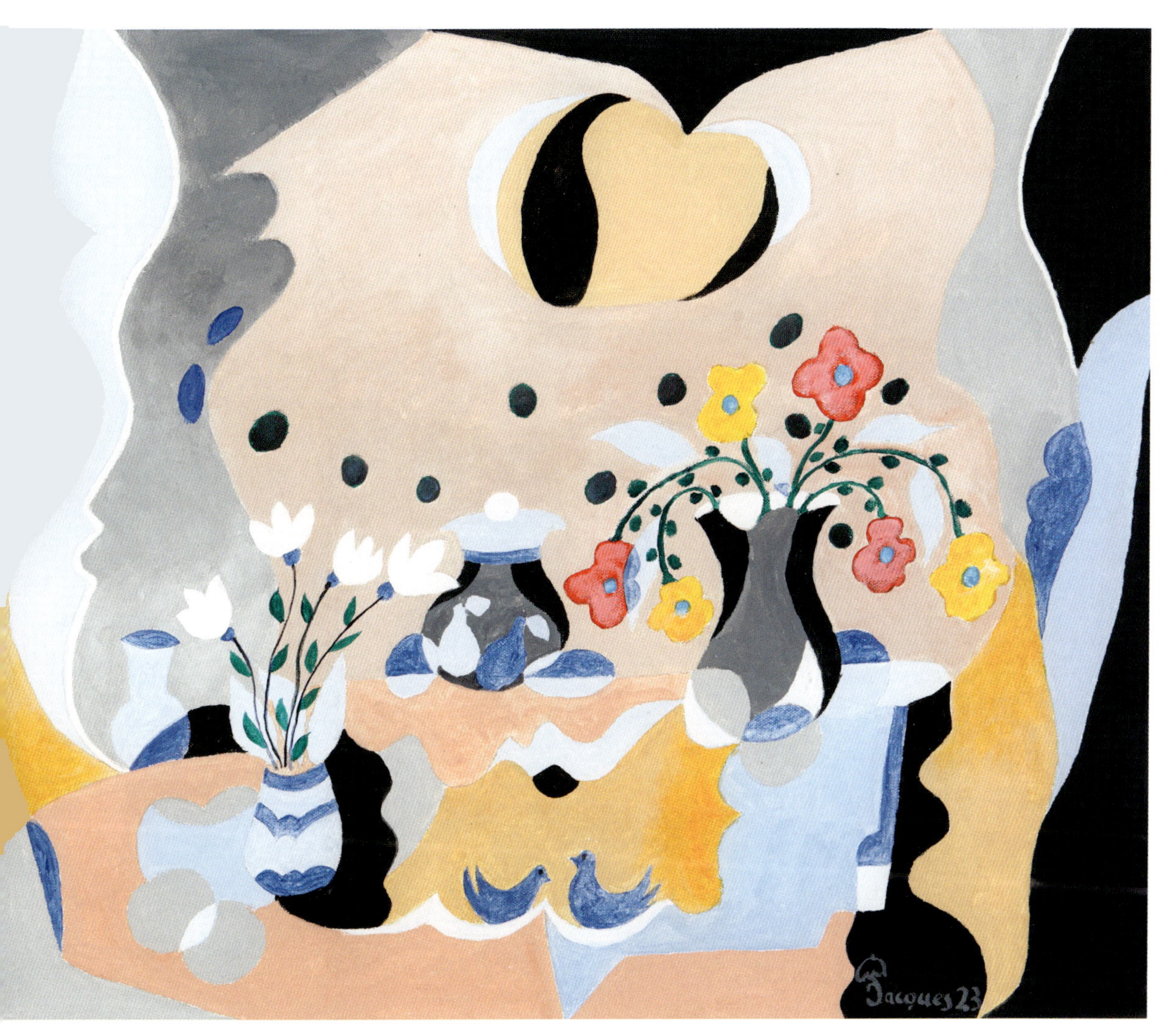

Tranquility, 2023

SAUTEED LAMB SHOULDER CHOP with MUSHROOMS

I find that the lamb shoulder chop, just like the Boston butt when you use pork, is one of the best parts of the animal. The shoulder chop is very moist, tender, juicy, and less expensive than the regular rack of lamb or lamb loin chops. Here it's simply sautéed and finished with a garnish of mushrooms.

Serves 1

1 lamb shoulder chop, 10 to 12 ounces

½ teaspoon salt

½ teaspoon freshly ground black pepper

½ tablespoon olive oil

1½ teaspoons butter

2 to 3 large white mushrooms, halved

1 large garlic clove, peeled and thinly sliced

1 tablespoon chopped fresh flat-leaf parsley or chives, for garnish

▸ Season the lamb chop with half of the salt and pepper. Heat the oil and butter in a heavy cast-iron skillet or grill pan over medium-high heat. Once hot, add the chop and mushrooms. Cook until golden brown on the first side, about 2 minutes. Turn the chop and the mushrooms. Season the mushrooms with the remaining salt and pepper, add the garlic slices, and continue to cook on the second side until it is golden brown, about 3 minutes more for medium-rare. If you prefer your lamb more well done, continue to cook until it's to your liking. Remove the pan from the heat, cover, and let rest for 5 minutes before serving. Garnish with parsley.

SAUSAGE en PAPILLOTE

Simple as a main course or great for a party, this dish can be changed by varying the ingredients to suit any occasion. Use leftover vegetables from the fridge for a quick meal or maybe something more special for a gathering.

Serves 2 to 4

2 pieces kielbasa (about 8 ounces), skin removed

2 Italian-style sausages (about 8 ounces)

2 potatoes, peeled and halved (about 12 ounces)

1 onion, peeled and halved (about 8 ounces)

5 to 6 garlic cloves

2 carrots, peeled and halved (about 8 ounces)

2 or 3 white mushrooms, cut into 1-inch pieces

1 large thyme sprig

2 bay leaves

½ teaspoon salt

½ teaspoon freshly ground black pepper

Tabasco sauce to taste

2 tablespoons olive oil

▸ Preheat the oven to 400°F.

▸ Spread a large piece of aluminum foil (about 20 inches square) on a flat surface. Arrange the sausages, potatoes, onion, garlic, carrots, mushrooms, thyme, and bay leaves on top. Season with the salt, pepper, and Tabasco (if desired) and drizzle with the olive oil. Fold the foil over the ingredients, making sure that there is space between the foil and the ingredients so steam is able to develop during cooking. Fold and twist the foil to seal the seams tightly. Transfer the package to a baking sheet and bake for 1 hour.

▸ To serve, using scissors, cut a slit in the top of the foil and peel it away to reveal the steaming ingredients. Be careful as you open the foil as the steam is very hot. You can serve directly from the tray or transfer the ingredients to a warm serving dish.

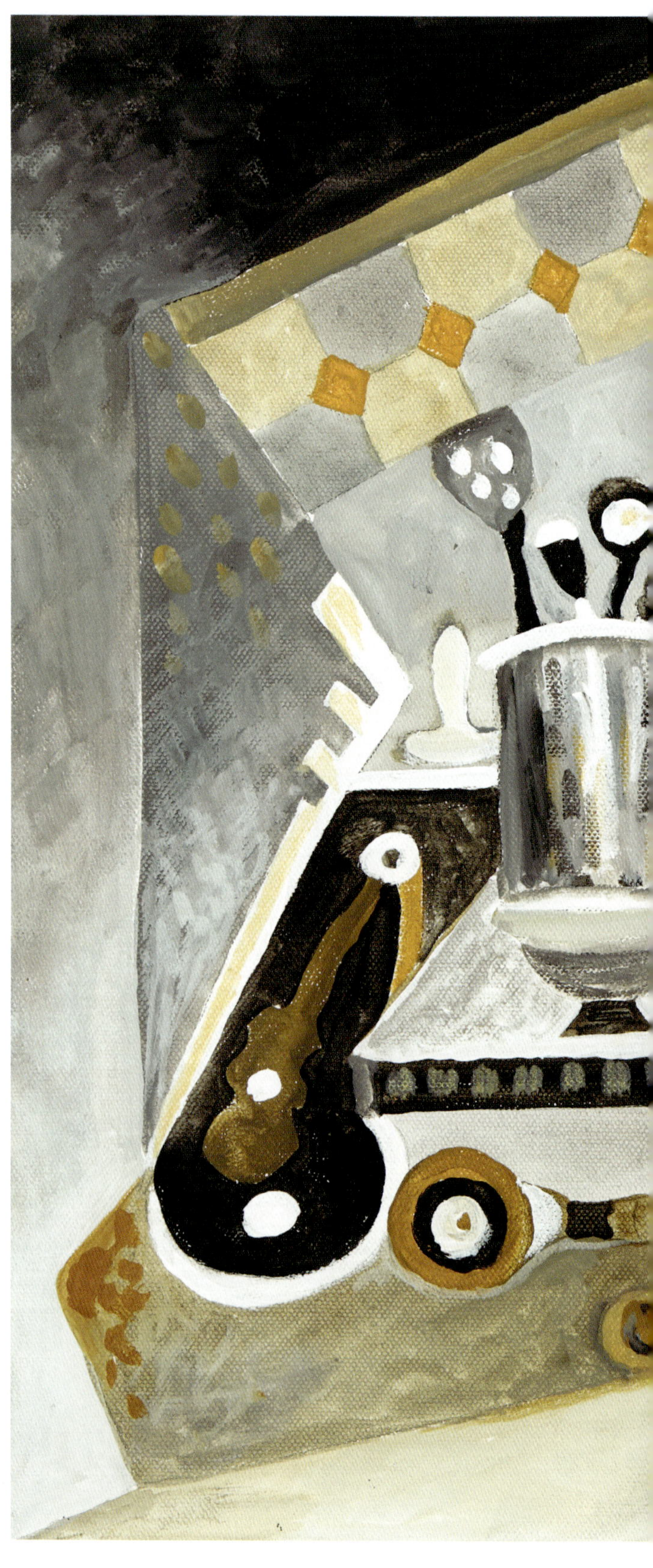

Gray Buffet, 2007

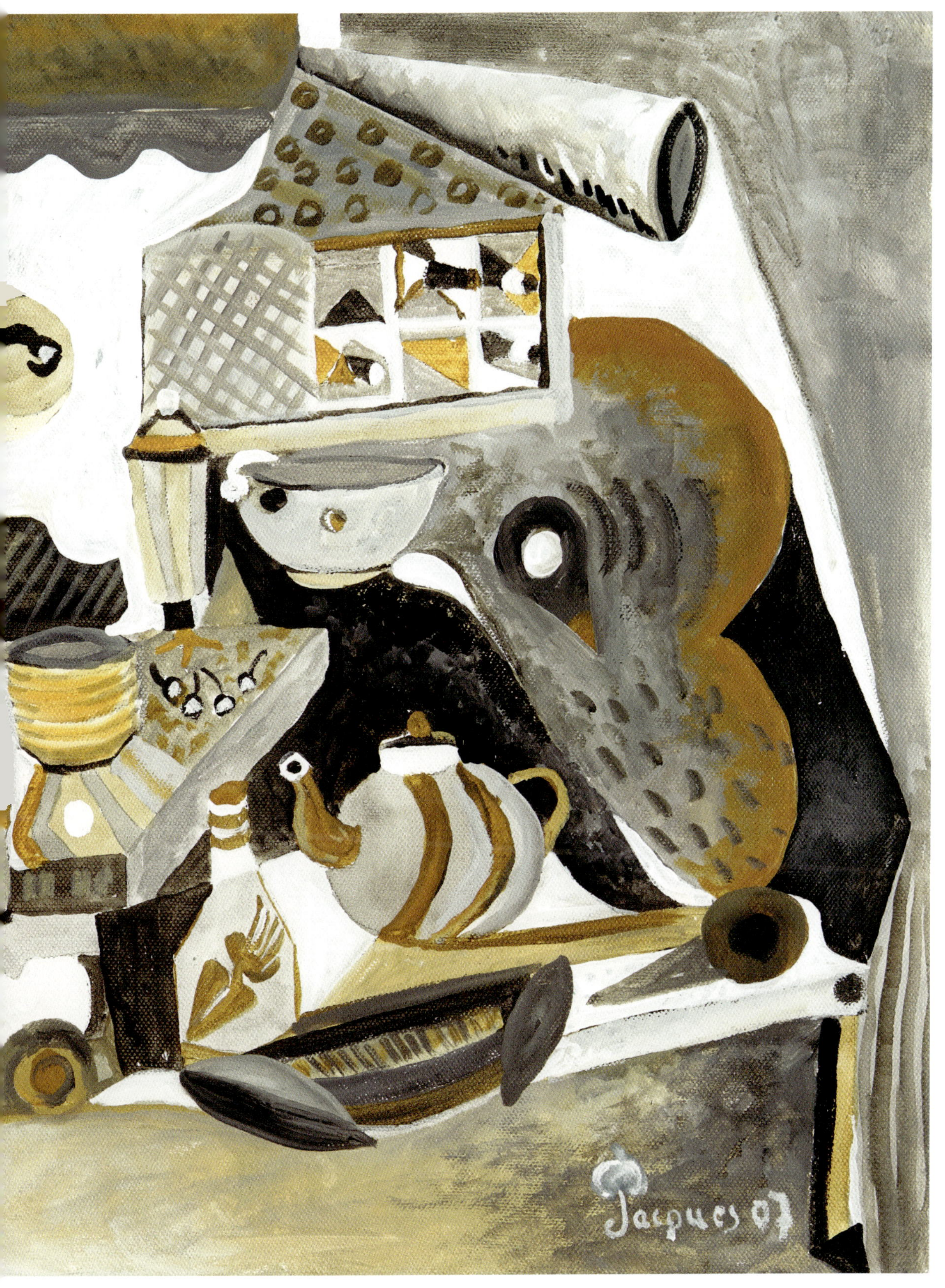
Jacques 07

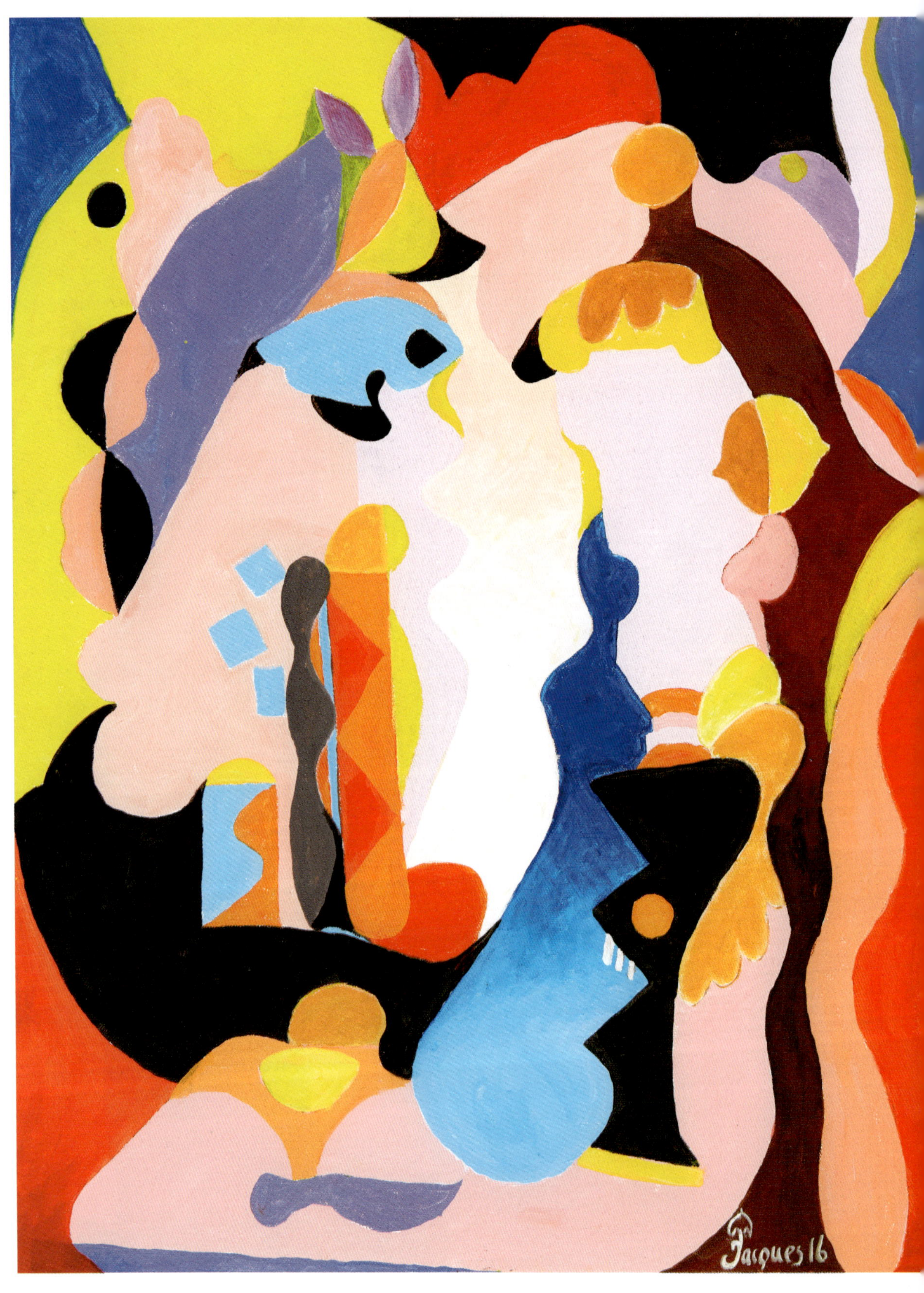
Jacques 16

PORK ROAST with RATATOUILLE

A pork butt is actually meat that is cut from the shoulder of the pig. The story is that in colonial New England, the shoulder cut was stored and distributed in barrels known as butts, and somehow the name stuck. It is a cut with some fat, which makes it flavorful, and in this recipe, the long, slow cooking makes it very moist and tender. Cooking the vegetables at the same time in a ratatouille makes this an easy one-pot meal.

Serves 4

1 bone-in pork shoulder butt roast (about 2 pounds)

1 teaspoon salt

1 teaspoon freshly ground black pepper

4 to 6 garlic cloves, peeled

½ teaspoon herbes de Provence or Italian seasoning

1 onion (about 10 ounces), cut into 1-inch dice

1 small eggplant, cut into 2-inch dice (about 12 ounces)

1 zucchini, cut into 2-inch dice (about 10 ounces)

1 large ripe tomato (about 10 ounces), cut into 1-inch dice

1 tablespoon chopped fresh chives, for garnish

▸ Preheat the oven to 275°F.

▸ Sprinkle the pork butt with half of the salt and pepper, rubbing it in well. Cut 2 of the cloves of garlic into five or six wedges and, using a small sharp knife, make five or six slits in the pork. Insert a wedge of garlic into each slit. Heat a Dutch oven over medium-high heat and, when hot, place the garlic-studded pork fat side down in the pot. Cook, turning frequently, until it is golden brown on all sides, 15 to 20 minutes.

▸ When the pork is browned all over, sprinkle it with the herbes de Provence. Add the onion, eggplant, zucchini, and tomato. Roughly chop the remaining garlic cloves and add them to the Dutch oven. Season with the remaining salt and pepper and cover. Place in the oven and cook until the pork is very tender, 1½ to 2 hours.

▸ Remove the cooked pork from the Dutch oven and let it rest for 10 minutes. Using a large spoon, transfer the vegetables and some of the cooking liquid to a serving platter. Slice the pork into thick slices and arrange on top. Sprinkle with chives and serve.

Facing page: *Shapes in Pink,* 2016

PORK KIDNEYS in RED SAUCE

Although some people shy away from organ meats, these pork kidneys are an excellent choice for a tasty, no-hassle dinner. Here I utilize readily accessible ingredients from around my kitchen to make this simple meal. Kidneys cook very quickly—just a minute or so on each side—making this a great choice for an on-the-fly supper on busy nights. I encourage you to give it a try. There is a layer of sinew in the kidney that has to be removed. Put your knife in the center of the kidney and cut down until you feel the sinew, then slide the knife out. Do the same in the other direction, then flip the kidney over and repeat. You will end up with four pieces of kidney, kind of like fillets.

Serves 2 to 3

2 tablespoons plus 1 teaspoon olive oil

2 pork kidneys, cleaned (about 8 ounces each)

¼ teaspoon salt

¼ teaspoon freshly ground black pepper

½ cup chopped onion

2 teaspoons chopped garlic

3 tablespoons white wine

⅓ cup spicy tomato juice, such as V8

2 tablespoons chopped fresh flat-leaf parsley

▸ Heat a large skillet (not nonstick) over high heat until very hot. Add 2 tablespoons of the olive oil. Season the kidneys with the salt and pepper and sauté 1½ minutes on each side. Transfer to a plate and let rest a few minutes. The kidney should be pink inside. Add the remaining teaspoon of oil to the pan and sauté the onion and garlic for 1 minute. Add the wine and cook for 30 seconds to 1 minute. Add the tomato juice and cook for an additional 2 minutes to reduce. Pour the sauce over the kidneys, garnish with parsley, and serve.

Facing page: *Kitchen Jumble,* 2022

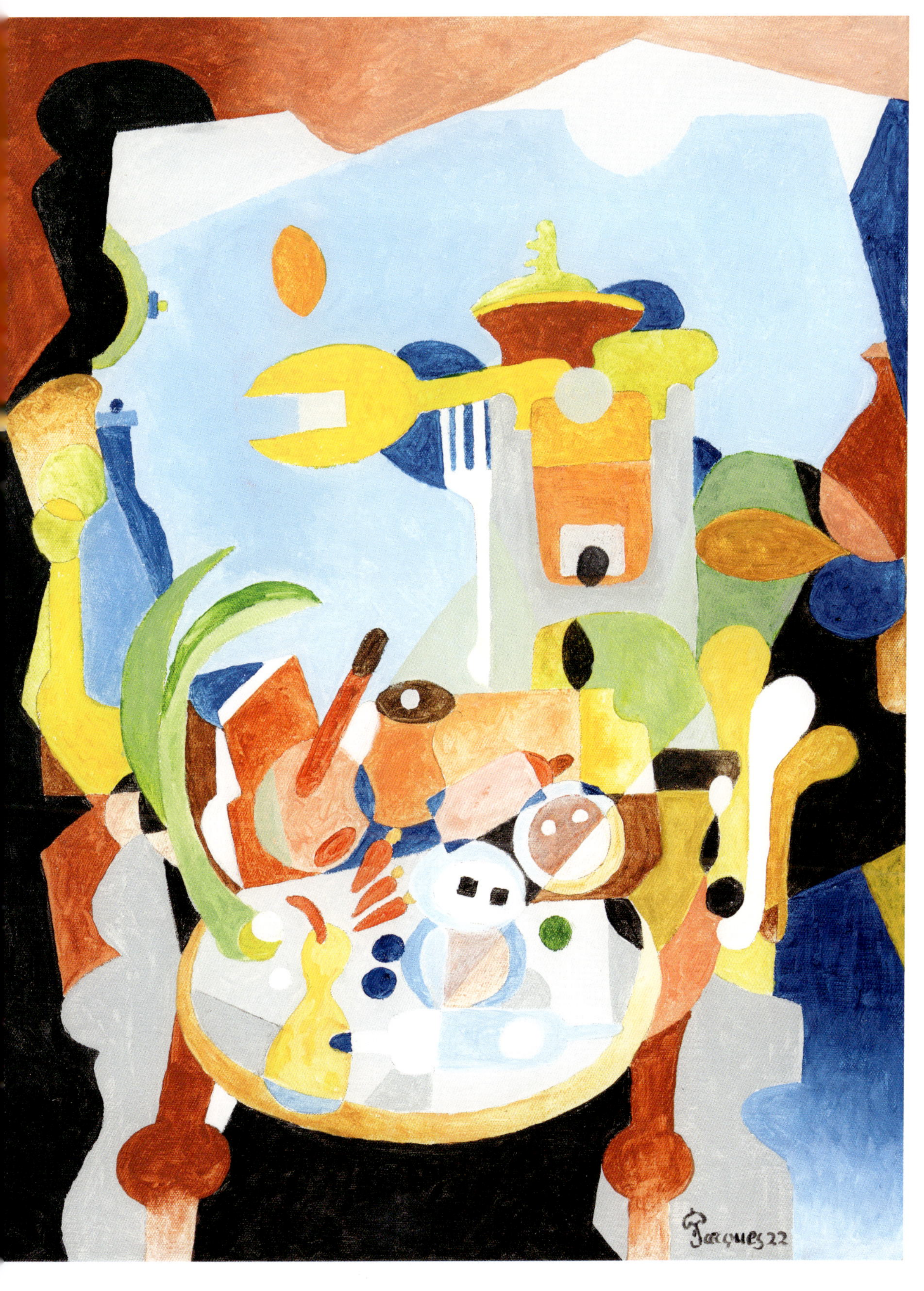
Jacques22

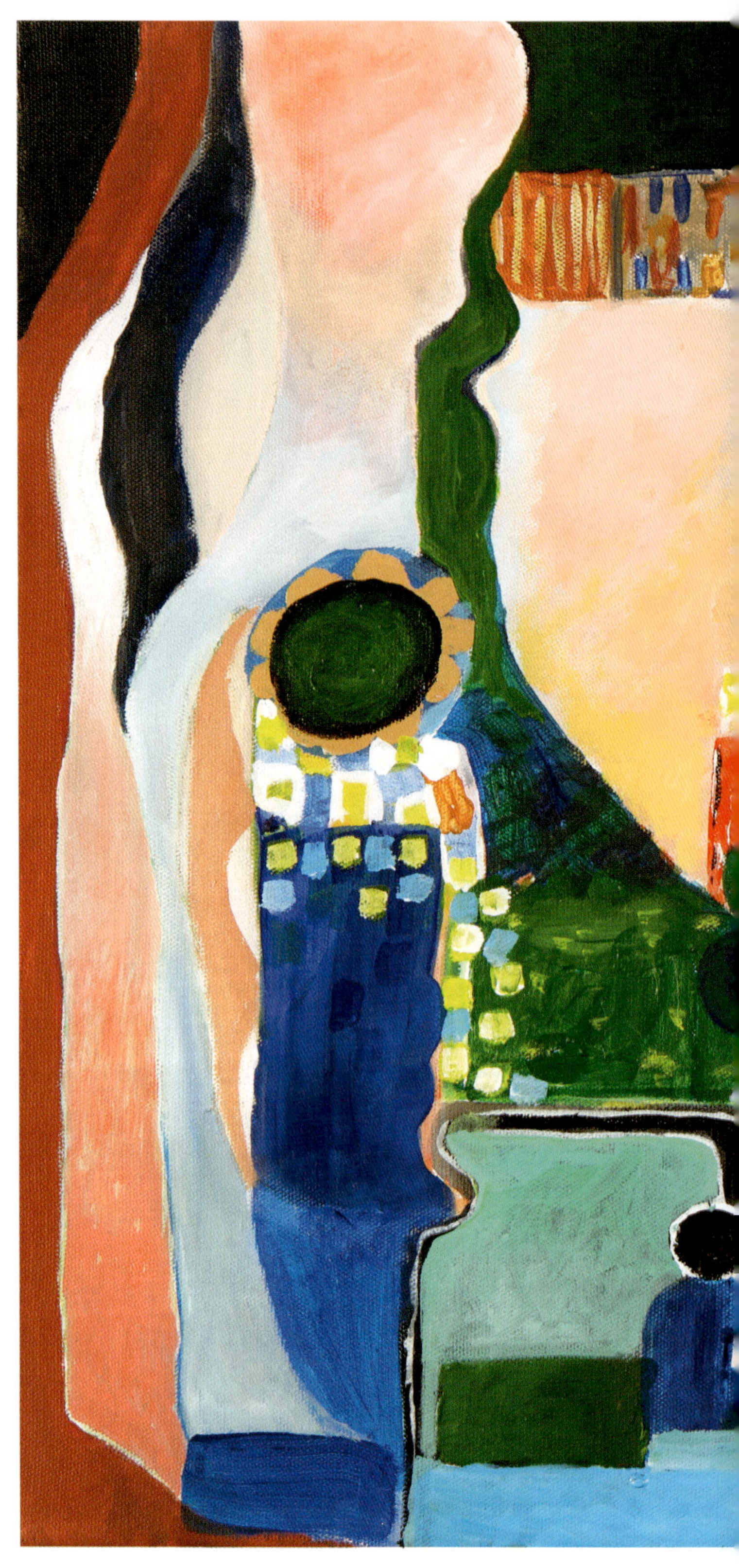

Le Pique-nique, 2016

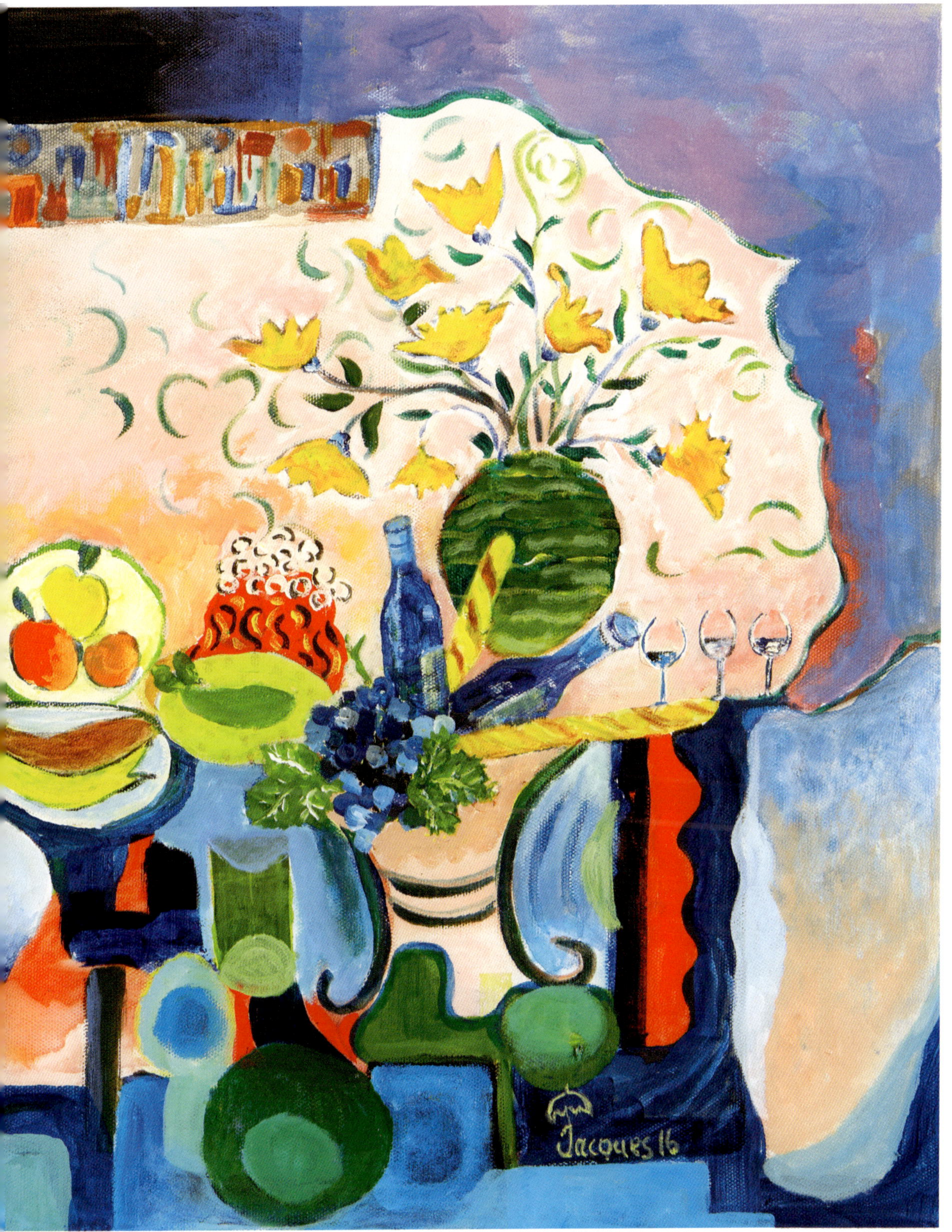
Jacques 16

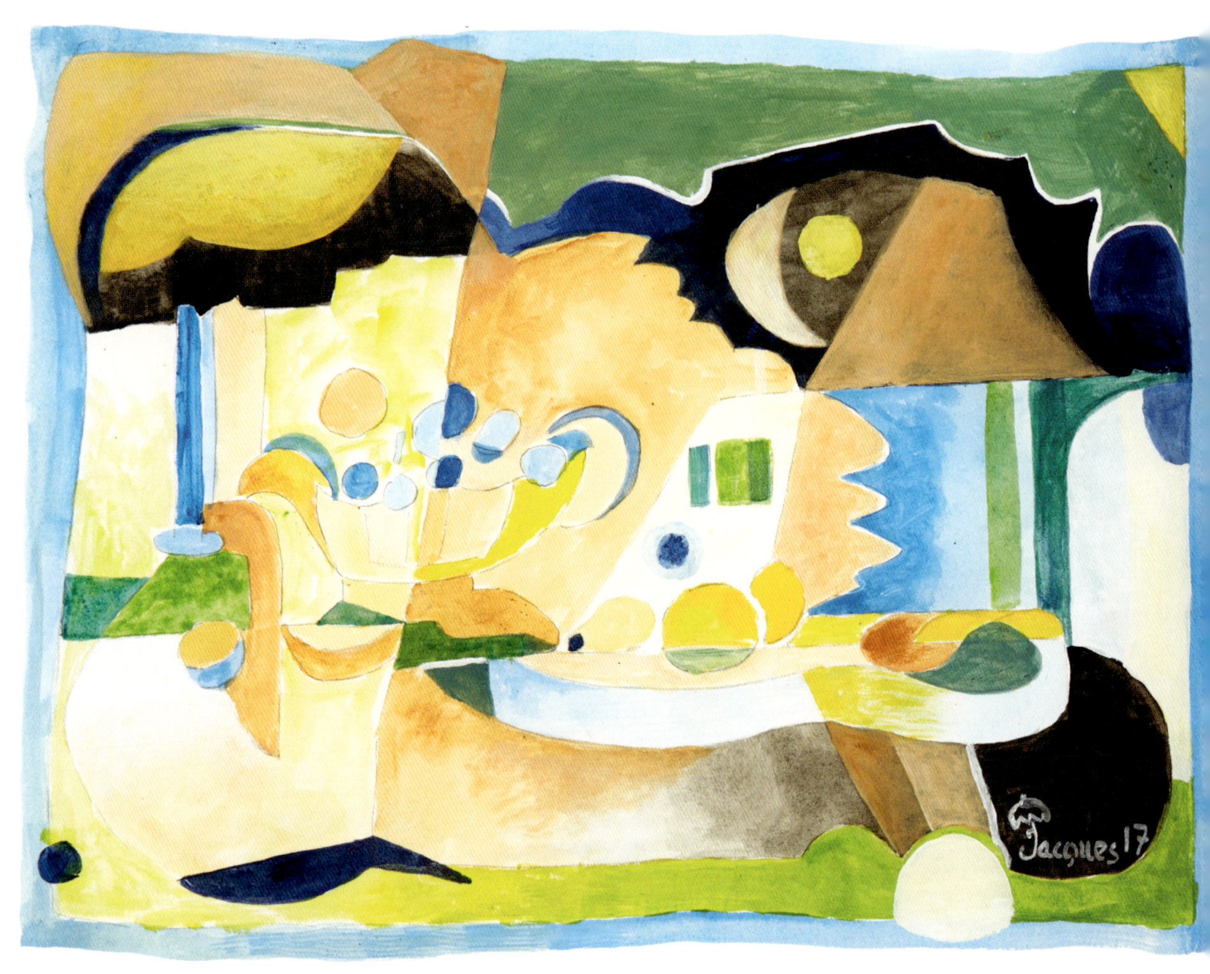

Sideboard 2, 2017

PORK TENDERLOIN with PRUNES

I like to cook pork tenderloin with prunes; it's a classic flavor combination. Pork tenderloin tends to be inexpensive and is easy to cook, and there are many ways to customize it to your liking. While it is often roasted whole, I sometimes like to cut it into steaks, sauté it, and serve it with a sauce. Here is one way I enjoy preparing it at my house—it would be very good with a side of mashed potatoes, pasta, or boiled semolina.

Serves 2

2 tablespoons butter

1 teaspoon olive oil

2 (4-ounce) steaks cut from 1 pork tenderloin (about 2 inches thick)

1/4 teaspoon salt

1/4 teaspoon freshly ground black pepper

1/2 teaspoon grated garlic

10 prunes

2 teaspoons Worcestershire sauce

1/2 cup tomato juice, such as V8

1 tablespoon chopped fresh chives

▸ Heat the butter and oil in a skillet until very hot. Season the pork on both sides with the salt and pepper. Add it to the hot skillet and cook for 3 to 4 minutes on each side, then transfer it to a plate and keep warm—it should be slightly pink inside. Add the garlic to the pan and cook for 30 seconds. Add the prunes, Worcestershire sauce, and tomato juice and bring to a boil. Boil gently for 1 minute. Pour the sauce over the pork, garnish with chives, and serve.

PETITS FILETS MIGNONS of PORK in PORT WINE

In this recipe, a fillet of pork is cut into small filets mignons, briefly sautéed, and served with a rich port wine sauce flavored with thyme.

Serves 4

- **1 tablespoon butter**
- **1 tablespoon olive oil**
- **1 large pork fillet (about 1¼ pounds), cut into 4 steaks**
- **¼ teaspoon salt**
- **¼ teaspoon freshly ground black pepper**
- **⅓ cup port wine**
- **½ cup chicken stock**
- **1½ tablespoons ketchup**
- **1 teaspoon chopped fresh thyme**

▸ Preheat the oven to 180°F.

▸ Heat the butter and oil in a large saucepan. Meanwhile, sprinkle the steaks with the salt and pepper. When the butter and oil are hot, arrange the steaks in one layer in the saucepan and cook them over high heat for 2½ minutes on each side.

▸ Transfer the steaks to a gratin dish and place them in the oven to keep warm while you finish the recipe.

▸ Add the port wine to the drippings in the saucepan, bring the mixture to a boil, and cook it over high heat for about 1 minute. Add the stock and ketchup and cook for 2 to 3 minutes. Add the thyme and mix well.

▸ At serving time, pour the juices accumulated around the filet in the port sauce, and stir to combine. Place one small pork steak on each of four plates and spoon some sauce around them. Serve immediately.

Facing page: *Blue Monochrome,* 2020

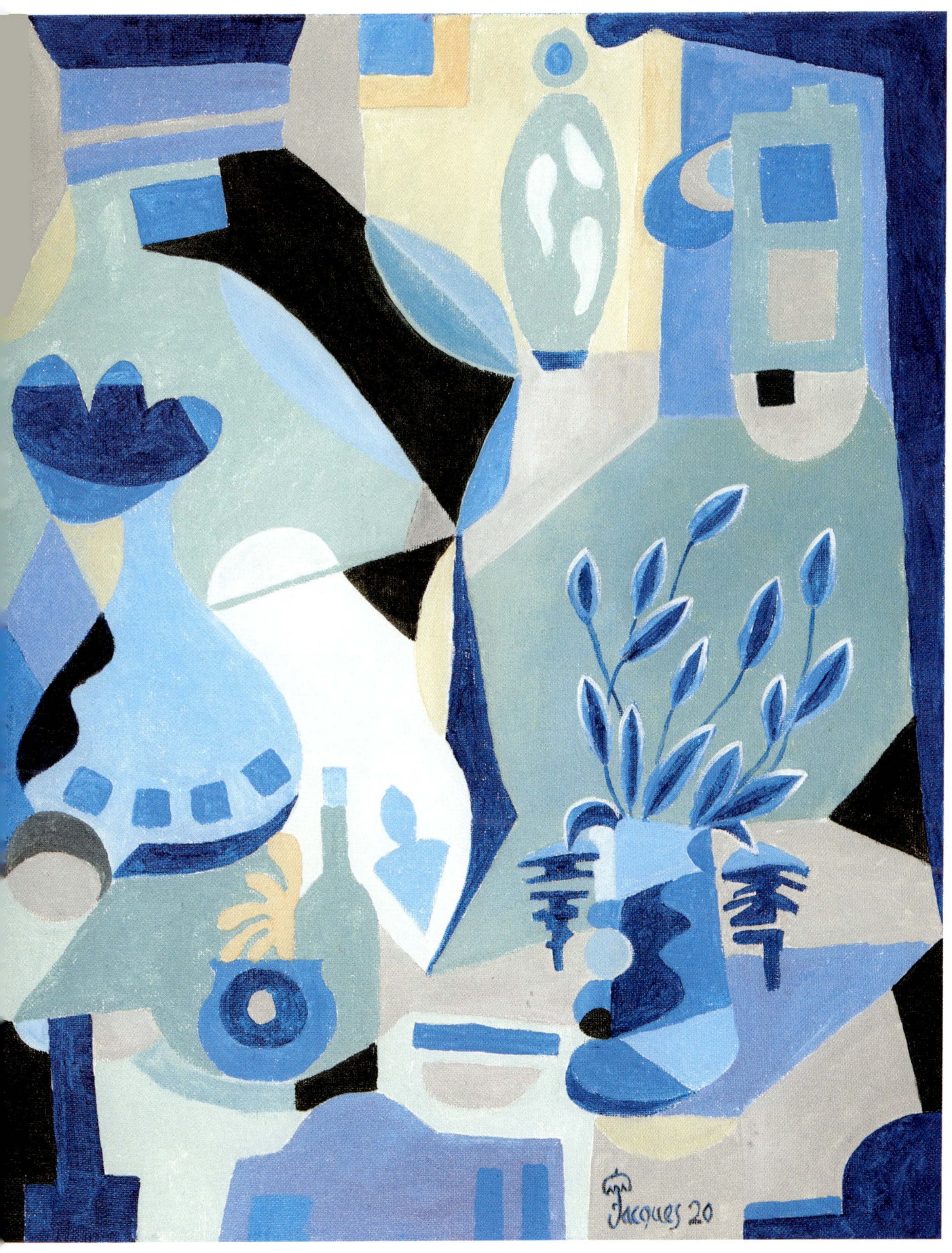
Jacques 20

TOURNEDOS of BEEF in MUSHROOM, MUSTARD & RED WINE SAUCE

Well-trimmed tournedos of beef—small, thick, round slices of meat that are usually cut from the tip of the tenderloin—are sautéed and served here on croutons in the classical manner. A light but flavorful sauce, made by incorporating reconstituted shiitake mushrooms, red wine, and mustard into the meat drippings and mushroom soaking liquid, lends a modern touch to this old favorite.

Serves 4

1 ounce dried shiitake mushrooms (6 to 8 mushrooms)

1 cup hot tap water

2 teaspoons canola or peanut oil

4 slices thin white sandwich bread

2 tablespoons butter

4 completely trimmed beef fillet steaks (1¼ inches thick; about 5 ounces each)

½ teaspoon salt

½ teaspoon freshly ground black pepper

½ cup dry red wine

2 tablespoons ketchup

1 tablespoon dry mustard

▸ Preheat the oven to 400°F.

▸ Place the mushrooms in a small bowl, cover them with the hot water, and set them aside to soak for at least 1 hour.

▸ Meanwhile, spread the oil lightly over the surface of a baking sheet. Using a round cookie cutter about 3 inches in diameter, cut a round crouton from each of the four slices of bread. Press the croutons lightly into the oil on the tray, then turn them over so they are oiled on both sides. Bake the croutons for about 10 minutes, until they are nicely browned on both sides and crisp. Set the croutons aside. Reduce the oven temperature to 175°F (if your oven does not reach 175°F, set as low as possible).

▸ After the mushrooms have soaked, drain them, reserving the soaking liquid (about ½ cup) in a bowl. Remove and discard the tough stems from the mushrooms and cut the mushroom caps into ½-inch pieces. (You should have about ¾ cup.) Transfer the soaking liquid to another bowl, pouring it slowly and discarding the sandy residue in the bottom of the original bowl. Set the liquid aside.

▸ At cooking time, heat the butter in a large skillet. Sprinkle the beef fillets (tournedos) with half of the salt and pepper and place them in the skillet. Arrange the mushroom pieces around them and sauté the tournedos over medium to high heat for about 2½ minutes on each side for medium-rare. Transfer the tournedos to a warm platter and set them aside to rest in the warm oven while you make the sauce.

▸ To the mushrooms in the skillet, add the reserved mushroom liquid along with the wine, ketchup, dry mustard, and remaining salt and pepper. Bring the mixture to a boil and boil gently for 3 to 4 minutes, until the sauce thickens slightly. (You should have about 1 cup of sauce.)

▸ Place a crouton in the center of each of four warmed dinner plates and place a tournedos on top of each crouton. Coat the meat with the sauce and spoon some of the sauce around the meat. Serve immediately.

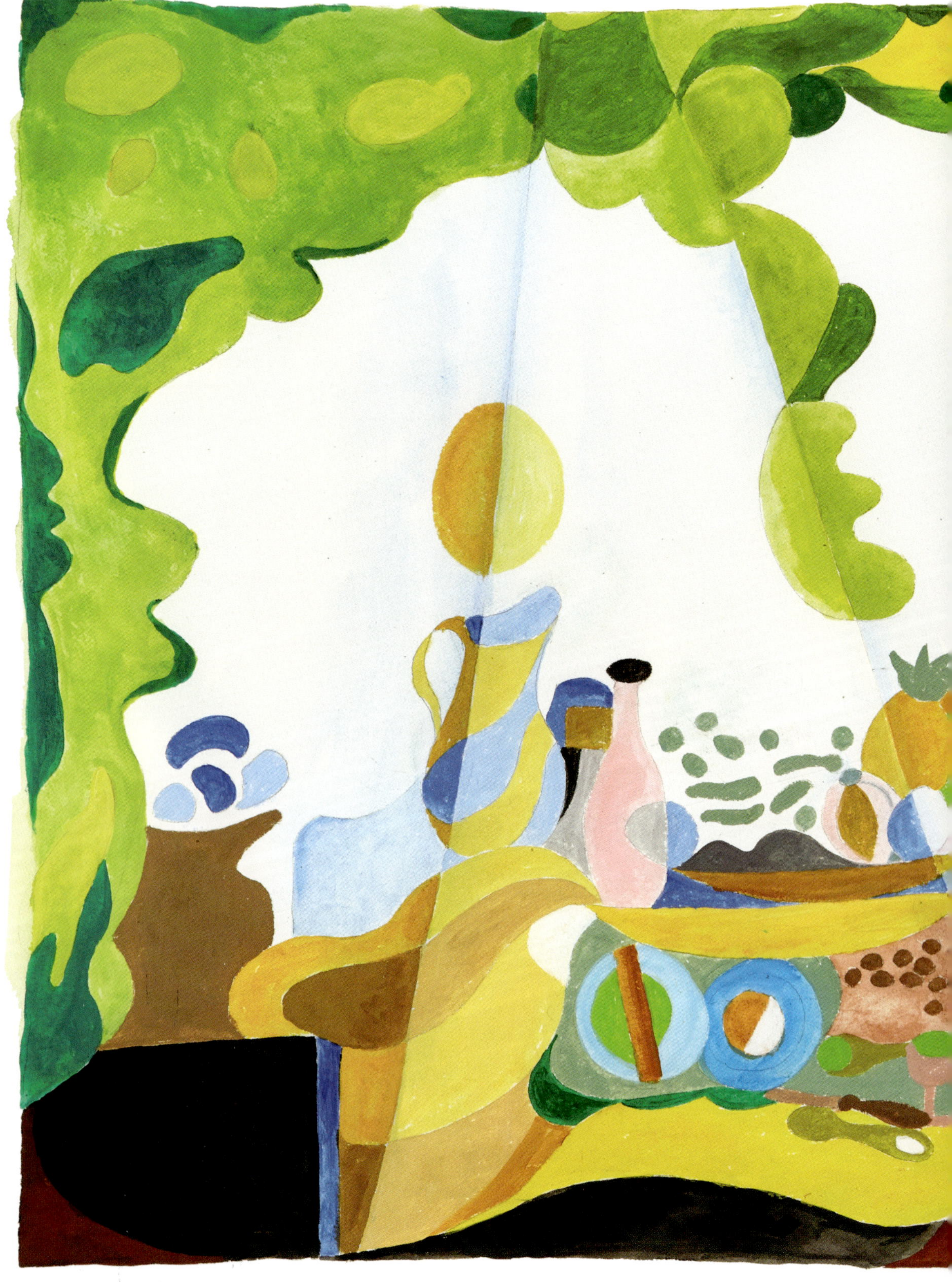

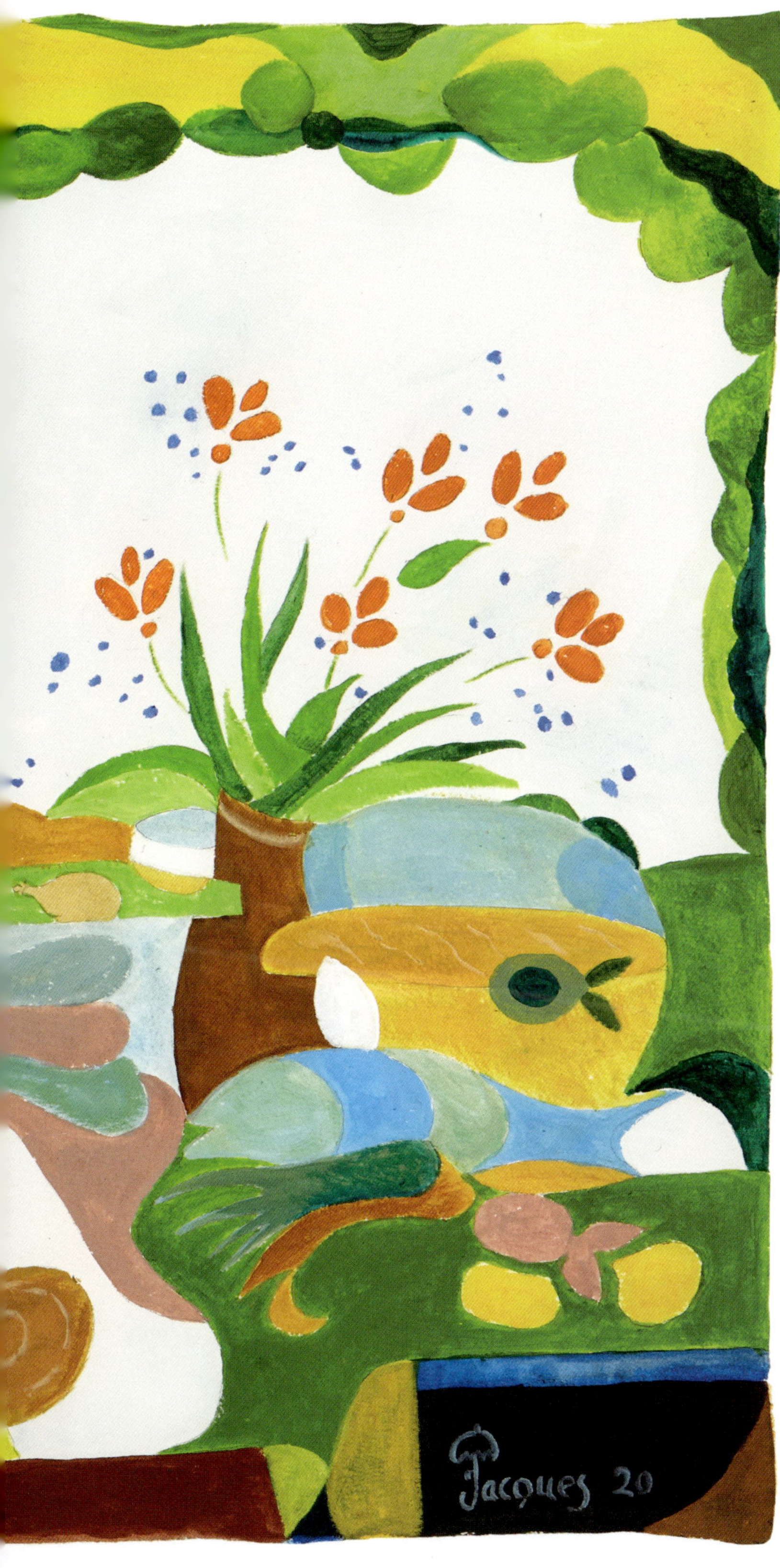

Picnic in the Woods, 2020

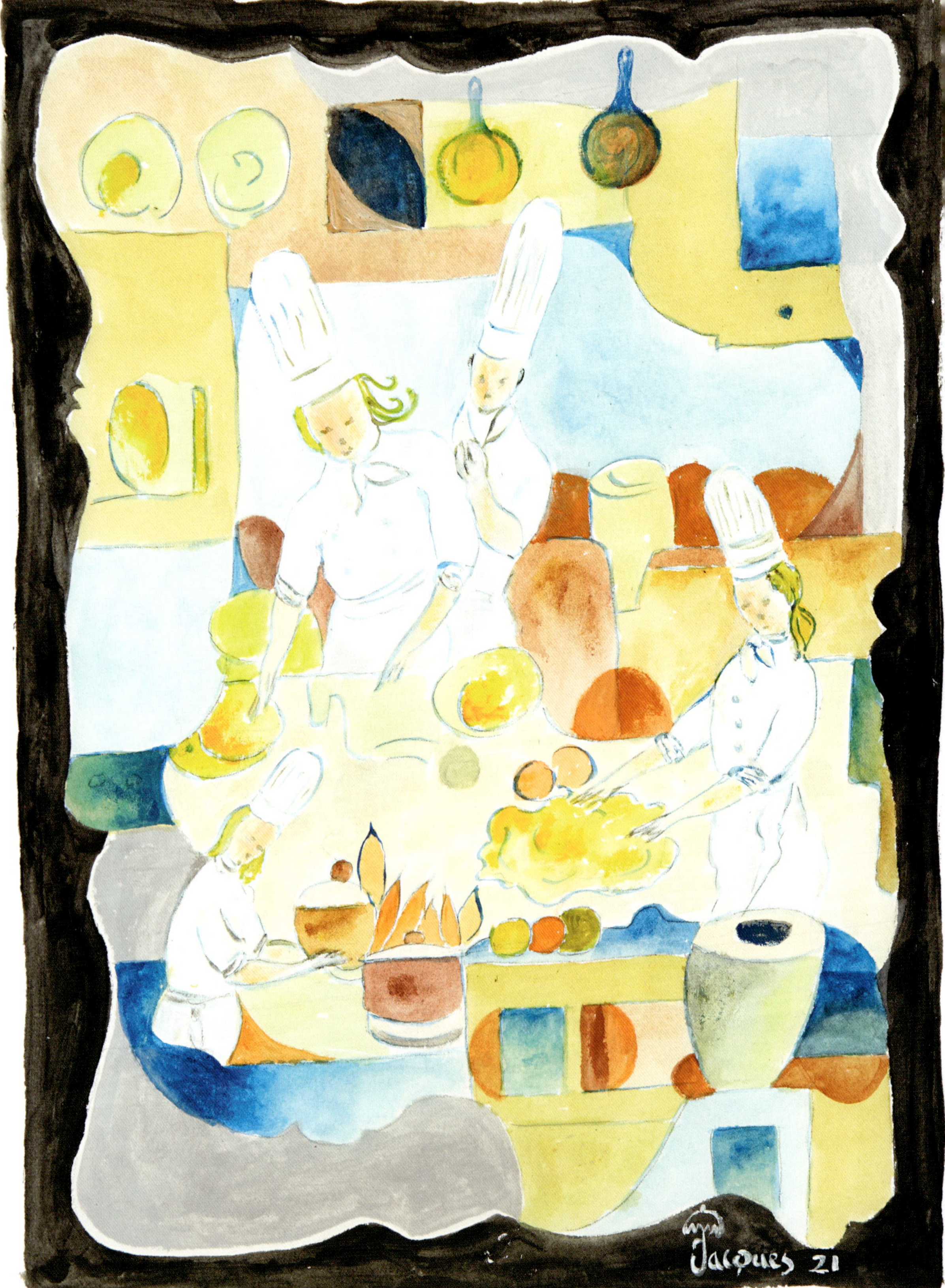
Jacques 21

FILLET of BEEF STROGANOFF with ZUCCHINI

This recipe can be ready in 5 minutes with a wonderfully delectable result. The beef fillet is expensive, but a small portion goes a long way—you need only 4 to 5 ounces per person. Make sure you use a very large, very hot skillet. I like to serve it with bright, just-tender cubed zucchini.

Serves 2

1 beef fillet (about 8 to 10 ounces), trimmed of all fat and sinews

1½ teaspoons smoked paprika

½ teaspoon salt, plus more for the zucchini

2 tablespoons butter

1 tablespoon olive oil

1½ cups coarsely julienned mushrooms

¼ teaspoon freshly ground black pepper

2 tablespoons medium or amontillado sherry

⅓ cup sour cream or crème fraîche

2 cups ¾-inch-cubed zucchini

1½ tablespoons olive oil

2 tablespoons chopped fresh chives

▸ Cut the fillet into ½-inch slices, then slice into thick strips or julienne about ½-inch thick. Sprinkle with the paprika and salt. Heat the butter and oil in a large skillet over high heat until lightly brown. Add the beef, spreading the meat in one layer so that it browns, and cook for 1 minute. Add the mushrooms and pepper and continue to cook on high heat, tossing occasionally, for 1½ minutes. Add the sherry and cook for 30 seconds. Add the sour cream, mixing well. Bring the whole mixture to a good boil and then remove from the heat.

▸ While the beef is cooking, place the zucchini in a microwavable glass bowl and sprinkle lightly with salt. Microwave on high for about 2 minutes, or until the zucchini is just tender but still crunchy. Drizzle with the olive oil and, using a slotted spoon, tip the zucchini onto a warm serving platter, making sure to discard any released liquid from the zucchini in the bowl.

▸ Spread the zucchini to the edges of the platter and spoon the steak and sauce into the center. Sprinkle with chives and serve immediately.

Facing page: *Busy Kitchen,* 2021

GRILLED STEAK with ZUCCHINI & ANCHOVY BUTTER

Part of what makes this steak visually appealing is the technique known as *quadrillage*, turning the meat on the grill to achieve a square marking. To do this you have to use an outdoor grill or a ridged grill pan, and it must be very hot. I garnish it simply with some zucchini and anchovy butter for extra flavor.

Serves 1

ANCHOVY BUTTER

½ stick (2 ounces) butter, at room temperature

1 tablespoon anchovy paste

1 tablespoon chopped fresh flat-leaf parsley

1 teaspoon lemon juice

¼ teaspoon salt

¼ teaspoon freshly ground black pepper

1 trimmed sirloin steak (1¼ inch thick; 8 to 10 ounces)

1 zucchini (about 6 ounces), halved and each half cut into 2 pieces

¼ teaspoon salt

¼ teaspoon freshly ground black pepper

1 tablespoon olive oil

▸ To make the anchovy butter, combine the butter, anchovy paste, parsley, lemon juice, salt, and pepper in a bowl and mix well with a whisk. Place on a piece of plastic wrap and mold into a log. This can be made ahead of time and will last for a few weeks in the refrigerator and months in the freezer. It is great served with any grilled meat, poultry, or fish.

▸ Heat an outdoor grill or grill pan over high heat for at least 5 minutes, until very hot. Season the steak and zucchini on both sides with the salt and pepper and coat with the olive oil. Add the steak to the hot pan with the narrow end facing you and cook, undisturbed, for 1 minute. Then turn it to the other side but in the same position, so that corresponding marks are made on the reverse. After another minute, turn it back to the original side, but this time have the wider side facing you. Let it cook for another minute, then do the same on the reverse, for four times total, marked beautifully on both sides with the quadrillage. You can also mark the zucchini the same way. Judge the doneness of your steak by gently nudging it with your finger—a piece of raw meat is very soft. If it gives some bounce back, it is still pretty rare in the center. If it's very hard, it's well done. When it is cooked to your liking, transfer the steak to a plate or cutting board and let it rest for at least 3 to 4 minutes. Place on a plate and garnish with any juice that accumulated while resting. Add the zucchini and top with 1 tablespoon of anchovy butter.

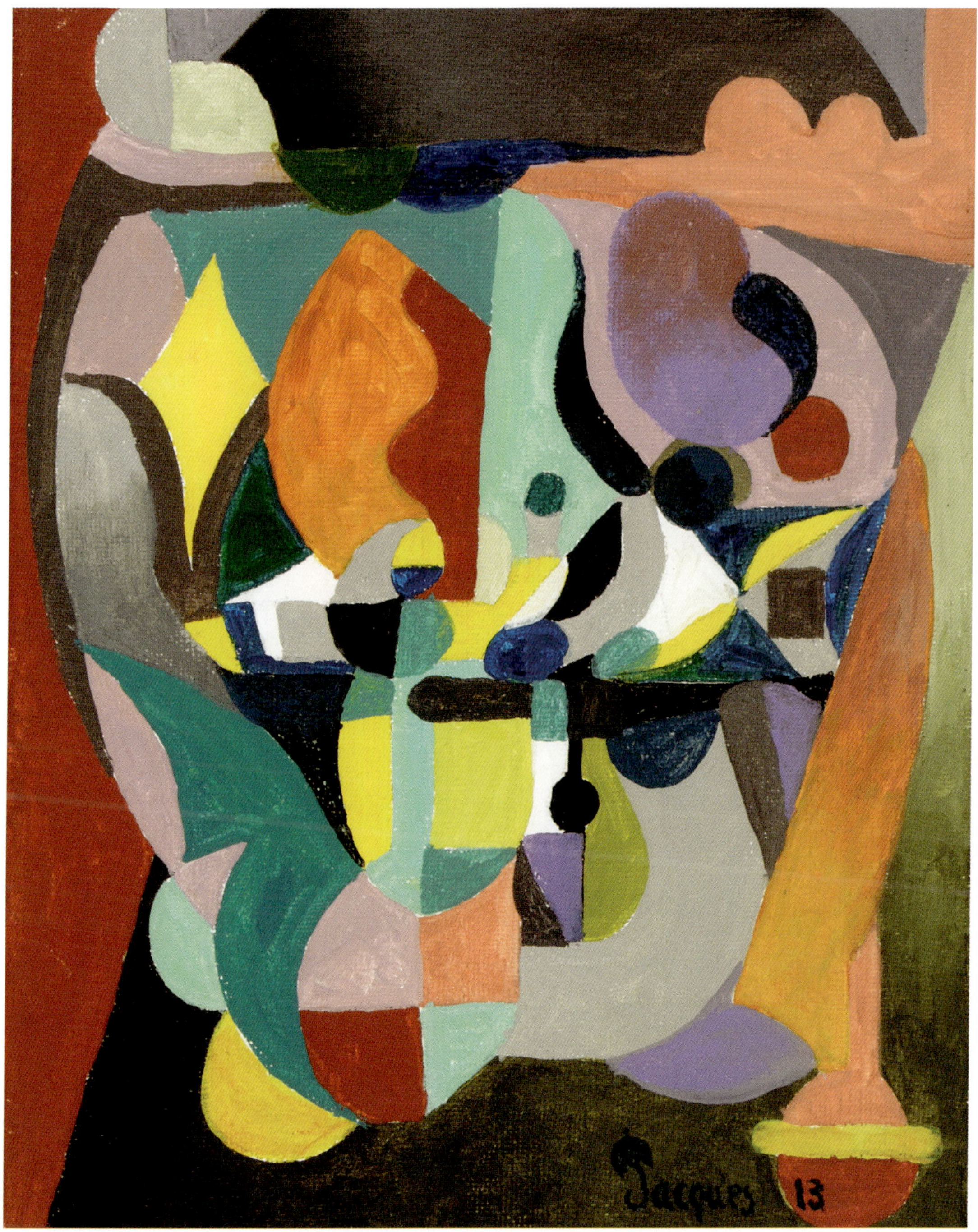

Intricate, 2013

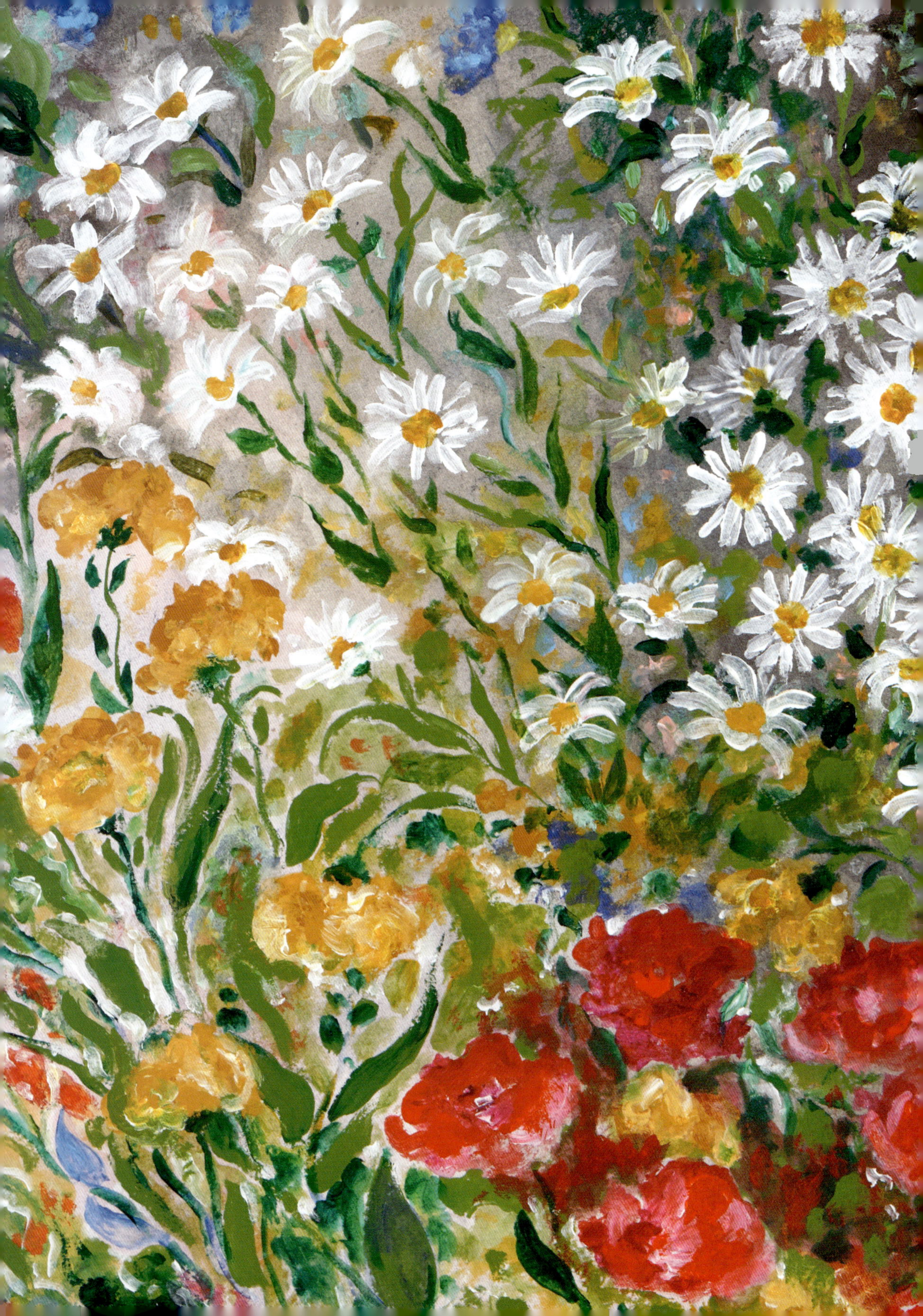

Desserts

ALMOND SHORTBREAD COOKIES

This is a delicious and simple cookie—perfect on its own or as a delicate accompaniment to any fruit dessert.

Makes about 4 dozen medium-size cookies

1½ sticks (6 ounces) butter, softened

½ cup sugar

2 cups all-purpose flour

½ cup blanched almonds, ground to a fine powder in a food processor

¼ teaspoon salt

1½ teaspoons almond extract

1 egg yolk

1 to 2 tablespoons heavy cream (as needed)

⅓ cup whole blanched almonds

▸ Place the butter and sugar in a food processor and process until smooth and creamy. Add the flour and ground almonds to the butter mixture and process a few times. Finally, add the salt, almond extract, and egg yolk and process another few times until well combined. (Note: If the dough seems dry and doesn't come together well, mix in enough of the cream to enable you to form it into a ball.) Refrigerate the dough for at least 1 hour.

▸ When ready to bake the cookies, preheat the oven to 375°F.

▸ Roll out the dough on a lightly floured surface until it is about ¼ inch thick. Cut into desired shapes and arrange on a baking sheet. Press a whole almond into the center of each of the cookies. Bake until cookies are light golden brown around the edges, 14 to 18 minutes, then cool on a rack.

Facing page: *Loose Flowers,* 2019

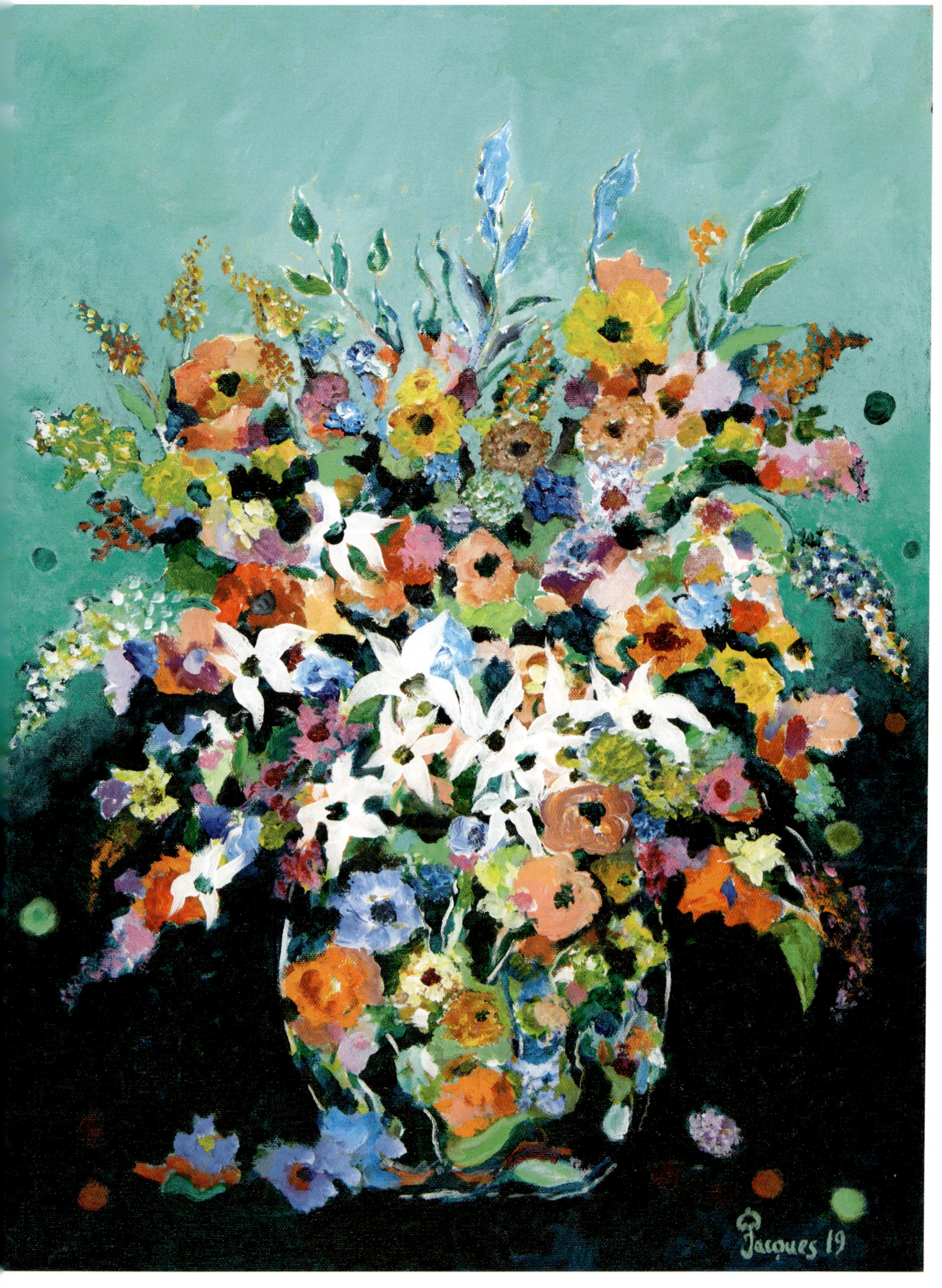
Jacques 19

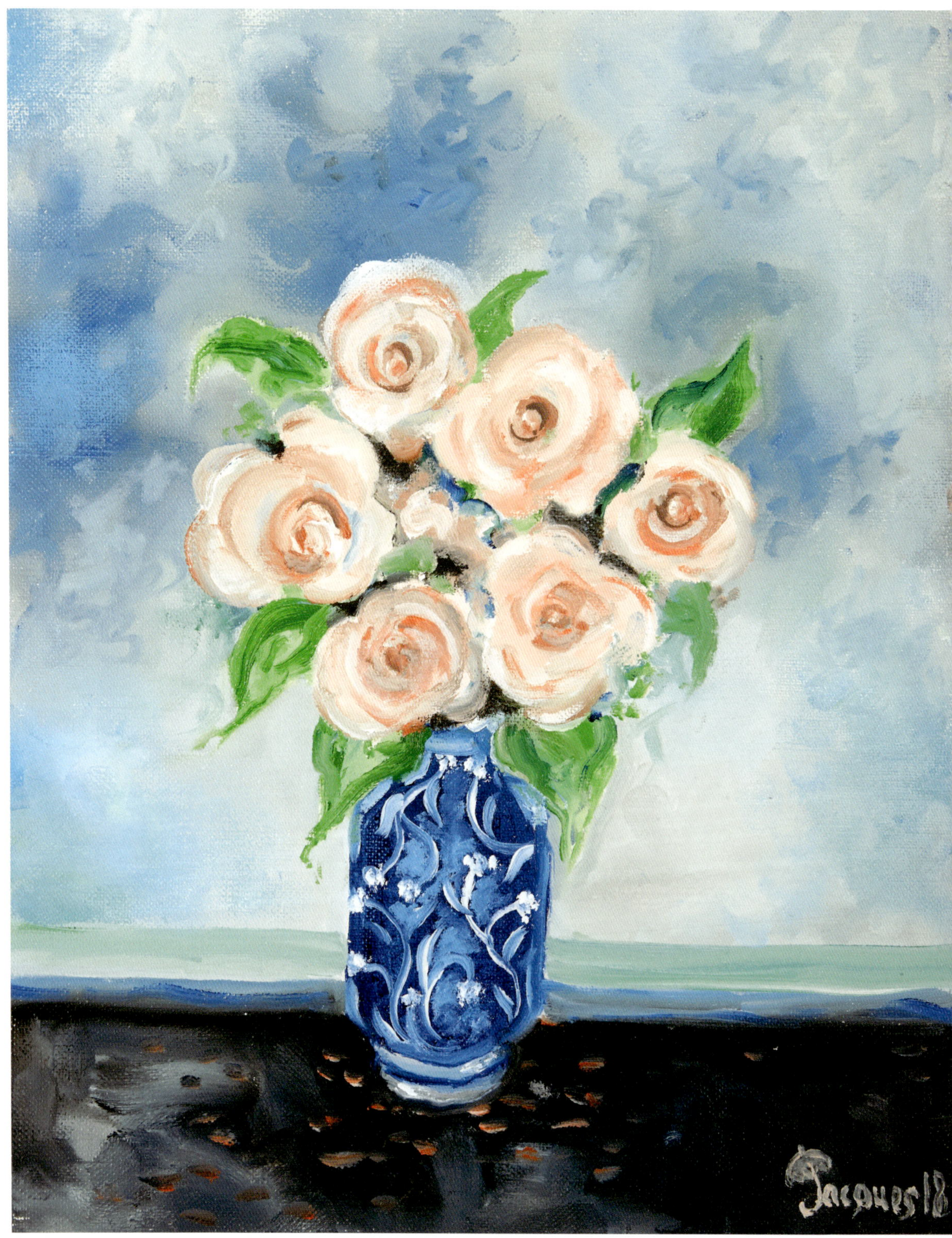

Roses, 2018

CHOCOLATE TREATS

I love to make these treats with my granddaughter, Shorey, for the holidays. Paper cupcake or muffin liners work well and are easy to peel away once the chocolate has set. If you use only nuts and dried fruit in your treats, you can keep them in an airtight container in the refrigerator for a month. However, if you use fresh fruit and mint leaves, they will last only a couple of days.

Makes about 12 treats

4 ounces bittersweet, semisweet, milk, or white chocolate, melted
12 pistachios
12 hazelnuts
12 pine nuts
12 dried cranberries
12 pumpkin seeds
12 fresh raspberries
12 fresh blueberries
Mint leaves (optional)

▸ Arrange up to 12 paper cupcake liners on a baking sheet. Pour about ½ inch of melted chocolate into each liner. Top with a selection of the nuts and fruit to your liking, pressing them into the soft chocolate, and top with a mint leaf, if desired. Refrigerate until set, at least two hours. To serve, peel away the papers and arrange the treats on a plate or tray. Serve as needed.

CREME au CHOCOLAT

This dessert will keep in the refrigerator for at least a week. Be certain to cover it well with plastic wrap; otherwise, the chocolate will absorb other flavors in the refrigerator.

Serves 4

1½ cups whole milk

1 tablespoon instant espresso granules

1 large egg plus 1 egg yolk

3 tablespoons sugar

1½ tablespoons all-purpose flour

5 ounces bittersweet chocolate, broken into a few pieces

1 tablespoon sliced almonds

Cookies, for serving (optional)

▸ Preheat the oven to 400°F.

▸ Bring the milk and instant coffee to a boil in a saucepan.

▸ Meanwhile, place the egg, egg yolk, and sugar in a bowl and mix well. Add the flour and mix it in well.

▸ Whisk about 1 cup of the hot milk and coffee mixture into the egg mixture in the bowl and combine well. Then, pour the contents of the bowl back into the saucepan and bring the mixture to a boil, stirring constantly with a whisk. Boil for 10 seconds.

▸ Transfer the hot mixture to a bowl, add the chocolate pieces, and mix every 2 or 3 minutes, until the chocolate has melted and is mixed in well. Cool, then refrigerate until serving time.

▸ Spread the sliced almonds on a baking sheet and place them in the oven for 6 to 8 minutes, until nicely browned. Set aside.

▸ Divide the cold dessert among four dessert bowls or cups. Sprinkle with sliced almonds and serve with cookies, if desired.

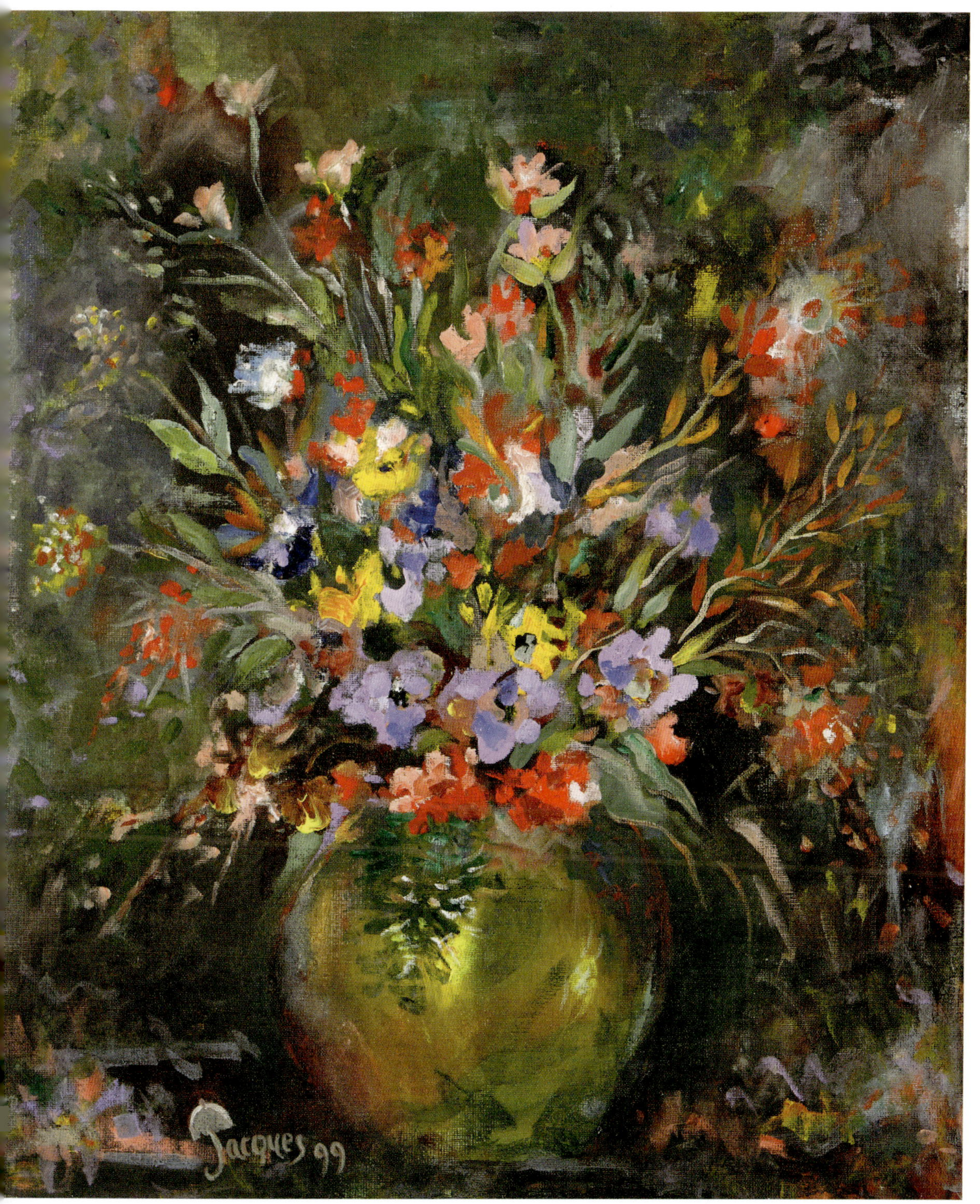

Golden Vase, 1999

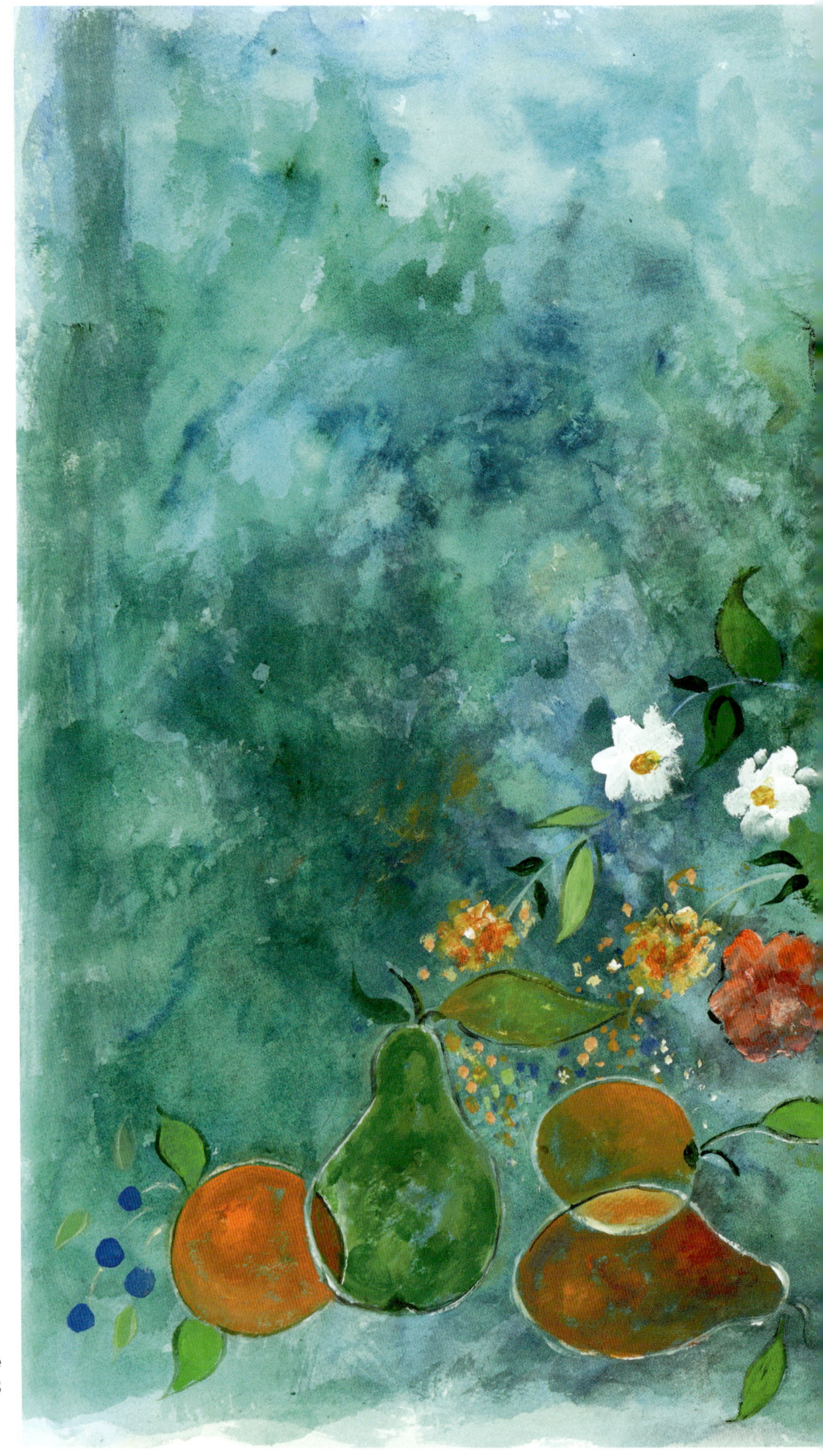

Flowers on Blue Background, 2023

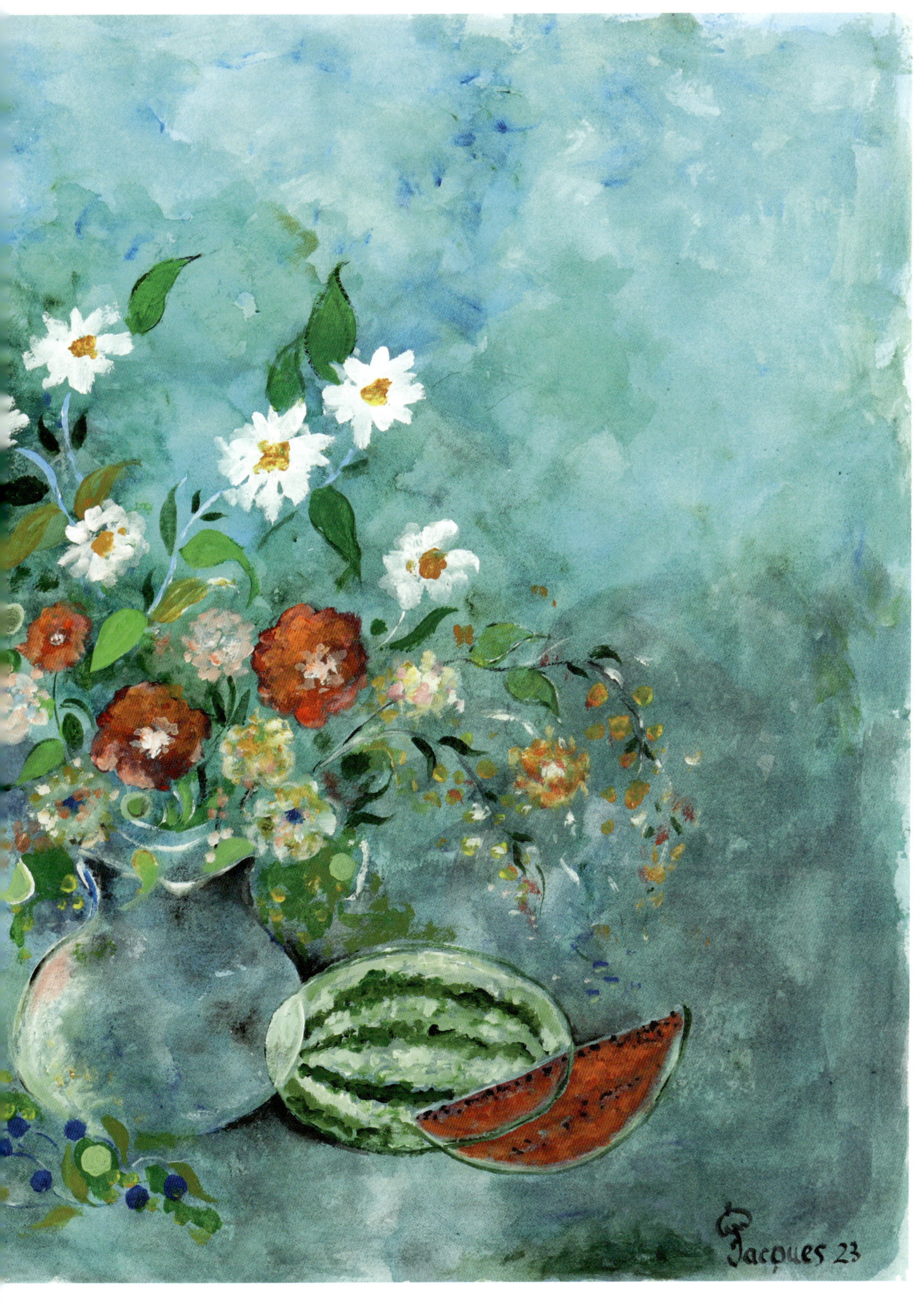
Jacques 23

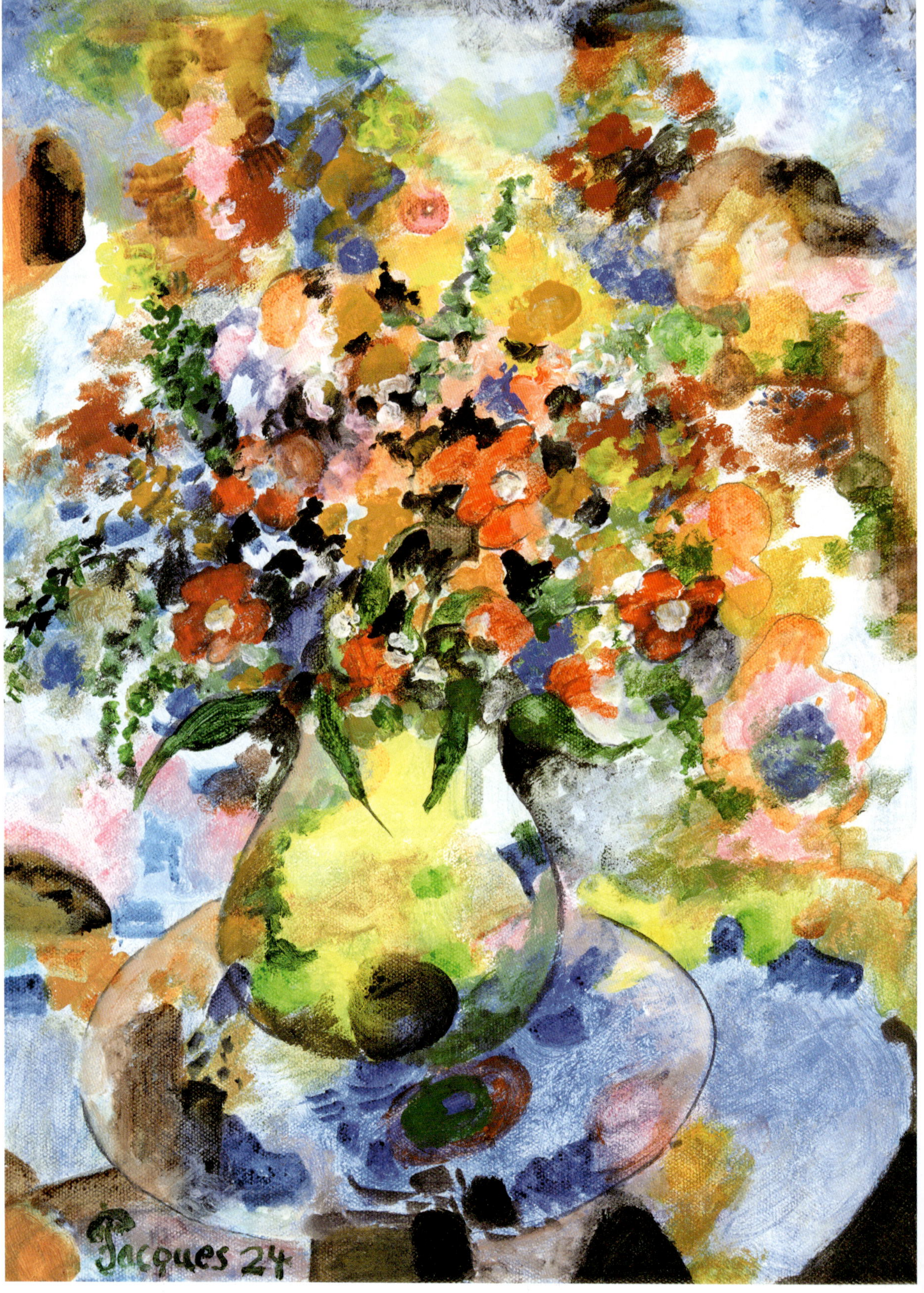
Jacques 24

BREAD PUDDING SOUFFLES with CHOCOLATE-BOURBON SAUCE

This dessert can be made ahead and refrigerated, then reheated at serving time until lukewarm in a regular oven, a microwave oven, or on top of the stove in a skillet, with the molds surrounded by water.

Serves 4

CHOCOLATE SAUCE

1 cup half-and-half, with 1 tablespoon reserved (see below)

2 tablespoons sugar

1 teaspoon cornstarch dissolved in the reserved 1 tablespoon half-and-half (see above)

3 ounces bittersweet chocolate, cut into 1-inch pieces

1 tablespoon bourbon, or 1 teaspoon pure vanilla extract

SOUFFLÉS

½ cup milk

3 thin slices white bread (2 ounces)

2 tablespoons golden raisins

2 tablespoons maple syrup

2 large eggs, separated

1½ teaspoons butter (for buttering the molds)

4 tablespoons seedless raspberry jam

▸ To make the chocolate sauce, place the half-and-half (minus 1 tablespoon) and sugar in a saucepan and bring the mixture to a boil. Add the dissolved cornstarch and bring back to a boil, stirring. Add the chocolate pieces and stir the mixture occasionally until the chocolate is melted. Cool to room temperature and stir in the bourbon. (If making the sauce ahead, refrigerate it, covered, and reheat to room temperature in the microwave at serving time.)

▸ To make the soufflés, preheat the oven to 350°F.

▸ Place the milk in a bowl, add the bread, and let the bread soak in the milk until it is well saturated, soft, and mushy. Add the raisins, maple syrup, and egg yolks and stir until the mixture is well homogenized.

▸ Beat the egg whites in a bowl until they form soft peaks. (They should not be too firm.) Mix the whites into the bread mixture.

▸ Butter four individual 1-cup molds. Place 1 tablespoon of the jam in the bottom of each mold and divide the bread mixture among the molds. Arrange the molds on a tray and bake for about 20 minutes, until just barely set. Remove from the molds and serve lukewarm with the chocolate sauce.

Facing page: *Memorable Bouquet,* 2024

FLAN à la VANILLE with CARAMEL-COGNAC SAUCE

This dessert is a classic crowd-pleaser, a great thing to have in your repertoire. The sauce is flavored with Cognac, but rum or Grand Marnier can be substituted, or the alcohol can be omitted entirely. The delicate part of this recipe is the cooking; the flan is cooked in a water bath that should not boil. If it does, the flan will cook too quickly, and when it is unmolded, the exterior of the custard will look like a sponge, with tiny holes all over it.

Serves 6

CARAMEL-COGNAC SAUCE

¾ cup sugar

2 tablespoons Cognac

1 tablespoon lemon juice

CUSTARD

4 large eggs plus 1 egg yolk

1½ teaspoons pure vanilla extract

⅓ cup sugar

3 cups half-and-half

Cookies, for serving (optional)

▸ Preheat the oven to 350°F.

▸ To make the caramel sauce, mix the sugar and ¼ cup of water together in a small heavy saucepan. Bring to a boil over medium to high heat and boil, uncovered, for 6 to 7 minutes, until the mixture turns a dark blond color. Pour about ¼ cup of the caramel into a 4- to 5-cup soufflé mold and move the mold so the caramel coats the bottom. (There should be just enough caramel to cover the bottom of the mold.)

▸ To the remaining caramel in the pan, add ⅓ cup of water slowly, to prevent splattering. When all the water has been added, mix well with a spoon and bring the mixture back to a boil. Stir again to ensure that all the caramel has melted and there is no thick layer of sugar underneath that might stick to the bottom of the pan. If this occurs, keep stirring until this sugary layer is dissolved.

▸ Transfer the caramel to a bowl and let cool. The mixture will thicken to the consistency of a heavy syrup. When the caramel is cold, add the Cognac and lemon juice and stir well. Reserve until serving time. (The sauce can be made ahead and refrigerated in a jar with a tight-fitting lid for several weeks.)

▸ To make the custard, place the eggs, egg yolk, vanilla, and sugar in a large bowl. Mix well with a whisk, then add the half-and-half and mix again until it is incorporated. Strain the mixture into the caramel-lined soufflé mold and place the mold in a saucepan. Add enough warm tap water to the saucepan so that it extends about halfway up the outside of the mold.

▸ Place the saucepan and mold in the oven and bake for 45 to 55 minutes, until the custard is set in the center. (Check to determine whether it is set by inserting the tip of a paring knife into the center of the custard; if the blade comes out clean, the custard is set, even though it may still look and feel soft in the center.)

▸ Remove the mold from the water and let cool for at least 3 hours (preferably overnight), refrigerated, before unmolding.

▸ To unmold the flan, run a sharp knife around the edge, making sure that the knife does not cut into the flan but follows around the inside wall of the mold. Place a platter on top of the flan and invert it, moving the mold gently to dislodge the custard. You will notice that some liquid will come out of the mold as the flan dislodges; discard this thin caramel and pour some of the thick caramel-Cognac sauce over the custard.

▸ Serve the flan with additional caramel-Cognac sauce and, if desired, some cookies.

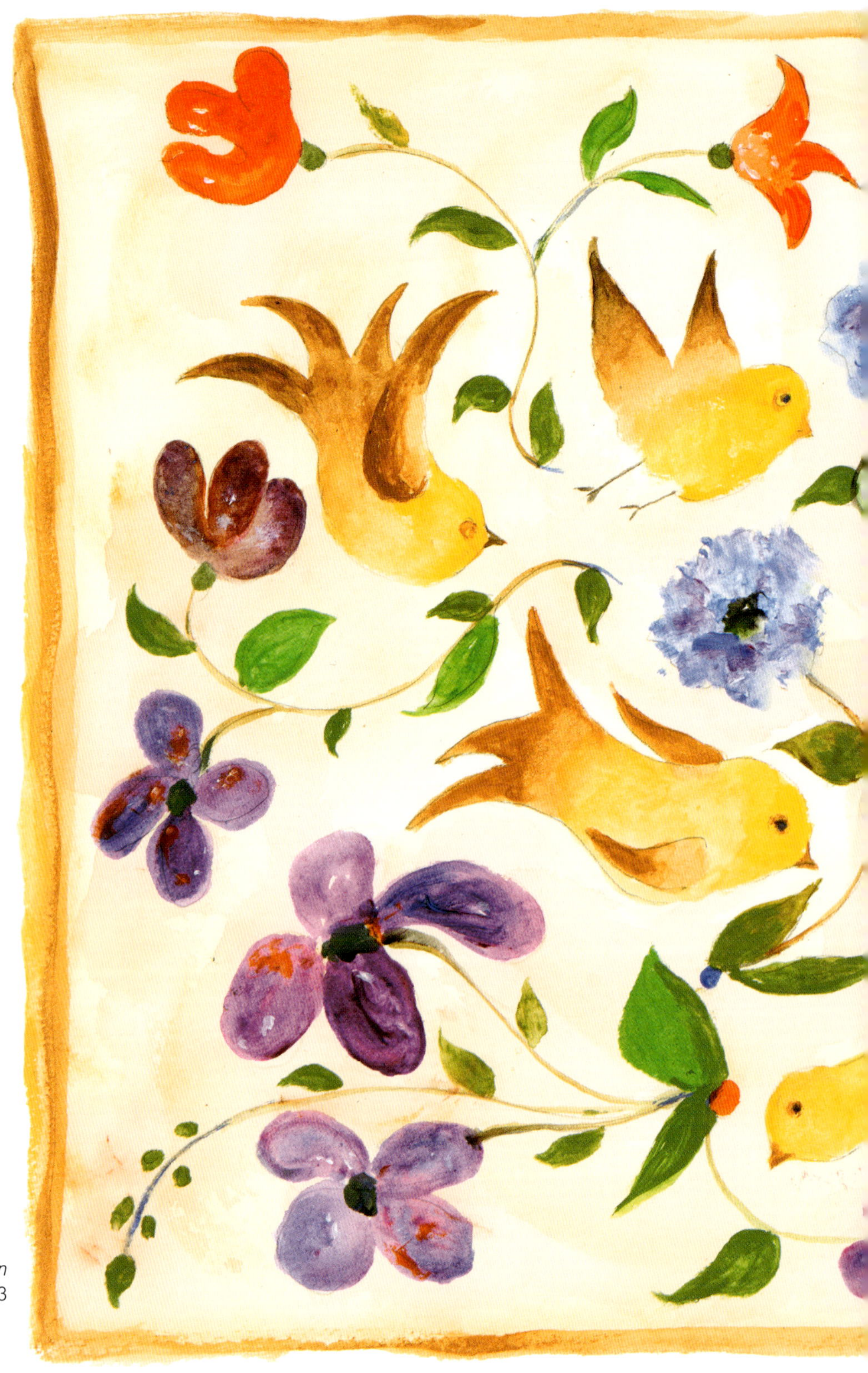

Birds in Flowers, 2023

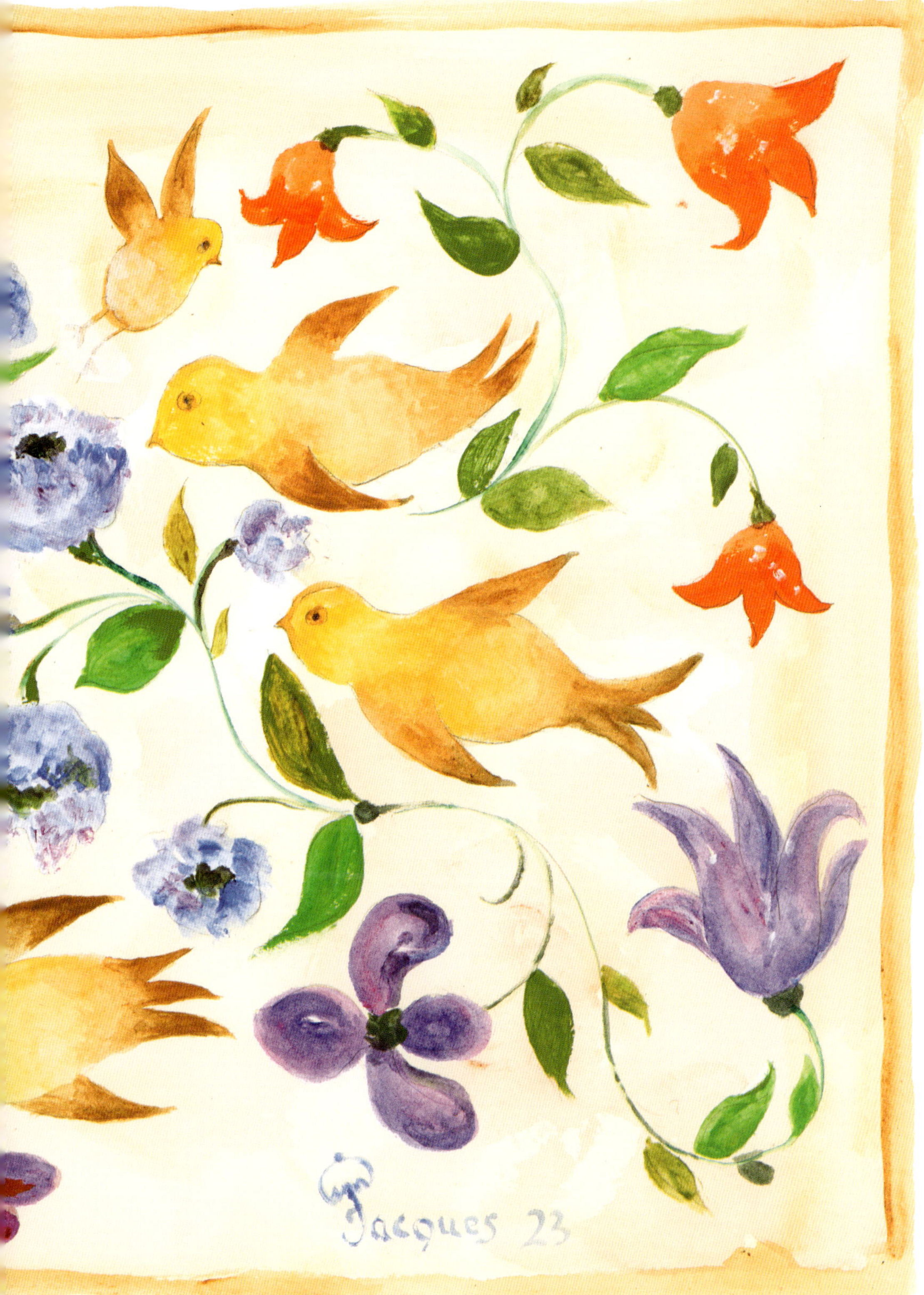
Jacques 23

RICE PUDDING with HONEY

When I go to a Chinese or Thai restaurant, I often end up coming home with extra plain white rice. This is a different way to repurpose that leftover rice for a quick and easy dessert.

Serves 4

About 1½ cups cooked plain rice

3½ cups half-and-half

⅓ cup golden raisins

½ cup honey

1 teaspoon pure vanilla extract

About ½ cup peach or apricot jam, for garnish

Sour cream, for garnish (optional)

▸ Preheat the oven to 350°F.

▸ Mix the rice, half-and-half, raisins, honey, and vanilla in a medium, ovenproof saucepan and bring to a boil over medium heat. Cover and place in the oven for 30 minutes—at this point the mixture will look soupy.

▸ Cool and serve with the jam spooned on top and a dollop of sour cream, if desired.

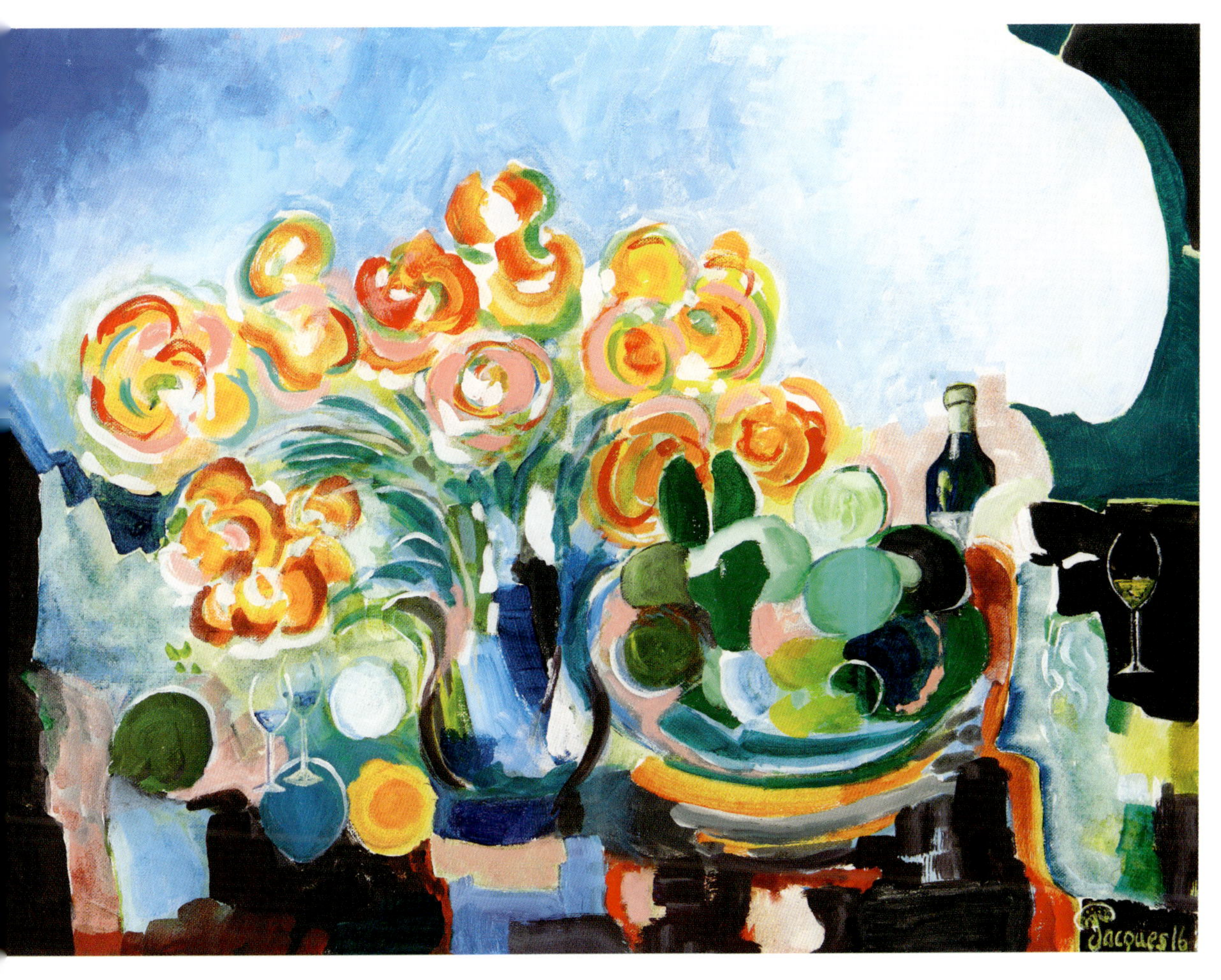

Flowers and Wine, 2016

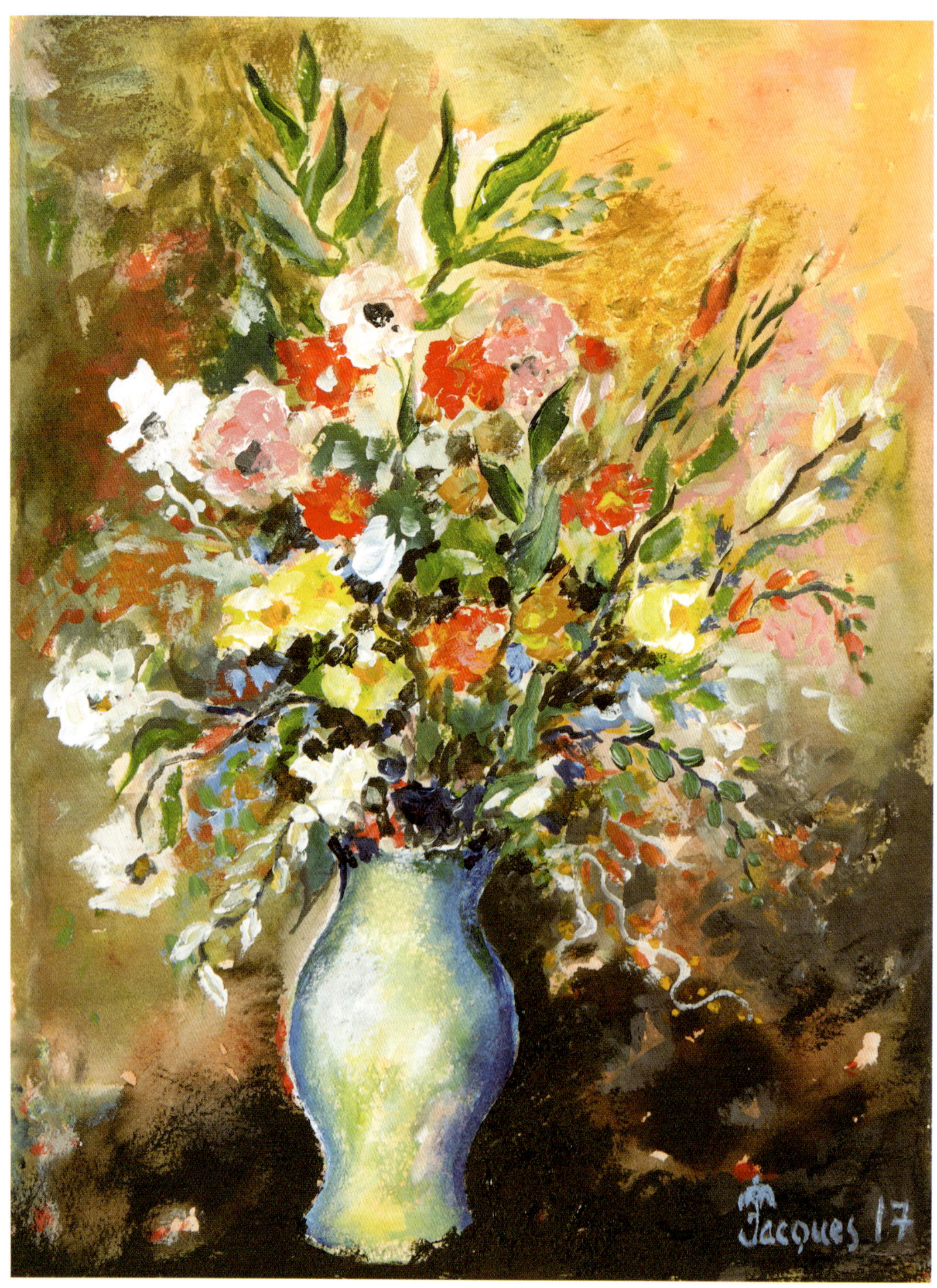

Bouquet in Blue Vase, 2017

APPLE COMPOTE

What we call "applesauce" was known as apple compote when I was a kid in France, and it was always served as a dessert at home. You can certainly use it as an applesauce or try it as a dessert with a garnish of sour cream and pound cake.

Serves 2 to 3

2 large apples, peeled, cored, and cut into 1-inch cubes (about 1 pound)

1 tablespoon butter

¼ cup apple juice

2 tablespoons sugar

½ teaspoon pure vanilla extract

Sour cream, for serving

Strips of orange zest, for serving

Pound cake, for serving

▸ Combine the apples, butter, apple juice, sugar, and vanilla in a medium saucepan. Bring to a boil over medium heat, reduce the heat to a simmer, cover, and cook until the apples are tender, about 15 minutes. Remove the lid and continue to cook until the liquid has reduced, about 5 minutes more. Using a potato masher, roughly mash the apples into a chunky puree to the texture of your liking. Allow to cool. To serve, spoon into a serving dish and top with a dollop of sour cream, the orange zest, and a slice of pound cake.

Pages 220–221: *White Peaches and Flowers,* 2023

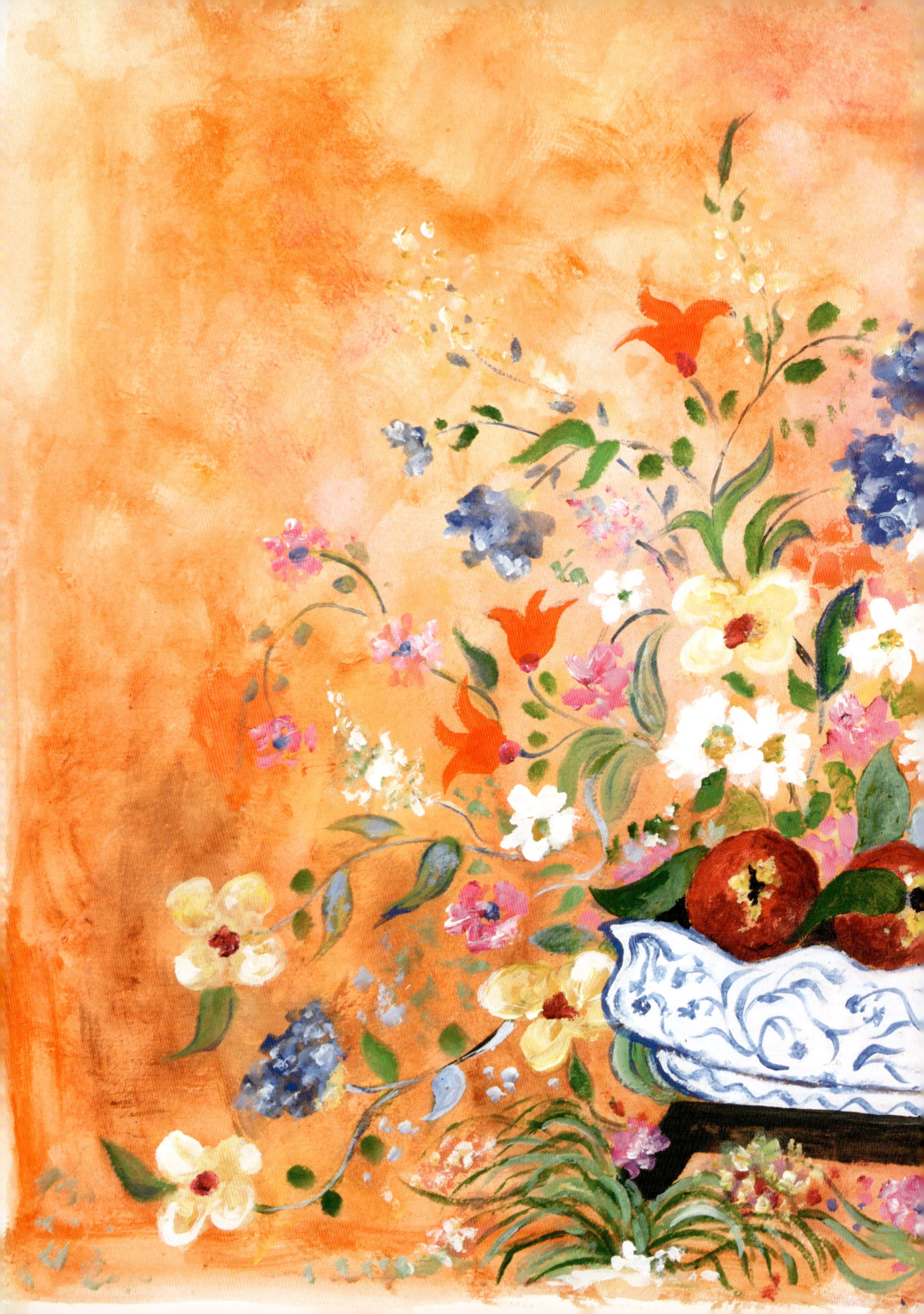

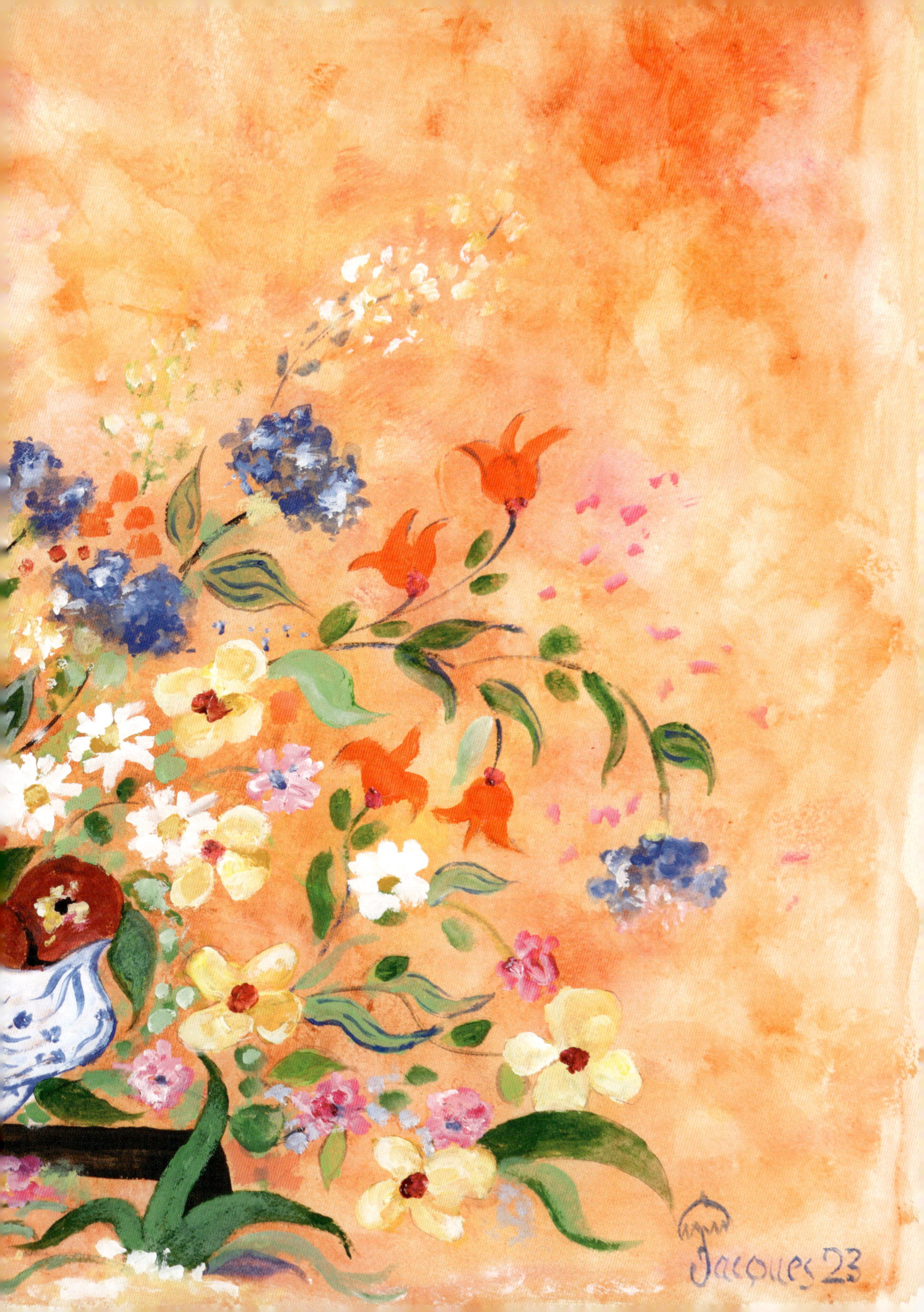
Jacques 23

BAKED APPLES (POMMES BONNE FEMME)

These baked apples are a classic dessert of my youth. My mother would also serve them in her small restaurant. A similar dessert can be made with pears. Everyone likes a baked apple—easy, sweet, and tasty. In the French style, I am flavoring them with jam and butter, but you may add cinnamon for a more American version.

Serves 2

2 large apples

1 English muffin, or 2 small slices leftover bread

3 tablespoons maple syrup

2 tablespoons apricot jam

2 tablespoons butter

▸ Preheat the oven to 375°F.

▸ Using an apple corer, remove the core from the apples. With the point of a knife, make an incision in the skin about a third of the way down each apple and cut through the skin ⅛ to ¼ inch deep all around. As the apple cooks, the flesh expands and the part of the apple above this cut will lift up like a lid. Without this scoring the apple could burst.

▸ Place the two muffin halves in a gratin dish or shallow ovenproof dish and set the apples on top. Drizzle the maple syrup over the apples and fill the center of each apple with 1 tablespoon of the jam and ½ tablespoon of the butter. Dot the remaining butter around the dish. Pour ½ cup of water around the edges of the dish. Bake until the apples are tender, about 1 hour. Allow to cool and serve at room temperature.

Facing page: *Flaming Flowers,* 2019

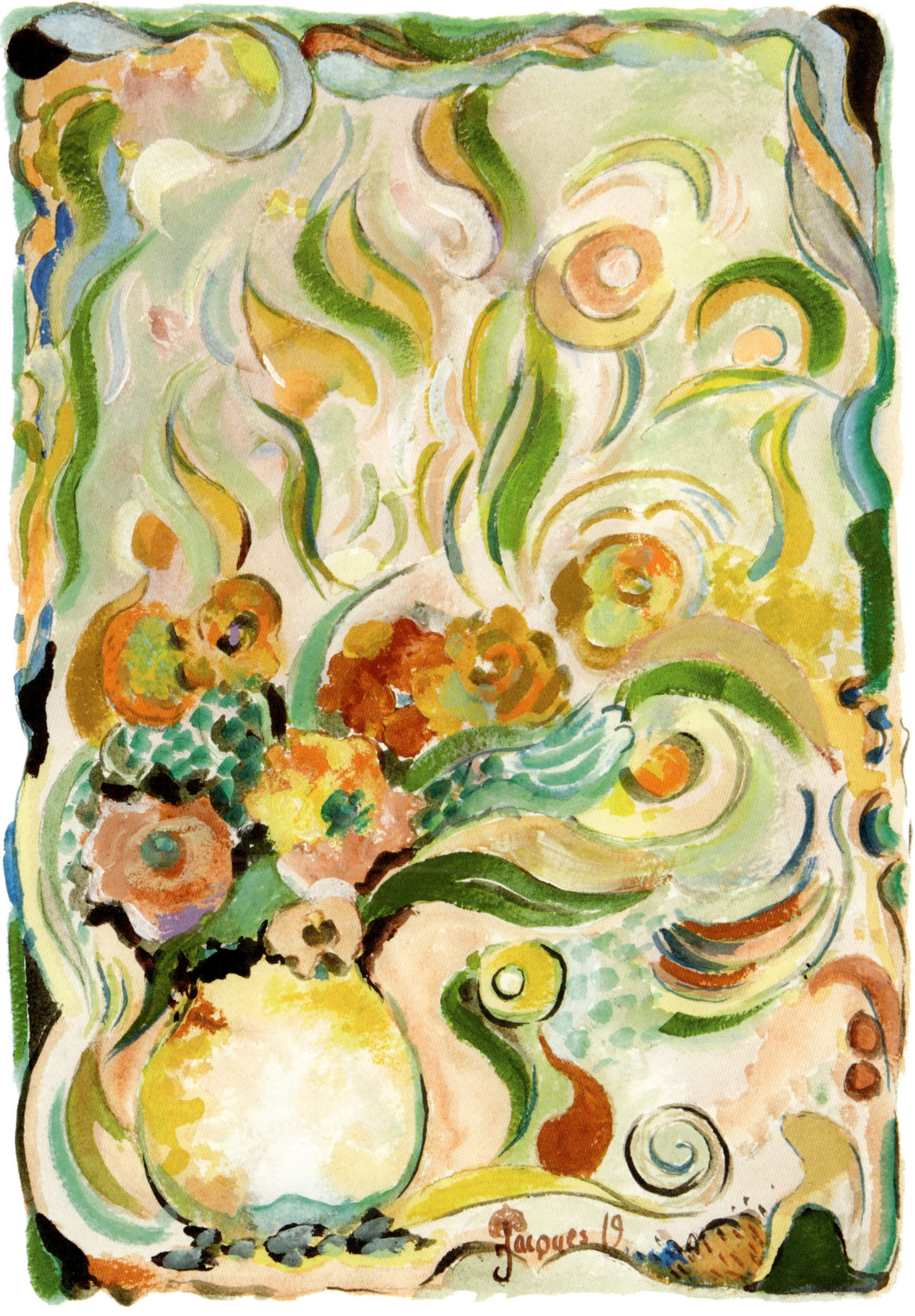
Jacques 19

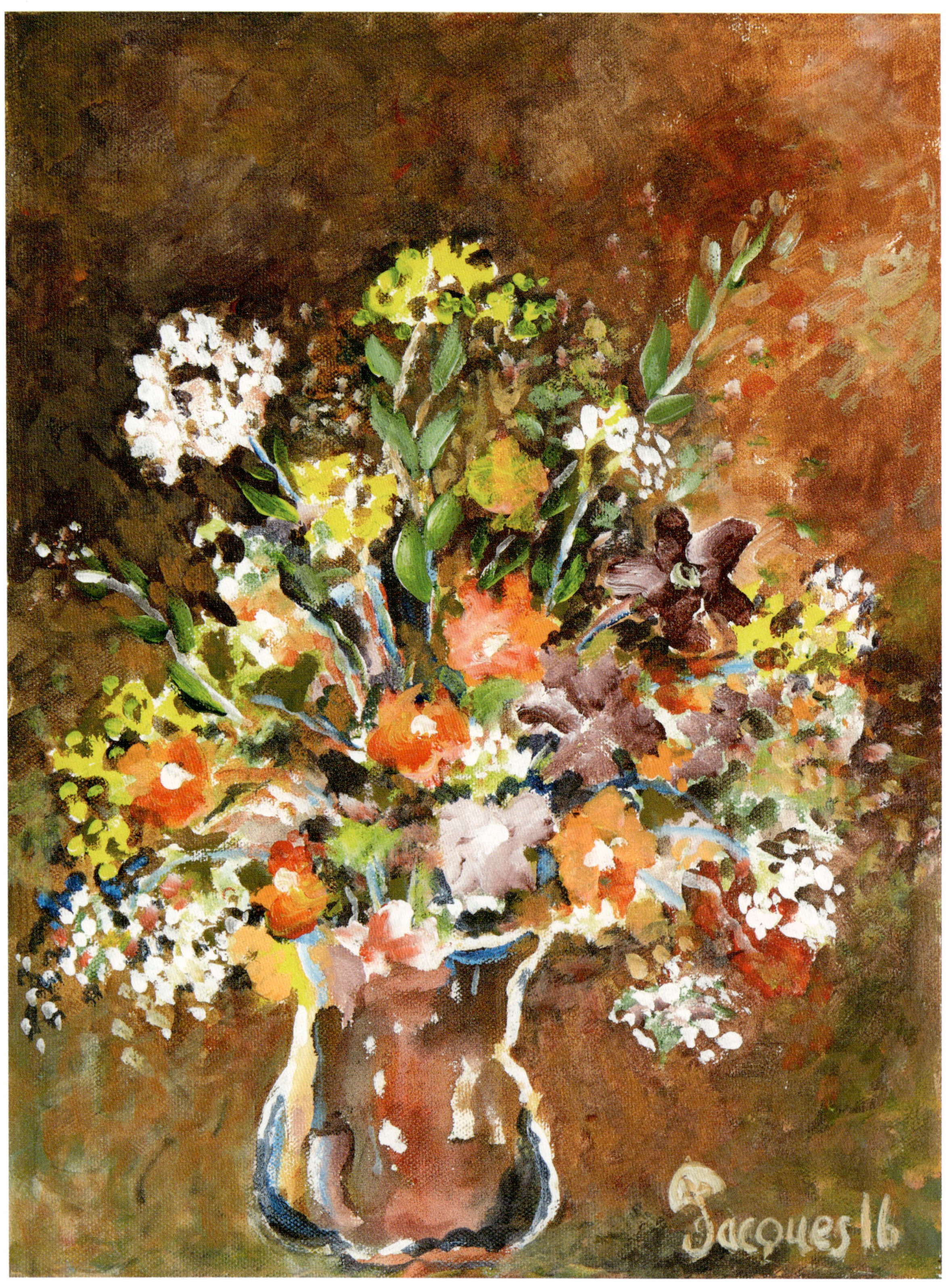

Mixed Bouquet 2, 2016

BANANA SHERBET

I do not like throwing food away, so when there are a few brown spots on bananas, I peel them and cut the flesh into pieces and freeze them to make this sherbet. You can use all frozen bananas, but they may need to thaw a bit as you are processing to make a smooth puree.

Serves 2 to 4

3 bananas, sliced, divided

Mint leaves, cut into chiffonade

2 tablespoons sour cream

3 tablespoons honey

⅓ cup peach preserves, for garnish

Mint sprigs, for garnish

▸ Spread the slices of 2 bananas on a baking sheet and place them in the freezer for at least 3 hours. Combine the frozen and the fresh banana, mint leaves, sour cream, and honey in a food processor. Process until the mixture becomes a smooth puree. If the mixture is firm enough, you can serve it immediately; if it is a little soft or if you prefer a firmer texture, return it to the freezer so that it firms up.

▸ To serve, spoon the sherbet into a serving dish and drizzle with the peach preserves. Garnish with a mint sprig and serve immediately.

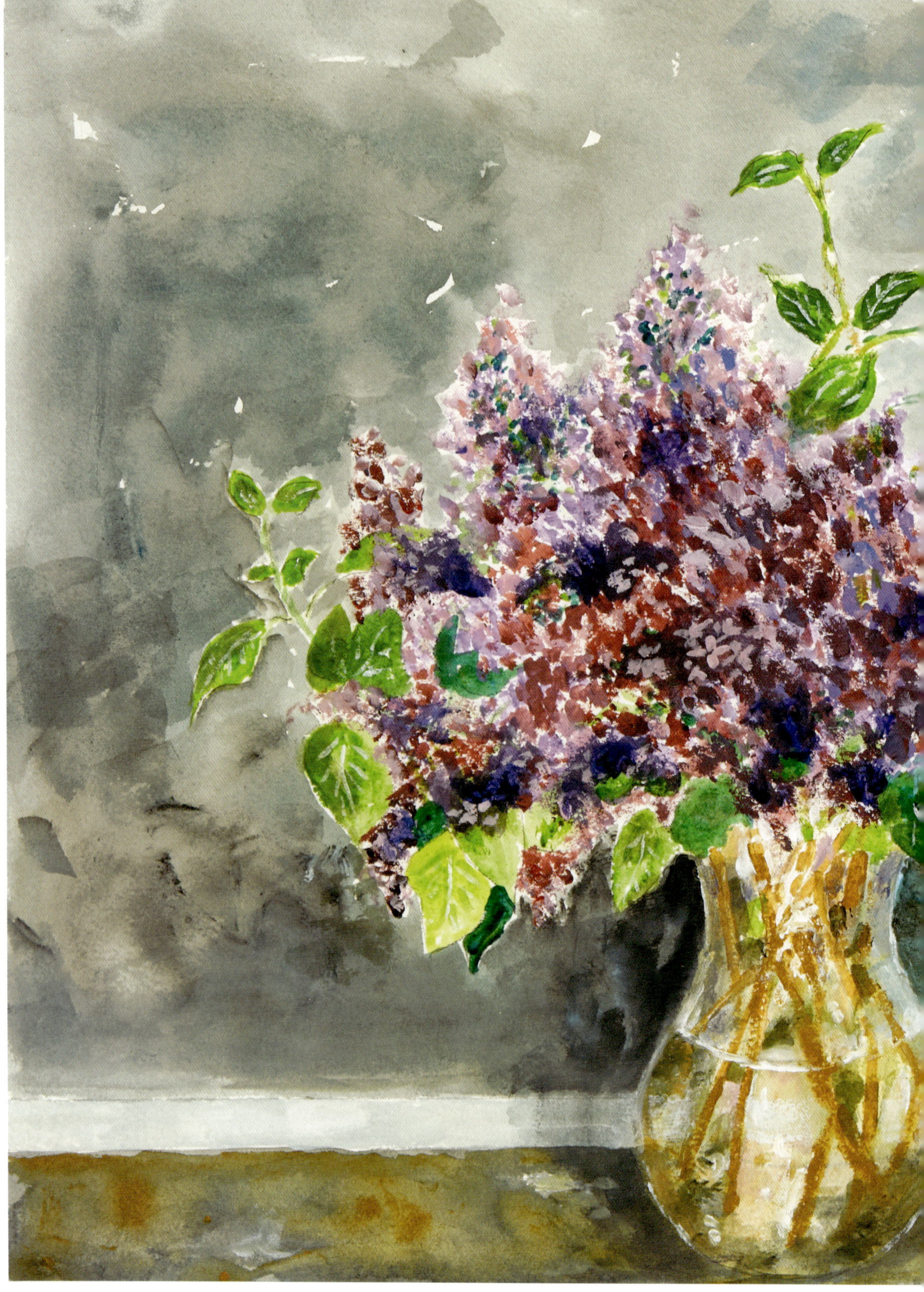

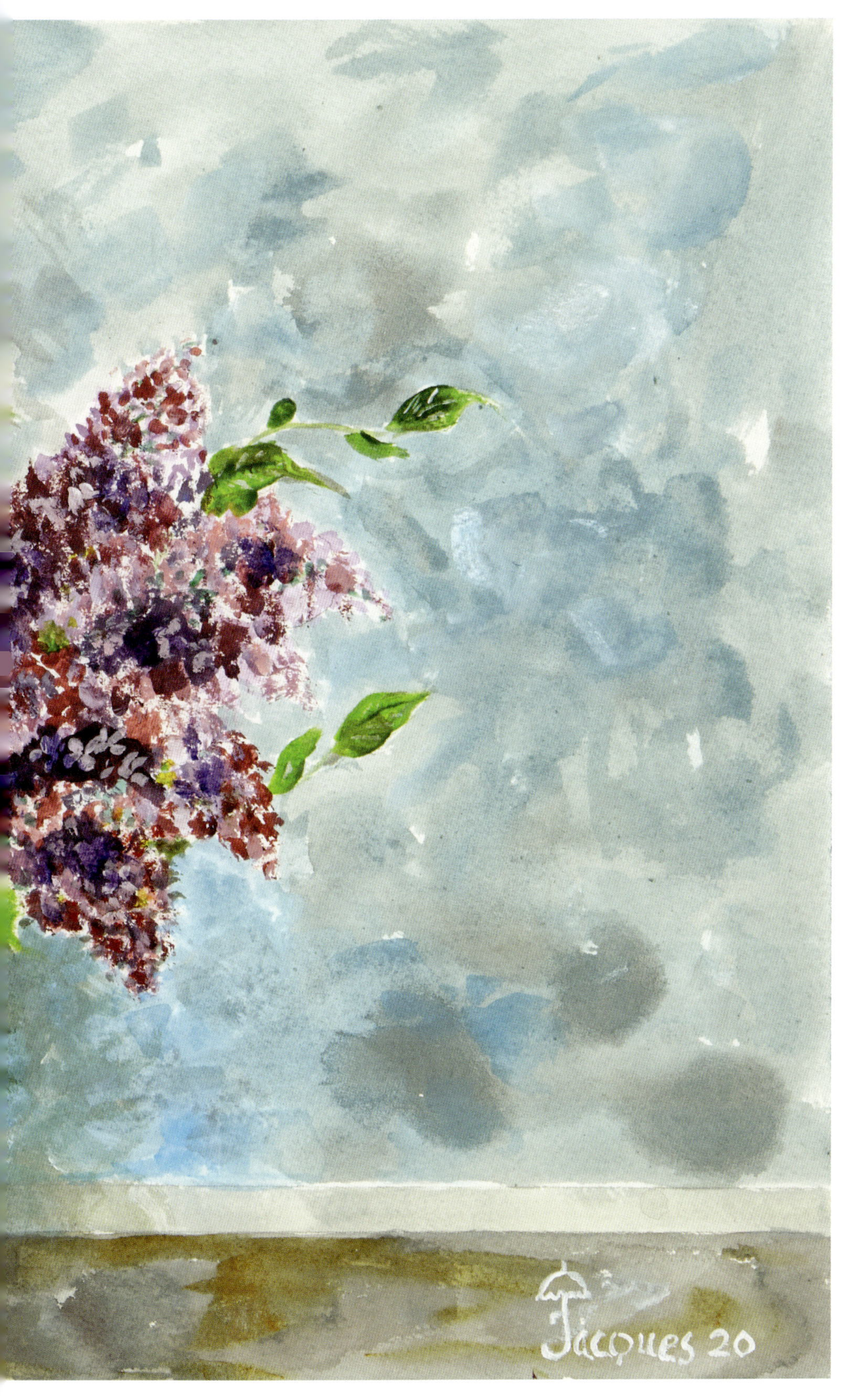

Lilas du Jardin, 2020

FLAMBEED BANANAS

I like bananas as a dessert, sometimes flambéed, sometimes baked, or even just sliced and served with lemon juice and sugar. Slicing them in half lengthwise, baking them in a gratin dish, and finishing them at the table with some rum makes for a dessert served with a flourish.

Serves 3 to 4

3 tablespoons butter

3 bananas, peeled and split in half lengthwise

¼ cup light brown sugar

1½ teaspoons grated lemon zest

2 tablespoons lemon juice

3 tablespoons dark rum

Sour cream, whipped cream, or ice cream, for serving (optional)

▸ Preheat the oven to 400°F. Butter a shallow gratin dish with the butter.

▸ Place the sliced bananas in a single layer in the dish and sprinkle with the sugar, lemon zest, and lemon juice. Bake until the bananas are soft and the sugar has melted, about 20 minutes. Remove from the oven, drizzle the rum over them and, using a long-handled lighter, carefully light the alcohol to flambé the dish. This can be done at the table. Spoon the bananas into dishes and serve alone or with sour cream, whipped cream, or ice cream.

PEAR in PUFF PASTRY

Sometimes I make my own puff pastry, but often I buy it ready-made from the market. I try to buy the kind that says "all-butter." The puff pastry comes frozen, usually in thin sheets that are about 10 inches by 4 or 5 inches. It must be thawed slowly. If you cut one sheet in half, that will be just enough to cover the two pear halves.

Make sure the pear is large, about 12 ounces and nice and ripe. The fruit is flavored with a bit of apricot jam, sugar, and butter, and I add a dash of water in the dish to help the fruit cook. This is a simple way to make an elegant dessert for 2 people.

Serves 2

1 large pear (about 12 ounces), peeled, halved, and cored

2 tablespoons butter, melted

2 tablespoons sugar

2 tablespoons apricot or peach jam

2 pieces puff pastry (each about 4 × 5 inches)

2 tablespoons sour cream, for garnish

▸ Preheat the oven to 400°F.

▸ Place the pear halves cut side down in a small gratin or ovenproof dish. Drizzle with half the butter and sprinkle with half the sugar. Spoon over the apricot jam and drizzle with 2 to 3 tablespoons of water.

▸ Place one piece of puff pastry over each pear, tucking it around the pear so that it forms into the shape of the pear. Brush the pastry with the remaining butter and sprinkle with the remaining sugar.

▸ Bake until the pastry is golden brown and crispy and the pear is cooked through, 30 to 35 minutes. Serve warm, alone or with a little sour cream, if desired.

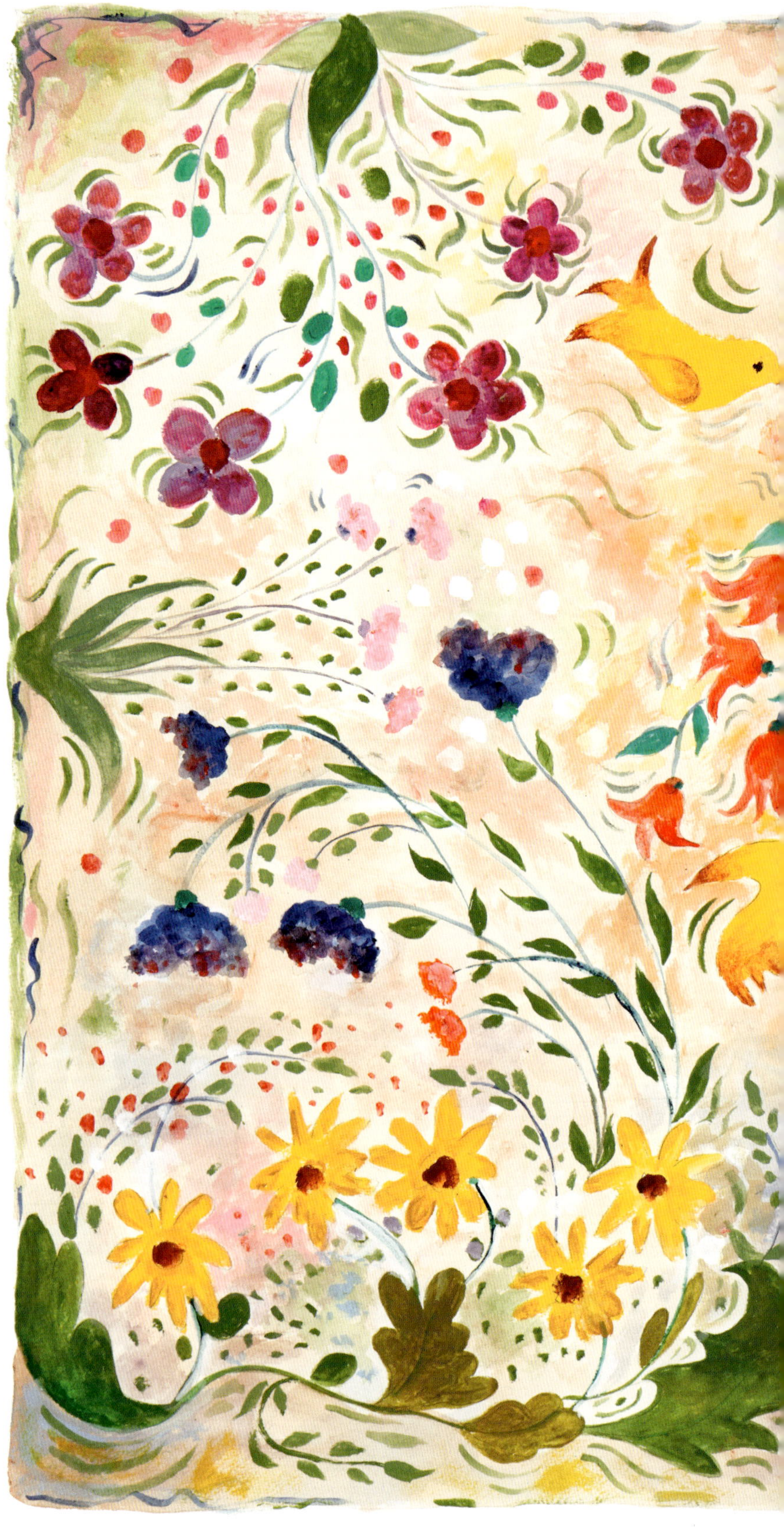

Catching Birds, 2023

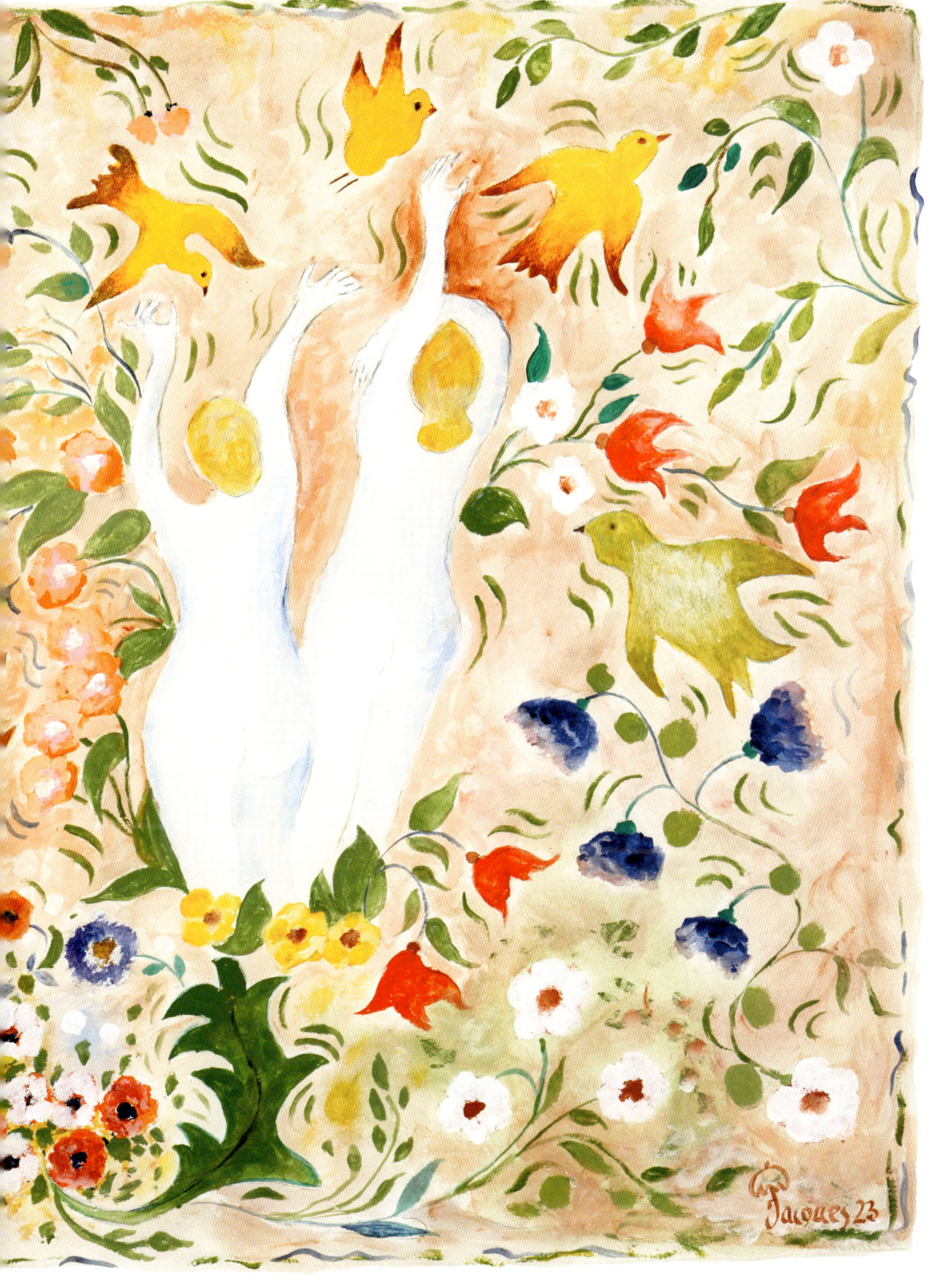
Jacques 23

RASPBERRY DELIGHT

This is an ideal recipe for when you have no time. It requires ingredients that are easily found in any supermarket, and it comes together in just a few minutes. A low salad bowl is nice for presentation. Here I moisten the pound cake with apple cider, but you could use apple or orange juice as well. An easy, impressive, and delicious dish, perfect to end a dinner party.

Serves 8

8 ounces pound cake

⅓ cup apple cider or other fruit juice

14 ounces crème fraîche

1 pint raspberries

⅔ cup seedless raspberry preserves, heated in the microwave for 1 minute

Mint sprigs, for garnish

▸ Cut the pound cake in ¾-inch slices and place in a serving dish in one layer. Sprinkle with the juice and spread with the crème fraîche. Cover with the raspberries, then glaze with the raspberry preserves. Garnish with mint sprigs and serve as needed.

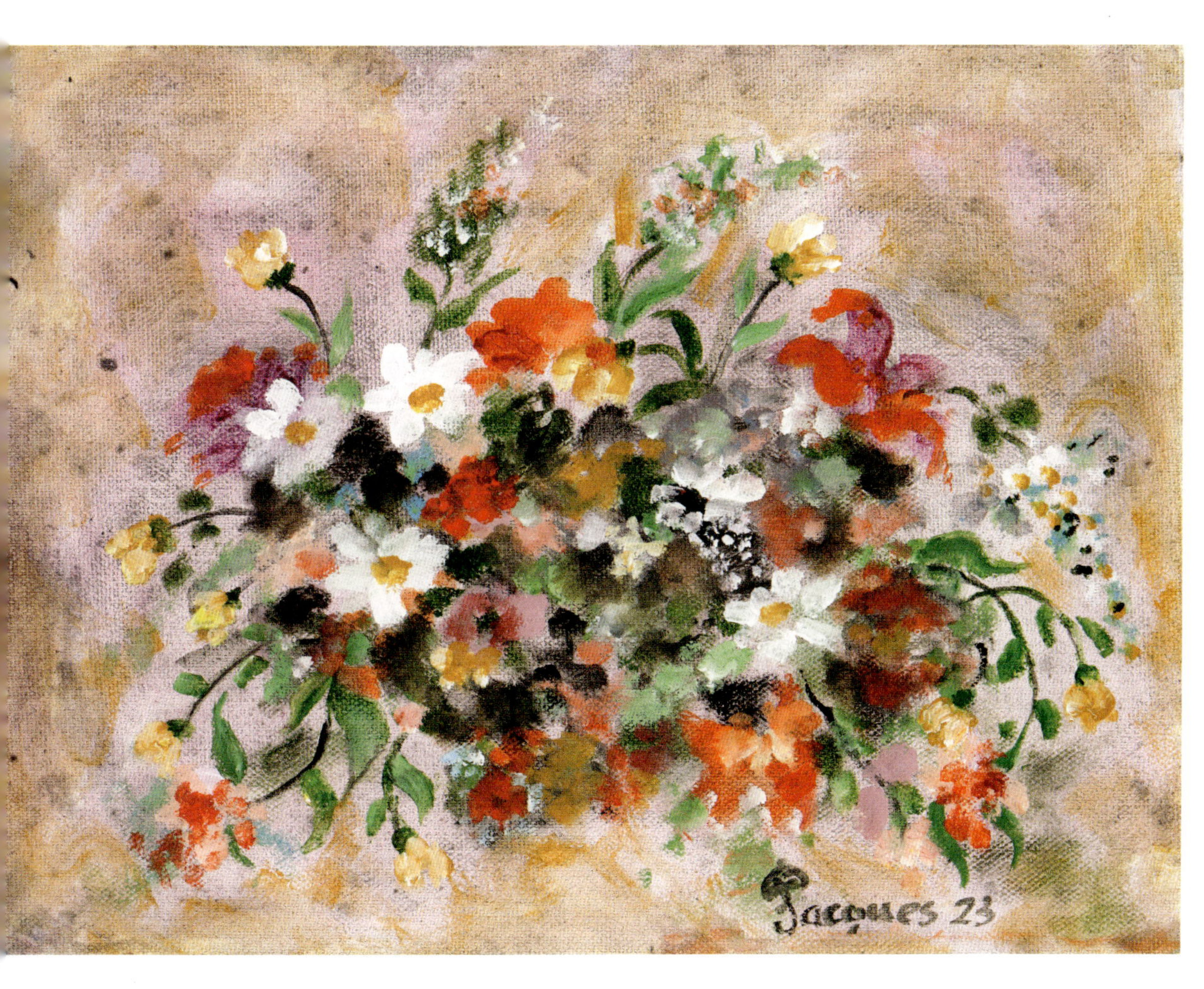

Wild Bouquet, 2023

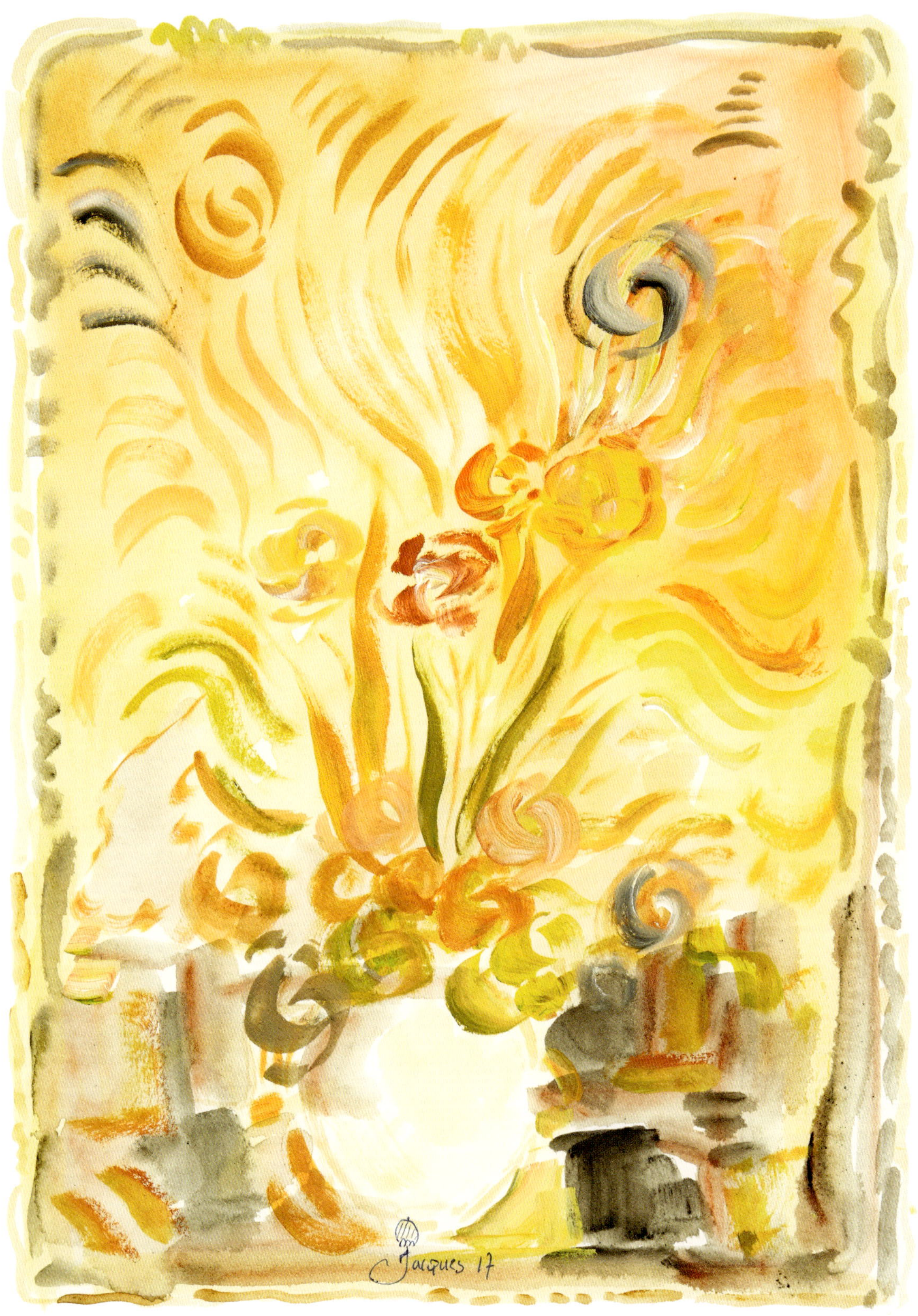

Dreaming Flowers, 2017

ORANGES in CARAMEL à la GLORIA

My wife read that Louis XIV enjoyed this dessert and asked me if I could make it for her—this is my interpretation. A royal dessert that is very inexpensive to prepare, it makes for a simple but impressive way to end a meal.

Serves 4

2 seedless oranges

⅓ cup sugar

4 mint sprigs, for garnish

▸ Peel the oranges, removing all the white pith, which is bitter. Cut into halves crosswise and place the oranges cut sides up on a platter. You will have four pieces of orange. Combine the sugar and 2 tablespoons of water in a skillet and cook, undisturbed, for about 5 minutes, until it turns into a blond to dark caramel. Pour over the orange halves. The caramel will harden on top of the oranges. Let sit for 15 to 30 minutes, until the caramel softens. Garnish with the mint before serving and enjoy.

Pages 236–237: *Red Flowers,* 2024

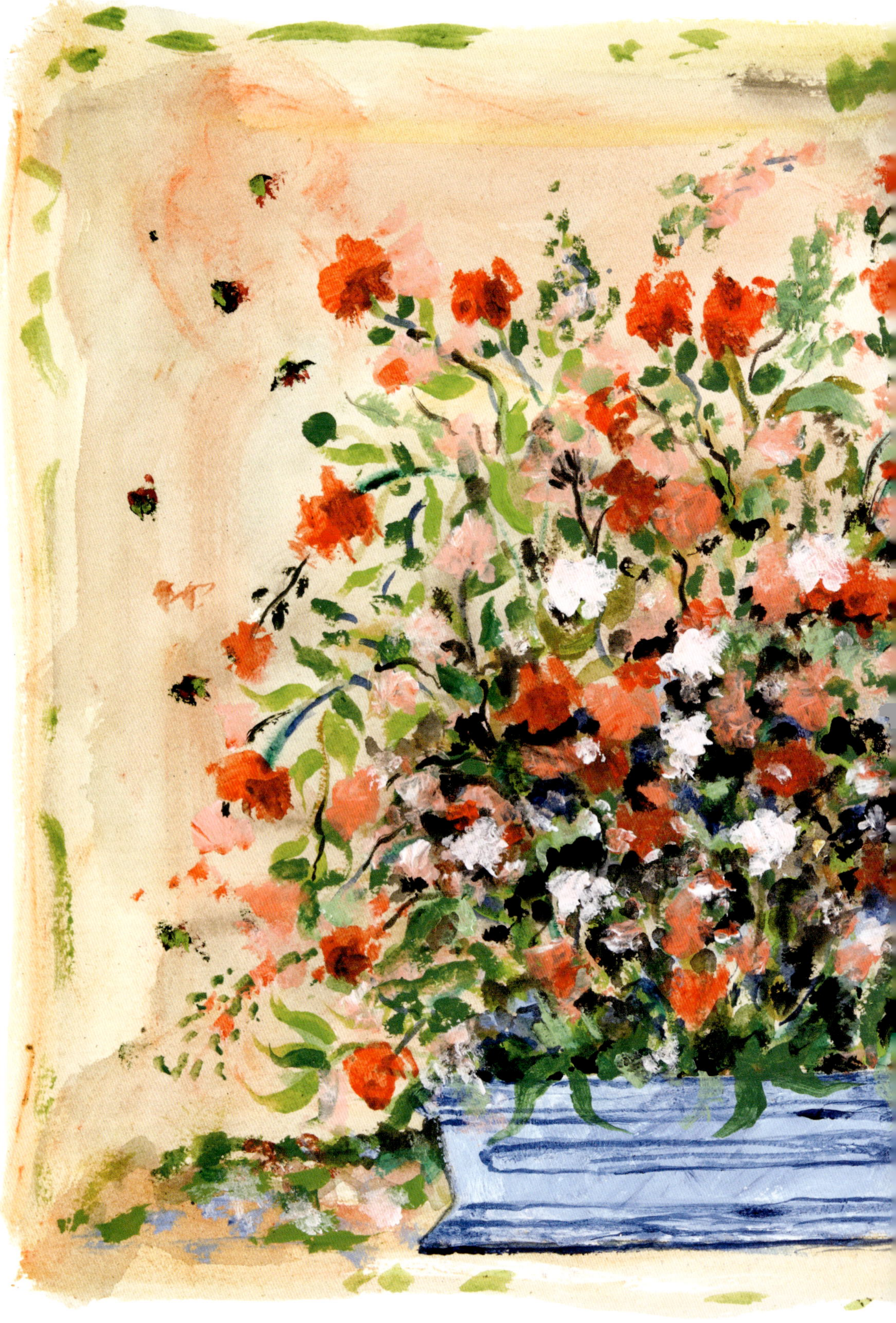

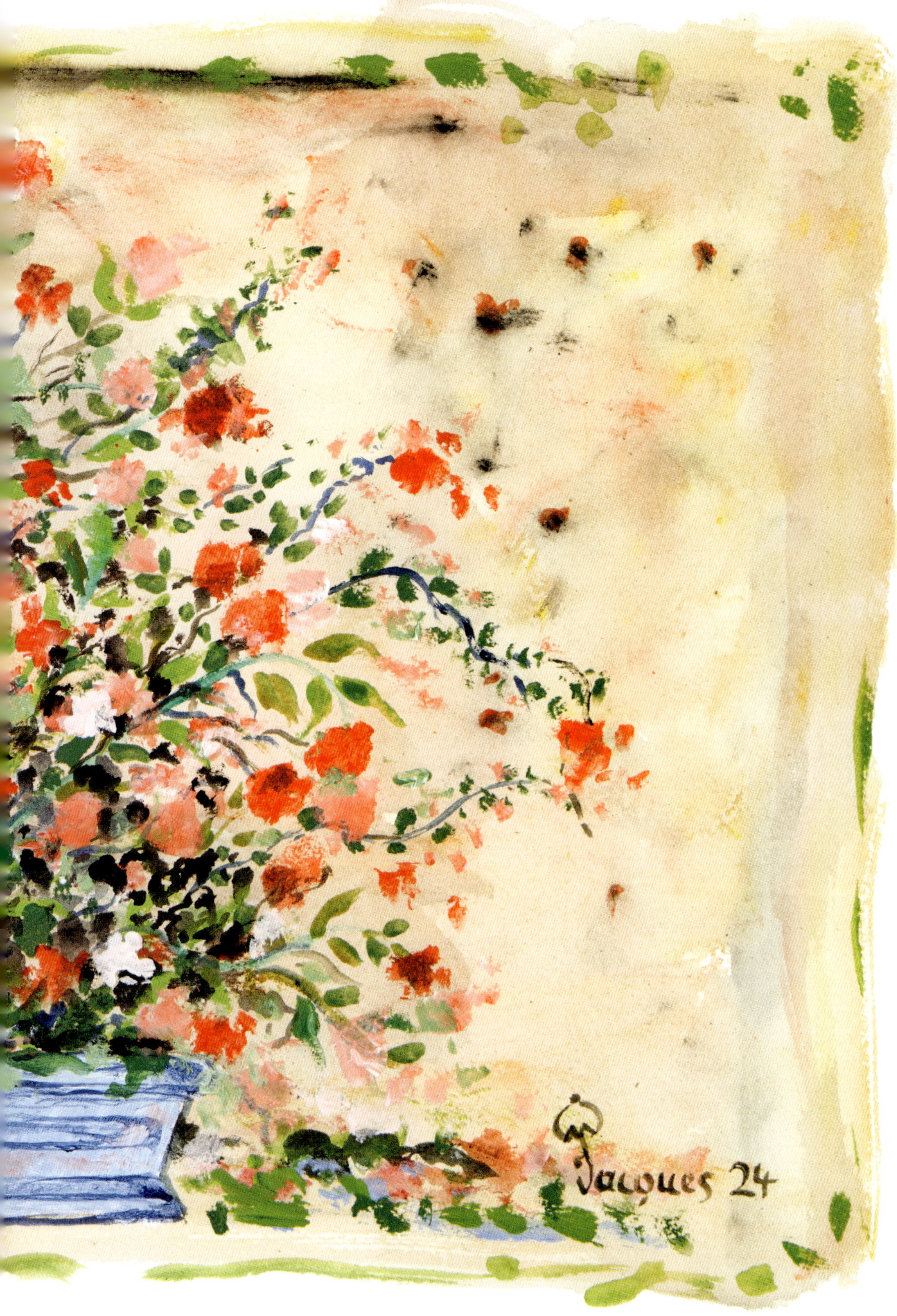
Jacques 24

GRAPEFRUIT SEGMENTS with APRICOT SAUCE

Refreshing grapefruit segments make a light end to a meal. This method also works well with oranges, especially blood oranges.

Serves 2

1 grapefruit

3 tablespoons apricot jam

Mint or basil sprig, for garnish

▸ Using a vegetable peeler, remove 2 strips of the zest from the grapefruit, being careful not to include any of the bitter white pith. Using a sharp knife, cut the zest into a thin julienne.

▸ Using a sharp knife and a sawing action, remove the skin and all the pith from the grapefruit. Position the grapefruit over a bowl to catch the segments and juice. Cut along the membrane to the center of the grapefruit on each side of one segment. Let it fall into the bowl below. To cut the remaining segments, cut along the side of the next segment, then twist the knife to cut along the other side of the segment and release it into the bowl below.

▸ Heat the apricot jam in a microwave for a few seconds, just until warm. Spoon jam into the center of two serving plates and then spread to thinly cover the base of the plates. Arrange the segments in a spiral with the julienned zest sprinkled around the edge. Add a sprig of mint or basil to the center for garnish and serve as needed.

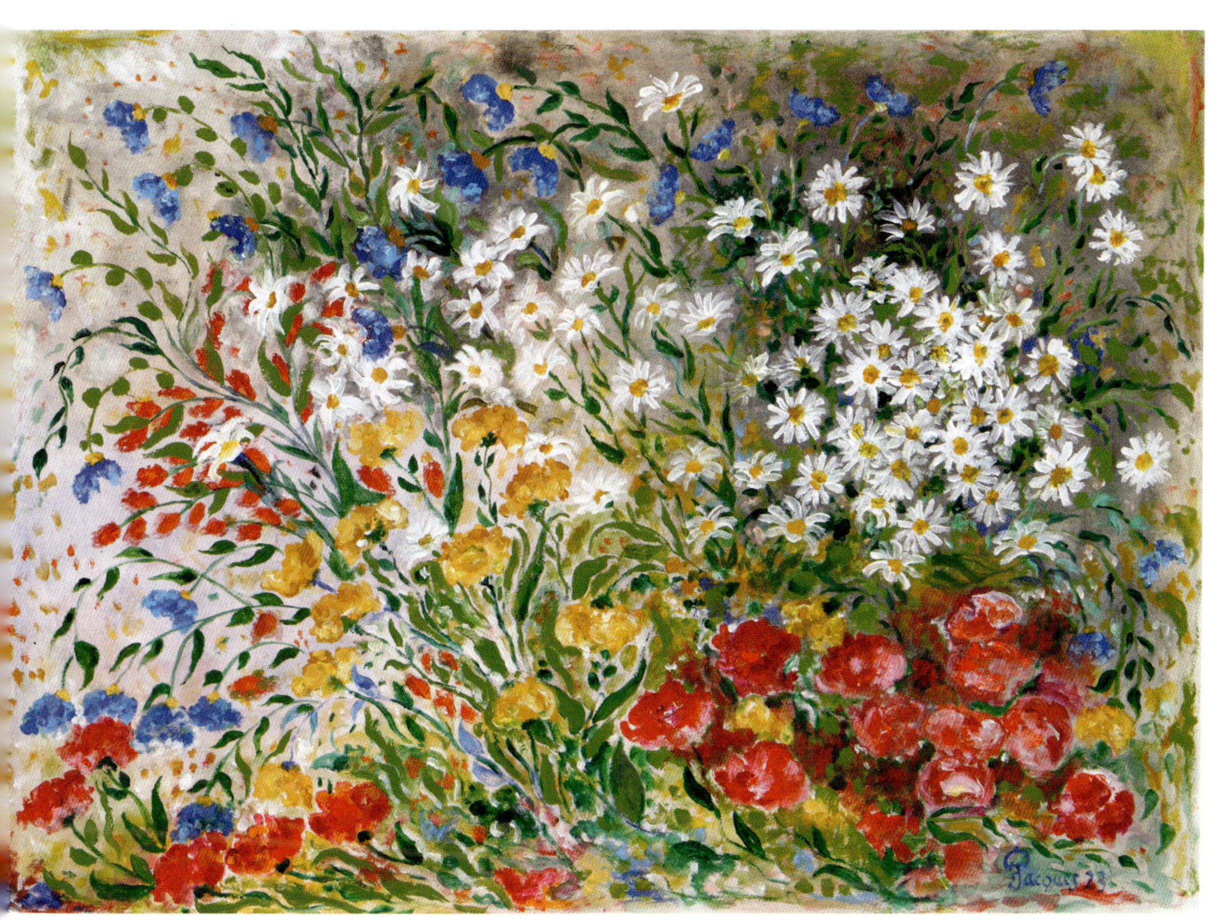

Field of Daisies, 2023

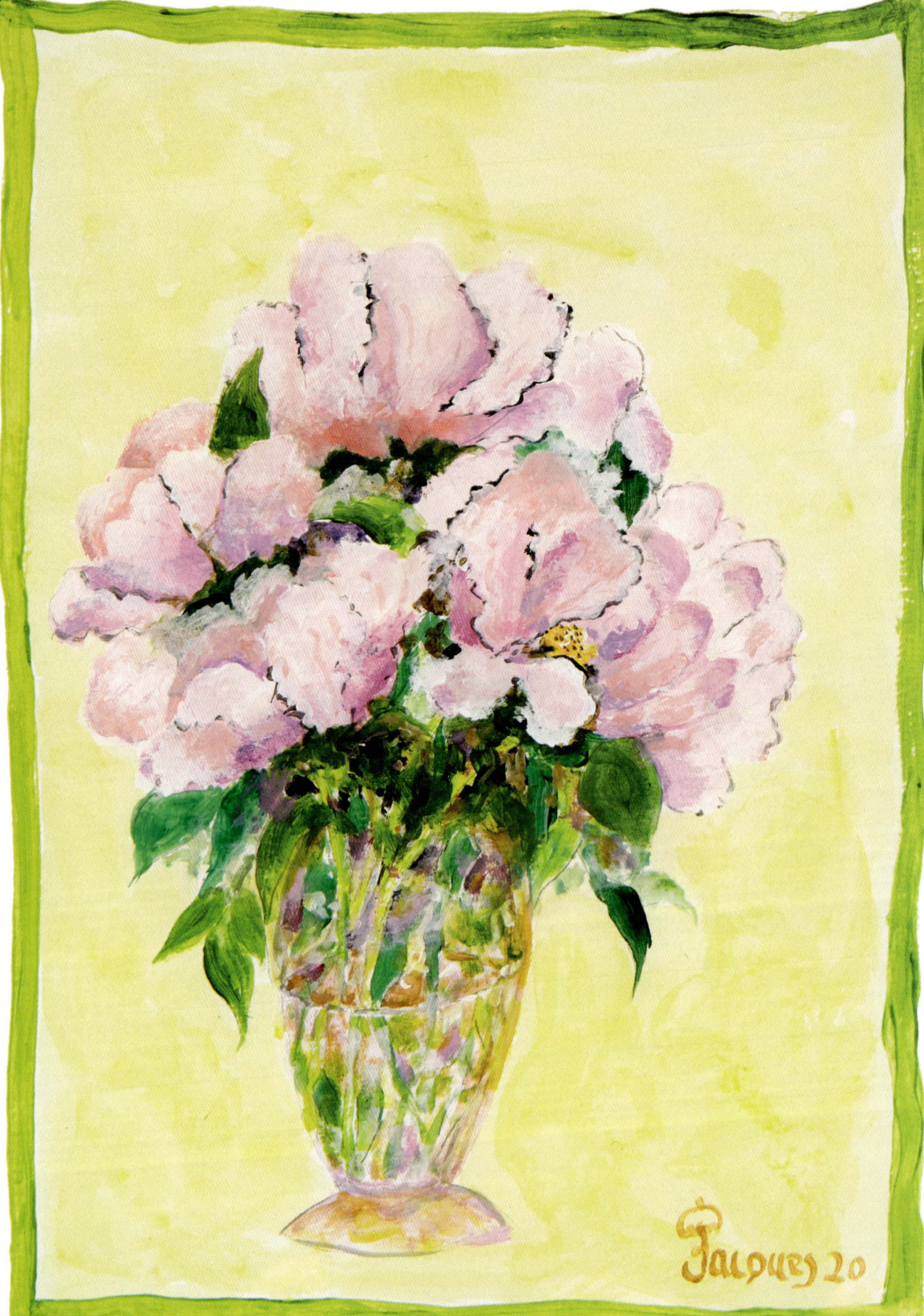

KIWI DELIGHT

I like fruit desserts; whatever fruit is in season or on sale at my supermarket. Kiwi is not a fruit I ate as a child, but I enjoy it now. In this recipe, I made one dessert with Nutella and one with crème fraîche. I often use pound cake as a garnish, or the small round sponge cake bases that are available at the market.

Serves 2

2 small round sponge cake bases or slices of pound cake

2 tablespoons Nutella

2 kiwis, peeled and cut into ½-inch slices

2 tablespoons crème fraîche

¼ cup apricot preserves

1 strawberry, halved, for garnish

▸ Set the sponge cake bases on two plates. Cover the first with the Nutella, then top with half of the kiwi slices. Spread the crème fraîche on the other and top with the remaining kiwi slices. Heat the apricot preserves in the microwave for a few seconds, just enough to liquefy the jam, and spoon it over the kiwi. Decorate with the strawberry halves and serve.

Facing page: *Les Pivoines,* 2020

PEACH à la MARTY

I call this Peach à la Marty after my good friend who once served a similar dish at her home. Fresh peaches are wonderful, but when it's not the season, canned can be just as good, especially in this simple and delicious dessert.

Serves 5

1 (16-ounce) can peaches (5 peach halves)

5 slices leftover bread, cut to fit the gratin dish

1½ tablespoons butter

2 tablespoons apricot preserves

Sour cream, for garnish

Mint sprigs, for garnish

▸ Preheat the oven to 350°F.

▸ Pour the syrup from the peaches into a gratin dish. Add the bread, turning to coat both sides in the syrup. Arrange the bread flat in one layer in the dish. Place a peach half on each slice of bread, cavity side facing up. Divide the butter and preserves among the peaches, place in the oven, and bake for about 25 minutes, until lightly browned. Cool to lukewarm and serve garnished with sour cream and sprigs of mint.

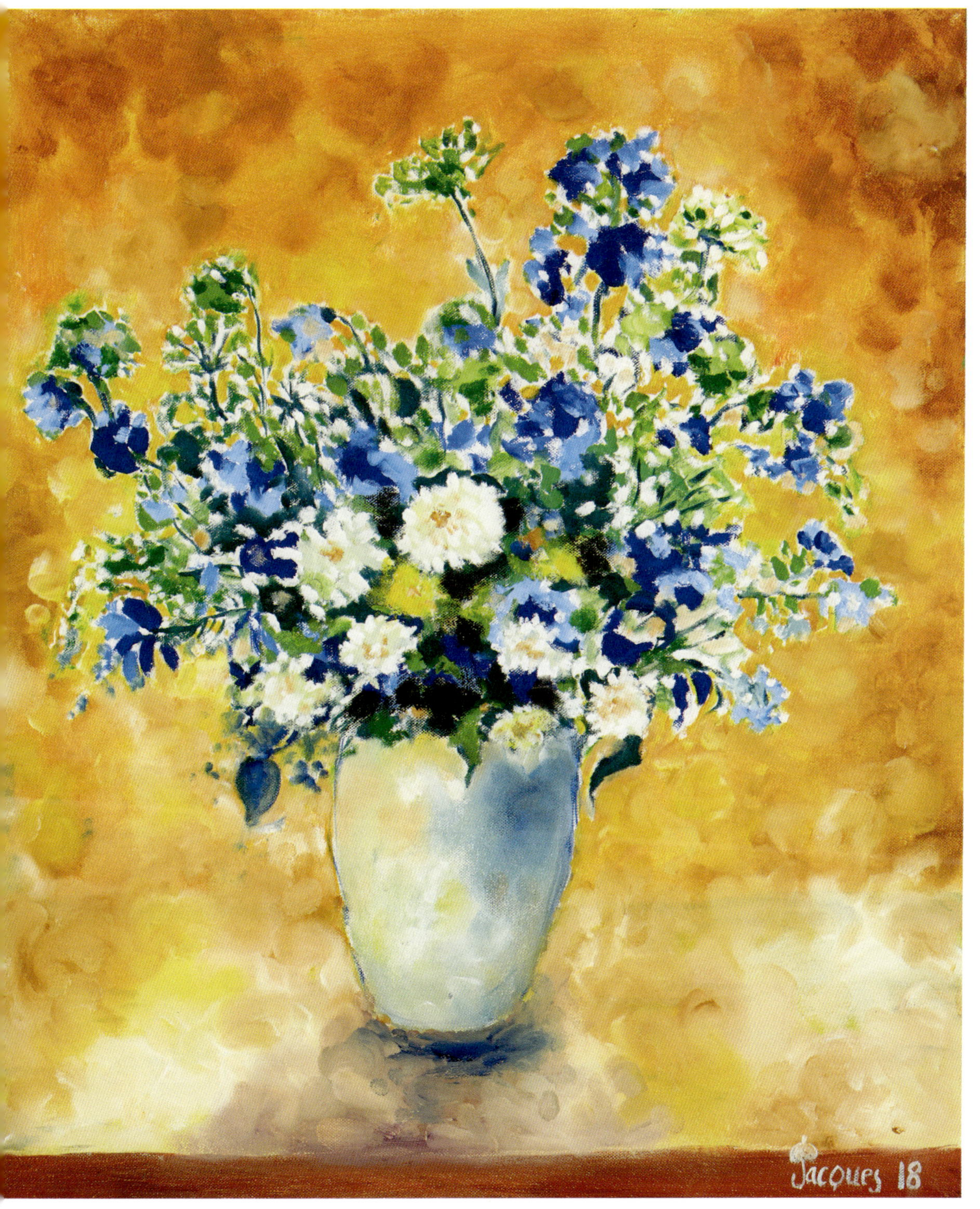

Blue Bouquet on Yellow, 2018

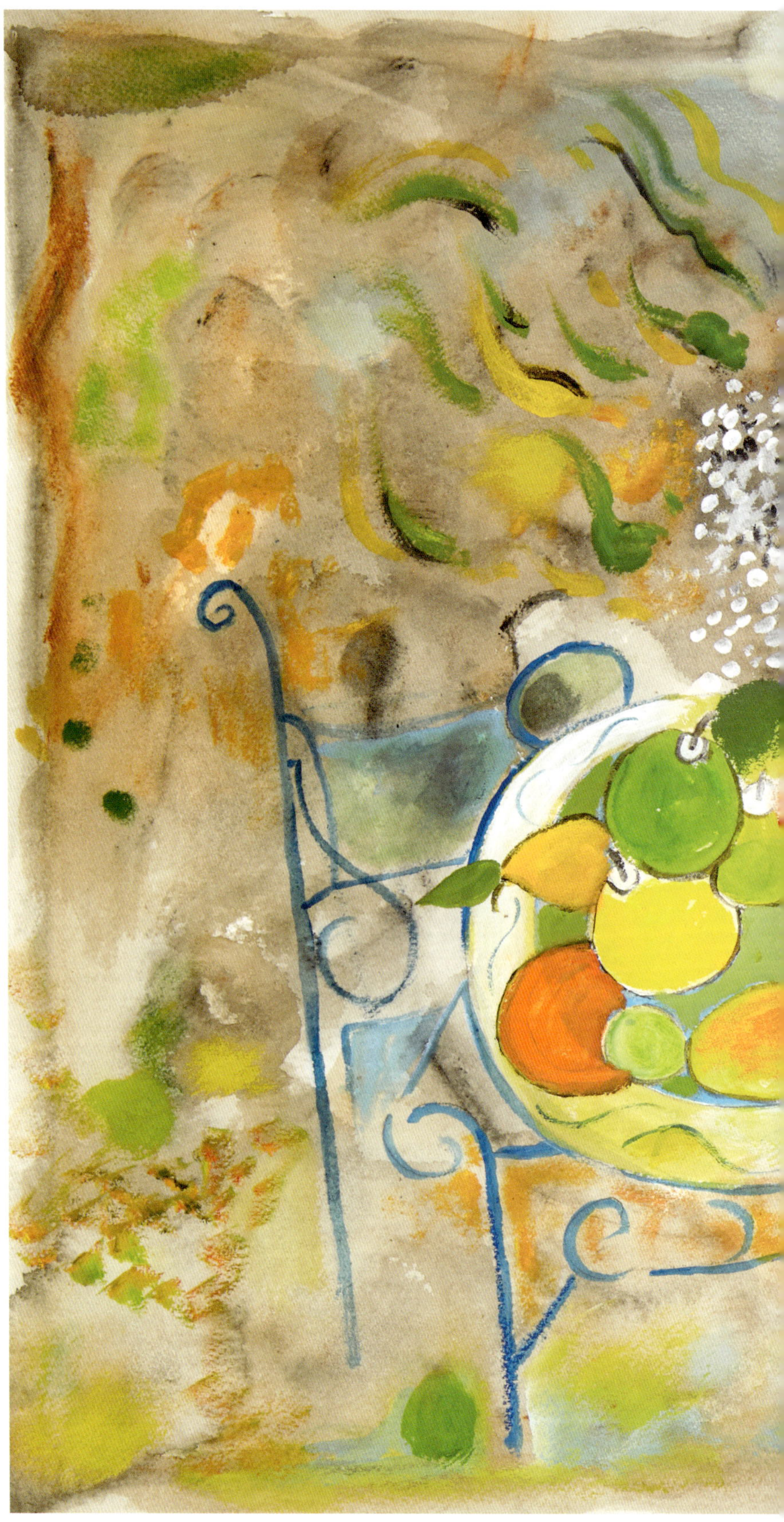

Flowers and Fruits, 2021

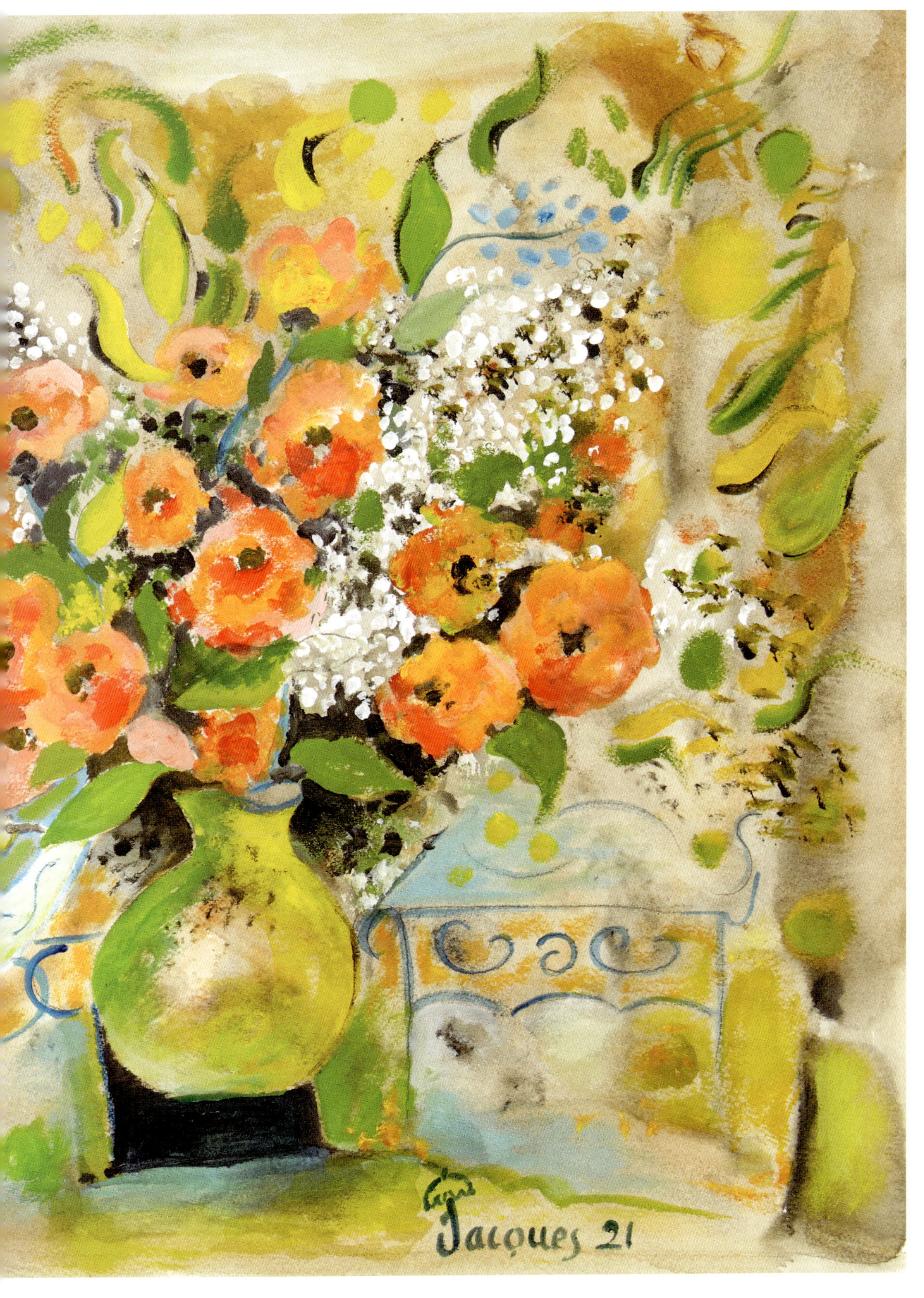
Jacques 21

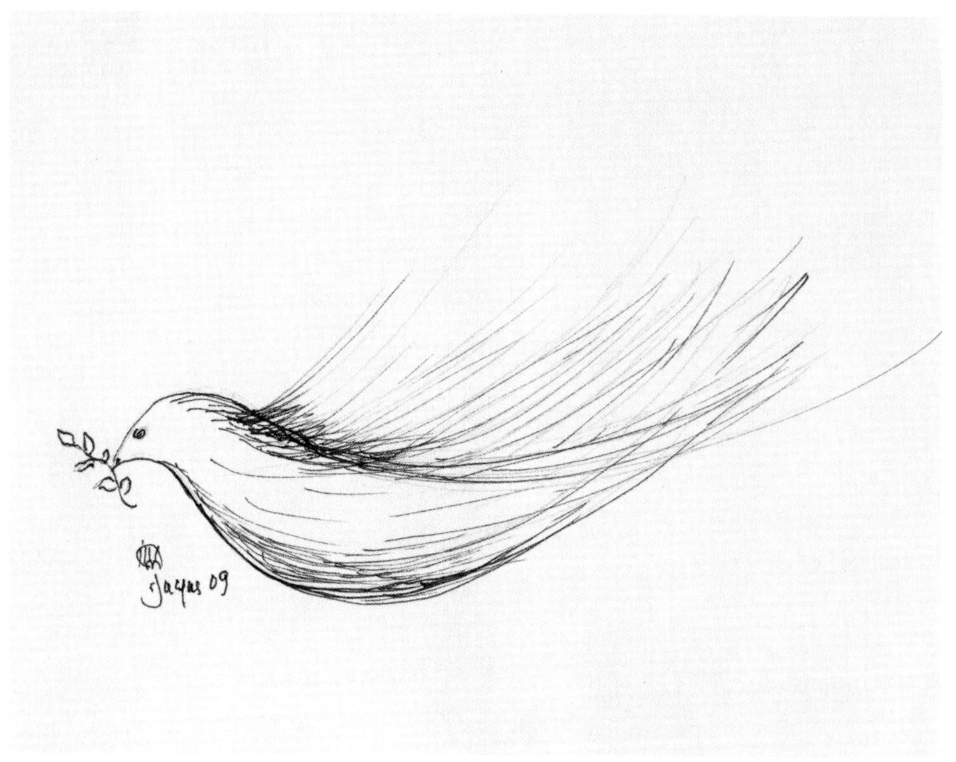

Songbird, 2009

Acknowledgments

THE MAKING OF a book is always a communal project. The idea of the book, the actual writing, the editing, proofreading, and production, all of these involve many persons and many talents. Thank you to Claudine and Rollie, my daughter and son-in-law, for their love, support, and input. Tom Hopkins for his unwavering help and talent, and Kelsey Whitsett, my assistant, for her patience and staunch endorsement and collaboration. Thank you to Sharon Burke for keeping the lights on for me. Thank you, Doe Coover, for your care and precious advice; Sarah Kwak, my editor, for your trust and belief in the book; and Sharyn Rosenblum and Odette Fleming for helping it reach an audience. My gratitude goes to Melissa Lotfy for the beautiful book design, along with Jacqueline Quirk, Heather Rodino, Amanda Hong, Kimberly Kiefer, and Jane Cavolina for their help and hard work. Finally, I send love and thanks to all my "boule" friends for their enduring affection and encouragement. I am indebted to you all. Happy cooking.

Index

E

F

G

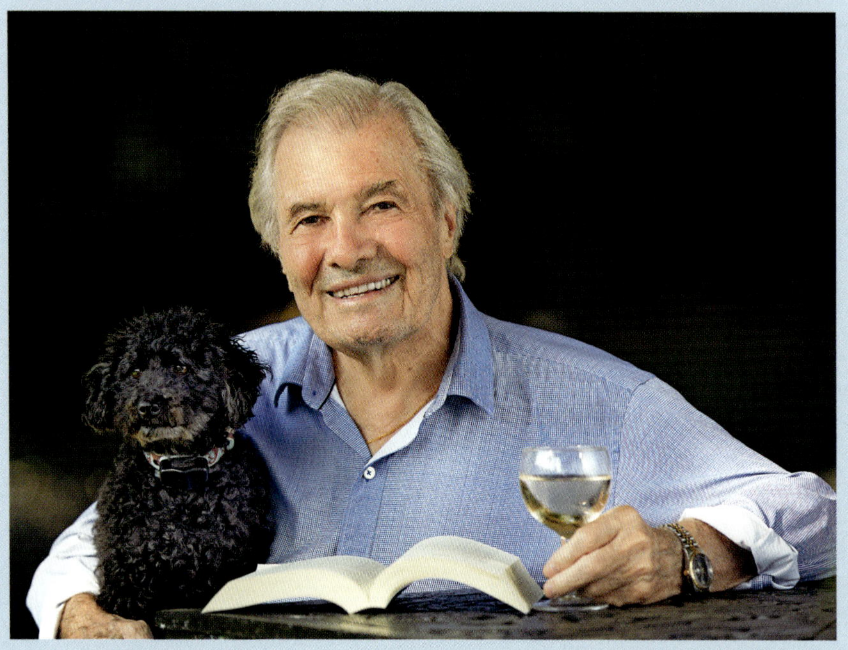

The winner of sixteen James Beard Awards and author of more than thirty cookbooks, including *The Apprentice*, *Essential Pépin*, and *Jacques Pépin Quick & Simple*, JACQUES PEPIN is a chef, author, television personality, educator, and artist, and has starred in twelve acclaimed PBS cooking series. His dedication to culinary education led to the creation of the Jacques Pépin Foundation in 2016.